W9-BRN-023

THE BELLE EPOQUE
in the Paris Herald

THE BELLE EPOQUE
in
THE PARIS HERALD

Hebe Dorsey

With 147 pages of illustrations, 16 in colour,
from the archives of the International Herald Tribune

THAMES AND HUDSON

INTERNATIONAL HERALD TRIBUNE

Printed and bound in Spain by Artes Graficas Toledo S.A.
D.L.TO-683.1986

THE NEW YORK HERALD.

COMPLETE NUMBER 12 PAGES. EUROPEAN EDITION—PARIS, SATURDAY, APRIL 16, 1904. COMPLETE NUMBER 12 PAGES.

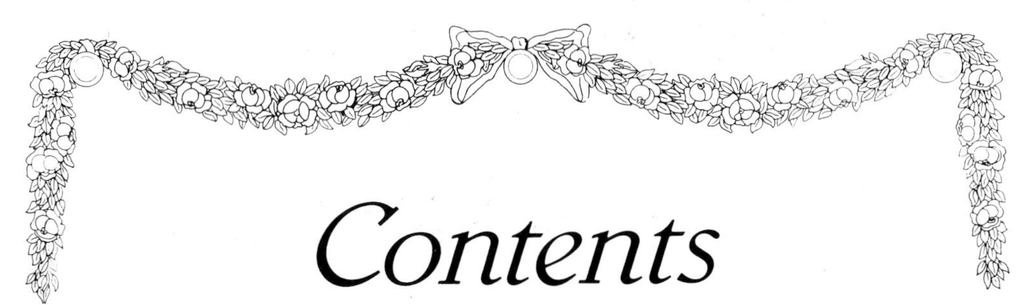

Contents

THE NEW YORK HERALD.

COMPLETE NUMBER 12 PAGES. EUROPEAN EDITION—PARIS, SATURDAY, APRIL 16, 1904. COMPLETE NUMBER 12 PAGES.

Introduction

THE BELLE EPOQUE is a dazzling mirage that many people have tried to capture in a nostalgic blend of frivolous "monde" and naughty "demi-monde," all of it bathed in a Proustian chiaroscuro of salon life.

It is associated with Paris at its most frolicsome – the Moulin Rouge and the cancan, Maxim's, where Russian Grand Dukes drank champagne out of the slippers of feather-bedecked cocottes – and, in counterpoint, with an innocent milieu in which pretty debutantes played croquet on summer lawns and sailor-suited children went to the Rond-Point des Champs-Elysées with beribboned nurses. In this carefree society, privileged people had everything they could ask for, including that most precious of today's commodities – time. To strains of Offenbach, they went from balls to receptions, and from spas to châteaux. Belle Epoque also conjures up society women strolling in the Bois de Boulogne, and salons filled with elegant, mustachioed men – who were always dropping in for tea, flirting round a shawl-draped piano with corsetted women in miles of rustling ruffles and dripping with pearls and diamonds.

Europe was like one vast kingdom, with emperors, kings and princes galore. Courts were magnificent stages for tiara-ed women and dashing officers in bright costumes slashed by rows of decorations. The court in London under Edward VII was the most elegant and exotic, with foreign princes and maharajahs reflecting the strength of the British Empire. St. Petersburg, with its Oriental influences and the tsar's immense wealth, was the most opulent. For European royalty, the Belle Epoque was the last act of an operetta whose actors did not know the end was in sight.

Arts were important and the Belle Epoque was a golden age for music, theatre and visual arts, superbly represented by such people as Verdi and Puccini, Ravel and Massenet, Tolstoy and D'Annunzio, Sarah Bernhardt and Eleonora Duse, and the Impressionist masters Monet and Manet. The period closed with the explosive, brilliant Ballets Russes.

Awkwardly, painfully, hesitantly, dangerously, sports became part of daily life. Balloons and bicycles, automobiles and airplanes as well as golf, tennis, swimming and skiing altered people's lives and mentalities – ending the boudoir society of the 19th century. The move was irreversible. Sportswear began to shape the looks of the 20th century. Automobiles led to the "Town and Country" view of life. With the improvement in steamships and railroads, Belle Epoque people started travelling a lot more – but always with style and plenty of servants.

To many of us, the Belle Epoque, in its hazy, shimmering splendor, simply means the end of La Belle Vie.

When exactly did the Belle Epoque take place? Opinions vary, although purists seem to place it between 1900 and 1914. But many feel that its spirit developed earlier. This explains why, as far as this book is concerned, the dates chosen are 1895–1914.

Nowhere are the Belle Epoque's golden days recorded more vividly and accurately than in the pages of the Paris edition of the *New-York Herald* – familiarly known as the "Paris Herald" – which began publication in 1887 and is still going strong today as the *International Herald-Tribune*. For if Belle Epoque stands out like a legend, so does the publisher of the Paris *Herald*, James Gordon Bennett, Jr., a wealthy American whose paper reflected his own flamboyant lifestyle. The events that determined this paper's creation were as bizarre as the man himself.

Tall, handsome, with blue eyes and a bristling mustache, Bennett was the rakish son of the owner of the *New-York Herald*. A noted eccentric, he was forced to leave New York in 1877 after committing a social offence at the home of his wealthy fiancée. The girl's brother gave Bennett a thrashing, to which Bennett responded by challenging him to a duel. Nobody died, but New York society rejected Bennett who, furious, went to Paris and remained there for forty years of self-exile.

In 1887, encouraged, according to legend, by the cry of an owl – Bennett's favorite animal, which became the paper's emblem – he launched the European edition of the *New-York Herald*, which his late father had founded in 1835. This Paris-based edition was all of four pages, cost 10 centimes, and was an instant success, putting across young Bennett's strong and very personal point of view. "I want you gentlemen to remember," he told his editors right off, "that I am the only reader of this paper. If I want the columns to be turned upside down, they must be turned upside down."

Bennett demanded news-news-news and names-names-names, but the latter were to dominate the *Herald*'s columns. Not just any names, for the publisher was quite a snob and interested mainly in kings and emperors, grand dukes and millionaires. On September 27, 1910, Bennett was proved right on target when the *Herald* published an interview with the King of Spain, "who greeted our correspondent with a handshake, more American in its warm frankness and friendliness than court-like." King Alfonso "praised the Herald" and said "he reads the European Edition every day. He finds it a new creation in journalism . . . likes the lively news columns, the short editorials and the society articles which allow the reader to locate many well-known people and friends."

There were very few bylines, for Bennett was a megalomaniac. All we know is that "Mistletoe" covered the races, that "An American Woman" was an excellent fashion/society writer and a mild but accurate gossip, and that the theatre column was written by a similarly incognito "Homme du Monde," until 1908, when it was signed by French playwright Pierre Veber.

With homes in Paris, New York and Newport, plus a villa on the French Riviera and a hunting lodge in Scotland, Bennett, who had inherited the New York paper from his father in 1868, preferred conducting his business from his 314-foot yacht, the *Lysistrata*. With a 100-man crew, a Turkish bath and an Alderney cow kept in a padded stall, this was said to be the grandest yacht in the world. Bennett was famous for all kinds of outrageous gestures, including riding a four-in-hand down the Champs-Elysées in the wee hours, roaring drunk and stark-naked, and sweeping tablecloths off restaurants' tables if he felt he was not being attended to. (After which, still according to legend, he would buy the restaurant.)

When it came to his newspaper, Bennett was a brilliant man, an astute promoter and a big spender who reportedly went through $40 million during his lifetime. Very much interested by all kinds of technical progress, he strove to get the news to his readers faster and more efficiently. He was the first to use the radio to receive news, and he introduced the linotype and the halftone print to Europe. A man with journalistic vision, he is remembered for having sent reporter Henry Stanley to Africa to find a missing British missionary, Dr. David Livingstone. The famous words "Dr. Livingstone, I presume," first appeared in the *Herald*.

As for his editorial standpoint, it was quite simple. Bennett was a wealthy man who accepted the class system and had his paper cater to a particular class: his own. E.D. Dewitt, publisher of *Editor and Publisher* and previously general manager of the *Herald*, wrote at Bennett's death in May 1918 (the only time that his name appeared in his paper): "The European Edition was probably read by more rulers, potentates and men of high officialdom than any newspaper published." Court news was important and so was international society.

Read by royalty and commoners alike, international from the start, the *Herald* covered the scene in all its brilliance from Paris to St. Petersburg and from Rome to London, taking in the shores of Dinard and Deauville, chic resorts like Newport, Nice and Biarritz and stodgier spas like Marienbad and Baden-Baden. Four major events dominated the Belle Epoque, all of them connected with royalty, and all amply recorded in the *Herald* on front page after front page: Queen Victoria's Diamond Jubilee (1897) and the coronations of Tsar Nicholas II (1896), Edward VII (1901) and George V (1911). The *Herald* was tracking royalty everywhere, even to such improbable, operetta-like settings as Serbia and Montenegro.

EUROPEAN HOTELS. | EUROPEAN HOTELS. | EUROPEAN HOTELS. | EUROPEAN HOTELS. | EUROPEAN HOTELS. | EUROPEAN HOTELS.

THE BUCHER-DURRER HOTELS

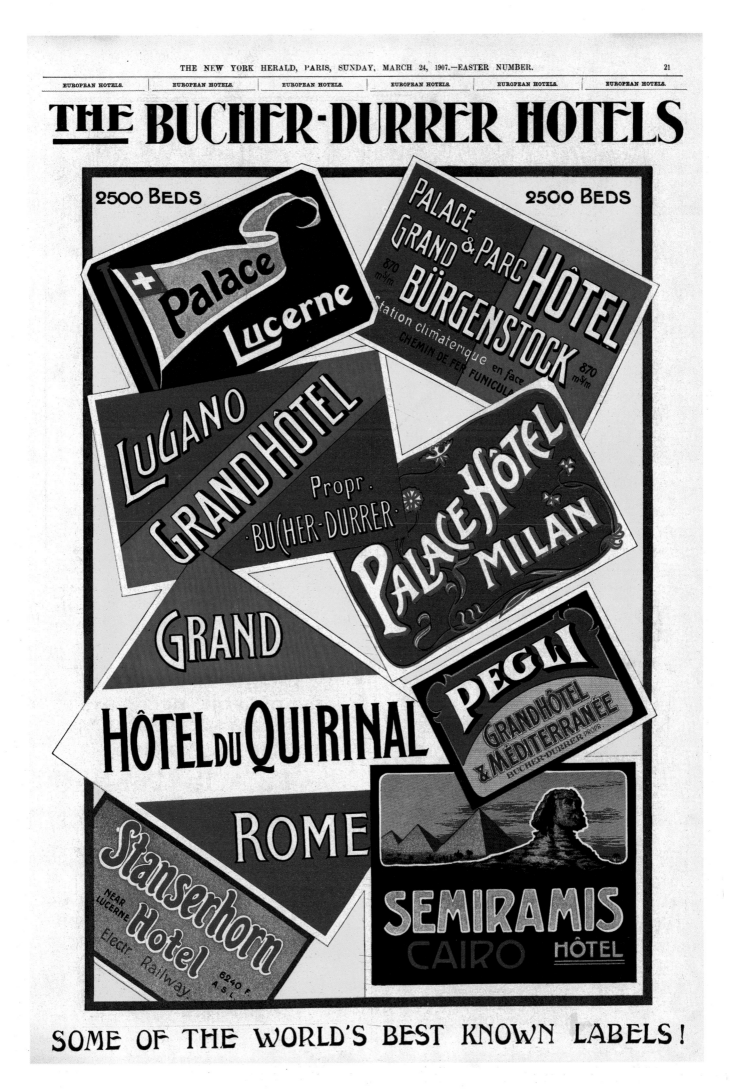

SOME OF THE WORLD'S BEST KNOWN LABELS!

Homeward Bound at Yuletide—Games on Board

BATTIER ❧ Pendant la Traversée — Le Colin-Maillard

EXCURSION. | EXCURSION. | EXCURSION. | EXCURSION. | EXCURSION. | EXCURSION.

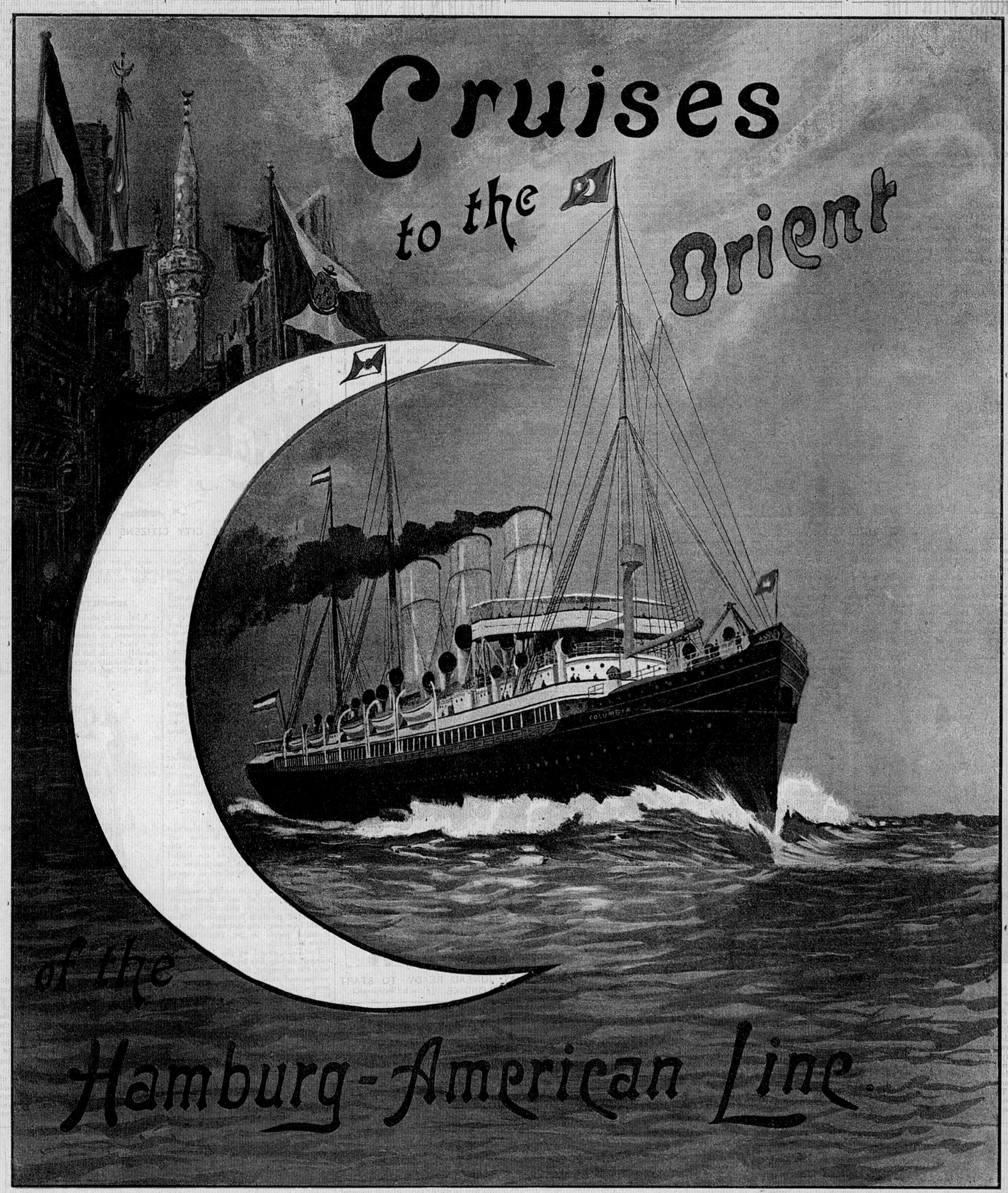

To the Amazing Wonders of Ancient Egypt.
To the Fascinating Places of the Orient.
To the Sacred Ground of the Holy Land.
To the Cradle Land of all our Art and Literature.

ON A SIX WEEKS' CRUISE OVER THE BLUE WAVES AND ROUND THE BEAUTIFUL SHORES OF THE MEDITERRANEAN

By the Transatlantic Twin-Screw Express-Steamers

"AUGUSTE VICTORIA" AND "COLUMBIA,"

Calling at GIBRALTAR, MALAGA, ALGIERS, GENOA, VILLEFRANCHE, (Nice), MALTA, TUNIS, ALEXANDRIA (Cairo), JAFFA (Jerusalem), BEYROUT (Damascus), CONSTANTINOPLE, ATHENS, CANEA, PALERMO, NAPLES and GENOA,

During **FEBRUARY** and **MARCH,** the balmy months of the Southern Spring.

Full particulars contained in a beautiful illustrated pamphlet will be sent free on application to :—

THE HAMBURG-AMERICAN LINE

HAMBURG
Dovenfleth 18-21

Passenger Department.

PARIS
3 rue Scribe.

The paper's coverage was strongly influenced also by Bennett's intense love of sports. He was a member of the Union Club, the Jockey Club and the youngest member ever to be admitted to the New York Yacht Club – which prompted his "Commodore" nickname. Fascinated by speed – on land, on sea and in the air – he was the winner of the First Transatlantic Yacht Race and created, besides the Gordon Bennett International Balloon Cup in 1906, an international automobile race that subsequently became the Grand Prix de France, an airplane race in which Louis Blériot participated, and a race for motorboats. He also introduced polo to America, bringing equipment, a team and instructors from England.

Spurred by Bennett's interest, the *Herald*'s reporters were everywhere – covering races, golf events, tennis matches, balloon flights and automobile races in minute detail, and always with a human touch. On August 13, 1909, the *Herald* reported that "Glen H. Curtiss, the American representative in the Coupe Internationale d'Aviation, arrived at Gare Saint Lazare, carrying his aeroplane as personal luggage, carefully packed in four cases." Bennett also spent a considerable amount of his personal fortune to get the kind of news he wanted in his paper, and did not hesitate to charter a yacht to cover the tsar's visit to Cowes, England, in 1909.

Called in the beginning "A sportsman's caprice" and "Bennett's favorite sport," the *Herald* soon grew into "The most serious of frivolous newspapers," and in the 1920s and 1930s, "The village newspaper for Americans in Paris," to quote *The New Yorker*'s Janet Flanner.

After Bennett's death the *Herald* passed through the hands of several owners, obviously changing in the process. The first was Frank Munsey, a publisher who had made a success with popular magazines in the United States. He bought the *Herald* from the Bennett estate in 1920, and four years later sold it to the Whitelaw Reids, who owned the *New York Herald-Tribune* and eventually called the Paris branch "The New York Herald-Tribune, European Edition" (after buying up the Paris edition of the *Chicago Tribune* as well). The Reids, in turn, sold both the New York paper and its European edition to John H. Whitney in 1959. When the *New York Herald-Tribune* folded in New York in 1966 Mr Whitney negotiated the merger of the European edition with the *New York Times* International Edition. A year later, the *Washington Post* came in as a partner. The result is today's *International Herald Tribune* – *IHT* for short. Four-fifths of its circulation is now outside of Paris and for the first time since World War I, a vast majority of its readers are not American.

This book takes us back to the early days of the Paris *Herald*, when it was delivered to kiosks, hotels and elegant homes by horse-drawn carriage. It took a lot of courage – not to mention money – to start an English-speaking newspaper abroad in that period. To understand the *Herald*'s outlook, it is important to remember that Bennett had spent most of his childhood in Paris. This may explain his cosmopolitan turn of mind and the fact that he eventually chose to become one of a long list of expatriates. As such, besides setting a pattern for generations to come, he understood the needs and wishes of Americans abroad and instinctively knew how to entertain, inform and cajole them. With the development and vast improvement of luxury transatlantic liners and railroads, more and more Americans came to Europe and a truly cosmopolitan class began to emerge, ready for the *Herald*. While retaining a strong American identity, Bennett's paper quickly identified with this new, glamorous and international set.

Bennett also knew the importance of Paris at the turn of the century and insisted that "a dead dog in the Rue du Louvre is more interesting than a devastating flood in China." He also told his editors: "I want one feature article a day. If I say the feature is to be Black Beetles, Black Beetles it's going to be." This attitude accounts for the number of lightweight stories and cartoons that were to give the paper its entertaining reputation.

Compared to today's tabloids, the *Herald* looked huge and, at first glance, fairly forbidding, with its solid columns of gray newsprint illustrated here and there by thinly drawn sketches. But despite a clumsy, cramped style, the reading was always lively and deliberately outrageous. Where else could you find such stories as one on Nana, a French poodle which had its "own room, bath and tutor," as well as a maid who cooked "special menus on special plates." This could only be topped by the headline: "Can Dogs Really Commit Suicide?" For Bennett, scandals rated the front page – as did the "Parisian Society Tragedy" of Comte de Cornulier, who shot his wife while she "was paying a visit to her business agent, which she did several times a week." Accurate to the last gory detail, the *Herald* also mentioned that, "After shooting her, he knelt down and said: 'Demand pardon of God. I pardon you.'"

The fashion stories were always from Paris, but lifestyle features often came from London – like the one during the hunting season about a "White Farm" where "every bird and animal [is] white and the effect is very pretty. There are little white bantams, white pigeons, white pheasants, white turkeys, peacocks, cows, horses; in fact, every obtainable English bird or beast."

From the start, the paper covered society extensively on Page Two with reprints in French from *Le Figaro*, as well as "London Court Circular," "Yacht Movements" and "Personal Intelligence," the latter on the comings and goings of prominent people. The weather, an important feature for yachtsman Bennett, was also on Page Two, illustrated with pretty sketches by Henry Tenré. Parties were amply covered and zeroed in on the *Herald*'s affluent readers. "Original Hints for Dinners" noted that "The very chic thing to do is to change knives and forks at each dish," as well as "Offering each woman an elegant corsage bouquet and placing a buttonhole before each gentleman guest." The paper also mentioned that "A very rich Lord had his table covered with mauve orchids with ribbons of the same shade. At the end of the meal, each woman was told to pick up the bouquet she liked best . . . and was surprised with a fancy trinket, a fan or a bag of ancient stuff, with a gold chain adorned with the most lovely, ravishing pearls."

The arts column, also a regular, held such exciting finds as the vernissage, in 1900, of Claude Monet's waterlilies at the Galerie Durand-Ruel and the 1905 Impressionist Salon with Monet and Renoir.

Towards the mid-1890s, the paper expanded to six or eight pages and the space used for extensive coverage of resort news. It was not unusual for the *Herald* to fill over two pages with "Society, Hunting, Kennel, Theatrical, and Racing News From All Parts Of The World." Bennett also added stunning Christmas, Easter, Art and Fashion Supplements, with stories, songs and poems printed on dazzling white paper, embellished with delightfully Art Nouveau flourish and illustrated with full-color engravings. Contributors included Gabriele d'Annunzio and Mark Twain, and the *Herald* was instrumental in helping shape French literature by serializing books of important authors of the times.

The fashion supplements, which must have been highly lucrative, were particularly charming. Of a smaller format, illustrated by some of the best artists available – including Bert, Brianz, Millière and Sabattier – and exquisitely laid out, they looked more like a magazine than part of a newspaper. They gave the *Herald* a strong fashion bent and couturiers such as Worth, Poiret, Doucet and Paquin were all happy to give exclusives to the *Herald*.

When the paper started using photographs, it chose such giants as Nadar and Reutlinger, whose pictures of Sarah Bernhardt or Lantelme often appeared in the supplements. The imaginative layout always included pretty frames in Art Nouveau ornament which today are a lesson in that period's flowery style.

In the end, the most remarkable thing about the *Herald* is that, with a unique combination of first-hand art and text, it delivered as pure, thorough and authentic a vision of La Belle Epoque as we can hope to encounter.

E NEW YORK HERALD

SPECIAL SUPPLEMENT.

EUROPEAN EDITION—PARIS, MONDAY. AUGUST 18, 1890.

NO

THE "HERALD" IN EUROPE.

A Few Facts About the Sudden Success of the Paris Edition.

NO REST FOR THE EDITORS.

The Enormous Increase in Business Compels Them to Change Quarters Again and Again — New Presses — The Rush of Visitors to the Famous Register.

We present to our readers to-day pictures representing the business and editorial rooms of the Paris Edition of the HERALD. They are a mile distant from each other, just as the editorial and advertising columns are a mile apart, each working independently of the other.

One of the most interesting things we can talk to our readers about, judging by the multitude of inquiries as to our success, is the HERALD itself, and particularly the Paris Edition. It has been called "the sauciest paper in Europe" and we admit it.

If anyone wants to know whether the Paris Edition is a solid and permanent success, let him look at the two substantial and extensive establishments which we illustrate to-day.

The growth of the HERALD's Continental work seems to surprise and delight all Americans who cross the ocean, and we have no lack of cordial congratulations from their Anglo-Saxon cousins who merely have to run across the Channel to reach the French metropolis and who already recognise what the HERALD has done to bring the peoples of the Old and New Worlds into a closer practical knowledge of each other. There are those who see in the international character of the HERALD, with its three centres in the three great capitals of the world, all united by electricity and working together as a common system, the beginnings of that cosmopolitanism which has been prophesied as the ultimate destiny of men.

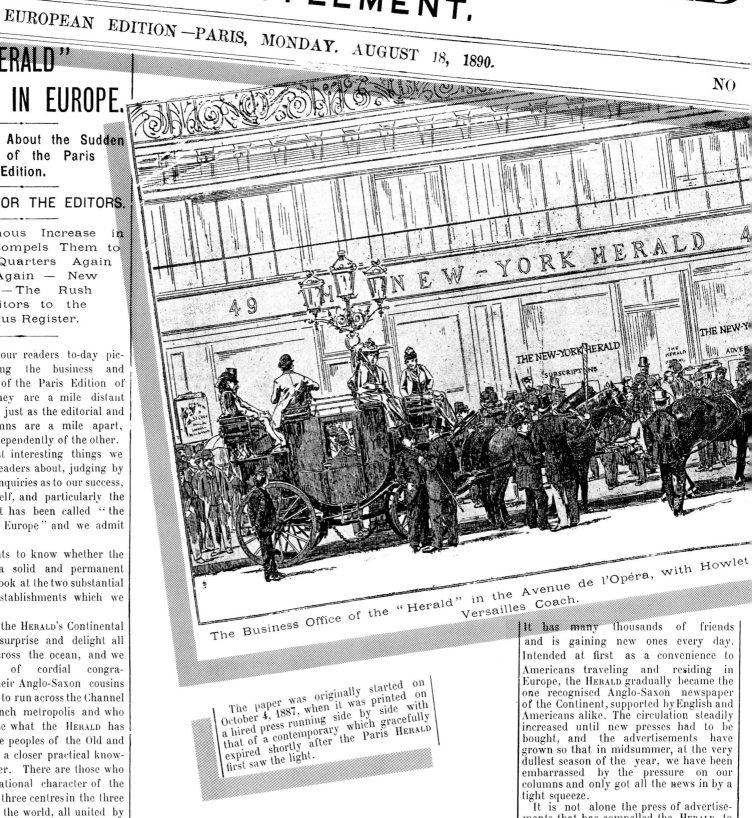

The Business Office of the "Herald" in the Avenue de l'Opéra, with Howlet Versailles Coach.

The paper was originally started on October 4, 1887, when it was printed on a hired press running side by side with that of a contemporary which gracefully expired shortly after the Paris HERALD first saw the light.

It has many thousands of friends and is gaining new ones every day. Intended at first as a convenience to Americans traveling and residing in Europe, the HERALD gradually became the one recognised Anglo-Saxon newspaper of the Continent, supported by English and Americans alike. The circulation steadily increased until new presses had to be bought, and the advertisements have grown so that in midsummer, at the very dullest season of the year, we have been embarrassed by the pressure on our columns and only got all the news in by a tight squeeze.

It is not alone the press of advertisements that has compelled the HERALD to constantly enlarge its facilities, but the extension of its system of gathering news has forced the paper to change its editorial quarters three times in order to get sufficient room to handle the volume of matter that comes from its correspondents in all parts of the world.

is the HERALD itself, and particularly the Paris Edition. It has been called "the sauciest paper in Europe" and we admit it.

If anyone w

A CHA

Of course, every English or American visitor to Paris knows the HERALD Office at 49 avenue de l'Opéra, where over a hundred thousand of its friends have registered their names and have looked through its long list of freshly arrived American and English newspapers and magazines. It is one of the institutions of Paris and by this time the picture which we print of it to-day will be as familiar to the average Anglo-Saxon as a picture of the Opera House or the Arc de Triomphe.

This is the place where the HERALD began the experiment which has proved such a remarkable success. From being a comparative stranger in Europe, the Paris Edition—for the American Edition has always been known abroad—has become the familiar friend and guide, not only of the traveling Anglo-Saxons, but of the residents of all the English and American colonies in Paris, Nice, Berlin, Dresden, Frankfort, Rome, Vienna, and, in fact, all places where the English tongue is understood.

And the centre of this extensive system, whose ramifications reach to St. Petersburg and even further, is the familiar and convenient office at 49 avenue de l'Opéra. Here almost every day travelers meet friends whose presence in Europe they had not suspected, and sometimes meetings of a very affecting character are witnessed there. Indeed, the business office of the Paris Edition has become such a recognised centre of communication that the famous Howlett coaches running to St. Germain and Versailles start from the office door, that being the one rendezvous which the manager of the coaches is sure every English or American visitor will know how to find.

Thousands and thousands of letters are addressed to persons on the Continent through this office, and almost every form of inquiry that a puzzled or belated traveler can imagine is presented there.

the
ally
It is
n the
npres-
of the
of the
es after
n set in
n enables
ate news
hour at
ave Paris
urope.
r presses
ating now
ur Paris
half an
Ve may
ffice in
he first
the

further along the apartment in which a corps of wo... are at work early in the morning preparing subscribers' copies for the post as if their lives depended on haste.

Every day the HERALD has to add to its equipment. The special fashion articles with illustrations drawn in the establishments of the great Paris dress creators, its piquant illustrations, its unrivalled personal intelligence, its close touch with everything from the doings of the world's Parliaments and the operations of armies to the latest whim of the European dilettante, its special cable news which alone costs as much as the whole staff expenses of any other Continental newspaper—these things and the readiness of the HERALD to open its columns to all comers, rich or poor, black or white, Christian, Jew, Pagan or Athesist are bringing in such a harvest that—well, we have looked at another new press.

A DUCHESS ... MEDICAL ASSIS...

mous

THE NEW YORK HERALD

Photograph of the "Herald's" Editorial Office in the Rue du Louvre, with a Group of Its Special Porters.

THE NEW YORK HERALD.

COMPLETE NUMBER 12 PAGES. EUROPEAN EDITION—PARIS. SATURDAY, APRIL 16, 1904. COMPLETE NUMBER 12 PAGES.

1 The Americans

THE DOLLAR WAS KING. On November 17, 1905, a front-page story listed John D. Rockefeller as being richer than the rich monarchs: "His Annual Income $30,000,000 Nearly Equal to Those of All Europe's Crowned Heads Combined."

The Tsar of Russia came second with a paltry $12 million, and the Emperor of Germany, who was third, had a mere $3,852,770.

Like the incalculable fortunes of today, Rockefeller's money, interestingly enough, came from oil. There was no such thing as Petro-dollars in his day, but princely dividends from his Standard Oil Company won Rockefeller the nickname of "King of Petroleum."

In 1909, when railway magnate Edward H. Harriman died, the *Herald* estimated his wealth at $400 to 500 millions, but calmed down a little later and valued his entire estate at between $75 and 100 million.

American millionaires lived in the grandest style, taking houses in London or Paris, sailing their yachts at Cowes, racing their horses at Ascot and marrying their daughters to European titles. By 1909, so many American girls were marrying foreign titles that a Judge James W. Gerrard, from New York, called it "a disgrace. We make ourselves a laughing stock for all Europe. Just because we've got money, we think we can buy anything."

Rich Americans also drove their powerful automobiles all over Europe. Bursting a tire was a major accident. In 1904, the *Herald* had a bucolic description of "Vanderbilt Auto Party Dining at a Swiss Inn." The party was touring Switzerland in a magnificent automobile when a tire burst in a tiny village in the Canton of Vaud. The chauffeur being unable to mend it, Vanderbilt wired to Lausanne for another tire. The hungry party went to the village inn "La Croix d'Or," whose proprietor, on discovering the identity of his guests, ransacked the village for delicacies. Ever so accurate, the *Herald* noted: "Champagne, however, was unobtainable."

Still, the party thoroughly enjoyed dinner and having the villagers at neighboring tables. Vanderbilt was charmed with the Swiss scenery and complimented the innkeeper on his dinner, "especially with regards to the wild strawberries."

All these millionaires, with names associated with extreme wealth – Whitneys and Vanderbilts, Astors, Armours and Drexels – were constantly in the *Herald*'s columns, which kept track of their various hobbies. Pierpont Morgan was an avid collector. J.J. Astor loved restoring old houses and A.G. Vanderbilt lavished his money on coaching and racing horses.

In 1900 the *Herald* described superb yachts owned by Americans. At Cowes and in the Mediterranean, they proudly floated like so many palaces. The largest of them was the *Nahma*, belonging to Robert Goelet (of the New York landowning family), with 1,806 tonnage and a crew of 67. Built three years earlier, she was equipped with broad passages, large and luxurious staterooms and saloons "full of simple richness." The paper also mentioned the *Utowana*, which belonged to Allison V. Armour, "a very practical yachtsman and his own master."

Very white and clean-looking was the *Safa-el-Bahr*, bought from the Khedive of Egypt by Colonel Francis L. Leland, of New York. This one was 669 tons and had a picturesque crew of fez-covered Turks, whom Leland took over with the yacht and whom he found very handy and clean, "and above all, sober." The yacht was trimmed with light oak paneling except for the boudoir, which was in satinwood.

In addition there was P.A.B. Widener's *Josephine*, "a pure and American yacht" decked up with a large reception room looking like a palm garden, with ceiling and walls of carved French walnut except for a grand boudoir, which was white and all in Louis XV style.

J. Arthur Hinckley's 429-ton *Calanthe* was equally handsome with oak-paneled grand and spacious saloon, a fireplace and modern bathrooms equipped with hot water faucets, "such as were specially invented for the Manhattan Hotel of New York."

As for the *Valiant*, which made the run from Le Havre to New York in nine days and one hour, a record time for yachts, she had a Louis XV main salon, with exquisite gold-and-white woodwork carvings. The Chippendale chairs, sofas and sideboards were all inlaid with brass and the upholstery was of crimson velvet.

The horsey set were also prominent in the *Herald*'s columns. Gordon Bennett, Jr., introduced polo to America and Americans cut a high-tone profile on such European thoroughbred race tracks as Ascot, Deauville and Longchamp. On June 15, 1908, a Vanderbilt horse, "North East," won the Grand Prix de Paris, acclaimed by 100,000 people. And on August 19, 1909, another Vanderbilt horse, "Messidor," won at Deauville.

In July 1909, Americans were backing their favorite American jockey, Danny Maher, at the Sandown race course in England. The King was there – in a dashing, bright blue bowler hat, dark blue suit and red tie. Americans complained that the day's racing at this pretty English track was spoiled by rain. There was a great shout of joy when Danny won and it was a feather in America's cap when Danny walked through the beautiful flower-bespangled paddock after the race.

Alfred Gwynne Vanderbilt, a London habitué, loved coaching, which prompted him to start a six-weeks London-Brighton coach service. The "Venture," with four magnificent grays and decked with red and gray ribbons, had a good send-off on May 1st, 1908, attended by many Americans (all very beautiful and wearing big hats), including Mrs. Vanderbilt, Mrs. Deering and a Mrs. King. Several automobiles followed, with their chauffeurs shouting: "Hurrah for coaching."

Other American millionaires were buying art with such systematic concentration that there was talk of "the rape of Europe." J. Pierpont Morgan was one of the most active. In April, 1904, the *Herald* listed among some of his purchases a Donatello bas-relief of the Virgin and Child from Florence, one of the master's most important works; an enameled jewel; and a pair of 16th-century candelabra from a Paris antique dealer. In 1906, the front page of an art supplement (which the *Herald* published at regular intervals) described the Pierpont Morgan collection at Prince's Gate, London, which included a series of exquisite miniatures.

In 1904, Morgan gave a work back to the Italian government, for it had been stolen from the cathedral of Ascoli.

In 1906, William Waldorf Astor restored the castle and hamlet of Hever, an ancient Tudor village in Kent with an 800-year-old church, where Henry VIII had often traveled to woo the ill-fated Anne Boleyn. Astor, who wanted no modern note in his castle, had moved in furniture and planned to make it his permanent home.

American women managed to keep themselves pretty busy in Europe. They came to Paris for fashion-shopping, but London was really their favorite setting for social acceptance. Their ultimate ambition was to be presented at court. Women who dressed soberly back home – "they wear too much black," as Paris designer Paul Poiret once remarked – came to Europe to display their toilettes and jewels – including most undemocratic diamond tiaras. Many of them married English titles and led appropriately grand lives.

As a result a bevy of brilliant social leaders in England were American-born, in particular the Duchess of Marlborough (Consuelo Vanderbilt), Mrs. George Cornwallis West (Winston Churchill's mother), and Mrs. Arthur Paget. The Duchess of Manchester, a long-time friend of Queen Alexandra, often played a clever bridge party with the King. The *Herald* considered a Mrs. Ronald to be the most genuinely popular; she gave beautiful parties in her house in Cadogan Place and was also the best amateur vocalist in London. When Lady Curzon, the American-born wife of the Viceroy of India, died in London in 1906, the *Herald* noted that "she will be long remembered as the first American woman to hold the nearly queen position which was hers in India."

One of the grandest American parties was given in July 1909 by Whitelaw Reid, at that time Ambassador to the Court of Saint James (and later owner of the *New York Herald-Tribune*), for the King and Queen, with such guests as Mrs. Cornelius Vanderbilt, Mrs. J.J. Astor and Mr. Pierpont Morgan. Mrs. Reid wore a dress of gray satin, brocaded with bunches of iris, its diamanté bodice jeweled with amethysts and its décolletage draped with Venetian lace fastened with diamond brooches and clasps.

The dinner was served at two tables decorated with colonial orchids in gold jardinières, tankards and gold candelabra.

The ballroom, its walls hung with Old Masters, offered a perfect background for rich dresses and flashing diamonds. All the royal group danced except for the King, who cared little for dancing and merely opened the royal quadrille with the hostess.

The *Herald* gave a detailed account of the splendid outfits the Duke and Duchess of Marlborough had provided for their son, when he was baptized with great magnificence at the Royal Chapel of St. James. Governesses, nursemaids and gardeners at Blenheim Palace were all interviewed by the *Herald,* which described the 12 dozen shirts, the plainest of which cost 200 francs, the eight dozen napkins at 50 francs each, bibs at 40 francs, capes at 800 francs, ending with: "Strange to say, the baby is supremely indifferent to all these costly articles as well as the $5,000,000 cheque sent to him by grandfather W.K. Vanderbilt for pocket money."

The wedding of John Jacob Astor's only daughter, Pauline, to Captain Spencer Clay was another display of riches. The bride was wearing a dress "of costly simplicity" with superb lace over white satin. Her father gave her a diamond comb and a black pearl necklace, pearl and diamond earrings and other jewels, as well as furs. The bridegroom came through with a diamond tiara, a ruby and diamond pendant, a diamond chain and a mounted dressing bag.

In June 1905, at a ball at Buckingham Palace for King Alfonso of Spain, the Duchess of Marlborough wore a Worth white satin dress brocaded with flowers outlined with diamonds, a diamond and pearl tiara, plus her superb dog-collar of 19 rows of pearls. Mrs. John Drexel of Philadelphia wore, over a blue chiffon under-dress, a magnificent gown covered with diamond embroideries, culminating in a band of diamonds round the hem of the skirt and a diamond bolero and the finest pearls in the room.

Mrs. Astor was a sensation, arrayed in white with an enormous diamond ornament on the bodice, plus a tiara of brilliants. A tiara again, of diamonds tipped with large, pear-shaped pearls plus seven or eight rows of pearls around one arm, for another American, Mrs. Potter Palmer of Chicago, who, on July 25, 1905, gave a dinner for the Whitelaw Reids. The entertainment was up to par with the first appearance in Europe of Chaliapin, "a great Russian bass, who came all the way from Russia to sing at this party." The *Herald* added that he was an enormous success.

The newly-wed Alice Roosevelt Longworth outdid them all when she visited London in June 1906. "Princess Alice", as she was quickly dubbed, was a piquant young matron, with nothing particularly striking in appearance or dress. To London society's astonishment, she gave each guest at her first party a hearty handshake.

On June 29, Alice made a spectacular entrance at court, where she was presented to the Queen wearing her wedding dress, the bodice literally blazing with diamonds, for there was a great *plaque de cou*, a stomacher of brilliants, a plaque of diamonds on the back of the bodice, epaulettes and a diamond tiara and necklace. Her train, white and silver brocade, had a trail of diamonds and silver roses down one side.

As hundreds of wealthy Americans in London began taking houses or places in the country, the servant problem became so acute that many people had to move to Paris. In 1908, a *Herald* upstairs-downstairs story told of one wealthy American hiring a butler for her Park Lane house. She was used to an 8 a.m. breakfast. The butler appeared tardily. "'Really,' he explained, half-awake, 'you caw'nt expect me to wake up before 8 o'clock.'" He was fired.

In 1906, a record year with 331,453 Americans in Europe, as against 261,978 the preceding year, 4,287 of them registered at the *Herald* in July. As more and more Americans came to Europe, the *Herald* became not only their favorite newspaper but their home away from home. After alighting from their trains with dozens of trunks signed Vuitton or Goyard, and quickly checking in at the Grand Hotel or the Continental, they would go to the *New York Herald*'s offices, at 49, Avenue de l'Opéra.

There they would catch up with the news, choosing from at least two dozen major American newspapers to be found in the *Herald*'s Reading Room. They would also faithfully register and, just as faithfully, their names would appear during the following days in long columns. The unprecedented wave of tourists in 1906 came from all States of the Union, including Maine and California and scores from Illinois. Paris was still the main goal of their pilgrimage. Hotels were taken by storm, cabs were busy and hundreds of Americans were enjoying themselves not only in Paris but in London, Berlin, Lucerne, Baden-Baden, Bad Homburg and St. Moritz, speeding in autos, bringing joy and prosperity, and prompting an innkeeper in Fontainebleau to remark (already!) that, "But for the Americans, hotelkeepers would starve."

Some liked it, others didn't. An American woman asked her husband what he thought of the Nice casino. "My dear," he said, "I think it's the wickedest place I ever saw."

*

Oddly enough, the Americanization of Europe started popularly with Buffalo Bill. Pierre Veber in 1905 denounced this rampant and alarming fad. "On a voyage of exploration along the French coasts," he wrote, "I want to draw the attention of the Minister of Instruction Publique to a great danger: Buffalo Bill." Totally deadpan, Veber described how children on beaches romped like Sioux, uttered horrible cries, pretended to steal horses and on and on. "Meanwhile," Veber sadly noted, "the Irish governess sits there, indifferent to this pantomime." If this Buffalobolism, as Veber called it, went on, he warned that governesses would quit and mothers would be forced to look after their own children, which had not happened for 300 years at least.

The Americanization of Europe was also being felt in people's drinking and dressing habits. During the September 1906 heat wave, the *Herald* announced, "American Drinks Cool Biarritz." In fashionable restaurants and hotels, French absinthe, Italian vermouth, Spanish chocolate and Scotch whisky had given place to American drinks, such as the Mint Julep, consumed in considerable quantities, the *Herald* reported, adding: "The flower of French, Spanish and Russian nobility are all drinking American cocktails with long thin straws."

Even eating habits were being revolutionized by the American visitors crossing the ocean. On December 8, 1906, theatrical producer Charles Frohman, who arrived on the *Lusitania* and stayed at London's Savoy Hotel, bought two plays from Somerset Maugham and another author for $100,000. Then he walked along Piccadilly to St. James's Street where he found a grocery that carried sweet potatoes, sweet corn and pumpkin in cans, all from New Jersey and, needless to say, at extravagant prices.

For Thanksgiving the same year, a fraternal gathering was held at Wyman's, a restaurant on rue Fontaine, Paris, decorated with French and American flags. As the *Herald* related, "They came early. The first event was the dinner party – with an American menu – captained by Major Burke. Two of his party were 'Al' Riel and Bandmaster 'Billy Sweeney', also of the Buffalo Bill aggregation. Jim Marshall was applauded till he blushed." Wyman, in conventional black Prince Albert of clerical cut and length, with black stock "but no diamonds," greeted guests, cracked jokes, rubbed his hands and made everybody happy. "This is no frost," said Wyman – and his assertion was confirmed by the attendance, the talk and the appetite of the Thanksgiving Americans.

In 1903, the *Herald* wrote that Paris was buried in six inches of confetti after the Mardi Gras celebrations. There was no cavalcade, though small bands of students paraded about singing and blowing horns. On the Grands Boulevards, where fun was rough and on a large scale, amid masqueraders, strolling musicians, terrific din and gaiety, several elderly American gentlemen were taking part in the festivities "with surprising vim and agility." Over in the Latin Quarter, fun-making started soon after 2 o'clock. Four American girls, including a tall, handsome blonde, took refuge under the awning in front of Café Soufflot. Feeling secure, they ordered coffee. Soon someone yelled "Les Americaines" and a young man rushed and covered them with confetti.

American girls were used to dealing with Paris "mashers" – as the *Herald* called these unwelcome Boulevardiers. One of them was given two *sous* to stop his advances. Needless to say, he followed the girl no further. Another young American was accosted by a well-dressed Frenchman who, doffing his hat and with a low bow, said: "'Pardon, Mademoiselle, but it is not the custom for such a pretty young woman to be seen alone in Paris at such an hour. Permit me to accompany you.' 'Pardon, Monsieur,' flashed the other, 'but je suis Americaine et j'ai l'habitude.'" The solicitous person made another low bow and was gone.

In 1906, thirty Kentucky girls, winners of a popularity contest and on their first visit to Paris, drew 1,500 people outside the Louvre Hotel, "giving them rude ratings." Photographers followed them all day, sightseeing and shopping. "It was horrid, perfectly horrid," said Anna Ford of Smith's Grove, Ky. The *Herald* reported their every move, including the fact that "Kentucky Belles in Sad Plight" had run out of chewing gum at Neuhausen, on the Rhine.

This last item proved too trite for an Old Kentuckian, who wrote an irate letter to the editor denouncing this disgusting notoriety, and pointing out, "We are sufficiently criticized and laughed at by Europeans."

Thanks to the automobile, American tourists were to be found in such assorted resorts as Carlsbad and Houlgate (Normandy); the latter was reported to be overflowing with many pretty American girls taking part in a ball at the casino. So many Americans were using automobiles throughout England in 1906 that the average Englishman was quite convinced that every visitor from the United States was in possession of at least one auto.

A Mr. George A. Kessler "of New York and Moet and Chandon fame" had his house on Avenue Raphael, Paris, equipped not with stables, but with a large garage for his collection of cars, which included a magnificent Panhard, a 60-HP Mercedes, a Renault and several other electric carriages. His decorator was Samson (who also did Boni de Castellane's Palais Rose) and the house was supposed to recall the Château of Marly.

American women were the first to drive powerful automobiles, as the *Herald* reported in "Who's Who Among Buyers of Autos." A Mercedes dealer mentioned that a Miss Hildger from New York had bought a 20-HP Mercedes from him. "They are all Americans, those lady chauffeurs," he said. "They handle the mechanism wonderfully and never seem to be afraid."

On July 19, 1909, a Mrs. Harriet Clark Fisher, manager of a foundry in Trenton, New Jersey, sailed on the *New York* for an automobile trip around the world accompanied by her chauffeur-secretary, her maid and a bulldog mascot.

Paris fashion held enormous fascination for all American women. A reader who signed herself "The American Girl Now in Paris" wrote to the editor with a thorough understanding of the magic behind Paris clothes: "The perfection is due to the absolute fit of every item. The first thing the Frenchwoman does is to have a well-fitting corset. Just to write about corsets would take a column." Paris was most attractive to women, she went on: "Dresses are designed for them, hats built for their heads, made to suit their side face and no one else's, shoes for every costume and parasols most enchanting."

In 1908 a fictitious character named "Fluffy Ruffles" appeared in the paper's pages and became the archetype of the young, pretty, naive but sassy American girl, eager to acquire the famous Parisian chic. She told her Uncle Joe that she wanted to go to Paris with her brother William, her French governess Sophie and her dog Teddy "to show them that nothing is more Parisian than a chic American." This in answer to a Frenchman, M. Ricaud, who, despite the fact that he had a wonderful time in America, pretended that American women could spend millions and still not look right.

After "the exquisite emotion" of arriving in Paris, Fluffy Ruffles' first remark was: "It's funny that an American, coming to Paris to acquire the supposedly unique Parisian chic, is confronted with an ostentatious display of English and American chic." Everywhere she went, she saw American shoes, English tailors and hatmakers. "What does this mean?" she asked. "Was it worth crossing the ocean?"

In the classic "Letter to My Uncle" format, she reported on the importance of the Rue de la Paix, with all those famous couturiers – glorious names over doors adorned with balconies or flower boxes. Shiny coaches were piled four-deep; elegant *valets de pied*, in white suede pants and beige or brown uniforms, lined up in front of each establishment as women got out of their coaches. Some rushed in, dresses rustling, through the big doors. Others, browsing in front of shop windows, brandished their lorgnettes on pearl necklaces "worth 100,000 francs each." "Trottins," mannequins, delivery boys rushed about, ever so busy. Very chic men, both young and old, stopped to feast their eyes on the beautiful clients stepping down from their autos. "It's heaven on earth," Fluffy Ruffles declared.

After a visit to a couturier, she decided that her corset was wrong, her skirt not voluminous enough. "I walk too brusquely, my hat is worn too far back and I'm too boyish."

Her brother – "Poor William," too tall, too colorful, shoes too yellow, buttonhole too big – did not fare much better. He simply could not escort her to chic tearooms. Fluffy Ruffles also shrewdly noted that Paris was full of deadbeats – elegant, distinguished young men with a habit of dropping in to their conversation the remark that chic people drink only champagne X and that the duke of such-and-such had ordered car Y.

Fluffy Ruffles became the heroine of a Broadway play in 1909 and Hattie Williams, the young actress who was to play the role, came abroad to study Parisian ways. Part of the play was to be set in the Pavillon d'Armenonville and part in London. The Bois, Miss Williams noted, was a "strict ritual" although the pretty Tour du Lac, so much in vogue under Napoleon III, had been abandoned in favor of the Proustian Allée des Acacias – which, she decided, was "straight as an arrow and frankly monotonous. But maybe better for the see-and-be-seen game."

To get the local color, Williams was given the grand tour, including the Folies-Bergère, the Pré Catalan, the Boulevards, the races ("but horses ran the wrong way") and the Fête des Fleurs, all by "Taximetre auto-cab – slow but sure." She also studied the café-concert queens of Montmartre, went to the "vernissage" of the Exposition des Artistes Français and had lunch at Ledoyen afterwards – a must, along with ordering "saumon sauce verte."

Williams said the play's costume designer need search no further than some of the dresses which were worn off the stage in Paris. And she concluded, "These Parisiennes are the limit of grace and attractiveness." In August, after the play's successful opening in New York, Williams changed her mind and told an interviewer: "The chic-est things in Paris are the American women. The cheekiest are the prices they pay for feeling chic."

Of all the American women who married across the Atlantic, Anna Gould encapsulated the saga of "American-heiress-marries-European-title-and-lives-to-regret-it." On February 8, 1895, a front-page item announced the official engagement of Miss Anna Gould and Count Boniface de Castellane. No time was being lost. The wedding was to take place within three weeks.

The couple had met in America, when the Count went to see the country and indulge in some Western shooting, which prompted the *Herald* to run the startling headlines: "Went to Shoot, Stays to Wed." Or, as Boni put it: "I hunted oftener and harder than any American. But I had no idea of getting married."

From the start, Boni was very nonchalant about money and declared to the *Herald*: "In regard to the settlements, nothing has been asked for or suggested by me. There may be two million more or less, or nothing." The *Herald* was more precise, stating that "Out of her fortune of $17 million, she settles $2 million on him the day of their marriage."

The Count was an aesthete who would come to be known for his exquisite taste in 18th-century furniture. But for the moment, he designed the wedding costumes. "Oh, yes! I know about such things," he told the

Herald, adding that the four bridesmaids were to wear white cloth trimmed with sable and the bride white satin and old lace. The bridal veil, a gift of the Marquise de Castellane, was of beautiful old *point* secured with clusters of lily of the valley.

The wedding was held on March 3, in George J. Gould's Paris residence, and police were needed to keep out the reporters of the sensational papers and sort out some 3,000 uninvited guests, from beggars to bankers, who had come from all over town to see what they could of the wedding. A wealth of roses, lilies and orchids covered all the walls and stairs. The bridal procession went down an aisle marked by white satin ribbon and covered by a sort of canopy formed of lilies, roses and orchids.

The jewelry was on the same scale. The bride wore a tiara of emeralds, pearls, diamonds and rubies worth $40,000, a gift from the Gould family. Frank Gould presented a chain of 200 diamonds and Howard Gould a large knot or cluster of diamonds.

The honeymoon took place in Europe, and on March 24 the couple were in Nice dining and doing some shopping. Anna chose a charming capote in green straw, surrounded with five large bunches of violets, trimmed with large pansies and bright green spangles and surmounted by an egret of feathers. After a brief stay in Paris at the Bristol, the Castellanes went to New York, where Count de Castellane was "to go about his business." The *Herald* also reported that provision had been made by which "not one cent of the Gould millions that will be the living expenses of the young people shall go out of this country."

It did not take long for Boni to show he knew better. The following April, the Goulds were back in Paris where Boni bought 5,000 meters of land in the avenue du Bois de Boulogne for 700 francs a meter. His idea was to build a mansion surrounded by gardens as an exact and complete reproduction of the Grand Trianon.

The mansion was completed in 1899 and on January 3rd the Castellanes, who had moved in a few days earlier, had the idea of inviting the entrepreneurs and all the workmen and their families, to wish them Happy New Year. At 4 p.m., about 1,000 people, including 400 children, arrived. From the vestibule, everybody admired this beautiful example of Louis XIV style, all in marble and pink bronzes. Then up the grand staircase, a wonderful reconstitution of the Ambassador's Stairway in Versailles. The Count and Countess were at the top with their two children, Boni, 3, and Georges, 11 months. The architect Samson and landscape artist Henri Duche shook people's hands while the host and hostess kissed the children. There was a guignol, flanked by two gigantic Christmas trees streaming with light, overflowing with toys and bibelots, and surmounted by two little flags, French and American. After the guignol – "a succès fou" – the children went to the trees to the strings of a gypsy orchestra.

The Castellanes later gave sumptuous dinners and balls, including one at which the ladies were asked to come as flowers and the men to wear colored dress coats. The hostess wore a beautiful red poppy dress, with a big poppy in her hair. Three duchesses arrived arm in arm as the flag of France: the Duchesse de La Rochefoucauld as a cornflower, the Duchesse de Luynes as a white carnation and the Duchesse d'Uzès as a red carnation.

By 1898, Boni had caught yacht fever, and on March 5 he entertained aboard the *Valhalla.* A special train conveyed the count's twenty guests to Civitavecchia on the coast near Rome. The lunch, which was served among wonderfully arranged flowers, began at noon to the strains of an excellent orchestra. The sea was like a mirror. At dessert, the yacht put out for a cruise. During this charming trip, a breeze arose and the 130 men of the crew, climbing the masts, went through maneuvres which enabled the yacht to stop engines and go on by sail.

With this kind of expenditure, it is little surprise that, in early 1900, Boni's financial troubles were all over the *Herald*'s front page. There were rumours that he had lost three million francs speculating on the Bourse and dumped millions of the Gould wealth into the gambling dens of Paris and Monte Carlo. This created a bit of scandal, although "everybody knows he is married to Miss Gould whose dowry was about $75 million, the capital of which remains in the United States." The Goulds had an annual income of about $4 million, paid to her. "Even in Paris," the *Herald* noted lightly, "one can make a show with that amount."

Boni spent money without counting. But the *Herald* noted that the splendid mansion in the Bois "must have been sweet to Mme de Castellane, whose dream was to go one better than M. Vanderbilt, whose palace on Fifth Avenue was a reconstruction of the Château de Blois." Boni was also alleged to be involved in a royalist conspiracy, toward which he reportedly made a 50,000 francs payment, but he denied these charges before a High Court. The *Herald* used a quote from the proceedings: "It is a fact that you attempted to pledge your yachts [plural]?" "No. I have not."

The couple left for New York amid speculation that one of Boni's brothers-in-law would rescue him from a momentarily embarrassing situation. "Many people will be surprised to hear that he is pressed for money with an income of $4 million," the *Herald* wrote, but New York was gearing up for the Castellanes' return, with dinners, balls and musicales planned in their honor. The *Herald* remained devoted to Boni and his financial troubles. On January 27, it was asserted that the count never exceeded his income and never called on the estate for funds, except for the Paris building. One informant, who called Boni "amusing, with extravagant speech," said that he really enjoyed the attention which he attracted.

THE NEW YORK HERALD.

Complete Number, 20 Pages. PARIS, SUNDAY, MAY 17, 1896.—CORONATION SUPPLEMENT. FRANCE, 25 CENTIMES.

H.I.M. NICHOLAS II.

TSAR AND AUTOCRAT OF ALL THE RUSSIAS.

(Specially drawn for the HERALD, by H. J. THADDEUS.)

GENERAL VIEW OF

THE PROCESSION.

ON THE WAY TO THE CATHEDRAL OF THE ASSUMPTION.

The passage of the Tsar and Tsarina down the Red Staircase of the Kremlin.

"Funds for Castellane" became a familiar headline as the Gould family, touched by the distress of the countess, kept coming to her rescue. In September, Edwin Gould prevailed upon George and the brothers, and 8 million francs were advanced to wipe out the count's outstanding debts and avoid the scandal of the Castellanes' mansion going on the block.

By November, the *Herald*'s front page announced that George Gould, with his sister's consent, had been appointed trustee of her estate by the Civil Court of Paris. The truth came out in glaring figures: 15 million francs spent in five years and 22 million in unsettled debts. The fantastic expenditure included almost 10 million francs for bric-à-brac and art objects.

On November 3, George, Helen, Edwin, Howard and Frank Gould agreed to pay the couple's debts, a gesture of family pride and affection for Anna; they did not want her "to be annoyed" by her husband's extravagance.

However, she was not yet ready to leave her husband. "She is fond of him and he of her. There is no occasion for scandal. The Comtesse will live in France as becomes her station and will not be forced to live in retirement or comparative penury, although her husband's reckless extravagance will end," the *Herald* reported.

If Boni ran short of money, it did not show. On March 19, he gave a dinner for a few friends, with a magnificent green Sèvres service and bouquets of pink cherry blossoms. The cuisine was splendid. The Duchesse de Gramont, Prince and Princess Edmond de Polignac and other guests then went to Princess Mathilde's salon on the rue de Berri. In 1904, the dinner the couple gave in honor of Princess Louis Ferdinand of Bavaria showed that "Comte Boni de Castellane dictates the elegance laws in Paris since his uncle, the Duke of Talleyrand, retired from the world."

The *Herald* somehow failed to report the divorce, but in 1908 Anna Gould – despite bitter opposition from her relatives – was preparing to marry the Prince de Sagan, who declared on April 14: "When trouble developed between Count Boni de Castellane and the Countess, I sought to aid them as a friend and was sincerely interested in their affairs."

Although he was old enough to be her father and was a bachelor who had never planned to marry, Sagan could not stifle his love.

HOTEL.
·OR,
·s-Elysées).
·ugh ; elevators
·rices, including
·ll Free.
à tables séparées.
UME, Prop.

·DENCE.

·PARK.
·ome for learning
·ift, bath, heater ;
·usson, prof. dip.

OEN. OF CITY
fr. a day ; bath

DES TERNES,
·e house, 2 sets of
·oarders ; arrange-

·ST-CLASS
PENSION.

· FRANÇ. DIST.,
· Gros, 25 avenue

·M.,TRES CONF.,
·r.Clément-Marot.

· well recom., exc
·. 10 rue Chalgrin

· WASHINGTON
·rs; French lessons

·EIVES 5 OR 6
·r Trocadéro ; ex-
· Office.

PRIVE AVEC
·ersonnes. Ecrire

·M.; BEST SIT
·av. Victor Hugo

·NSION.
·e de la Michodière
·1 8 to 12fr. all inc.

·LY OWNING
·inutes from Paris
·ur) would receive
ladies wishing to
families ; facili-
·es for painting,
literary evenings
·, very luxurious
·kitchen ; bicycle
·akes, stable and
·tor of the Villa
·ne.

DE FAMILLE,
cleanliness, and
Mme. Mansfield,

·ARD DE COUR-
·ass pension, com-
·ont rooms ; high-
·oom ; telephone.

· diplomatist, Am.
· 93 r. Miromesnil.

·le Armée, receives
·ns ; terms mod.

·comf.; large gar.;
·rue Boileau, Paris.

·11 rue Poisson
·v. Grande-Armée
·th room ; heater

DE FAMILLE
·u Dôme (Etoile).

·, family rec. 3 or
·class ; from 10fr.

·ées.—Pension and
·good table ; sepa-
·families ; baths,
·euve Noir et fils.

BREMEN TO INDO-CHINA, JAPAN AND NEW GUINEA.

Leave Southampton. Genoa. Naples
SACHSEN .... Oct. 12... Oct. 20.... Oct. ·
BAYERN .... Nov. 9... Nov. 17...·
PRINZ HEINRICH... Dec. 7... Dec. ·

BREMEN TO AUST·
Leave S·
GERA.......
DARMST·

OCEAN STEAMSHIPS.

·ATES MAIL STEAMERS.
·AMPTON direct to NEW YORK.
Every Saturday at noon.
·PARIS.........Sept. 26 | ST. LOUIS.......Oct. 3
NEW YORK.......Sept. 29 | ST. PAUL........Oct. 10
Passengers booked at through fares from Paris.
Reduced winter rates.
Apply to N. MARTIN, 9 RUE SCRIBE, PARIS.
RICHARDSON, SPENCE & Co., Liverpool and Southampton, and 3 Cockspur-street and 116 Leadenhall-street, London.
BAGGAGE STORED AND FORWARDED UNOPENED FROM PARIS TO STEAMERS.

ANCHOR LINE
UNITED STATES MAIL STEAMERS
GLASGOW TO NEW YORK.
First Class Through from Paris $70 to $90.
ANCHORIA......Oct. 1 | ETHIOPIA.........Oct. 8
ARTHUR H. GROVES, 5 rue Scribe, Paris.

ATLANTIC TRANSPORT LINE.
Every Thursday.
LONDON TO NEW YORK.
All twin-screw steamers. No steerage or second-cabin passengers carried. All state-rooms amidships. Electric light through ship. Surgeon and stewardess. Fare strictly first-class. Time, London to New York, ten to eleven days. For particulars apply to Managers,
WILLIAMS, TORREY and FEILD (Limited),
108 Fenchurch-street, London, E.C., or to
S. STAMFORD PARRY, Paris Agent, 23 rue d'Hauteville.

CUNARD LINE.
For New York. For Boston.
CAMPANIA .....Sept. 26 | SERVIA ....Sept. 26
UMBRIA ....Oct. 3 | SCYTHIA.........Oct. 1
LUCANIA ....Oct. 10 | CARINTHIA......Oct. 6
BAGGAGE forwarded unopened from Paris to Liverpool at fixed rates. Apply to the CUNARD STEAMSHIP CO. (Ltd.), 38 avenue de l'Opéra.

HAMBURG-AMERICAN LINE
Maintains a direct service between the European Continent and New York with Twin-Screw Steamers
HOLDING THE RECORD FOR FASTEST TIME ON THIS ROUTE.
The steamers of this line now touch Cherbourg on their way from Hamburg and Southampton to New York.
The Hamburg-American Line's special train (with dining-car attached) from Paris (Gare Saint-Lazare), Fridays at 8.35 a.m. to Cherbourg in 6½ hours, connects directly with the steamer.
Shortest and Most Convenient Route
FROM PARIS without Channel Crossing TO NEW YORK.
Sailings from Southampton and Cherbourg.
Augusta Victoria .Sept. 25 Columbia.........Oct. 9
Fürst Bismarck....Oct. 2 Normannia ....Oct. 17
HAMBURG-AMERICAN LINE,
PARIS, 3 RUE SCRIBE.

NETHERLAND AMERICAN STEAM NAVIGATION COMPANY.
Weekly Mail Service between Rotterdam and New York via BOULOGNE-SUR-MER.
SCHIEDAM ....Sept. 26
VEENDAM..................Sept. 30
Baggage booked and forwarded unopened from Paris to steamers.
Apply to Company's Offices. 1 rue Auber, Paris; 36 rue des Ecoles, Boulogne-sur-Mer. Telegraphic address: NASM.

RED STAR LINE.—ANTWERP-NEW YORK.
FRIESLAND, for New York .... Sat., Sept. 26
KENSINGTON, for New York...........Sat., Oct. 3
Baggage forwarded unopened to the steamers.
Apply to von der Becke and Marsily, Antwerp; Al. Peters, 49a Friedrichstrasse, Berlin; Red Star Line, 14 Kartnerring, Vienna, or to N. Martin, 9 rue Scribe, Paris.

WHITE STAR LINE ROYAL MAIL STEAMERS
LIVERPOOL TO NEW YORK.
BRITANNIC ....Sept. 30 | TEUTONIC...:...Oct. 21
MAJESTIC ....Oct. 7 | BRITANNIC ......Oct. 28

·a Sq·
CA·

BADEN-BADEN HOTEL DE·
First-class, with eve·
Lawn Tennis.

ST. MOR·
HOTEL ENGAD·
6,130 FEET ABOVE ·
First class. Best situation. Open summer an· Patronized by the élite of society. Oldest hotel of · 250 beds and many private sitting-rooms. Largest and · and corridors. Lift, electric light, steam heating on· Excellent Orchestra. Asphalt Lawn Tennis Court. Ice R·

MERAN. HOTEL ERZH·
HIGHLY REPUTED FIRST-·
every modern comfort. Magnificent public rooms. Most beautiful large ga· Post and telegragh offices in the Hotel. Favorite residence of American an·

VENICE. HOTEL BRITANNIA. Grand ·anal. El·
GENOA. HOTEL DE LA VILLE. First·
Only hotel with a view of sea. ·
BOZEN. (Tyrol).—HOTEL VICTORIA. New prop· First clas· comfort. ·

HOWLETT'S STABLES,
24 RUE DES BELLES FEUILLES.
NOTED COACHING TEAMS,
FOR COUNTRY DRIVES AND DRIVING LESSONS
Also on hire
ALL KINDS OF CARRIAGES WITH GOOD HORSES
by Day, Month or Year.
HORSES TAKEN IN AT LIVERY.

LONDON.
MASSAGE, HERB-SCENTED AND ELECTRIC Pine Bath.
Madame D'Allen, assisted by the Misses Julien, Lisle, Claret and Trilby, from 11 till 9, Sundays included, at 37 Old Bond-street (Piccadilly end).

LADIES' ATTIRE.
Mme Clément JOYEUSE
DRESSES AND MANTLES
PARIS 44, Rue du Colisée.

STYLISH DRESSES at very moderate prices. Mme. LEGER, late first fitter from first-class rue de la Paix houses. 24 rue Caumartin.

TO be well dressed ladies should apply to Mlles. Gercte 62 rue du Bac. For this reason: they make very pretty foulard dresses at 140fr.; dresses in woollen at 90fr.

SHIPPI·G.
AMERICAN EXPRESS COMPANY
Head Office: 65 Broadway, New York.
6 RUE HALÉVY, PARIS.
3 WATERLOO-PLACE (Regent-st.), LONDON
Local Agencies at most prominent points in Europe.
Merchandise, packages, baggage transported to and from the United States, Canada, Mexico and Europe by fastest steamers. Only company under above title authorized by the United States Government to carry goods IN BOND from New York and Boston direct to inland points of entry in the United States and to Canada and Mexico. NO CHARGE FOR CUSTOMS, BROKERAGE OR CARTAGE at New York or Boston on goods shipped IN BOND. Travelers' cheques, money orders, cable transfers. Uniformed agents meet steamers on arrival at New York. Rates and information furnished at any agency in Europe or America.

AMERICANS SHOULD SEE PITT AND SCOTT for STORAGE and FORWARDING

I·
BERLITZ ·
Latin Quart·
BOARDING AN· ladies. 51 rue S·
CHATEAU D'AU· 16 r. d'Auteuil, ·
COLLEGE FOR · Mmes. Cherion et·
INSTITUTION · Malakoff, Dr. H. · table, splendid roo· Universities Fre·
MR. HERBER· late Cav. Fran· to give lessons in v· address 81 Blenheim·
RUDY INST·
ST. GALL, INT· SWITZERLAND. Dr. S· and e·
ST. MARGAR· the household. Address·
ST. PAUL'S SCH· Villeneuve-l'Etang; arrang. perfect, excellent· for youths of 7 to 20; · Apply to Mr. Herman, ·
THE REV. JAMES· Prepares for Eng. and Ame· for boys under 15. Ex· boarders. 6 av. Montespa· la Pompe. Class-work re·
AU·
First-class. Electric Light. CARL· ANGER·
CARLSBAD, ·
CARLSBAD,·
ISCHL. Fa· Under personal manag·
VIENNA. H· Favorite re·
VIENNA. First-class and best sit· English and American· sanitary arrangement· and attendance) fr·

LESS FLIRTING ON OCEAN LINERS.

Orders to Officers to This Effect Issued by the Cunard Steamship Company.

NOTICE SENT FROM LIVERPOOL.

Result of Too Much Attention Paid to Women Passengers During Transatlantic Voyages.

[BY COMMERCIAL CABLE TO THE HERALD.]

BOSTON, Saturday.—Orders have been received here from the managers of the Cunard Steamship Company in Liverpool to the effect that the officers of the line must pay less attention to the women passengers hereafter.

It is understood that the order is the result of letters of complaint received from passengers with regard to the recent flirting indulged in by the officers with women passengers during voyages.

SAILINGS FOR EUROPE.

Mrs. Harrison Kerr and Mr. and Mrs. Hanna Among Those Sailing from New York.

[BY COMMERCIAL CABLE TO THE HERALD.]

NEW YORK, Saturday.—Sailing to-day on the Vaderland are Mmes. Harrison Kerr and H. W. Curtiss, Dr. Grace Dewey, Mr. and Mrs. Frank R. Hanna, Mr. and Mrs. George F. Parmelee, Mr. and Mrs. Eugène Pool, Mr. H. T. Richardson, Mr. and Mrs. Thomas E. Satterthwaite.

On the Pretoria are Mr. and Mrs. Lowell M. Palmer, Mrs. E. G. Scott, Judge C. H. Wickham, Mr. Calvin Whitney, Mr. Herbert N. Casson, Mr. and Mrs. George H. Campbell and Mrs. Lloyd Harris.

HONORS FOR NOTED SURGEON.

[BY COMMERCIAL CABLE TO THE HERALD.]

PHILADELPHIA, Saturday.—Sir Frederick Treves, the noted English surgeon, will be the recipient of an honorary degree at the commencement exercises of the University of Pennsylvania on June 13.

PHILADELPHIA HORSE SHOW.

New York Exhibitors Win Again, Mr. Reginald Vanderbilt Being of the Number.

[BY COMMERCIAL CABLE TO THE HERALD.]

PHILADELPHIA, Saturday. — The New York exhibitors at the horse show here yesterday won six firsts out of fourteen entries. Mr. Reginald Vanderbilt captured the blue ribbon for ponies in harness.

Mrs. J. B. Grosvenor received three blue ribbons and Messrs. J. H. Moore and Eben D. Jordan one each.

TIE AT ELEVEN INNINGS.

Great Game of Baseball Between Cincinnati and New York, of National League

ATLANTIC PASSAGE RATES.

Break Up of the Pool Controlling the Fares Between England and New York.

[BY THE HERALD'S SPECIAL WIRE.]

LONDON, Tuesday.—It is announced on good authority that the steamship pool that has for a number of years controlled the price of passages between Southampton and Liverpool and New York, has been broken, and that the transatlantic traveler will enjoy lower rates in the immediate future at least.

This pool, which was formed several years ago, comprised among its members all the leading transatlantic companies, such as the Cunard, White Star, American, North German Lloyd, Hamburg-American and the French. The minimum winter rate for a first class passage was £15, the minimum second class rate averaged £8. This applied only to the first class steamers of these companies.

Yesterday I found upon investigation that several companies were offering rates below the minimum. A gentleman showed me a letter in which a well-known company offered him a minimum price of £12 first-class to New York. I called at the offices of the American Line, in Cockspur-street, and in the absence of the agent, I ascertained from a clerk that, while they had no authority to make a rate to-day less than £15 first-class, they expected to make a £12 rate on March 1. The rumor was current that the White Star Company intended to meet a cut on the other lines by making a £10 rate first-class to New York, but this lacked confirmation. The minimum second-class rate, it is understood, will be reduced to £7.

ered from this
inspired by the
are anxious to
is no truth in
nsidered harm-
to its action.
no representa-
rable to trouble
circles is that they
Germany.—Daily

ADOPTED.

powered by the
to Declare

via HONG KONG,
ublica," the Filipino
es that the Malolos
a new constitution,
onfidence in General
powered him to de-
nericans whenever

f women held in
nthusiastically re-
al Aguinaldo for
ce of men in the
dependence and

rred last night,
y killed a Filipino
e Tondo outpost.
ely excited and
rdly assassina-

GED.

nos Who At-
e Ameri-
s.

ONG-KONG, Thurs-

VEXATIONS FOR RETURNING AMERICANS.

They Must Make a Declaration of the Prices of All Articles Purchased Abroad and Paste a Copy on Their Trunks—Questions of Value to Be Settled by Appraisers.

[BY COMMERCIAL CABLE TO THE HERALD.]

NEW YORK, Thursday.—Persons returning from abroad after February 1 will find that they must comply with still another unpleasant formality of the law with regard to such articles as they may have purchased abroad.

By a recent ruling of the Treasury Department they will have to declare in detail to the customs officers any and all articles they have purchased abroad. This will not be agreeable news to transatlantic voyagers, for heretofore they have been required to declare their purchases in a general way, only giving the total value, and if that proved to be less than $100 then the purchases were exempt from duty.

A NEW RULING.

This will not be the case hereafter. This ruling of the Treasury Department was brought about, the collector of the port, Mr. Bidwell, explained to me last evening, by a combination of circumstances. An inspector of customs, he said, had had charges preferred against him for failure to declare certain articles dutiable. The inspector appealed to the collector, asserting that his action was justified by the Tariff Act and other acts of a similar nature, which were cited, and for his future guidance the collector, Mr. Bidwell, referred the whole matter to the Treasury Department for a ruling. In response to the inquiry he received the following instructions:—

THE TREASURY'S DECISION.

TREASURY DEPARTMENT, Jan, 13, 1899.

"Sir,—In referring to your letter of the

questions at issue between the United States and Great Britain have been prepared.

Mr. Harris, the new Minister accredited to Austria, has received his instructions and is now at his home making preparations for proceeding to Vienna.

A. H. GARLAND DEAD.

Mr. Cleveland's Attorney-General Has a Fit of Apoplexy in the Supreme Court Room.

WASHINGTON, Thursday.—Judge Augustus H. Garland, Attorney General in President Cleveland's first Cabinet, fell in an apoplectic fit while arguing in the Supreme Court room here to-day, and died almost immediately.—Daily Telegraph.

Law and Politics.

Judge Garland was born in Tennessee in 1832, but went to Arkansas with his parents. He studied law and was admitted to the bar in Washington, Ark., in 1853. He was an opponent of secession but on the outbreak of the war espoused the Confederate cause and served as a Senator until the close of the rebellion. He was elected a United States Senator in 1867, but was not allowed to take his seat. He subsequently became Secretary of State and then Governor of Arkansas, and in 1876 was elected to the United States Senate and served from March 5, 1877, to March 5, 1885, when he took his seat in President Cleveland's first Cabinet as Attorney-General. A sad incident of his life was the suicide of his daughter, Miss Daisy Gar-
er 27, 1893.

NEW

His Solicit
His

[BY THE
LONDON, Fr
Earl Poulett
George yeste
tion on the
former organ
body was br
Wednesday
met by a larg
was borne in
estate trade
night by the
was deposite
north side of
remains of t
have died du
The Centr
Hinton Poul
reported to
his residence.
Henry buildi
that a doctor
he had prono
be suffering f
great measur
TH
With regar
is stated the
Hall, has adv
take his seat
effect a forci
of the estates,
for the mere
claim which,
unassailable to
the path of th
not look perfe
istence of an
has in his fa
law, possession
of tenants an
gagees. If, as s
ton is guided
will happen w
the rents shal
ant. No dou
made on beha
agent or colle
a dilemma fr
only by due p
THE
This is the
by Mr. Hall.
stated in a le
that a resettl
fected in 185
claimant and t
ton Poulett, t
marriage, mus
inherited. Th
late earl was
there were fou
title, he gave
which left him
ing, as he af
limited life int
death, by the
passes to a co
Earl Poulett s
person calling
but it also ba
he always reco

Y AND AMERICA.

Resolution Addressed to McKinley by the American Colony in Munich.

g is the text of the resolu-
the members of the Ameri-
Munich, to which reference
been made in a despatch from the HERALD's special correspondent in Munich:—

To His Excellency the President:—

SIR—A meeting of Americans temporarily residing in Munich was held on January 23 in the reading room of the American Church, at which the following declaration of sentiment was unanimously adopted:—

We, American citizens sojourning in Munich, feeling that we are to some extent cognizant of the true sentiment of the people of both the United States and Ger-
express our regrets at the
which tend to strain
the two nations. We
iefly due to a too great
rt of the public in the
sponsible statements and wilful exaggerations of the sensational press, and we believe we represent the thinking classes of both countries when we say there is no real cause for unfriendly feeling between the United States and Germany.

We have the honor to be, sir, your obedient servants, G. Monroe Royce, chaplain of the American Church in Munich, chairman; John M. Stillman, Stanford University, secretary; R. Meyer, New York, and George W. Patterson, University of Michigan, the committee.

and also voted
on in aid of the
was signed by
are to remain

shed at the con-
day between the
ipinos. It is ru-
at the next meet-

HOW THE RULE WILL ACT.

The collector, Mr. Bidwell, says that the new regulation will go into effect on February 1, and he believed that, while at first it might cause some complaint on the part of passengers, it would ultimately be found beneficial. He said the rule now was that returning passengers were not obliged to declare any personal baggage they had purchased abroad that was valued at less than

.—The Filipino
been instructed
t the Philippine
at Malolos, the
y last.—Globe.

eneral Otis.

—Two long cable
Otis were received
t yesterday, but
anspire as to their

written on the back of the passengers' trunks.

PERTINENT EXAMPLES.

"For example," Mr. Bidwell said, "suppose a passenger has a comb in his baggage and declares that he purchased it for $4. The inspector will say, knowing the market value, of course, that the comb sells here for $6. In such a case the comb would go to the appraising officer, who would fix the duty to be levied upon it. A man again

CAIRO

Stated that
Present

[BY THE
LONDON, Fr
current yeste
Cairo to the
"Pall Mall Ga

AMERICAN VISITORS IN THOUSANDS.

All the Transatlantic Companies Regard This Year as One of the Best on Record.

THOUSANDS WAITING TO RETURN.

Bookings on All the Lines Extend to September and Incoming Steamers Full.

[FROM OUR SPECIAL CORRESPONDENT.]

LONDON, August 30.—An evening paper has been endeavoring to get at the number of Americans who have visited Europe this year. It has failed in the attempt, but its investigations are still interesting, and point to 1895 as a record year in the history of the American invasion.

The London agent of one of the principal Atlantic steamship companies said an American had gravely informed him that there had been at least 200,000 Americans in Europe this year, and that at a reasonable estimate they would leave $200.000,000 behind them. "Of course," said the agent, "these figures are absurd. But this American's calculations set me wondering how many really had come across the Atlantic during the year."

The American visitor, says the journal I have mentioned, though thousands have gone home, is still to be found at every turn, not only in London, but all over England, Scotland, Wales and Ireland.

THOUSANDS WAITING FOR RETURN BERTHS.

There are thousands upon this side of the Atlantic now who are desirous of taking ship for America, and who are unable to secure even a berth.

"We have done 30 per cent. more business this year than in 1892," said Mr. Berting of the Hamburg American line, "and 1892 was our record year up to that time. On such ships as the Normannia, Fürst Bismarck, Columbia and Augusta Victoria the bookings are full up to September 1. We have a few berths up to September 27 and four cabins up to October 7. I do not see how many of the people who are in a hurry to get back will succeed in doing so, as other large companies are pushed as hard for room as we are. We also have a line from New York to the Mediterranean ports and *vice versa*, and upon this our bookings have been very large this year. Our steamers coming this way are coming full, and I don't know how long the rush will last. No! I do not know how many Americans have come to Europe this year. May be 50,000; may be 100,000."

Though the office of the American line was crowded with people, who seemed anxious to get out of the country, Mr. James Parton found time to answer all the questions put to him. "We are practically full," he said, "until the middle of October. There is always a bare chance of a berth, and occasionally somebody gives up a room. But outside of those chances we are booked up to the middle of October. This is the greatest year we have had since 1889. That year may have been as good for business as this, but I have not looked into the matter. The year 1892 was also a good one. We are now running three ships, the St. Louis, the Paris and the New York, between Southampton and New York. Our new ship, the St. Louis, is in every way satisfactory. She was given a trial last week and steamed fifty-two miles against tide at the rate of 21 knots per hour, and fifty-two miles with the tide, at the rate of 23 6 knots per hour. That is an average of 22.3 knots. She has not made what we call a fast trip across the Atlantic yet, but when she is called upon I think she will do some surprisingly fast work."

CUNARD AND NORTH GERMAN LLOYD LINES.

"How many Americans have come to Europe this year? That is beyond me; perhaps 50,000, but that is only a guess."

Mr. East, manager of the London office of the Cunard line, which has six boats running between New York and Liverpool, said: "Our passenger traffic this year has been the greatest since the Jubilee year. Our favored boats are the Lucania and Campania, probably because they make the fastest passages across the Atlantic." Mr. East, however, would not attempt to even try and estimate how many Americans had come to Europe this year.

The North-German Lloyd line is hard pushed for room like its competitors. On the Trave, which sailed from Southampton on Sunday, the company found it necessary to build a number of temporary state rooms, in order to accommodate passengers who begged to be taken home, and who had been booked for the Aller, which was due to sail last Wednesday, but had the misfortune to break her shaft.

The White Star line is at present badly in need of more room also, and its agents tell the same story of a prosperous business. Indeed, all the companies agree that this is one of the very best years they have ever had.

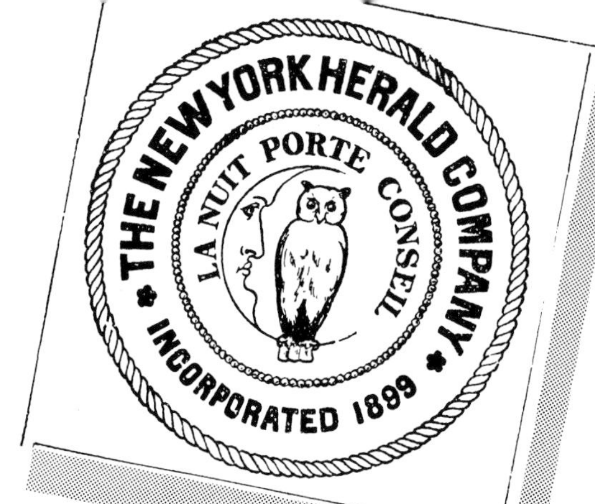

NEW YORK HERALD

(EUROPEAN EDITION)

49 AVENUE DE L'OPERA, PARIS.

The NEW YORK HERALD is published in New York and Paris every day of the year. The European Edition is sold at 15c. per copy (Sundays excepted). Sunday edition, 25c.

Money for subscriptions can be transmitted direct by cheque or draft on London or Paris, or by Post Office order. All money remitted at risk of sender.

In order to ensure attention, subscribers wishing their addresses changed must give their old as well as their new addresses.

TERMS TO SUBSCRIBERS, FREE OF POSTAGE, DAILY, INCLUDING SUNDAY.

	Paris and Brussels. Francs.	France and Belgium. Francs.	Abroad. Francs.
ONE MONTH	4.50	5	7
THREE MONTHS	13.50	15	21
SIX MONTHS	27.00	30	42
ONE YEAR	50.00	58	84

SUNDAY EDITION ONLY.

	Paris and France. Francs.	Abroad. Francs.
THREE MONTHS	4	5
SIX MONTHS	8	10
ONE YEAR	15	20

All letters must be addressed NEW YORK HERALD (European Edition), 49 AV. DE L'OPERA, PARIS.

All correspondence intended for publication should be authenticated by name and address of the writer, not for publication, but as a guarantee of good faith.

Manuscripts and other communications will always receive prompt and careful consideration, but the HERALD refuses to return, or to enter into correspondence about rejected articles submitted for approval, even if stamps be enclosed.

ADVERTISING RATES.

	Fr.C.
ORDINARY ADVERTISEMENTS:—	
Last page, per line	2.00
Inside page, opposite editorials, per line....	5.00
Other inside pages, per line..................	3.00
COMMUNICATED ADVERTISEMENTS:—	
Editorial page, per line......................	25.00
Other pages, except first, per line............	15.00
PERSONALS:—	
Editorial page, last column, per line........	5.00
SITUATIONS WANTED:—	
On Mondays, special tariff, three lines for....	0.50
Other days, per line	0.25
APARTMENTS OR HOUSES TO LET OR FOR SALE, on Tuesday and Friday, three lines for	1.00
BIRTH, MARRIAGE and DEATH NOTICES:—	
Not exceeding three lines....................	10.00
Additional lines (per line)..................	2.00

TO ADVERTISERS.

The NEW YORK HERALD (European Edition) is taken by special agents on board all incoming Transatlantic steamships at HAVRE, QUEENSTOWN, LIVERPOOL, SOUTHAMPTON, etc.

C. CHRISTIANSON, Manager.

NEW YORK—Herald square, Broadway and 35th street.

WASHINGTON—No. 1502 H street, N.W.

LONDON—"Daily Chronicle" buildings, 81 Fleet street, E.C. For advertisements and subscriptions 1 Trafalgar Buildings, Northumberland avenue.

The HERALD will not guarantee to distribute circulars received as answers to advertisements.

THE NEW YORK HERALD HAS A LARGER CIRCULATION THAN ANY OTHER NEWSPAPER PRINTED IN ENGLISH ON THE CONTINENT.

72nd YEAR - - - - No. 52.

TO ENSURE TELEGRAMS BEING SENT BY THIS ROUTE THEY SHOULD BE MARKED "VIA HAVRE COMMERCIAL," WHICH INSTRUCTIONS ARE NOT CHARGED FOR.

PARIS, THURSDAY, Feb. 21, 1907.

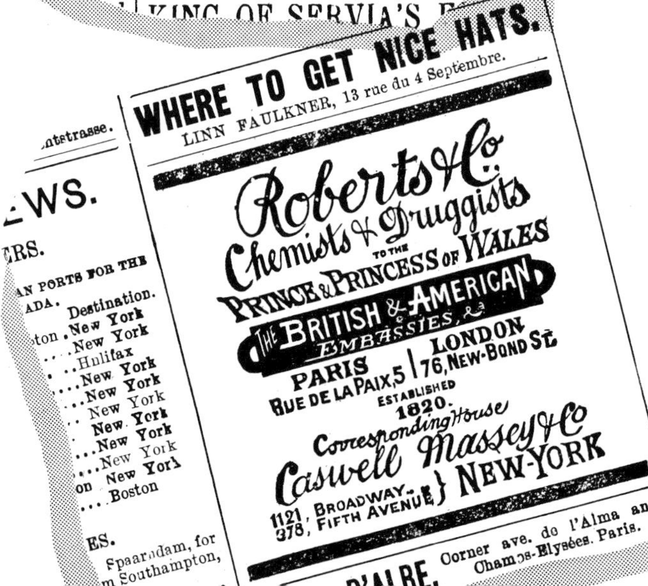

"HERALD'S" WEATHER SERVICE.

IN PARIS.

Beginning with a wet and sloppy morning, to which Parisians are accustomed and hardened, yesterday's weather had fits of fair periods, alternating with black clouds which distributed patterings of rain here and there. The g l impses of sunshine were attractive, for there are many more or less truthful persons in Paris who declare they have seen the sun only twice since November. The temperature was far from tropical.

At three o'clock this morning the sky was overcast and the barometer registered 748mm. and was falling, having dropped 6mm. during yesterday.

The Meteorological Observatory, Tour Saint-Jacques, reports:—

	February 20 Min.	February 20 Max.	February 21 Midnt.	February 21 3 a.m.
Temp. (Cent.).	3.5	10.5	4	2

VELOCITY OF WIND PER HOUR.

In miles	45	37½	22½
In kilomètres	72	60	36
Direction of the wind	WSW		WSW

February 21, 1906.

The weather one year ago to-day was fair, with some rain. The minimum temperature was 1deg. and the maximum 8deg. Cent.

In the United States.

[BY COMMERCIAL CABLE TO THE HERALD.]

NEW YORK, Wednesday.—Hazy and overcast weather prevailed to-day in New York City. The temperature ranged from zero Cent. (32deg. Fahr.) to 3.5deg. Cent. (38deg. Fahr.) There was a fresh north-easterly breeze. The outlook is somewhat threatening, and the barometer is unsteady to-night.

Fair weather prevails in the central valleys, the Lake region and in the west, but a depression on the central North Carolina coast is moving north-east and causing considerable cloudiness in the Atlantic States. The temperature is near the normal in the country generally, but is rising in the north-west.

Overcast weather and strong north-east breezes are indicated for the western Atlantic from latitude 35deg. to 50 deg. north.

The HERALD'S correspondent at Bermuda reports: Fair; gentle southerly breeze; temperature, 19.5deg. Cent. (67 deg. Fahr.); barometer, rising.

The HERALD'S St. John's (N.F.) correspondent reports: Cloudy; gentle south-westerly breeze; temperature, —1deg. Cent. (30deg. Fahr.).

The HERALD'S Cape Race correspondent reports: Cloudy; strong north-westerly

FORECASTS FOR TO-DAY.

Cross Channel Steamers Will Have Rough Passages.

OVERCAST.

The HERALD predicts overcast weather with high winds and some rain for to-day.

breeze; temperature, —2deg. Cent. (28 deg. Fahr.).

At Dover.

DOVER, Wednesday.—At the Burlington Hotel, at noon to-day, the temperature was 6deg. Cent. The weather was cloudy, the wind north-westerly and the sea moderate.

At Folkestone.

FOLKESTONE, Wednesday.—At the Pavilion Hotel, at six p.m. to-day, the temperature was 7deg. Cent. The weather was fair, the wind north-westerly and the sea rough.

TAKING THE HEIGHT.

"What are you doing now, Patrick?"

"Sure your mother towld me to see how high the thermometer was."—Leslie's Weekly.

Weather at Fashionable Resorts.

AIX-LES-BAINS.—Hotel Regina, 10 a.m., 5deg. Cent. Splendide and Excelsior Hotels, noon, 6deg. Cent. Rainy.

ALGIERS.—Mustapha Hotel St. Georges, noon (on the terrace), 22deg. Cent. Very fine.

BARCELONA.—Grand Hotel, noon, 18deg. Cent.

BERLIN. — Hotel Bristol, noon, 3.5deg. Cent. Cloudy.

BEAULIEU. — Petite Afrique, minimum during the night, 7deg. Cent.; maxi-

VIENNA.—Hotel Bristol, noon, ... Cent. Fine.

WIESBADEN.—Hotel Nassau (Nassauerhof), 11 a.m., zero Cent. Hotel Kaiserhof, noon, zero Cent. Hotel Rose, 2 p.m., 4deg. Cent. Snow.

From Centigrade to Fahrenheit.

TO THE EDITOR OF THE HERALD:—

I am anxious to find out the way to figure the temperature from Centigrade to Fahrenheit and vice versâ. In other words, I want to know, whenever I see the temperature designated on Centigrade thermometer, how to find out what it would be on Fahrenheit's thermometer.

"OLD PHILADELPHIA LADY."

Paris, December 24, 1899.

"MISTLETOE'S" SELECTIONS.

Pronostics pour Auteuil:

PRIX SAUVETEUR—Chevalier, Gavarni.
PRIX DU PHALANSTERE—Le Miracle, Cabriole
PRIX DU VIADUC—Saint-Laurent, Diégo.
PRIX CASTIGLIONE—Alcyon II, Argentine.
PRIX BEAUMANOIR—Le Miracle, La Chaldée.
PRIX DE LA FAISANDERIE—Liliac, Petit Frère.

"MISTLETOE."

Yesterday's Gale in Paris and France.

Paris and the rest of France were yesterday swept by a gale of hurricane-like violence. The wind was of unusual velocity. At the Tour Saint-Jacques Observatory high clouds were seen moving at the rate of 66 mètres a second, or more than 237 kilomètres an hour. The storm did considerable damage, particularly to telegraph and telephone lines, telegraphic communication with England being almost entirely interrupted.

The damage to property was also considerable. The balloon house of the Aéro-Club at Saint-Cloud was completely wrecked at an early hour yesterday morning, and all day chimney-pots were flying and scaffolding and palisades were a source of public danger.

ART INSTITUTE FOR BRUSSELS. THE formation of a great International Art Institute has been undertaken by the Belgian Government, as the outcome of resolutions adopted at the Liége Exhibition, and the main lines of the new organization, which has the support of many European and American cities, have been laid down. Details appear on page 9.

ENDING "GRAFT" AMONG POLICE. GENERAL BINGHAM, the Police Commissioner of New York, who, before he accepted that arduous post, was regarded as the "social dictator" at the White House, is not seeking to dodge responsibility. He has just had introduced a bill at Albany which ha... purpose the extension of his p... passed General Bi... minate "graft" ... police force or ... failure to do so. ... news on this s... page 7, where a ... personal intel... latest arrived ...

"FEMMES ...

the attemp... what is to ... tion: cab... to pass ... licences began ... streets of the capital ... sketch of their experiences will be ...

Christi. The Tacoma ... gos.

The ...

It is reported ... de Paris" that ... œuvres will be h... usual so that ... direct them befo... on May 23. Th... be the western ... understood that ... Admiral Fourni... tary Medal.

GENERAL ...

Destroye...

[SPECIAL ...

MALTA, Wedn... troyer Nikh stea...

THREE JAPA... AR...

Squadron to R... Organized f... a...

HONOLULU, T... cruisers Matsus... sukushima arriv... its were exchan... the local author... remain here a ... organized for t... and men.—Tem...

YACHT...

MARSEILLES, ... steam yacht M... quhar owner, ha... (From Watso... agents.)

CANNES, W... steam yacht S... owner, and par... for Ajaccio. (F... builder.)

Excu...

MALTA, Wed... cursion steame... of 200 on boa... Tunis.

PERSONA...

Mr. W. B. S... Hotel Contine... Carlo.

The "Temps" ... at the Mairie ... rondissement, ... brated of Mlle. ... of the former ... C. Coxe, Ame... neral in Paris, ... Coxe, of Buffal...

At ...

Christmas Eve Procession in Honor of the "Old Philadelphia

To the Editor of the New York Herald:—

Sir,—Less than three weeks have now to elapse ere as many years will have passed away since **THE OLD PHILADELPHIA LADY** burst into perpetual bloom on your editorial page, and I beg to suggest that a little celebration in the form of a procession be organized in honor of the anniversary of the date on which she penned her classic query. As it will be Christmas Eve her countless admirers can make a day as well as a night of it. I am not used to business nor to organizing things, having in early manhood fortunately inherited enough from another dear old Philadelphia lady to enable me to move promptly to Paris and live at my ease, but I sometimes refresh my memory of my boyhood's home by perusing the conundrum which holds the Continent enthralled. Therefore I leave the organizing to others, who have knowledge of such matters, but permit me to roughly sketch my idea of what such a procession should be. The organizing committee can fill in details of badges, music and such things.

The procession to form at the Washington statue near the Trocadéro at noon, and proceed in the following order:—

The American Ambassador and staff, mounted and in carriages.

Portrait banner of the "Old Philadelphia Lady," flanked by an American flag and the coat-of-arms of Philadelphia (on a flag), borne by Heralds.

Portrait banners of Mr. Fahrenheit and Monsieur Centigrade, borne side by side by other Heralds, each preceded by a Herald blowing a trumpet in honor of his own particular banner.

The American Consul-General and staff in carriages, carrying portraits of some o the former Consul-Generals.

Americans of the smart set in Paris i their automobiles.

Prominent American business men o Paris in carriages and headed by the presi dent of the American Chamber of Com merce.

The American jockeys (those still left i country by police), mounted on thorough breds. Colors, the Stars and Stripes.

The American artists of Paris on bi cycles, leading the American art student on foot, wearing American-made shoes

H SUPPLEMENT. COMLPETE NUMBER: 20 PAGES.

-ady" Suggested by an Admirer.

Ordinary but real Americans to wear ot hats.

Extraordinary but naturalized Ameri-ans, high hats.

Busted Americans of either class.

The route to be viâ the rue Lincoln to he Champs-Elysées, place de la Concorde, ue Royale and the boulevards to the venue de l'Opéra and the HERALD Office, hich will be superbly decorated in honor f the occasion, and will be saluted and heered by each section as it passes. hence to the two great American shrines f Paris, the Grands Magasins du Louvre and the Bon Marché, the first half of the procession dispersing at the former and the second at the latter shrine, the busted Americans withdrawing to the rue Volney.

In the evening illumination of the HERALD Office, and all day from noon until midnight Quaker Oats lunches to be supplied free at Henry's Bar and the Café Américain to all Americans who produce railway passes or dead-head tickets. Those from Philadelphia to have two helpings.

SCHUYLKILL DE RITTENHOUSE.

Paris, Dec. 4, 1902.

HERAL

1906.—TWELVE PAGES.

ommercial Cable.

R DOG; HIS LINER.

Obliged to Hire Tug- ke the Departing voie.

N THE DOCK.

Voyage and Broke ust as Vessel d.

: TO THE HERALD.] .—A little yellow l to a sea voyage aster to lose the to-day. The two and the dog was ward.

a "ki-yi" and a e gang plank. The ith longshoremen The collie turned er ran south and e dog and returned e master rushed up the Savoie out in had to hire a tug- og and his trunks

AKING RECORD

Off Sable Island e—Averaging Knots.

THE HERALD.] The Provence o'clock this nch line's

the er-

AMERICAN FOODS FOR LONDON HOTELS

Big Consignment of Many Delicacies Now on Way Across the Atlantic.

FIRST FRESH FOOD SHIPMENT.

Terrapin and Oyster Crabs on List Intended to Tickle Yankee Palates on Foreign Shores.

[BY COMMERCIAL CABLE TO THE HERALD.]

NEW YORK, Thursday.—Packed in a special storeroom on the Kaiserin Augusta Victoria, sailing to-day, was a ton of the choicest things known to the American palate. In the lot were terrapin, kingfish, bass, flounders, softshell crabs, oyster crabs, redhead, mallard and canvasback duck and Virginia hams, all intended for London hotels.

This is the first time that fresh American food in such quantity and variety has been sent to England, so far as is known, and M. August Keller, the manager of the restaurant on the Kaiserin Augusta Victoria believes that this exportation will open new fields to London chefs, and perhaps induce Paris and Berlin to try the same means of pleasing visitors from the United States.

HORSE SHOW IN BALTIMORE.

Fine Weather for the Opening Day—Many Fashionable People Among the Spectators.

[BY COMMERCIAL CABLE TO THE HERALD.]

BALTIMORE, Md., Thursday.—Sunny skies and soft breezes made the opening lay of the Horse Show a brilliant suc- Fifty-eight boxes were occupied, grand stand was fill with ut-of-t

AGAINS

In the An this morning will be found York Herald's automobile spe American high timely cartoon.

DIGEST OF T LONDO

Items from the "Mo Chronicle," "St News" and

[BY THE HERALD'S LONDON, Friday. summary of the news this morning's papers

The Spanish Marriag

The "Morning Post," Princess Victoria Eug says: "The impending young couple appeals sentiments which are dee low-countrymen. The t which bind England to S on the old-time appreciat nation learnt in times bot of rivalry, to entertain They needed no such eve their strengthening or ren Royal marriage is sure t them."

Lord Milner Honored.

A banquet in honor of V ner was given at the Hote night, when the toast of " was submitted by Mr. Chamb made an eloquent reference vice which the noble lord ha in a great crisis in the nation and strongly repelled the adv cisms which had been passed u Milner's policy and conduct o In acknowledging the toast, Lor expressed deep gratitude for the ment paid to him, and indicat anxiety as to the present situa South Africa.—Standard.

Mischief of House of Lords.

Speaking at Liverpool last nig Lloyd George referred to the Ho Lords as a "house of mischief" an clared it was intolerable arroganc

HOTEL PROPRIETORS TALK ABOUT "TIPS."

Information of the Most Complete Description Given in Answer to the "Herald's" Circular.

GRATUITIES APPROVED.

The System "Has the Advantage of Encouraging Certain Little Attentions on the Part of the Employés which No Fixed Wages, However High, Would Ensure Regularly."

"GIVE WHAT YOU LIKE."

Most Nations Condemn the Custom of Giving "Tips"—In Theory—In Practice They Find It Better to Do as Did Their Fathers.

WHAT NATION GIVES THE MOST?

It is only a couple of days since the HERALD sent out a circular to the principal European hotels asking for an authoritative statement on the subject of "tips," and already the answers that have arrived roll up into the hundreds. The idea of seeking information from the hotel proprietors was prompted by a genuine shower of letters that followed a request to the HERALD to guide some inexperienced traveler through the mazes of the "tip" question. How much should he give, he asked, and to whom should he give it? The answers supplied by correspondents were so contradictory that in order to thoroughly exhaust the knotty subject, the HERALD has applied to the best source of information—that is, the hotelkeeper in person.

To-day the first selection from the answers received is given below. The circular consisted of the following questions:—

NEW YORK HERALD.
(European Edition.)

BUSINESS OFFICES: 49 AVENUE DE L'OPÉRA.
Paris, ... 1896.

M . . . . . .

Dear . . .

Will you kindly answer the following questions on the subject of "Tips," or as many of them as possible, and then return the circular to the Editor of the HERALD, 49 avenue de l'Opéra, for which purpose a stamped envelope is enclosed.

And oblige, yours truly,
C. CHRISTIANSON, Manager.

QUESTIONS.

1. Do you approve of gratuities or "tips" being given to the various employés and servants of your hotel?
2. What is the proper amount to be given by a single traveler after one week's stay—
   To the maître d'hôtel?
   To the hall porter?
   To the waiter in the restaurant?
   To the waiter who brings the first breakfast in the bedroom or private sitting-room?
   To the chambermaid?
   To the boots?
   To the luggage porters?
   To the omnibus driver?
3. What is the proper "tip" to be given to each of the above by a party of two persons after a week's stay at the hotel?
   By a married couple?
   By a family of three?
   By a family of four or more?
4. State a general rule to guide travelers as to the proper sums to be given in gratuities.
5. Are the servants in your hotel led to believe that "tips" are a regular and steady portion of their remuneration?
6. Do the servants in your hotel receive regular wages independent of "tips"?
7. Do the servants in your hotel receive no wages at all, but are expected to obtain their remuneration solely by means of "tips" from visitors?
8. Would you personally like to see the "tip" custom abolished?
9. Would you personally like to see the "tip" system maintained as it exists all over Europe to-day?
10. What are its advantages?
11. What are its disadvantages?
12. Have you any suggestions to make about "tips"?
13. Should "tips" be given when the visitor arrives, when he leaves, or when he requires any special or extra attention?
14. When "service" is charged in the bill, does or does not this imply that "tips" are not expected?
15. From your observations visitors of which particular nationality are most opposed to the "tip" custom?
   Which nationality most favors it?
16. Which nationality gives the biggest "tips"?
   Which nationality gives the smallest "tips"?

The answers are numbered in the same order as the questions.

certain little attentions on the part of the employés which no fixed wages, however high, would ensure regularly.

11. That very generous visitors may be attended to with zeal, sometimes to the prejudice both of the proprietor and of other less lavish guests.
12. That the opinion of the manager of the hotel should be asked as to the best way of making a general division of what it is intended to give.
13. Generally on the occasion of services which are not absolutely obligatory and then a present at the moment of departure if the service has been satisfactory.
14. As a general rule the servants always expect something, though naturally they ought not to claim it as a right.
15. Americans certainly, and by far.
16. French, decidedly.

HOTEL DE L'EUROPE AND MÉTROPOLE, LYONS

1. No.
2, 3 and 4. No
5, 6, 7 and 8. Th[...] sufficiently [...] wages an[...] pared to in[...] the custom[...]
9 and 10. No [...]
11. Tips tend t[...] to certain [...] of the ge[...]
12. The suppr[...] about gr[...] and less [...] calculat[...] the slac[...]
13, 14, 15. N[...]
16. The Ge[...] the m[...]

ETABLISSEM[...]

1. Yes.
2 to 7, 9, [...]
8. No.
10. The [...] tra[...]
12. Serv[...] en[...]
14. No [...] b[...]
16. Th[...]

1. C[...]
2. [...]
3, 9[...]
4. [...]
5. [...]
6. [...]
8 [...]
1[...]

2. Head waiter 5fr., porter 5fr., waiter at restaurant 5fr., shoeblack 3fr., driver of omnibus 2fr.
3. Two persons traveling together, a family of two 5fr., three persons 10fr., four or more persons 15fr.
4. On an average each traveler should give daily to each employé who serves him a minimum of 50c.
5. No.
6. Yes.
7. All the employés are appointed.
8. No.
9. Yes.
10. Tips stimulate the zeal of employés and make them more attentive to passengers.
11. The suppression of tips would lower the attention of the staff to travelers.
12. No answer.
13. When the traveler leaves and when he requires special attention.
This does not imply that the staff does [...]

[...]ericans are most liberal; [...]rtain classes of English

[...], PARIS.

be impossible to dispense [...]

[...]n the class of the hotel in [...]

[...]nd 10 per cent., according [...] of hotel.

[...]ld otherwise be impossible [...] *personnel*.

[...] it is impossible.

[...]ble.

[...]The hotels at Innsbruck tried [...]pedient of posting up notices [...] the guests to give no "tips." [...]sult was such a very unsatis[...]y service that the guests tried to [...]a improvement by giving "tips" [...]te of the notices—just as at the [...]issance with the *ouvreuses*.

[...] week or month in the case of a [...] stay, otherwise when leaving.

[...]ght to be so, but it is not.

[...]in theory, but they are not in [...]ctice.

[...] particular nationality. The people [...]o have traveled much give freely [...] order to [...]

3fr.
2fr. to 5fr.
3fr. to 10fr.

3. It is difficult to say, for there wou[...] be too much divergency.
4. The traveler can take as a basis t[...] attentiveness of the servants and t[...] amount he intends to spend.
5. No. My servants are well paid, and I [...] not concern myself with their tips.
6. Yes.
7. No answer.
8. Yes, but we should only find servan[...] with difficulty and at exorbita[...] wages.
9. Ditto.
10. The advantages are that the servant[...] expecting a "tip" at the traveler[...] departure, are more attentive a[...] polite. In spite of the strict orde[...] given by the office to forestall t[...] desires of guests, some servants a[...] impatient, and such may be affect[...] by "tips."
11. "Tips" make beggars of the servan[...] and sometimes to obtain them th[...] do not hesitate to wrong their em[...]ployers. The custom of "tipping" [...] old and well established, but is pe[...]nicious from my point of view.
12. "Tips" might be paid into an i[...]surance office and used as a pensi[...] fund for servants, but it would [...] very difficult to organize and contr[...] such an arrangement.
13. Generally on leaving.
14. The service charged in the bill is not f[...] "tips," and the servant may therefo[...] expect a "tip."
15. The Russians, and then the English a[...] the French.
16. The largest "tips" are given by t[...] Germans, French, Swiss, Dutc[...] Belgians, &c.; the smallest by t[...] Russians, English, Spanish, &c.

HOTEL D'ANGLETERRE, TROUVILLE.

1. In principle, no.
2. I consider that a traveler may calcula[...] 1fr. per day to be divided among t[...] servants, which should be given eith[...] to the proprietor or manager, so as n[...] to give without knowing who gets t[...] money. Porter and omnibus driv[...] separate.
3. In the same proportion except whe[...] there are many travelers in compan[...] in which case a reduction of 25 p[...] cent.
4. See clause 1.
5. They all reckon their wages as scarce[...] half what they get.
6. Yes.
7. Yes, but they reckon on tips.
8. Yes.
9. No.
[...] notorious that every servant a[...] [...]to a customer who pays w[...] [...] to another, and that se[...] [...] when they do not g[...]

would be in no
advantage, for
would be forced,
aise his servants'
arily his prices, both
s and board.

ving.

nglish.

PARAMÉ, PARAMÉ.

of pourboires would
press.

mployé is well paid.
3fr., according to the
rendered.

r.
r.

fr. (accordidg to the num-
runks).

proportion, but certainly

a traveler stopping a
distributed.

as become an established

employés are paid : for
chambermaid, 30fr. a
valet de chambre 40fr. a
ut all expect to receive

fer its suppression, but it
icult. Travelers would
suppress it.

who expect a good pour-
e attentive to travelers ;
e, of advantage to those
ned to be generous.

ntage to people who are
to be generous.

nding among the hotel-
Europe to raise the wages
ervants and inform travelers
servants are forbidden to
tips." This result might
e obtained by putting service
ll, under the head : "Service
to Servants."

enerally given at the moment

charge for service do not
that the servants do not

tipping" being widely
, it is natural that the
e the most generous.

hich "tips" are not
urally furnish the
to the supple-

HOTEL DE FRANCE
AT SAINT-MALO.

1. Yes.
2. At the wish of the guest, according to the services rendered and the willingness of each of the employés to please the guest.
3. As above.
4. That is the guest's affair.
5. Yes and no.
6. Yes.
7. No answer.
8. In cafés, yes ; but in hotels, no. The services rendered are not of the same nature.
9, 10, 11 and 12. No answer.
13. When the guest leaves.
14. An intelligent hotelkeeper should never put the service in the bill.
15. Frenchmen outside of Paris and the inhabitants of the big cities.
16. The Parisians and the English, the most ; the American is above classification—he pays for everything very liberally.

HOTEL DES BALANCES, LUCERNE.

1. No answer.
2, 3 and 4. According to the giver's ideas.
5. Some receive a fixed sum, others have reduced wages.
6. Yes.
7. No answer.
8. Yes ; but the visitor should pay extra for his personal demands and services.
9. Yes ; for extra services and the goodwill of the employé.
10. The employé will be attentive.
11. The employé would be negligent and would only do what was necessary.
12. I am personally opposed to pourboires, but we would then have employés less attentive and less good, and the guest would want to pay less or demand more comforts. There are guests who are always contented and satisfied. There are others who are always asking for things and are never satisfied. These latter ask the employé for things for which he cannot be paid. They ask him for all sorts of work—that the porter should clean his clothes, brush his shoes several times a day, that he should run errands. The demands on the femme de chambre are still more exacting : she is looked upon rather as the guest's own servant than as an employé of the hotel. Both those who are exacting and the satisfied ones pay the same price to the hotelkeeper. This is why these extra services ought to be paid extra.
13. No answer.

The service counted in the bill is rather ... otelkeeper on the price ... at, as well as lighting, ... sed in the price of

vants ...
tips.
11. That of stimulating servants ... on which they reckon ... bait of a tip.
12. I approve the American system, which is generalised in England, but it would be very hard to suppress "tips" in France, where one cannot go to the hairdresser's or elsewhere without giving them, not to speak of the cabmen.
13. On le ... stay ... fri
14. No, ... b
15. A
16. F

... the most ; the least.

(LYONS).

r rooms include ed to pay. Our s and we ignore es" altogether.

HOTEL ... (MONTREUX).

1. Yes.
2. 1fr. 50c. each, with the ...
3. 50c. a day.
4. Unanswered.
5. Tips are a part of their remuneration.
6. All except the two janitors.
7. All my servants are paid except the janitors.
8. Yes.
9. No.
10. The only advantage of tips is that the guests are better served.
11. It is demoralizing for the employés.
12. No.
13. At the departure.
14. It does not imply the giving of tips.
15. The French nation.
16. The German, Russian and Swiss the biggest, the French the smallest.

HOTEL —— PARIS.

1. Yes.
2. At the rate of 50c. per day.
3 and 4. No answer.
5. No.
6. Yes.
7. No answer.
8. No. In the first place the customer, if he is generous, is better served.
9. Yes.
10, 11 and 12. No answer.
13. When he leaves.
14. Service is not reckoned ; it is optional.
15. No answer.
16. Dutch the largest ; English the smallest.

GRAND HOTEL AND HOTEL DE FRANCE
(BORDEAUX).

MANAGER OF THE HERALD :—

I am in receipt of your list of questions respecting "tips" in general and the considerations which result therefrom.

My staff receive an adequate monthly salary, but I am persuaded that they are not insensible to the gratuities they consider ought to be paid them by travelers who are satisfied with their services.

As far as I am concerned I take no interest in the question, still I consider it natural that a traveler, when leaving, should distribute some token of satisfaction at the attention bestowed on them by those who wait on them.

VEUVE LOUIS PETER.

... nal unders... between hotelkeep...
Unanswered.
...ly it is the custom of employés to expect "tips."
...RIA, 10 CITÉ D'ANTIN, PARIS.

the question ...

HOTEL RICHMONDE

1. Yes.
2. 5fr. to 10fr.
3fr. to 5fr.

not consent to suppress it.

10. Hotel seravnts who expect a good pourboire are more attentive to travelers ; it is, therefore, of advantage to those who are inclined to be generous.

It is a disadvantage to

inhabitants of ... g cities.

16. The Parisians and the English, the most ; the American is above classification—he pays for everything very liberally.

HOTEL DES BALANCES, LUCERNE

THE CASTELLANES MEET THE GOULDS.

Arrival of the Parents of the Comte de Castellane, Fiancé of Miss Gould.

ACQUITTAL OF CAPTAIN HOWGATE

The America's Cup Committee Meet and Accept Mr. Iselin's Resignation.

DEATH OF GENERAL J. B CARR.

Mrs. Sarah Havemayer's Will Contested by Her Son, Whom She Disinherited.

[BY COMMERCIAL CABLE TO THE HERALD.]

NEW YORK, Feb. 25.—The Marquis and Marquise de Castellane and Comte Henri de Castellane were met at the dock yesterday on their arrival by Comte Jean de Castellane and M. Raoul Duval.

Mr. Gould's carriages were in waiting, and the party went to Mr. Gould's residence, where they are guests.

After a welcome by Mr. and Mrs. Gould Comte Jean de Castellane entered the drawing-room with Miss Anna Gould on his arm. The marquise gave her prospective daughter-in-law one searching glance, then a motherly embrace.

Then they had luncheon, which was followed by a family talk over coming affairs.

AT A MUSICALE.

The Marquise de Castellane accompanied Mrs. Gould to Mr. Bagby's musicale at the Hotel Waldorf this morning. Among the guests were the Earl of Caithness, Prince Loewenstein and Mmes. Wilmerding, Kernochan, Ronalds, Burden and Roosevelt.

Friends deny the rumor that Miss Gould has become a Catholic.

The Rev. Dr. Madison Peters, a sensational preacher, made the coming marriage the text of an offensively personal sermon yesterday, imputing mercenary and ambitious motives.

The Custom House authorities exacted $2,500 duties on the wedding gifts which the Castellanes brought from Europe.

A NOTABLE ENGAGEMENT.

New York society, at home and in the clubs, is talking of little else but Miss Gould's engagement, rumors of which were set afloat weeks ago. It is considered the most notable of the season. The Comte de Castellane has been, since his first meeting with Miss Gould last November, an untiring lover. He seems to have been considered entirely acceptable by the relatives of the young lady, to whose entertainments, whether at Lakewood or in town, he was always a welcome guest.

The Comte de Castellane was at Mr. George J. Gould's house party at Lakewood in December, and was one of the most expert riders who followed the hounds. Recently he was one of Mr. Gould's guests in a party which visited the ice carnival at Montreal. It was during this visit to the Canadian city that the engagement was made.

[BY COM
NEW Y
Committe
Lord Dun
provisional
day for the
The comm
that a keel
out delay.
been allowe
of 17ft. d
shortened a
speed. In
will be a re
The latte
nary trial
They
from the
who have
the gripp
York.

Mr. C.
the America
in a vessel
for the selec
the challengin
the committee
this action, b
the right man
the Cup defen

Miss
[BY COMMER
NEW YORK
announced fr
and Mr. Hor

Secreta
[BY COMMF
NEW YO
is ill with

GENERA

The Disting

[BY COMM
NEW Y
Joseph
N.Y., of

General Jo
in 1828, and w
of the Americ
into the war as
Volunteers, fou
Army of the
general. In p
was three time
1885 he was
Lieutenant Gov
General Carr
several years
Hospital on
operated upon
house surgeon,
For some
experienced
however, the si
his cheek bega
the growth has
The cancer was
afflicted General
which was though
performed last A

Medical In
[BY COMMERCIA
NEW YORK, F
Frank L. Du B
the Portsmouth
aged fifty-sev
THIRTY-
Medical In
from Pennsyl
on May 22,
passed assista
surgeon on

Miss Gould has just passed her twenty-first year. She was educated at a seminary near Boston, where she remained until her father's death. It was not long after she left the seminary and while she was still in mourning for her father that rumors of her engagement to Mr. Henry M. Woodruff, a member of Mr. Charles Frohman's company, were set afloat. Mr. George J. Gould promptly denied the stories, and assured his friends that when his sister was ready to marry he would, as head of the family, make the announcement.

In February, 1894, the formal announcement of Miss Gould's engagement to Mr. William M. Harriman was made at a dance given at Mrs. Paran Stevens's house, 1 East Fifty-seventh-street. Early last spring Miss Gould sailed for Europe, ostensibly to prepare her trousseau. She came to Paris, where she became the guest of Miss Fannie Reed, the sister of Mrs. Paran Stevens, who has all along been Miss Gould's most devoted friend. Miss Gould was introduced to the fashionable world in Paris, and met most of the prominent men and women in the city.

Society was startled several weeks after Miss Gould's arrival in France by the news that the Gould-Harriman engagement had been broken by mutual consent. From that time on rumors of the young woman's engagement to men of more or less prominence in social life abroad were circulated. They were all promptly denied by the members of the Gould family. Miss Gould, who was expected to pass the winter in Europe, returned to New York in the autumn, and it was not long after her arrival that a report of her engagement to Mr. Woodruff found its way into print. It was at once denied. The Comte de Castellane next came upon the scene and won the prize.

inspect
two ye
sea ser
Hospita
he was a

[BY CO
NEW
vice-pre
Bank,
years.
Sami
Americ
confer
to-day
years.

Mrs.
[BY C
NEW
Sarah
son, M
disinheri
He ch

[BY CO
NEW
late Fre
Washing
in thous
This af
were hel
of all pa
conveye

MISS ADELAIDE MONTGOMERY,
A Bridesmaid at Miss Gould's Wedding.

PREPARING FOR THE GOULD WEDDING.

Detectives and Police on Hand to Keep Out Reporters of Sensational Papers.

CRANKS' THREATENING LETTERS.

Mr. Smalley Defends M. Paul Bourget from the Attacks of Mark Twain.

[BY COMMERCIAL CABLE TO THE HERALD.]

NEW YORK, March 2.—Mr. and Mrs. George J. Gould gave a dinner last night in honor of the Marquis and Marquise de Castellane. There were twenty guests, including Mr. and Mrs. Burden, Prince Del Drago, Marquis Imperiali, Prince Lubecki, Sir Roderick and Miss Cameron, Mr. Brockholst Cutting, M. Raoul Duval, Mr. Morris Bagby, Lady Gwendoline Little, Count Ruspoli, Mr. Richard Peters, Mrs. Paran Stevens, Mrs. Russell Sage, Mrs. De Witt and Mr. and Mrs. Frederick Coudert.

The bridesmaids were invited to a luncheon to-day.

Elaborate preparations are being made for the wedding on Monday. There will be numerous detectives and police in and about the house on the wedding day to keep out cranks and reporters. Threatening letters have been received from the former, promising to blow up the whole business.

OUTRAGEOUS JOURNALISM.

Some of the newspapers have gone to such outrageous lengths that the Goulds have decided that no reporters shall be allowed on the premises.

The Comte de Castellane says that the HERALD is the only paper that has treated him decently. One sensational sheet produces an alleged facsimile of a love letter from Miss Gould to the Comte and gives pictures of the trousseau down to the minutest and most indelicate details.

As the *Sun* says, the reporters of some contemporaries never before did such lying as has been done in connection with the Gould-Castellane wedding, incredible as that statement seems.

rriman,
ert H.
K. H
eral and
Mrs. Ric
and M
ederick Pi
Prince and
Stevens, Mr.

MISS BEATRICE RICHARDSON,
A Bridesmaid at Miss Gould's Wedding.

itchie,

Mr. and Mrs.
onel and Mrs.
C. Furman,
. Eckert, Mr.
B. Schackford,
nn, Mrs. J.
S. Miller, the
Mrs. Paran
Mr. Charles

2ND EDITION.

MISS ANNA GOULD WEDS THE COMTE DE CASTELLANE.

Alliance of the American Financier's Daughter to a Noble French House.

AT MR. GEORGE J. GOULD'S HOUSE

Archbishop Corrigan Performs the Ceremony Under a Canopy of Flowers.

FOUR BEAUTIFUL BRIDESMAIDS

A Wealth of Roses, Lilies and Orchids Covered all the Walls and Stairs.

[BY COMMERCIAL CABLE TO THE HERALD.]

NEW YORK, March 4.—Miss Anna Gould youngest sister of Mr. George J. Gould and daughter of the late Jay Gould, was married shortly after noon to-day at Mr. Gould's house, on Fifth-avenue, New York, to the Comte de Castellane, son of the Marquis de Castellane, of Paris.

Archbishop Corrigan, of New York, performed the ceremony. The floral decorations and musical selections were elaborate. After the ceremony the happy couple received the congratulations of the guests. Then followed the wedding breakfast, after which the Comte and Comtesse left for Lyndhurst. They are soon to visit Paris.

THE FLORAL DECORATIONS.

The Gould residence was given up last night to florists, fifty of whom began work after the family had retired. All the greenhouses from Boston to Philadelphia seemed to have been bought out. Wagon-loads of roses, lilies and orchids arrived, and by morning the walls, ceilings, doorways and staircase balustrades were covered with magnificent floral decorations.

The handsomest and most lavish were those in the East India room, where the ceremony took place. The large mirror between the windows was concealed by Imperial purple tapestry, embroidered with gold and carried up to the ceiling and forward, making a canopy, under which Archbishop Corrigan stood.

The aisle for the bridal procession through the music room into the East India room was marked by white satin ribbon, supported by rare flowering plants. The entire leng h of the aisle was covered by a sort of canopy forme l of lilies, roses and orchids. The arch under which the couple stood was composed of the rarest possible flowers. Not far distant, at the foot of the grand staircase was a screen of palms and ferns behind which was the orchestra. The effect of the whole magnificent outlay was lavish yet artistic.

end Burden, Mr. Barry, Mr. P. F. Collier, Miss Brogden, Dr. and Mrs. George F. Shrady, Mr. and Mrs. Reginald H. Ward, Count Zaorma, Mrs. Emma Louise Smith Mr. and Mrs. Samuel Sloan, Mr. J. Nor man, Dr. Whitehouse, Mr. and Mrs. Willia A. Perry, M. Patenôtre, the French Amb sador ; Count Hadik, the Marquis Imperi Chancellor and Mrs. McCracken, Mr. J. Harrison, Mavroyeni Bey, Mr. A. M Bagby, Mr. Charles A. Baldwin, Wilmerding, Mr. and Mrs. William Bu Mr. and Mrs. Dwight M. Harris, M Madison Jones, Mr. H. Maitland K the Comte and Comtesse Laugier-Vill the Comte and Comtesse de Montsaul

THE WEDDING PRESENTS.

Each of the guests received soli heart-shaped boxes containing cake. The boxes were half an thickness lined with gold. On was a comte's coronet in gol which were the letters "G De C

The ushers and the bridesmai diamond pins with the initials G. a

Among the bride's presents were a brooch fashioned in the shape of a heart. In the centre is the famous Esterhazy diamond, surrounded by eleven diamonds, each large enough to be worn as a single stone. This was the gift of Miss Helen Gould.

Mr. and Mrs. George J. Gould's present was a collar of superb pearls of ten strands, each pearl the size of a good-sized pea. The strands are crossed by ten bars of platinum, each holding twelve large diamonds.

Mr. Frank Gould presented a chain of two hundred diamonds. Mr. Howard Gould gave a large knot or cluster of diamonds, each end of which has, as a tassel, a superb blue and pink diamond.

THE MARQUIS' GIFT.

The Marquis and Marquise de Castellane gave a superb necklace of five ropes of pearls. At one end of the necklace, securing the five strands, is a magnificent square of emeralds surrounded by twenty-four diamonds. Another present from the Marquis de Castellane is a ring of superb rubiess and sapphires. The Comte Jean de Castellane gave a present of a diamond hat pin of exceeding beauty. The Prince del Drago gave a diamond horseshoe pin.

MISS CATHERINE CAMERON,
A Bridesmaid at Miss Gould's Wedding.

General and Mrs. Eckert gave a diamond star.

One of the most superb and rich presents was a tiara of diamonds from Mr. and Mrs. Edwin Gould.

In addition to these there were many lesser ones—scarfs, lace, bonnet and hat pins, studded with diamonds, and gifts of every description. Among others were a silver box *repoussé*, from Mr. and Mrs. Russell

THE COMTE AND COMTESSE DE CASTELLANE.

...ted came from ...ing the streets ...e police arrived ...crowd, contain... ...st all classes, ...move on. ...y ten o'clock. ...ss suggested ...rs and busi... ...andoned the ...e what they

...ith children, ...smothered in ...ook the affair ...d back to per... ...s to approach. ...arry, were on

... number of ...t house, as ...elatives only ...e ceremony ...lowing: Sir ... Mr. Duncan ... Mrs. Sidney ...tting, Miss ...r. and Mrs. ...r. Cornelius ... Mr. and Mrs. ... Mrs. Henry ... Mrs. J. B. ... Mr. and Mrs. ...ionel and Mrs. ... C. Furman, ... T. Eckert, Mr. ... B. Schackford, ...unn, Mrs. J. ...l S Miller, the ...i, Mrs. Paran ... Mr. Charles ... Russell Sage, ...s. Peter Cooper ... Northrup, Mrs. ...iss Pomeroy, ...zelton, Admiral ... and Mrs. F. C. ...ry Belmont, Mr. Miss Maude Bacon, ... and Mrs. Bronson,

Archbishop Corrigan, who assisted by the Rev. Father Co... arrived at noon, and a little while aft

MISS HELEN GOULD,
A Bridesmaid at Her Sister's Wedding.

noon the bridal procession was formed on the library floor, above the drawing-room, descended the grand staircase and entered by the music-room into the East India room.

THE MUSIC.

A musical programme had been arranged by Mr. Morris Dagby. There was an orchestra of twenty strings, of which M. Victor Herbert was conductor. Mr. Pecher, the organist of the cathedral, was at the large organ in the hall. The soloist was Mme. Sucher, of the Metropolitan Opera House.

While the bridal party was assembling the following selections were given in rapid succession : Handel's "Largo," for orchestra and organ ; Greig's "In the Spring," for orchestra ; and "Elsa's Dream," from "Lohengrin," sung by Mme. Sucher. The bridal march from "Lohengrin" was next played. During the service, Mme. Sucher sang Gounod's "Ave Maria," accompanied by organ, harp and violin. This was followed by the orchestra playing the

ORIE...

The Oroya ... Still Fas...

[SPECIAL ...

NAPLES, M... Oroya, Capta... ashore this n... As the first ... were unsucc... land the pa... three of the ...

The Oroya ... The British s... to her assista... no Italian me... to be able to

INFLUE...

The City A... ing Medic... Sit...

[SPECIAL ...

MUNICH, M... have made a... Town Hall, ... had with the ... find that the ... here has been...

The numbe... cases which ...

PRINCE LO...

[SPECIAL D...

MUNICH, M... Bavarian Cabi... the political w... ment of Prin... Russian Min... considered a... peace.

Under the ...

COSTUMES IN THE COMTESSE DE CASTELLANE'S TROUSSEAU.

[This is the picture the New York "World" attempted to obtain by bribing a HERALD employé.]

on palpitations and other cardiac disorders in timid and impressionable people.

The way in which this kind of sport may be harmful, or even dangerous, is in the exertion required in

taken a week's time on the part of Court, jurymen, counsel and many witnesses to establish the fact that the plaintiff has suffered no real injury, and that the newspaper has done her no injustice.

Grotesque as this suit and claim may

Gould has frequently been asked to allow her little boys to serve as pages at weddings of her friends, but she has never permitted it till now. They are very handsome boys, with dark hair and eyes, and although two

with white aigrettes, with steel foundati and wings and sets.

VISITORS IN PARIS.

The following names have been regi at the New York Herald

THE COMTESSE DE CASTELLANE.

Pretty Dresses and Exquisite Lingerie for the Wedding and Traveling.

ONLY HALF A DOZEN HATS.

Her Millinery to Be Purchased in Paris—Description of an English Bonnet.

The Herald presents to its European readers to-day the picture of the Comtesse de Castellane's trousseau reproduced from the New York Edition. The picture has become famous owing to the attempt of the New York *World* to secure it by bribing Herald employés. A description of the wedding outfit was published in the New York Edition on February 24, from which the following is taken:—

Her bridal dress is pure white satin, the skirt being plain, falling in full, graceful folds at the back. The loose-fitting bodice-blouse effect is sparingly trimmed with tufts of point lace and mousseline de soie, and sprays of natural orange blossoms will be placed in front and fasten the folded satin sash. She will wear a tiara under ... which is the gift of her mother-in-... de Castellane. It is of ... bouquet will be

costume ... roses and ... They will carry bou... worn. Mr. George Gould will ... roses. The best man will be ... bride away. Jean de Castellane, the Comte's brother, and ... the ushers Howard Gould, Prince del Drago and M. Duval. These are the arrangements finally completed. The Catholic wedding service will be the only ceremony and Archbishop Corrigan will officiate.

LINGERIE AND DRESSES.

Her lingerie is extremely beautiful, composed entirely of silk, linen and real lace. It is all French hand-made and imported from Paris. A very pretty petticoat was thrown over a model of Miss Gould at the modiste's. It was of palest blue and gold moiré antique, flounced with lace and trimmed with ribbon. Another beautiful skirt of lilas glacé silk was striped with lines of black and adorned with four or five Vandyke frills, each edged with lace.

The bride's traveling costume consists of blue velvet, with a perfectly plain skirt, and lined throughout with tan silk shot with ... The smart, tight-fitting coat to the ... finished with a little French cape, ... flounces falling over ... low the belt

Holme, ... Harrison and ... Kerr, ... Grand Hotel. Ferris, Alexandre M. and ... Mass.; Grand Hotel. Robbins, Milton and Mrs ... Hotel de France.

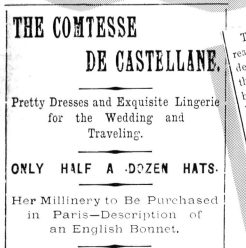

M. LE BARGY DO

To the Editor of the H...

I saw in the Heral... criticised Mr. Grattón, of t... for keeping his hands in ... the stage.

Does M. Febvre forg... *sociétaires* of the Com... Bargy, has the same fau...

Paris, March 1, 1895.

OF INTEREST TO

The vogue, without ... products that are k... sometimes more co... new article, the exc... any shadow of doub... is happening just n... a specialty for the ... ation of the pe...

DOINGS OF "TOUT PARIS."

Comte and Comtesse Boni de Castellane Give a Magnificent Dinner and Ball.

LADIES DRESSED AS FLOWERS.

Many Charming Costumes—The Grand Duchess Anastasia of Mecklenburg-Schwerin Present.

The dinner and dance given by Comte and Comtesse Boni de Castellane at their magnificent house in the avenue du Bois de Boulogne took place on Tuesday night.

The ladies had been asked to come as flowers and the men to wear colored dress coats. Nothing could be more brilliant than was this gathering of beauty. The costumes were all charmingly carried out and most original, while the bright-colored coats, red, white, green, gray, cream, lemon, etc., of every shade, with different facings, had a most happy effect and did away with the dismal black that usually dims the brightness of a ballroom.

The Dinner.

A hundred and fifty guests sat down to dinner at small tables, each laid for six, which were set in the long hall surrounding the great staircase. And what a lovely gathering of beautiful flowers it was.

The hostess wore a beautiful red poppy dress, with a big poppy in her hair.

Princess Henry of Pless, looking exquisitely fair, wore an Ophelia dress, representing the sweet-scented jasmine, long garlands of pretty flowers falling from her hair, with diamond dewdrops shining among them. The dress, of the palest green tulle, was covered with sprays of jasmine and embroidered with diamonds.

Another sensational entrance was that of three lovely women, who came arm-in-arm, representing the national flag of France, the Duchess de La Rochefoucauld as a cornflower, the Duchesse de Luynes as a white carnation and the Duchesse d'Uzès as a red carnation.

But it is impossible to describe or do justice to all the beauty and charm of this gathering of fair "mondaines," among whom were:—

A Water Lily.

Comtesse J. de Castellane, most handsome as a waterlily; Princesse J. Murat, as a white poppy; Princesse E. Murat, as a Parma violet; Countess Roman Potocka, as a most beautiful dragonfly; the Duchesse d'Harcourt, as a purple pansy, with sprays of diamonds embroidered on the leaves and on the big pansy in her hair.

The Marquise de Balleroy, as a sweetbriar rose; Comtesse Czernin, wearing a dress trimmed with wisteria and a dragonfly in her hair; the Duchesse de Rohan, as a four-leaved clover; Mme. de Saulty, most effective as a blue cornflower, with a dark blue skirt; the Marquise de Bailleul, in rose petals, with a big rose in her hair.

The Vicomtesse Léon de Janzé, most effective as an arum lily, with big lilies in her hair; the Comtesse d'Harcourt, as a blue cornflower; the Comtesse de Contades, as a mauve orchid; Comtesse Lafond, as a "morning glory"; the Marquise de Loys-Chandieu, as a purple poppy; Baronne de Berckheim, as a cornflower

Galliffet. The pretty favors, representing various flowers, were much admired.

The garden was beautifully illuminated, and, as the weather was so charmingly mild, all the fair living flowers formed lovely groups against the dark trees and illuminated lawn.

The cotillon was followed by a "sit down" supper at small tables, after which dancing began again and was kept up until the early hours of the morning, thus prolonging what was certainly the most beautiful fête given this season.

FUNERAL OF THE PRINCE DE JOINV[...]

Buried in the Family Va[...] —An Impressive [...]

The special train [...] left the Saint-Laza[...] 7.45 yesterday mor[...] the late Prince de [...] neral service was [...] house by Abbé Fle[...] lippe du Roule, ass[...] Only the members [...] were present.

The train arrive[...] Sous-Préfect and [...] the Western Railw[...] ing to receive it. [...] considerable crowd[...]

The railway wag[...] was brought opposi[...] tion. The coffin wa[...] of black velvet faste[...] It was immediately [...] which was drawn b[...] housings, each le[...] prayers had been [...] of Dreux the pro[...]

Among those [...] tesse de Paris, P[...] leans, the Duche[...] Duchesse de Chartr[...] of Denmark, the Co[...] cess Blanche d'Orlé[...]

Chief Mourner.

The Duc de Cha[...] Duc d'Orléans was [...] him came the Duc [...] Henri d'Orléans, [...] Magenta, Comte [...] Prince August o[...] Pierre d'Orléans-[...] dôme, Mr. Micha[...] Plenipotentiary, r[...] of England; Prince [...] lon, representing the [...] M. de Hegermann-Lin[...] of Denmark; M. de Sou[...] ing the King and Queen [...] Kikiphoroff, and the Fre[...] gret, Humann, Sée, Cail[...]

As soon as the coffin [...] the hearse the processi[...] which were the carriag[...] then set itself in motion[...]

At the door of the chap[...] angel of the resurrection. [...] this symbolical image that [...] arrived at eleven o'clock, a[...] steps leading to the church. [...] deposited in a catafalque, [...] of which the late prince's [...] with crape, was placed. [...] were silver "lampadaires[...] fifteen candles. The ch[...] léans family, Abbé Grom[...] in the course of which t[...] sung by M. Muratet, [...] mei" by M. Delpouget.

The stone of the vau[...] quarter past twelve, an[...] princesses retired with [...] remaining mourners we[...] the crypt.

FASHIONABLE [...]

Items of Interest fr[...] ing Papers, Sent [...] "Herald's" S[...]

[BY THE HERALD'[...]

ARRI[...]

The Grand[...] Duches[...] h[...]

COMTE BONI DE CASTELLANE.

COMTE DE CASTELLANE WOUNDS M. DE RODAYS.

The "Figaro's" Editor Receives a Bullet in the Thigh—He Is Expected to Recover in a Week or Ten Days—Bullet Not Yet Extracted.

FOUGHT AT THE VÉLODROME DU PARC DES PRINCES.

Comte Boni Untouched by His Adversary's Fire, Makes Kind Inquiries, and Then the Two Shake Hands—Clandestine Spectators.

The de Rodays-de Castellane duel is over. M. Fernand de Rodays has received a ball in the thigh. The count and the journalist have shaken hands and it is now hoped by the friends of the two combatants that the "truce" recognized on the "field of honor" will be lasting.

The reason for the meeting is well-known.

Over night it had been stated that the duel would be strictly private and that not a single newspaper correspondent should be present.

Early yesterday morning I called on Comte Albert de Dion at his flat in the avenue Mac-Mahon. He was out. Then I went to his offices in the avenue de la Grande-Armée, and he had not arrived. "Indeed," said M. de Villepin, his secre-

M. FERNAND DE RODAYS.
(Who was wounded in the duel.)

each wearing a silk hat. Both looked calm.

The scene was curious, for the two adversaries, with their seconds and doctors, had only exchanged the "parliamentary bow" as they took their respective places.

Comte de Dion, when the two men were in position, standing on the further side, opened the box containing the two loaded pistols and, with his silk hat in his hand, went to M. de Rodays first. Leaving a weapon in the last-named gentleman's hand, he crossed the ground and handed Comte de Castellane the other.

Comte de Dion then, from the centre, addressed both the combatants. At this point his words were almost inaudible, but when he cried, "Messieurs, veuillez armer vos pistolets," and "Messieurs, êtes-vous prêts?" his stentorian voice rang out through the chilly air.

I noticed, however, that M. de Rodays fired immediately after the word "feu," without waiting for the regulation words, "un, deux, trois." M. de Rodays was in his right.

Comte Boni de Castellane, on the other hand, took matters more calmly. M. de Rodays had not "pinked" him. Between the words "two" and "three" he raised his pistol, took aim and shot.

M. de Rodays did not fall, but his hand fell to his right thigh.

Immediately Comte de Dion and Comte Boni de Castellane rushed towards him. The ball had lodged about fifteen centimètres below the groin. A few inches higher the wound would have been fatal.

M. de Rodays was carried by Comte de Dion, M. Périvier and the two doctors to the vélodrome [...]

THE NEW YORK I

MISS VANDERBILT BETROTHED.

Her Engagement to the Young Duke of Marlborough Formally Announced.

TO MARRY BEFORE JANUARY 1.

Prince of Wales Notified by a Cable Despatch Sent by the Nobleman.

[From the NEW YORK HERALD, Septembe 21.]

Miss Consuela Vanderbilt, daughter of Mrs. William K. Vanderbilt, will before the end of the year become the Duchess of Marlborough.

The engagement was quietly announced to the families and intimate friends of the contracting parties yesterday. It was confirmed beyond any question last evening.

As the engagement is of such recent date only few details of the approaching marriage have yet been arranged. The ceremony, however, will be held in this city within the next few months. It will be performed in accordance with the ritual of the Protestant Episcopal Church, conforming with that of the Church of England. Bishop Potter will probably officiate, and the services, it is thought, will be in open church.

The Duke of Marlborough cabled the news yesterday morning to the members of his family and intimate friends in England and on the Continent. Included among those to whom the information was conveyed was the Prince of Wales, who is godfather to the duke. It is expected that several of the intimate friends of the duke will cross the Atlantic to be present at the wedding.

CHARLES RICHARD JOHN SPENCER CHURCHILL (*Ninth Duke of Marlborough*).

Intimate friends of the duke last evening, in speaking of the engagement, of which they had full cognizance, said that the duke regarded the approaching mar...

arrived in this city, on his first visit to this country, his valet, who was the only person to accompany him, inscribed his master on the register of the Hotel Waldorf as plain Charles Spencer.

The young duke is a strong contrast in appearance to the general run of the Churchills, although he bears a family resemblance to the portraits of the first duke, who was the greatest general of his age. He inclines more to the Hamiltons, his mother having been Lady Alberta Hamilton, daughter of the Duke of Abercorn. She is still alive. Like his father, he is somewhat below the average size and slender, with a sallow complexion, a high forehead, aquiline nose and dark brown hair.

His face is without hair, with the exception of a light moustache, and his favorite attitude in conversation is to stand with his arms crossed on his breast and one hand stroking his chin. His manner is entirely unassuming, while the acute observer may occasionally detect a look of boredom in his eye or what might be taken as a cynical curl on his lip, but those who know him best say that his cynicism is only skin deep.

OF A NOTABLE FAMILY.

Of a family whose every member has been conspicuous in one way or another, one the greatest soldier of his day, another the best talker, still another the possessor of the handsomest leg, the young duke, in his matter of fact way, has already shown that he has some of the family traits strongly developed.

He went to Cambridge, where he soon showed that he had reached his proper sphere by flooring the boldest examiners of whom Trinity College could boast. He speedily became a member of the Pitt, the Athenæum, the True Blue, the Carlton and other organisations of the students. He played polo and cricket, the latter with great precision and accuracy of style. His rooms became noted as showing his excellent

MISS CONSUELA VANDERBILT.

taste, and he was well known to the Bond-street dealers in the antiques. He is a bold horseman as well, and with all these he was an excellent student, history being his favorite study, while for mathematics he entertained a strong dislike.

After the year of mourning consequent on his father's death the young duke's coming of age was commemorated by a ... historical Bl...

STOC...

In Capel ... Quiet, b...

WALL ST...

Decline i...

[BY COMMER...

WALL STRE... general tone of ... though some st... Cotton was... transactions i... bales. Wheat... The final bi...

Atchison 4s., T...
Atchison, Inc., T...
Atlantic and Pa...
Buffalo and Roc...
Can Southern Fi...
Can Southern Se...
Chesapeake and C...
Ches. and Ohio Ge...
Chic. Burl. & Qui...
Denver and Rio G...
Det. Mack. and I...
E. Tenn. V. and...
Flint and Père M...
Lehigh Valley c...
Long Island 4s...
Metropolitan E...
Missouri, Kans...
Missouri, Kans...
Mobile Ohio Gen...
N.Y., Chic. and...
N.Y., Lake Erie...
Northern Pacific...
Northern Pacific...
Northern Pacific...
Peoria and Easter...
Philadelphia and...
Phil. and Read 1s...
Phil. and Read 2...
Phil. and Read. 3...
Pittsburg and W...
Rio Grande We...
St. Louis and Se...
St. Louis South...
St. Louis South...
Southern Railw...
Texas Pacific...
Texas Pacific...
Toledo, St. Lou...
Union Pacific...
Wabash 1st Mo...
Wabash 2nd Mo...
West Shore 4s...
West N.Y. and Pe...
Wisconsin Cent. ...
U.S. Two per Cent...
U.S. Funded Loan...

Alton and Terre Ha...
American Cotton C...
American Cotton O...
American Sugar R...
American Tobacco...
Atchison Stock, all...
Buff., Roch and...
Bell Telephone...
Boston and Mo...
Calumet and He...
Canada Southern...
Canadian Pacific...
Central Pacific...
Central and South...
Chesapeake and Oh...
Chicago Brewing...
Chicago Brewing...
Chicago Gas...
Chicago and North...
Chicago and Nor...
Chicago, Bur...
Chicago, M...
Chica...
Ohi...

... which was published in a London magazine.

He gave, in a very interesting way, the history of the well-known Palace in Woodstock, Oxfordshire, from the time when Queen Anne, in 1705, in accordance with an address of the Commons, granted to the first duke the Royal estate, of which Woodstock was the centre, with money to build a house. How costly the building was is apparent from the fact that the £500 000 voted for the purpose did not suffice for the completion of the work.

It was in this palace, about a year and a half ago, that he entertained the young girl who is destined to become its mistress. Named Consuela, after the Duchess of Manchester, who was Miss Yznaga and an intimate friend of Mrs. W. K. Vanderbilt, the young lady is just such a girl as might be supposed to attract a young man like the duke.

Now about eighteen years old, she is strikingly tall, a dark brunette, with black hair and eyes, and very rich coloring. Her face is small, and she is decidedly *japonaise* in type. She is very slight, but carries herself well, and will undoubtedly be a very handsome woman. She has unusual sweetness and charm of manner, and although she has few intimates these few say that this sweetness of manner and disposition make her most lovable, and they are devoted to her.

She is one of the most thoughtful of hostesses, and at all the entertainments at Marble House, in Newport, this summer, her attention to the wants of her own and her mother's guests have been constantly remarked. In a word, she is yet a thoroughly simple, sweet, and unspoiled girl, and if she can carry through her future life, with its heavy responsibilities, the same characteristics of manner and temperament which she now possesses, she will surely be a notable woman in her day.

HER SIMPLICITY OF DRESS.

She dresses very simply, generally in white, of crépon or muslin, and her only ornament is usually a red rose or carnation in her back hair. At the recent Marble House ball she wore a fillet of red carnations, which was wonderfully becoming to her. She has been educated at home by a private governess, who is still a member of the family. She is well read, and while not possessing any particular accomplishment, is said to be unusually cultivated. She is the eldest child, but is not yet too old to enjoy a game of romps with her brothers, William K., Jr., who is now about fifteen years old, and Harold, who is about ten.

On the north wall of the ballroom in the Newport House there hangs a full-length ... Miss Vanderbilt by Carolus-D...

Distilling and C...
Edison Electric I...
General Electric...
Great Northern...
Illinois Central
Lake Erie and W...
Lake Shore and M...
Long Island
Louisville and Na...
Louisville, New A...
Manhattan Cons...
Michigan Central...
Missouri Pacific
Missouri, Kansas...
Mobile and Ohio...
Nashville, G. and...
National Lead Tr...
National Lead Tr...
National Linseed
New Jersey Centr...
New York Centra...
N.Y. and New E...
N.Y., Chicago and...
N.Y., Chic. and St...
N.Y., Lake Erie an...
N.Y., Lake Erie an...
N.Y., Susq. and W...
N.Y., Susq. and W...
Norfolk and West...
Norfolk and West...
North America ..
Northern Pacific.
Northern Pacific...
Ontario and Weste...
Ontario Silver .
Oregon Improvem...
Oregon Short Line...
Pacific Mail S.S. ...
Pennsylvania ....
Philadelphia and...
Pitts., Fort W. an...
Pullman's Palace
St. Paul and Dulu...
St. Paul and Oma...
St. Paul, Minn. an...
Silver Bullion Cer...
Southern Pacific
Southern Railway...
Southern Railways...
St. Louis South-W...
St. Louis South-W...
Tennessee Coal and...
Texas Pacific ...
Union Pacific....
Union Pacific, Den...
United States Exp...
United States Cord...
United States Cord...
Wabash, St. Louis...
Wabash, St. Louis...
Wells Fargo Expre...
Western Union Te...
Wheeling and Lak...
Wheeling and Lak...
Wisconsin Central...
• Last sale.

London, sovereign...
Paris, dollars.....

Cotton (Spot) in N...
The closing price...
Cotton in New...

	Yesterday
Oct.....	8.72
Nov....	8.75
Dec.....	8.82
Jan....	8.89

Wheat, in Chica...
Dec 61
Corn, in Chicago...
Dec...... 27¾

UNION OF WEALTH AND TITLE.

By this marriage there will be united the representative of one of the most distinguished families of Europe and the eldest daughter of one of the richest families of America.

Charles Richard John Spencer Churchill, the ninth Duke of Marlborough, who, in choosing for his wife an American girl, is following the fashion set by his father and his uncle, the late Lord Randolph Churchill, will be twenty-four years old on November 13 next. He attained his majority four days after his father, the late duke, died.

In addition to being Duke of Marlborough, he is the Marquis of Blandford, and will be until he is the father of a son, who will assume that title by courtesy. He is also Earl of Marlborough, Earl of Sunderland, Baron Spencer of Wormleighton, Baron Churchill of Sandridge, Prince of the Holy Roman Empire and Prince of Mindelheim, in Suabia.

THE VANDERBILT-MARLBORO' WEDDING.

Names of the Bridesmaids, Bride's Trousseau and Her Mother's Dress.

PRECAUTIONS NECESSARY.

Presents to the Bridesmaids to be Given According to English Custom.

[From the NEW YORK HERALD.]

Beyond the few details of the wedding of Miss Consuelo Vanderbilt to the Duke of Marlborough, printed from time to time by the HERALD, there is at present very little to say, for the reason that the plans are not entirely completed.

As has been before stated, the duke's best man will be his cousin, the Hon. Ivor Guest, eldest son of Lord Wimborne, who has been here for about five weeks, but the entire list of ushers is not yet completed.

However, among those who will act in that capacity are Messrs. Reginald Ronalds, Mr. R. T. Wilson, Jr., and Mr. Brockholst Cutting. No one will come over from England especially to act in that capacity. The Duke of Marlborough will give a farewell bachelor dinner during the coming week, but he has not yet mentioned the time or place.

Miss Vanderbilt's bridesmaids will be Miss Marie Winthrop, Miss Evelyn Burden, Miss Kittie Duer, Miss Elsa Bronson, Miss Daisy Post, Miss May Goelet and Miss Julia Jay, who have already been mentioned, and in addition to these Miss Morton, eldest daughter of Governor Morton.

CHURCH WILL ...

Invitation...

Paris. These dresses will be sent to Blenheim. The very important dress of the trousseau, the bridal dress, has been made in New York and by Mme. Donovan. The first authentic description and cuts of the bridal dress appear in the HERALD.

Next to the richness of the materials, the predominating and most pleasing feature of the dresses to be worn by the immediate bridal party is the refinement of coloring. The satin used in the wedding dress is of a peculiar creamy tint, a trifle deeper than ivory, and matching perfectly the rare point lace flouncing, twelve inches deep, with which it is trimmed. This combines the patterns known as point d'Angleterre and point appliqué, being made especially from designs suggested by Mrs. Vanderbilt herself. The lace was made in Brussels.

FLOUNCE IN HORIZONTAL ROWS.

Without cutting, this flounce is arranged in four horizontal rows across the front and sides of the skirt, entirely concealing the satin, and crossing the flounces diagonally on the right side is a long spray of orange blossoms. The front of the corsage is draped with chiffon, gathered very full from neck to belt and covered in turn with a deep fall of the lace, gathered into a high stock collar covered with the same rare lace and hanging thence unconfined to the satin girdle.

Triple revers of the lace project over the enormously full sleeves, which are pleated into the armhole, and cut in gauntlet style below the elbow without trimming of any sort. A spray of orange blossoms is fastened on the left shoulder.

The most distinctive feature of the dress, however, is the court train, five yards in length, which is fastened at the shoulders some five inches below the neck band. This, which falls in double box pleats from top to bottom, is bordered down both sides and across the lower edge with a two-inch wide embroidery of pearls and silver, representing rose leaves tied together at intervals with a true lover's knot. The veil to be worn with this dress is of exceedi... ...els net and will b... ...et of...

STOC...

Very Little ...
Pric...

HOLIDAY...

Quotati...
fected...
St...

[BY TH...

LONDON, Nov... day were flat a... to a very... practically suspe... to realize forced p... deal largely in v... and the absence of... real condition of... American were a... quotations were r...

The closing pr...

2¾ per Cent. Ac...
2½ per Cents. (1...
2¾ per Cents. (1...
Indian 3½ per C...
Indian 3 per Ce...
Canadian 3½ p...
Cape (1883)...
Egyptian Unified...
Egyptian Prefe...
Natal...
New South Wale...
New South Wale...
New Zealand 4 ...
New Zealand 3...
Queensland 4 pe...
Queensland 3½...
South Australia...
Victoria 4 per C...
Victoria April-C...

Great Eastern...
Great Northe...
Great Northe...
Great Northern...
Great Western...
London and B...
London and B...
London, Chath...
London, Chat. &...
London and No...
London and Sou...
Metropolitan...
District...
Midland...
South-Eastern Or...
South-Eastern De...
Caledonian Prefer...

ANOTHER AMERICAN DUCHESS.

Miss Consuelo Vanderbilt Wedded to the Duke of Marlborough.

TWO BISHOPS OFFICIATE.

St. Thomas's Church Completely Lined with Flowers—Magnificent Concert.

WAITING FOR HIS BETROTHED.

His Grace Kept Standing in the Aisle for Nearly Twenty Minutes.

ARRIVAL OF THE BRIDE.

Enters the Church on the Arm of Her Father — Eight Bridesmaids.

BEGINNING OF THE SERVICE.

Flowers Distributed to the Guests While the Register is Being Signed.

A MOST BEAUTIFUL WEDDING.

[BY COMMERCIAL CABLE TO THE HERALD.]

NEW YORK, Nov. 6.—The wedding of Miss Consuelo Vanderbilt, daughter of Mrs. W. K. Vanderbilt, and Charles Richard John Spencer-Churchill, ninth Duke of Marlborough, was celebrated to-day, at noon, at St. Thomas's Church, with the utmost pomp and ceremony.

Two bishops, Bishop Potter, of New ... Bishop Littlejohn, of Long ... stood behind

BLENHEIM PALACE.
Ancestral Home of the Marlboroughs.

arches ... altar and garlands sus... gave the building the appearance ... perfect bower of flowers.

The concert lasted from eleven o'clock until noon. At twelve o'clock precisely the ...

THE BRIDES' DRESS.

sl... as... cit... alw... and... one... their... prec... entra... of ad... sonall... carefu... one b... church...

Exper... persons ... is neces... who real... ceremony,... very wis... Departmen... order out... the unbidd... quently a co...

... girdles ... satin ribbon, almost a

Alexander... Angelo... Benoni... Black Reef P...

were the prospects there.

"Is there any skating?" exclaimed M. Eckart, secretary of the Cercle des Pa-

culars of a serious stabbing case at Charenton:—

A working cooper, named Louis Mar- ... on his way to his work at the ...int-Bernard, was attacked in ...aris by two men. One of them ...s, while the other stabbed him ...tween the shoulders. The un...an fell to the ground uncon-

...kmen who were passing suc...resting one of the assailants. ...his name as Ernest Cloin, a cooper, ...ad stated that his reason for stabbing Marchand was that the latter was courting his wife.

IN MEMORY OF THACKERAY.

Saturday being the thirty-fifth anniversary of the death of William Makepeace Thackeray, his bust in Poets' Corner, Westminster Abbey, was decked with a number of floral wreaths. The grave of Charles Dickens, situated almost below the bust of Thackeray, was also decorated with floral tributes.—Observer.

of a nature to call for investigation by the press."

The "Figaro" publishes this morning a more detailed contradiction which M. Bard has made through the Havas agency. The only communication which he had with Lieut.-Colonel Picquart was to inform him one day, at the request of the president of the Court, that he could not be heard on that day, and this was in the presence of the two gendarmes in whose custody he was. M. Bard adds that he has only broken through his rule of ignoring misstatements because the polite note which he sent to the "Temps" was published by that paper and might have been taken for an unsatisfactory rectification.

M. ESTERHAZY'S THREAT.

How He Is Said to Have Secured Col. von Schwartzkoppen's Silence.

The following statement, which, if true, tends to prove the relations existing between Major Esterhazy and Colonel von

SOCIAL LIFE AT NEWPORT.

Bevy of Handsome Girls Who Will Be Prominent in New York This Winter.

YOUNG MR. HENRY CLEWS' FAD.

He Creates a Mild Sensation by Wearing White Silk Socks at a Dance.

[From the NEW YORK HERALD.]

NEW YORK, Sunday.—There will be a bevy of handsome girls in society this coming winter, some of whom have been "half" out either at the opera or small dances. The Newport contingent, now very much in evidence, will come in for a good share of attention. Among these are Miss Laura Swan, Mrs. Elisha Dyer's daughter; Miss Sallie Van Alen, whose resemblance to Cléo de Mérode is frequently alluded to; Miss Marion Fish, who rides a good deal with her mother; Miss Fanny Jones, for whom a good many parties are being given, and Miss Evelyn Blight.

Possibly to this list may be added the Misses Mills, who are likely to be seen occasionally in society during the winter, although they will probably not be formally introduced.

All these mentioned may be classed among the athletic girls of society, for they seem to live in the open air, golfing, swimming, riding or playing tennis. The Misses Mills have already distinguished themselves as golf champions, and they will figure at the coming horse show in several classes. They drive extremely well, and no doubt will carry off some of the prizes.

A singular feature of summer life, especially where the automobile is extensively used, is the absolute fearlessness displayed by the women. It is a remarkable sight, to say the least, to see two or three elegantly dressed women, without maid or groom, speeding to or from a dinner in one of the elegantly appointed "bubbles" that are so much favored. This is a common sight, especially at Newport, more often in midweek, when the husbands are away at business. But Newport has such excellent roads that there is no apparent danger, and women are decidedly expert in running the machines.

Milk White Socks.

Young Henry Clews, Jr., has set a fashion decidedly noticeable, but probably not to be widely followed. The other night he appeared at a dance with milk-white socks—silk, of course—which, in contrast to his black pumps and evening dress, made him the butt of kindly merriment. The colors of socks have run the entire gamut of shades, and even a screaming scarlet or the palest blue might escape without comment, but white, never.

Mr. Clews, Jr., does not confine himself to the wearing of white socks in the evening, but in the day time as well this part of his attire is noticeable. When running his "bubble" he has a fashion of throwing one leg over the other so that one foot rests on the other knee, thus displaying an expanse of pure white footgear. Thus it is that extremities set the fashion—red-headed women and white-socked men.

One of the most elegant dinners of the summer was given a few nights ago by Mr. and Mrs. Heber R. Bishop, at Friedheim, their first of the season. Their

port as the guest of Dr. and Mrs. John H. French.

Mr. and Mrs. Joseph Harriman ... to have Mr. and ... Herbe... as their guests. ...il. Whether

Dr. and Mrs. a while longer ... dinner Sunday e... all appear... cluded Mrs. Scot... skating park ... Henry Bowen ... French and ...ntinued M. Ec-

Mr. Barto...ent, is not thick ... port to spend ...timètres as yet.

Mrs. C. Alb...orning if there ... lightful dinner has been keep-

For the first ...ecount of the ... and Mrs. Luth...o know what ... port, the guest all inquiries, ... R. Bishop, who...o, there is to ... Theodore Have... Bellevue aven...vy, the park ... formally intro...d by an eager ... daughter to s...id: "Ma foi! ... ranged to sail ...w how the ice ... turn to New Yo...e is only three

Mr. and Mrs...s thick, but if ... have found the...here the park ... nished home, at...e glanced at ... Fifth avenue a...ner keeps on ... cool and comfort... enough by ... in town all sum...e ice must be ... for Europe sh...ck to allow of ... propose to mak...f people skat- ... France, Germa...on that if it ... may not return ...ght, which is ... until next Febr...ty of skaters

No date has y...e end of the ... wedding of Mis... of Mr. and Mr... Mr. Langdon B... Mr. and Mrs. H... engagement was ... ago.

...RAMP.

...living at La ...ty, Seine-et-...stmas night, ...man was dis-...house by a ...l been al-...He made his ...the "Temps," ...to the autho-

Engagements A...

Several inter... announced last w... the information ... daughter of Dr. ... fin, and half-sis... varro, former... American stag... gagement to H... well-known por... of Professor H... tinguished p... Griffin, who ... has made he... last ten year... well known in... though an Am... all his life in L... some apartm... Lowndes squ... year ago last ... a reception ... sion he was a... and Miss Ma... will be celebr...

...PARIS.

...até de Nuit, ...out a thousand ...ons in Paris, ap-...cast-off cloth-...he most needy ...us refuges on ...ressed to the ...uges at the fol-...de Tocqueville, ...oulevard de Cha-... the Seine, and ..., on the south

Announcem...fetch any gifts ... gagement of ... contributions ... daughter of ...received. ... Pomeroy, of N... Jenkins, of Sta... roy, who has n... sented, is an att... favorite. The da... not yet been decid...

Mr. and Mrs. J... West 126th street, ... ment of their daugh... ta Crandell, to Dr... prominent physicia... Miss Crandell com... cestry, her paterna... tors having been a... in the Rhode Isla... colonies. Dr. Ke... this city, and afte... ther course at t... burgh. He is a m... tive medical socie... Westchester count... clubs of Yonkers. ... early in the autumn...

Formal announcem... gagement of Miss F...

NEW REVISION OF THE FOUR HUNDRED.

Mrs. John King Van Rensselaer Is Bringing Out a Series of Books on Old New York Families Which She Intends to Be a Guide to Social Rank.

MANY WELL KNOWN NAMES ARE OMITTED.

[From the NEW YORK HERALD.]

Mrs. John King Van Rensselaer, in order to establish clearly the identity of the descendants of New York's early settlers and those who have married into their families, has compiled an elaborate work, entitled "New Yorkers of the Nineteenth Century." This work, it is announced in the prospectus, "will be the standard of rank in New York," that it, it is intended to show what families were prominent here in the days of "old New York," or Man-ha-ta.

According to Mrs. Van Rensselaer, the originally prominent New York families are now represented, in descendants or membership by marriage, by about seven hundred families or about 3,500 individuals, although she confines her list in the first book of the series to the descendants of these twenty families:—

BARD,	JAY,
BARCLAY,	KING,
BRONSON,	LYNCH,
BUCHANAN,	McVICKAR,
DELAFIELD,	MORTON,
DUER,	RENWICK,
EMMET,	RUTHERFORD,
FISH,	SCHUYLER,
GLOVER,	STUYVESANT,
HOFFMAN,	VAN RENSSELAER.

Other books which are to follow will include one hundred other families, the total of 120 households, representing New York society of seventy years ago.

There are exactly 689 households, Mrs. Van Rensselaer finds, which are entitled to places in this genealogical record. As only "old New York" families are dealt with, from her list are missing the names of many New Yorkers included by Ward McAllister in the "Four Hundred." She does not include the Astors, Bloodgoods, Whitneys, Morgans, Winans or Goulds, and Mr. George Vanderbilt is the only member of that family included in the work. He owes this to his recent marriage to Miss Edith S. Dresser, who is of an old New York family.

For the same reason barely a dozen of those present at the first assembly in the Waldorf-Astoria on Thursday evening are referred to in her book by Mrs. Van Rensselaer. Neither Mr. Worthington Whitehouse, nor Mrs. Almeric Hugh Paget, who led the cotillon on that occasion, is mentioned.

Mrs. Van Rensselaer's latest book, which is handsomely printed on Dutch handmade linen paper, with binding of an old Dutch style, is designed to be the foremost genealogical record of its kind, and is expected to take the place here as to local families, that is filled by England's Burke's "Peerage, Baronetage and Landed Gentry."

AUTO SPEED IN NEW YORK.

[BY COMMERCIAL CABLE TO THE HERALD.]

NEW YORK, Saturday.—The discussion as to what is the "proper" speed for an automobile in this city continues. The aldermen threaten to pass an ordinance which will establish a ridiculously slow maximum.

In the meantime, however, an agreement has been made whereby some of the prominent "chauffeurs" are to take the aldermen out riding and give them a practical demonstration. The Tammany braves will be whisked over the park roads and shown the ease and safety with which automobiles can be handled.

oristes

rche de Noé," avec
de Rostand, et
ni ses meilleurs en-
e panneau de Fa-
racieux de ces des-
ains envois, comme
toujours péché,"
ur...," ont quel-
galant des ar-
ècle.
ésolument dans
eaucoup, parmi
arelle en quatre
itation," Aéro-
me," "Naviga-
ui déforme avec
e signalerai, entre
e. Mistinguett et
sant la valse cha-
orde, avec des évo-
à la Henry Mon-
vec la série si pim-
; M. Bac, avec ses
"La Dame et le
Le Jardin public,"
Gerbault, M. Gui-
e de Régina Badet),
uettes de Peaux-

avec ses têtes de
proclame la souve-
ture française. M.
œuvres, un excel-
dessins, où, sous le
n à l'Epatant," il
ypes parisiens con-
roqués.

moins bien repré-
l'humour lui fait
convient de men-
nt M. Charles Pou-
le manœuvres sont
M. Ricardo Florès,
s choses, une aqua-
s serrée, "Les Apa-
M. Emmanuel Bar-
hemise."
a signé un panneau
n moulin de Mont-
lors que ce quartier
la campagne).
e a quelques très
sées par les spiri-
il a le secret. Je
nt: "Les Désen-
d'amateur," "Les
petites chéries,"

ore parmi les bons
Neumont (décora-
e à coucher); de
Sévigné et danc-
et, neuf panneaux
de ballerine.
figure une série
o, qui n'est pas
de l'exposition
ositions rétros-
de Grévin.

DROUOT

uste de jeune
expirant," mar-
siècle, a trouvé
les porcelaines,
r deux soupières
le Saxe décorées
pour un sucrier
le en même porce-
sonnages dans des
t d'eau. Au nom-

Tiffany & Co.'s New Establishment Is Another American Triumph in Paris

A CORNER OF THE SALEROOMS.

AN EXTERIOR VIEW.

Artistic Quarters, Just Opened in Equitable Building, Present Many Novel and Beautiful Ideas.

American enterprise in Europe has not been lacking in conspicuous instances, but perhaps nothing of that character in recent years has attracted so much attention as the establishment, just now completed, of a famous American business firm in a new American building in the heart of Paris. For a long time the avenue de l'Opéra has been pleasantly called an American thoroughfore. The place de l'Opéra now becomes even more entitled to that designation, with the opening of Tiffany and Co.'s new store in the Equitable building, at the corner of the rue de la Paix and place de l'Opéra.

There is declared to be nothing in all Europe like this establishment. The only one in the world with which it can be compared is Tiffany's, in New York. By this it is meant that the new shop is constructed on lines entirely different from those employed in the typical jewelry shop in European cities. Its novelty, its artistic beauty and its conveniences for customers set it apart from even the most famous places of its kind, and make it one of the show places of Paris, not only for Americans but for Parisians themselves.

Carefully Planned.

In preparing to occupy their new quarters, Tiffany and Co. took advantage of a long delay in the erection of the building, and went studiously about making the establishment as nearly perfect as possible. The interior design and construction of the store were placed in the hands of Mr. Charley Knight, the architect, son of the well-known painter, and a graduate of the Ecole des Beaux- beautiful and original American jewelry. This jewelry is made at the Tiffany factory in New York, under the personal supervision of Mr. Louis C. Tiffany. Chiefly American stones are used—turquoise, kunzite, zircon, peridot, sapphire, tourmaline and Mexican opal, for examples. This jewelry is different from anything made in Paris, especially as to color. It is the aim of Tiffany and Co. to secure perfect harmony in tones. In a brooch with a central blue stone, for instance, the other stones used in it will not be of opposite or contrasting color, but of harmonizing hues; and even the gold or platinum will be given a tint to match the stones or to blend with their lights.

Another specialty is the Tiffany favrile glass, bronze and translucent enamel ware, made in the furnaces on Long Island, N.Y. This ware is already famous the world over, and a beautiful display of it is to be seen in the new store.

A great deal of time and great ingenuity have been expended on the equipment of Tiffany's, apart from the features already described. The offices on the second floor are all in glass and mahogany. In the two basement floors are the massive safety vaults; the ventilating plant for the renewal of the atmosphere three times an hour; the electrical sterilizers; the hot and cold air plant to regulate the temperature, and the machinery for the pneumatic tubes and parcel carriers.

Here is placed the first Edison storage battery seen in Paris, kept in reserve against any contingency by which the regular electric service might be interrupted. Still another novelty is the electric manipulation of the outside iron shutters, which disappear into the basement below the windows by the simple turning of a lever.

The first Tiffany store was established in Paris in 1845. The new place is the fourth into which this firm has moved following the demands of trade.

HOTEL-KEEPERS' SYNDICATE FAVORS "CURE" TAX

Measure to Impose Payment on Visitors to Resorts Finds Favor, Says Secretary.

The recent voting of a "cure" tax to be levied in health resorts and watering tax on visitors, in imitation of the German Kur-tax, the Mayor declared that he was absolutely opposed to the imposition of such a tax.

"If the Government decided to allow watering-places to exact a 'cure' tax I should do all I could to prevent it being

Au M
Héro

—

Le Poulain de
Hurgente,
Autres Gag
Lenoir; Ho
Gauvreau;
Fléole et E
lier; Grenad

—

La réunion d
Cloud a bénéfi
température.
tionnelle le spor
Le prix Vich
de pur sang (for
et formule cont
huit partants.
gagné la course
en est sortie
mené devant Fe
yère. Hyo éta
face Fémina pa
de loin. Ecuy
place devant Ga
Hors d'Œuvr
ses adversaires
tête devant Hi
bois il n'a jama
dépassait aux
celui-ci reprenai
la ligne droite.
Hauterive a
style le prix de
proché à aucu
et Hourra se so
tenus derrière
ordre. Le fav
prendre que la
Hérode a gag
lière de bout e
Hérédia et Han
écuries, où elle
Hurgente, qui
devant Hautbois
Fléole s'est ad
Oise en suivant
précédents gagn
route ses concur
tueuse l'ont su
perdu à la fin les
et Gandia.
Germinal, favo
a paru ne pas
figuré. Grenade
Francklin et Ga
le même jusque
Francklin venai
avait même un
la pouliche de M
victoire sur le
troisième tout
fort bon quatriè
Dans le prix
vori Etourdi a s
sait sans effort
plaçait seconde
à l'entrée de la
d'Etourdi. Celu
ment le meilleur

(TR

The trotting
yesterday was
weather. The p
ly interesting to
The Prix Vich
thoroughbreds,
The victor was
race at Caen.
Fémina, Fleuret
site the stands

SUNDAY, JULY 10. 1898.-

NEW YORK SOCIETY IN WAR TIMES.

Fashionable People Who Are in Town Dine Now on the Roof of the Astoria.

NEWPORT'S CROWDED SEASON

"Coaching at Sea," the Latest Fad, Is Expected to Become Popular.

[BY COMMERCIAL CABLE TO THE HERALD.]

NEW YORK, Saturday.—That portion of society which is drifting through or is caught in town makes a grand rendezvous on the roof garden of the Astoria every night for dinner. Between seven and eight hundred people dine there now every fine night. It is a marvellous and new feature of New York. To eat under the stars and the moonlight so far above the dirty, smelling city is almost as pleasant as to be at Newport or Lenox.

Newport, by the way, was never so full before. Every cottage is occupied. Quiet, however, reigns, as no one is in the mood for much jollity. Mrs. Oliver Belmont has given a picnic at the Crag, and Mrs. Potter Palmer another at the old tea house. Dinners, luncheons and golf fill up the rest of the time.

Few yachts are in the harbor. The decision of the N.Y.Y.C. not to hold the annual cruise, and the fact that there will be no Goelet Cup races, impelled most of the owners not to put their yachts in commission.

One yacht, however, is having a very busy time about New York in a grand enterprise of coaching by sea, if the "bull" can be excused. The Calypso begins to run Monday in conjunction with the "Good Times" coach from the Astoria. The coach leaves the hotel at half-past ten o'clock in the morning daily and connects with the yacht at an uptown pier. The yacht sails up the Hudson, down to the Narrows and up the Sound. Luncheon is served on board.

The trip is limited to twenty-five persons daily. The round trip is ten dollars. It is expected to become very fashionable, that is to say, by the fashionables who are so unfashionable as to be in New York in July.

Mr. William C. Whitney is gathering a grand stable. He has just paid $25,000 for Plaudit, the winner of the Kentucky Derby. Mrs. Whitney's condition is still sufficiently serious to prevent her removal to Bar Harbor.

AMERICAN SOCIETY NOTES.

[From the EVENING TELEGRAM.]

Formal announcement is just made of the engagement of Miss Frances Dana Archbold, daughter of Mr. and Mrs. John D. Archbold, of No. 20, East Thirty-seventh street, to Mr. Frederick Collin Walcott, of New York Mills, N.Y. Miss Archbold is a sister of Mrs. Michael M. Van Beuren, whose marriage took place a couple of years ... uptown ... the Hudson, where ...

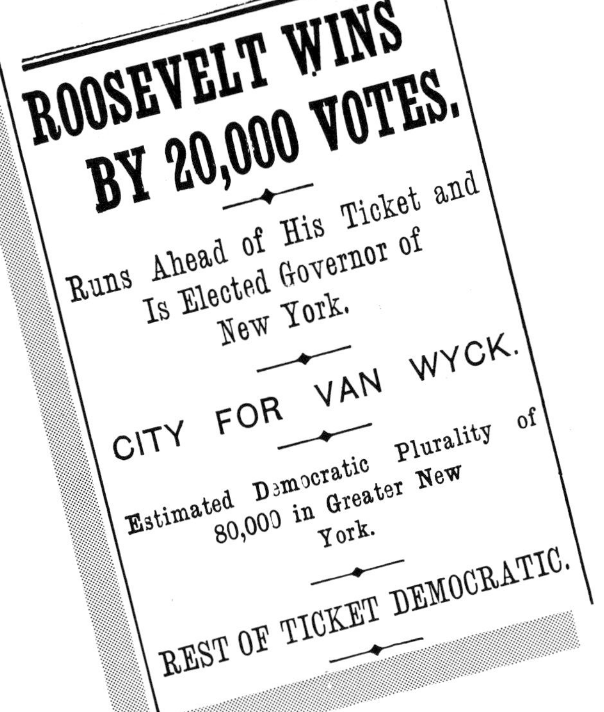

ROOSEVELT WINS BY 20,000 VOTES.

Runs Ahead of His Ticket and Is Elected Governor of New York.

CITY FOR VAN WYCK.

Estimated Democratic Plurality of 80,000 in Greater New York.

REST OF TICKET DEMOCRATIC.

A PERSONAL VICTORY.

Colonel Roosevelt the Only One of His Ticket Elected.

[BY COMMERCIAL CABLE TO THE HERALD.]

NEW YORK, Wednesday.—The personal character and the gallant war record of Colonel Theodore Roosevelt have won him a victory, made all the more remarkable by the fact that he is the only one of his ticket elected. The Lieutenant-Governor, State offices, and Congressmen, all went down before the sturdy attacks of the unterrified Democracy. The Rough Rider alone galloped through and over all opposition, and is landed in the Governor's seat this morning by the votes of men who broke all party ties and plumped votes, true and straight, for the soldier and gentleman.

It is too soon to speculate upon the curious condition of affairs with a Republican Governor and Democratic State officers. The Legislature, however, is Republican on the joint ballot, which insures a Republican successor to Senator Murphy.

...out the HERALD office seem ...the enormous concourse at ...ty election.

...ime, at nine o'clock, re... ...in fast, and yells of grati... ...ay are following fast and ...e displayed on the bulle...

...Y ABOUT 79,000.

...k Has that Lead in ...r New York.

...CABLE TO THE HERALD.]

...uesday.—The Tammany ...et is undoubtedly elect... ...running right up with ...aly is running slightly ...but will undoubtedly ...25,000 majority.

...is running much bet... ...cted in the city of New ...

...not give Judge Van ...0,000, Brooklyn about ...and Richmond counties ...

...te shows about 79,000 ...ority for Governor in ...rk.

...f, for Lieutenant-Governor, ...nd his ticket.

...the Statte show great Re... ...es in Monroe, where Colonel ...but 1,450 majority, and in ...the Democrats have car...

...'s City Majorities.

...CABLE TO THE HERALD.]

...sday.—The results, esti... ...ut of the 1,516 election ...er New York, give Judge ...ities of: in New York ...King's County, 16,835; ...2,100; in Richmond ...tal, 80,985.

...ATE SENATE.

...en Ahead in the As... ...Control the ...slature.

...BLE TO THE HERALD.]

...day.—The present fig... ...State Senate of twenty... ...nforth is elected Lieu...

...reply of the Vatican to ... telegraphic communication concerning the rights acquired for German Catholics by His Majesty on Mount Sion was considered extremely curt, while on all important occa-

...cordial ... to the great general who had learned his first lessons in soldiering within her borders.

When the special train drew up at the

COLONEL ROOSEVELT.

sions the French Consul-General has been present in order to uphold the position of ...

station, says the "Daily Telegraph," Lord ...

THOUSANDS VIEWING THE ELECTION RETURNS OF THE HERALD

ver the State of New York, and in the ity, too. First the election of one side and hen that of the other seems assured.

The returns received so far indicate that udge Van Wyck carries Greater New

Pennsylvania. New Jersey is doubtful. The Republicans sweep Philadelphia.

CONTR... THE SENAT...

nathy for Spain and a warning to the United States.

It would in any case be a proof that the ... American Government, ... the "Figaro," to

ceedings were of an entirely private character.

DEGREE ...

[BY COMMERCIAL CABLE TO THE HERALD.]

NEW YORK, Wednesday, 12.30 a.m.—The HERALD's figures indicate the undoubted election of Colonel Roosevelt by about 20,000 plurality. The Democratic headquarters, however, concede nothing.

Of greatest interest to Europe is the complexion of the United States Senate and the House of Representatives. There is nothing in the figures to aid or encourage Spanish hopes. The Senate has gained at least six Republicans, and that party now has a clear majority, having lacked one of a majority before the election.

NEW YORK, Wednesday.—The personal character and the gallant war record of Colonel Theodore Roosevelt have won him a victory, made all the more remarkable by the fact that he is the only one of his ticket elected. The Lieutenant-Governor, State

the ant... more th... votes b...

The c... to exce... the last...

For t...

THE NEW YORK HERALD.

COMPLETE NUMBER 12 PAGES. EUROPEAN EDITION—PARIS, SATURDAY, APRIL 16, 1904. COMPLETE NUMBER 12 PAGES.

2 The Monarchs

Edward VII

THE DASHING EDWARD VII – also known as the First Gentleman of Europe – was the true father of La Belle Epoque, the Edwardian era, as it came to be known in Britain. A natural and simple man who "never showed any flashes of wit nor was he a brilliant conversationalist," according to a French friend who knew him for half a century, Edward "had rigorous common sense, unfailing tact and . . . a great desire to amuse himself without attracting attention or curiosity." Paris was his favorite city, and he visited it every spring incognito except for his 1903 State Visit. Invariably recognized, he was extremely popular, as the *Herald* recorded in 1905 when, on his way from Marseilles, the king received a hearty welcome from Parisians "singing 'God Save the King' in front of the Bristol [Hotel] and under the rain."

Reading about his antics in the *Herald* (which guilelessly but faithfully recorded everything he did) is getting to know a true Belle Epoque gentleman. In Paris, he worked every morning with two secretaries until 10.30 a.m., then, "Wearing the rosette of the Legion of Honor, he had lunch at the Elysée, went to the races and the Comédie Française . . . and also visited Cartier – he had promised Pierre Cartier in London." He might have been doing some shopping as well, for on June 12, 1906, the *Herald*'s correspondent wrote: "I hear the king has given Lady Mary Hamilton a Cartier necklace of diamonds, mounted on black velvet." Another of his flames, actress Lillie Langtry, wore in *The Degenerates* (October 31, 1900) "magnificent Worth costumes and the longest chain of diamonds that has ever been made. Made for her by Cartier, Paris, it is . . . so long that it falls from the neck to far below its tall and graceful wearer's knees."

Under the dainty heading "Une petite indiscretion," the *Herald* wrote on January 21, 1895, that "The Prince of Wales spent 48 hours in Paris last week incognito to see a few intimate friends. Coutumier de ces petites escapades the prince, to avoid indiscretions, did not stay at the Bristol as usual. Even more, he got an ordinary fiacre that took him around, escorted by Lord Fortescue." But during his State Visit, the king dropped his bachelor habits and stayed at the British Embassy. With flags, banners and triumphal arches in all the streets, he did the tour of the city with President Loubet in a Calèche de Gala "drawn by four splendid dark bay horses and ridden by four outriders in the blue and gold livery of the presidency." The crowd, estimated between 250,000 and 300,000, chanted "Vive le Roi" and "Vive l'Armée." Despite a few incidents – a priest in Vincennes cried: "Vive la Liberté" while a midinette at Les Halles shouted: "Vive Edouard" – "the king was greatly pleased and raised his hand to his plumed hat, almost without intermission." There were many popular songs about the king. "Edouard VII à Paris" went:

Il tient a sa suite,
Une Bande de Milords,
Ces Anglais d'Elite,
Vont nous couvrir d'Or.

Abundantly illuminated for the occasion, Paris richly deserved its nickname *Ville Lumière*. On Rue Royale, letters of light in front of Maxim's – that legendary temple of Belle Epoque cavorting – spelled out: "Welcome to the King."

Edward, "whose knowledge of the theater was singularly intimate," predictably ended his stay at the Comédie Française, where, notable womanizer that he was, he "turned his glasses with evident pleasure towards Mlle Baitet, who filled the role of Claire in 'L'Autre Danger'." Earlier, "With his usual thoughtful kindness, the King informed M. Claretie that he will dispense with the ancient ceremonial used on royal visits, which requires that the administrator of the Comédie Française should receive him, holding a lighted candelabra in his hand."

On private visits, the King, "who had a preference for melodrama and the lighter, brighter form of entertainment," was more likely to go to the Boulevards to see such plays as *Chantecler*, *La Vierge Folle* or *Le Vieux Marcheur*. In 1909, on his way back from Biarritz looking "hale and hearty," he stopped at the Bristol for a couple of days, had dinner at the hotel, "then went to the Variétés to see 'Le Roi'." He was an habitué of the Opéra, where, for *The Barber of Seville*, he sat "down below the Royal Box, in the omnibus box which he is so fond of."

Edward had a great deal of style. When President Loubet came to London in May 1908, a gala performance was held at Covent Garden, "with all the boxes decorated with two shades of roses, pink and crimson, except for the royal box, all crimson, while the whole of the box itself was lined with orchids."

The King was above all a strong individual, a keen yachtsman who raced the *Britannia* for years, a golfer and a thoroughbred horse owner who had three Derby winners. He also liked traveling in what was then racy company, the equivalent of today's Café Society. His circle was a cocktail of beautiful women, American millionaires and several Rothschilds. It was at the home of a Rothschild that, in 1898, the Prince of Wales slipped, hurt his knee and made front page news. "The baron was worried, but the prince reassured him: 'I hope dear old Ferdie Rothschild won't be worried about this,' he said. 'It is too bad to go to a man's house and then fall down his stairs.'"

Edward smoked cigars or cigarettes "all day," loved dogs and owned, the *Herald* reported, "a piping bullfinch which is generally kept in his dressing room and wheeled in to the morning room while he breakfasts."

Very much a man of his time, year in, year out he went to Marienbad to lose weight. He took the waters "at the celebrated Kreuzbrunner, which looks like a Greek temple with columns." Traveling as Lord Renfrew, he was mobbed as he walked up and down the colonnade "like any Cur-gast" but he did not go "en queue," or "goose march" as the Germans call it. The water was brought to him by a servant from Klinger's.

When the Victorian era ended in 1901, the new King imposed strict mourning at court, "expecting all those who have been presented to wear mourning until July 22" – much to the ladies' distress, because it meant no colors at Ascot. But the King was too much of a *bon vivant* to let gloom settle for long. On May 23, the day when his wife, Queen Alexandra, "made her first appearance in the park this season," the King dined with Sir Ernest Cassel, "and no fewer than 34 were bidden to meet him." He also told Lord Onslow "that he could not countenance any entertainment called a dance, but if people were dining and afterwards chose to dance, that was a different matter."

To stylish men the world over, Edward was to establish British leadership in matters of elegance in the 20th century – a tradition that seems to keep jumping one generation, since it was picked up after him by his grandson, the Duke of Windsor, and today by the Princess of Wales.

After Victoria's death, the *Herald* described the new King as "invariably well dressed. He will no doubt set the fashion for men." Everything he chose to wear or not wear – be it gloves, vests or silk hat – was avidly followed.

Edward VII was Marienbad's most famous guest for many reasons, including his sartorial eminence. On a typical visit, "The king's presence here has attracted swarms of young dandies from Berlin, Budapest, Vienna and other cities, as well as numerous tailors and outfitters, all intent upon obtaining hints as to the latest fashions from 'The First Gentleman of Europe.' Eager eyes scan minutely details of His Majesty's dress each time he appears in public."

Every morning, the King favored for his early promenade an easy-fitting gray or brown suit with a soft brown or gray hat. "If the suit is brown," the *Herald's* fashion reporter noted, "the hat is gray and vice versa."

Red was obviously the King's favorite color, "for whatever other changes he makes, he invariably wears a red necktie and red socks, while, in the afternoon, he always puts a red band around his straw hat. Already, all young dandies are wearing bright red ties and socks and red ribbons around their hats, exactly like the King. The tailors have put red in their windows."

The King's love for color was unrestrained, as in the "purple ties and pink carnations" that both he and the Prince of Wales wore at Ascot in

June 1904. Edward earlier landed on the *Herald*'s first page (July 11, 1897) with the rumor that he had started a new fashion in the form of a "broad-brimmed, fluffy beaver hat." The *Herald* duly interviewed Messrs. Lincoln, Bennett & Co., "a famous house in Piccadilly who personally attends HRH for headgear. 'An extraordinary statement,' was their icy comment, while A.J. White, of Jermyn Street, dismissed it as 'All twaddle'."

During his 1905 Paris trip, Edward made fashion waves by wearing gloves with baguettes "in town, on visits, to the theater and while traveling," causing panic among glovemakers who were "overwhelmed with demands, because nobody would risk appearing with gloves sans baguettes." Edward's taste for hats was equally personal. Besides introducing the homburg to England, he started a fad for Tyrolean hats in 1897, buying eight of them at Marienbad. The English all followed suit and the *Herald*'s reporter crowed: "At last I am proud to say I am in a position to offer the readers of the '*Herald*' the most decisive evidence on this matter. The Prince of Wales has bought eight hats and wears one constantly."

Edward's fondness for American millionaires made London a power base for prestige- and politics-hungry railway barons and their equally ambitious spouses. *Princess Dollar* was a topical and popular operetta in his day. A seemingly endless number of American millionairesses were marrying British titles, and Americans fell into the habit of coming to London regularly. Renting splendid houses, they gave equally splendid parties and could not wait to be presented at court. On July 1, 1905, a Mrs. Kessler gave a party, for which she "had a gondola specially built in one of the courtyards of the Savoy Hotel, in the center of which 22 guests sat. Surrounded by water and scenes of Venice painted all around, she had the ceiling painted dark sapphire blue with stars. A pontoon bridge was erected across while waiters brought various dishes."

At Ascot that year, the King had lunch with "society leader" John Jacob Astor, one of his favored Americans, who had emigrated to England. Edward was "dressed in a light gray frock suit" and wore, yes, "a new shaped hat, with the brim rather curled and the hat itself bell-shaped."

Edward was particularly fond of the Ogden Goelets, who were "old New York," had been "influential in building Newport's palatial homes" and were worth $50 million. Goelet, who founded the Goelet Cups, valued prizes of the New York Yacht Club, kept an impressive new yacht, the *Mayfair*, at Cowes in 1897. (He also died on it in August of the same year.)

Goelet was a great friend of the Prince of Wales, "who introduced him to Queen Victoria on April 7, 1897, aboard the Britannia." On April 27, 1895, the *Herald* explained the Prince's fondness for the Goelets, whom he was visiting on the Riviera. He enjoyed them not only "because they were a devoted husband and wife but also because he has hit upon a house in which the arrangements and appointments exactly fit his royal taste. The

English on the Riviera are a very rag-and-bobtail lot, impecunious to a degree, very undesirable associates for the First Gentleman of Europe. . . . The Goelets have the best house on the Mediterranean. Mrs Goelet is very charming and as full of tact as a nut is of meat. She entertains divinely, has the best cook, and being an American, is quite removed from any suspicion of courting royalty for the sake of what royalty can do for her in England. The Prince enjoys, above all things, just that sort of informal comfort which he can get at the Goelets, and nowhere else on the Riviera. No wonder he cultivates them and did we ever hear of a New York lady who would not be pleased to make His Royal Highness comfortable?" If all this sounds curiously familiar, it may be because we have here the essence, the very texture, of Edward VIII's infatuation with Wallis Simpson years later.

Queen Victoria

In her own private way, Queen Victoria too was a Belle Epoque character, who launched Nice as a resort with its famous Promenade des Anglais. She visited the Riviera every year around March – except during the Boer War. Like the Prince of Wales in Marienbad, she was naturally a privileged guest and awarded ample security. She was protected by a quadruple guard, including eighteen train detectives.

On March 17, 1895, she was taking her first drive in Nice in an open landau preceded by an outrider and followed by one of her Indian servants on horseback. That day, the Prince of Wales had lunch with her but did not go to the Bataille des Fleurs on the 22nd, at which Her Majesty arrived at 3.30.

The municipal band struck up "God Save the Queen" amid frantic applause. The mayor offered the Queen two baskets, containing bouquets of violets tied with scarlet ribbons, and the battle began. As the carriage passed, bouquet after bouquet was thrown to the Queen, who retaliated by flinging flowers.

In 1896, it was reported that the Queen, who had met the Empress Dowager of Russia for lunch, drove out in her donkey carriage drawn by Jocko in the gardens of the Villa Liserb and came back at one o'clock. The next day, during her drive, charmed by the picturesque landscape, she made a sketch of the Vallon de la Madeleine in the sketch book that she always took on excursions.

Nicholas II

Another monarch who figures prominently during the Belle Epoque and whose name appeared constantly in the *Herald*'s pages was Tsar Nicholas II. Saint Petersburg was a capital of staggering opulence and the Tsar's lifestyle loomed larger than life.

The last Tsar's coronation in Moscow was the most splendid Europe would ever see: 69 million rubles were spent on refurbishing gold carriages and bringing in 320,000 pounds of fine crystal and silver and gold plate and tons of table linen, specially manufactured in England for the banquet that took place after the coronation.

A hundred thousand hands were at work – cleaning, arranging, getting ready. The vast, rose-tinted Kremlin Palace, the unique, grotesque, savagely beautiful and splendidly barbarous heart and greatness and glory of Moscow, was entirely renovated. The banquet took place in the famous Granovitaya Palata, the finest room in the palace, with vaulted golden ceilings.

For the trip from Saint Petersburg to Moscow, three new Imperial trains were built. One for the Tsar and Tsaritsa, one for royal guests and one for the suite. The Tsar's light blue, seven-carriage train, solidly carpeted in rich gray drugget, its handles of bronze gilded eagles, included a saloon, a dining room, three private staterooms, and a kitchen, plus three cars for luggage and one for the electric plant. A mosaic door led from the olive-silk-upholstered saloon into the dining room, decorated with a fine mirror and a magnificent lustre. The dark green leather nursery was between the Tsaritsa's room, upholstered with sand-colored silk, and the Tsar's nut-brown chamber featuring a massive Renaissance writing table.

The city itself was dressed up for the occasion. A perfect forest of flags waved in the air, backed by long festoons of evergreen, along the fronts of houses and public buildings. At every likely spot was a pretty obelisk, or tribune or kiosk. Seven Russian artists, each of whom had duly received his diploma from the Imperial Academy, decorated Moscow with towers, pavilions, garlands, flags, triumphal arches and greenery.

Delegates from all over the Empire were sent to present to the Tsar and Tsaritsa the bread and salt which, under its modestly sounding name, had assumed a highly expensive form, the plate (on which the bread was presented) often being very large and of gold studded with precious stones.

Asked how much Moscow was prepared to spend, a merchant replied: "As much as is needed."

Foreign countries apparently agreed, for France alone spent one million francs, half of it for a ball on May 17 to which the Tsar had accepted invitations. The only exception was the United States, which prompted the *Herald* to note: "A great pity."

The dress protocol was elaborate and strict. On the day of the solemn entries of Their Majesties, the Department of Ceremonies decreed that ladies had to wear a high-necked dress and hat. A court train was to be worn for the coronation, for the grand banquet and for the gala ball at the Granovitaya Palata. For the gala spectacle, a long décolleté dress was required and for the popular fête on the Khodinskoe Field, a high-necked dress and hat.

By order of the Tsar, the court dresses and mantles worn at the coronation and the court fêtes by the ladies of the Russian Imperial family had to be made in Russia. Exception, however, was made for the gown of the Dowager Empress, mother of the Tsar, which had to be made of white velvet embroidered in gold because she was wearing widow's mourning. This dress was turned out by Mme. Nicaud in Paris. As most foreign women ordered their dresses from Paris, Nicaud shared honors with Rouff, Raudnitz, Worth and Redfern.

When the big day arrived, nine guns signaled the entry of the sovereigns into Moscow. The grand procession opened with a glittering and flashing band of Oriental magnates, riding two and two, a vast geography of the Empire illustrated in gorgeous outfits and fantastic embellishments.

Then came the Cossacks of the Don, the Black Sea, the Caucasus, Astrakhan, Orenburg, the Ural, Siberia and Trasbaikalia, dressed in various styles of closely fitting caftans. In a roar of popular greeting, mingled continuously with bells and music, the ceremony's central and chief figure, the young Tsar, rode alone on a noble steed, sublimely solitary and followed by a galaxy of Grand Dukes and a gleaming array of princes and Russian generals. Across his dark green soldier's coat he wore the azure ribbon of Saint Andrew, and two or three stars of gold and diamond glittered on his breast.

The high point of the procession was a unique collection of sixty State carriages, including ten splendid, silver-gilt ones, drawn by six to eight white horses, which brought to mind the splendors and luxury of Eastern courts in the 18th century. The Tsaritsa's two-seated carriage, sent by Prussia's Frederick the Great to Empress Elizabeth Petrovna in 1746, was the richest. It was of the heaviest gold repoussé, with the double-headed Russian eagle of large size in diamonds on the door. On the top of the carriage was the Imperial crown, inlaid with precious stones and at the four corners sat the Imperial eagle in gold.

Sitting all alone in her splendid golden carriage, drawn by eight milk-white horses, the beautiful Tsaritsa, Empress of All the Russias, was dressed wholly in white, bedecked with diamonds. As she slowly passed along, she looked like a marble saint in a golden shrine.

In the Cathedral of the Assumption, the Tsar sat under a splendid gold-and-scarlet canopy of the Diamond Throne, which, even in the dim light of the cathedral, coruscated with an irrepressible and almost phosphorescent gleam. Incrusted upon the costly original material of the chair were nearly a thousand diamonds, over a thousand rubies and three rows of large but unshapely pearls sewn upon ancient silk velvet between lines of Persian turquoises.

Unfortunately, the Coronation fêtes ended in tragedy. All the rejoicing turned into mourning as thousands were crushed on Khodinskoe Field at a great popular fête to which two million poor and lowly moujiks came from all parts of Russia.

*

Throughout the *Herald*'s report on Nicholas, one finds a striking ambivalence between opulence, not likely ever to be seen again, and simple, earthy stories of a tragically miscast ruler who longed to be Mr. Everybody. One side of life was a giant merry-go-round, with cruises on the Imperial yacht, called the *Standard* and the largest yacht afloat in 1895 with a crew of 400 men; the Imperial Maria Theatre, decorated to represent winter, with masses of white material hanging from the boxes and balconies; regal flower battles in Moscow, where, in June 1901, there was a moving platform of flowers on which violinists played.

The social season, lasting from January to March, was a succession of brilliant balls and theatrical performances. Decors included the entry of a large ship, completely covered with flowers, at Grand Duke Vladimir's ball in 1900, and footmen in gorgeous liveries alternating with tartars from Crimea in national costumes on the steps of a marble and gilt staircase – the latter at a ball given by Prince and Princess Youssoupoff in their magnificent palace. The Tsaritsa wore a superb, star-spangled balldress and a tiara of magnificent diamonds. Supper was served on solid gold plates.

At the Winter Palace there was quite a difference between Concert Balls (held in the concert hall), with only 800 guests, and Grand Balls and Hermitage Balls, with 3,000 to 4,000 people. At the second Concert Ball of the 1900 season, to which only members of the highest aristocracy were admitted, the Imperial cortege entered at 9 o'clock, the Tsar in a uniform of the Guards, the Tsaritsa in a splendid costume of light mauve silk with a diadem and necklace of diamonds.

Each ball was more magnificent than the previous one. At Grand Duke Vladimir's ball, Princess Orloff shimmered with gold and precious stones, like a princess in a fairytale, her dress of gold cloth clasped at the waist by a marvelous girdle of diamonds and emeralds. In her hair, she wore six large diamond sprays. Princess Kantakuzen was in strawberry velvet, her right shoulder strap a row of diamond stars.

The *clou* of the 1903 season was the Boyard Fête, unique in the annals of the Russian court, at which a young Grand Duke had one million rubles' worth of jewels attached to his costume. Another used great cabochon stones of priceless value for buttons and one had the fastening of his cloak studded with diamonds.

In contrast, the *Herald* was also inclined to run all kinds of stories about the normal, often rustic lives led by the Imperial couple. An article entitled "Daily Life of the Imperial Russian Family at Yalta" took the view that "A happier couple than the emperor and empress it would be impossible to find. Both love the quiet far more than the pomp and parade of court. They are never happier than when they can get away to relative peace and quiet, such as they have found to some extent at Livadia."

Happy days for them were those when they could watch their three little girls playing on the sand, accompanied by their tidy, cheery-faced English nurses or riding in baskets on pony backs about the grounds of the palace. The Tsar and Tsaritsa spent a lot of time in the nursery. The little princesses had no costly toys, because the Tsaritsa wished to inculcate in them a taste for simplicity. The costly toys sent to them by their great-greatgrandmother, the Queen of England, were brought out only on great occasions. Livadia, where they spent holidays, was not a magnificent dwelling; it was only big enough to house the Tsar and Tsaritsa and their family. Every evening, the Tsar dined with his wife "en tête à tête."

Christmas 1900 was spent at Tsarskoe Selo, where a grand tree was lighted in the Riding School of the Imperial Stables. The tree, ablaze with electric lights, was decorated with fruit, sweets and gingernuts. There was a balalaika orchestra, with Cossacks dancing popular Circassian dances.

Gage are just as dead as Jeff Davis. Must our feeling toward the English be guided by living interests of to-day or by what our great-great-grandfathers did to their great-great-grandfathers or *vice versa*? Now that we have ceased to flourish the bloody shirt, why should we continue to twist the lion's tail? W. C. SCOTT.

Nice, March 11, 1898.

TROUBLE IN THE NEAR EAST.

Latest News of Turkish Armaments Explained by Russian Intrigues in Macedonia.

LONDON, Saturday.—I learn from a reliable source that the Government is not at all pleased with the sensational, excited tone of certain London newspapers over the state of affairs in the Far East.

On the other hand Lord Salisbury feels somewhat uneasy with regard to the suspicious look of things in the Near East, notably in Macedonia and along the Servian-Bulgarian frontier. The Russian rouble "roule dans ces parages"—in fact, that sinister coin is said to have been in lively motion ever since ex-King Milan returned to Belgrade last October, and Lord Salisbury has heard of its movements. The paper rouble is also at work in the districts mentioned, but the effect is the same in both cases: they spell brewing mischief in the Balkan and explain the latest news of Turkish armaments.

LATEST FROM CONSTANTINOPLE.

CONSTANTINOPLE, Friday.—It is understood that as soon as the British and French Governments have laid before the two Parliaments the conditions of guarantee of the Greek loan, a Note will be handed to the Sultan informing him that on payment of the first instalment of the debt he will be

QUEEN VICTORIA LEAVES FOR NICE.

Reception by the Cherbourg Authorities Upon Landing from the Victoria and Albert.

PRESENTATION OF FLOWERS.

Departure of Her Majesty and Princess Beatrice at Half-past Ten o'clock.

Her Majesty Queen Victoria passed a good night on board her yacht Victoria and Albert at Cherbourg, and appeared yesterday morning to be in a good state of health.

At nine o'clock, says a telegram to the *Temps*, the band of the 1st Regiment of the Marine Infantry played the prettiest pieces of its repertory before the Royal yacht. Vice-Admiral de Maigret, Marine Prefect; General Ragaine, the general of division in command of the 10th Army Corps; Rear-Admiral Gigon, Major-General Aubry de La Noé, Chief of the Staff; M. Poirson, Prefect of the Manche, and others, proceeded to the landing stage, which was richly decorated, to salute Queen Victoria as she landed.

Her Majesty showed herself very sensible of the marks of sympathy of which she was the object and of the reception which was given her. She expressed her warm thanks.

A magnificent bouquet of flowers was presented to her by Mr. William Eddy, secretary to the president of the board of directors of the Compagnie de l'Ouest.

Then the Queen took her place in the Royal railway carriage, accompanied by Princess Beatrice and her children. The crew of the yacht, in full uniform, were drawn up on the deck until the departure of the train at half-past ten o'clock. The band played the National Anthem, the troops drawn up in échelons on the route to the platform presented arms and the bugles called to arms.

Immediately after the Queen's departure the vessels which escorted her weighed anchor. The cruiser Australia fired a salute of twenty-one guns, the French flag flying at the mainmast. The arsenal battery replied to the salute. The Mersey saluted the flag of Rear-Admiral de Penfentenyo with thirteen guns, and the Bouvines replied with a similar number of shots.

The Victoria and Albert left the arsenal at half-past eleven o'clock for Portsmouth. The other vessels followed, and at noon disappeared on the horizon.

THE QUEEN AT THE WINDOW OF HER SPECIAL SALOON CARRIAGE.

SWISS PASSION PLAY.

The people of Selzach, a village between Soleure and Bienne, in Northern Switzerland, have decided to again take up in 1898 the Passion play performances which they inaugurated with such success in 1896, and the following are the dates fixed for the days of the play: June 19, 26, 29; July 3, 10, 13, 17, 24, 31; August 7, 14, 15, 21, 28, 31; September 7, 11.

As in 1896, play begins at 11 a.m., and lasts, with an hour's intermission at one o'clock, until 5 p.m. Two hundred and fifty actors, singers and musicians will part in the play, the character of improved by the addition scenes. The whole covering

Kenny, and is stated to have had the best of the spin.

MATRIMONIAL OFFER.

A Prince of highest position desires to marry a very rich lady. Address P. R J. 1895, HERALD Office, Paris.—(*Communicated*)

THE PRINCE OF WALES.

His Stay on the Riviera—Intimacy of His Royal Highness with Mr. Ogden Goelet.

[From the New York *Recorder*.]

A great deal of talk is heard about the Prince of Wales' intimacy at Cannes with the Ogden Goelets

The reason is quite clear.

It is not that the Prince has at last met a devoted husband and wife upon both of whom he can fairly dote, but it is because he has hit upon a house in which the arrangements and appointments exactly suit his royal taste.

The English contingent on the Riviera are a very rag-and-bobtail lot, inpecunious to a degree, and very undesirable associates for the first gentleman in Europe.

The Goelets, on the other hand, have the best house on the Mediterranean.

Mrs. Goelet is a very charming woman, and as full of tact as a nut is of meat.

She entertains delightfully, has the best cook and wines procurable, and being an American, is quite removed from any suspicion of courting Royalty for the sake of what Royalty can do for her in England.

The Prince enjoys, above all things, just that sort of informal comfort which he can get at the Goelets, as nowhere else on the Riviera.

No wonder he cultivates them, and did we ever hear of a New York lady who would not be pleased to make H.R.H. comfortable?

PICTURES OF THE CHAMP DE MARS.

People desirous to buy pictures exhibited at ... de Mars should apply to LES ARTS ... ENUE DE L'OPÉRA.—(*Communi-*

from making
ty-five years

SITUATION.
orrespondencia
ate despatch
t in a family
rsday evening
e Cuban ques-
rted to have
t as long as
r the Yankees
ps.

OTILLA.
orpedo flotilla
e Cadiz owing
the weather
e Canaries.—

RIALS
Wire a Great
ism.
HE HERALD.]
ropos of the
Key West by
HERALD this
A mechanical
our staff of
, which will
t as the news
of the world
at its fingers'
ent in the idea
s."
nly reparation
mand is that
y cut of this
ric rule shall
sensibilities,
nd of mediæ-
m on this side

torial on the
says: "It is
r any of the
the Pacific,
opriation will
ase of war."
talk is still
n the streams
hither from
se treasury is
etal is not in

duty of the
elf that peace
d so achieved
while the
United States
provoke us to

NION.
China"—such
signed by M.
aro, the main
the fulmina-
articularly of
gainst Russian
nothing but a
e both Russia
Africa.

ADVICE.
ALD:—
ll of General
ALD, European
, 1898). "It
out a Sugges-
ALD, European
398).
not a yellow
old, a caterer
g, sensation-
n population?
ar akin to the
e sheets that
f "American"

9.50 5-1
dent and Qua-
lacteur, Feuille
14 to 1; and
same distance
was ridden by
Three-year-olds;
es.
... 37.00 4-1
... 23 00
.. 38.00 8-1
so ran: Monfino,
lf; two lengths
artholomew, was
Race; 3,000fr.;
0.... 35.50 6-1
50.... 18 50
50 ... 18 00 5-1
Also ran: Sparticus
nini, 16 to 1; and
; a length and a
Barese, was ridden
ndicap; 5,000fr.;
... 19.00 3-1
... 8.50
.... 14.00 8-1
0. .. 9 50 9-2
L. 8 to 1; Sinha,
erois', 14 to 1;
Selika, 25 to 1
between second
d, was ridden
ee-year-olds;
8.50 1-2
6.50
1.00 12-1
Quettehou,
1. Won by
and third.
n by Barlen

his share of
appended his
its will be paid
ertained that the
y proceeds apace.
it is stated to have
rmit the passage
of the ironclad
gunboat of the
Crete, which are
Black Sea dock-
vessels of the
gh the straits
wo first men-
iarbekr, who
consequence
year by M.
ssacre at that
of Bassorah,
ned notoriety
a Bey affair,
mand of the
received the
taché to the
in audience
nted to His
n military
Emperor
SIA.
g to
Russo-
post of
meeting
uter.
T.
tate-

truth
one
atte
diag
"co
give
to h
of t
been
jew
geo
the
for
"
O
Tur
arri
stri
in
visi
afte
bro
seen
hors
cour
who
befo
dee
occ
For
Fro
her
leav
air
O
part
Hou
Par
cess
and
wer
of
set
Dur
atte
in I

RACE WEEK AT BADEN-BADEN.

Splendid Weather and a Brilliant Gathering of Rank and Fashion.

FOUR COACHES TURN OUT.

Many Charming Toilettes on the Course—Evening at the Casino Bazaar.

[FROM OUR SPECIAL CORRESPONDENT.]

BADEN-BADEN, August 26—Never has the "Baden-Baden week" opened more brilliantly. The weather is perfect—plenty of sun, but none too warm. Plenty of rain to water the race-track on the eve of the opening day, yet none too much, for the ground could well stand the twelve hours' sousing it got overnight.

Socially, the gathering could scarcely be more brilliant, while the sportive element points proudly to the fact that we have here the winners of three Derbies—Omnium II. of the French, Sansoretto of the Italian, and Recluse the winner of the German Derby.

PRINCE OF WALES AND MISS DE KEYSER.

THURSDAY, AUGUST 29, 1895.

ıd, with had its below it. ·rrange ·h

on the roof Baron E. Oppenheim, Count Grote, Mr. S. von Berckheim, Mr. von Winslow, Mr. L. Berendt, Mrs. L. Berendt, Mr. H. Suermondt and Mr. P. Sergezeff. And so th... The...

wi fe

BADEN-BADEN WEEK.
Prince Fürstenberg in the centre.

THE PRINCE OF WALES.

brimmed straw hat, ... feathers.

Mrs. Langtry was there and very naturally attracted a deal of attention. She was quite equal to the occasion, and yielded to none in point of elegance. Her toil... was a superb one, and no on...

laugh... ber of... sea...

EUROPEAN EDITION—PARIS. SUNDAY, MAY 24, 1896.—WITH SUPPLEMENT.

Many Happy Returns of the Day to VICTORIA, R. et I.

AS AN INFANT.

AT TWENTY-ONE.

AT EIGHT YEARS.

AT FORTY FOUR.

THE QUEEN'S BIRTHDAY.

Her Majesty Attains the Age of Seventy-seven Years To-day.

DOYENNE OF SOVEREIGNS.

Many happy returns of the day! Victoria, by the grace of God, of the United Kingdom of Great Britain and Ireland, Queen, Defender of the Faith, Empress of India, attains the age of seventy-seven years to-day, having been born on May 24, 1819.

Her Majesty, who succeeded to the Throne on the death of her uncle, William IV., on June 20, 1837, is the *doyenne* of the sovereigns of Europe, the next in seniority being the Emperor Francis Joseph of Austria-Hungary, whose accession dates only from December 2, 1848.

The Queen has now reigned over her loyal subjects for fifty-eight years eleven months and four days, a period which has only been exceeded by one English monarch, her grandfather George III. who occupied the throne for fifty-nine years three months and four days, but who only reigned in name during the last nine years of his life. To but two others of Her Majesty's ancestors, Henry III., who reigned fifty-six years, and Edward III., who reigned fifty years and a few months, was it given to celebrate their jubilee.

In point of age Queen Victoria must yield precedence to four reigning sovereigns. At the head of the list stands His Holiness Leo XIII., who was born in 1810, followed by the Grand Duke of Luxemburg, who is seven years younger, and the King of Denmark and the Grand Duke of Saxe-Weimar-Eisenach, both of whom were born in 1817.

The illustrious lady whose birthday is celebrated throughout the "empire on which the sun never sets" to-day, is therefore the fifth on the list, and the HERALD heartily wishes her many happy returns of the day.

NICE WELCOMES THE QUEEN OF ENGLAND.

Her Majesty Reaches the Shore of the Mediterranean in Queen's Weather.

A SPLENDID RECEPTION.

Great Gathering of the French from All the Towns on the Coast.

[SPECIAL DESPATCH TO THE HERALD.]

NICE, March 15.—Queen Victoria of England, Empress of India, arrived here this afternoon at exactly four minutes past four, accompanied by Princess Beatrice and her suite. With her she brought what has come to be known to every British subject as Queen's weather, and which means that the weather was superb, with a balmy temperature and a bright, but not too warm sun shining.

The people ...

ARRIVAL OF THE PRINCE OF WALES.

[BY THE HERALD'S SPECIAL WIRE.]

LONDON, May 24.—The *Evening Standard* states that the Prince of Wales left Marlborough House yesterday morning on a visit to the Queen, to-day being the seventy-seventh birthday of Her Majesty. On arriving at Windsor, the Prince drove to the Castle, which the Duke and Duchess of York had just quitted. The Duke and Duchess of York's children visited the Queen in the afternoon.

CELEBRATION IN BERLIN.

["EVENING STANDARD" TELEGRAM.]

BERLIN, May 23.—A luncheon will be given by the Emperor and Empress at noon to-morrow at the New Palace, Potsdam, in honor of the Queen's birthday. The members of the British Embassy have been invited and covers will be laid for seventy guests.

CELEBRATED IN PARIS.

Dinner Given at the British Embassy by Lord Dufferin.

In celebration of the Queen's Birthday the Marquis of Dufferin and Ava gave a dinner last night at the British Embassy.

Among the guests present were the Marquis of Anglesey, Right Rev. Bishop Wilkinson, Hon. Alan Herbert, Sir George Errington, Bart., Mr. Phipps, C.B., Mr. David Gill, C.B., Mr Henry Howard, Colonel Douglas Dawson, C.B., Hon. C. Hard[illegible] Mr. Grah[illegible]

DEPARTURE OF THE TSAR AND TSARINA.

Their Imperial Majesties Leave St. Petersburg for the Ancient Russian Capital.

AN EMPIRE EN FÊTE.

Every Province, City, Town and Commune Getting Ready for the Coronation.

PREPARATIONS AT MOSCOW

The Next Three Weeks to Be One Long Succession of Gorgeous Functions.

NICHOLAS II.'S GENEROUS INITIATIVE

A Proclamation to Be Issued Abolishing Corporal Punishment Throughout Russia.

GERMAN HONORS FOR THE TSARINA.

[SPECIAL DESPATCH TO THE HERALD.]

ST. PETERSBURG, May 17.—The Imperial train preceded by that of the Tsar's suite, left here this evening at eleven o'clock. It will arrive at Moscow to-morrow afternoon at half-past four.

PREPARING IN MOSCOW.

The Whole City Working Feverishly to Get Ready for the Celebration.

[BY THE HERALD'S SPECIAL WIRE.]

LONDON, May 18.—In continuation of the story of the coronation written by the *Daily Telegraph's* special correspondents at Moscow, Dr. E. J. Dillon contributes the following, which was telegraphed yesterday and appears in the *Daily Telegraph* this morning :—

MOSCOW, May 17.—If one may judge by the elaborate preparations which cause the streets of Moscow to resemble the cells of a beehive, by the vast sums of money which public bodies and private individuals are lavishly expending on all sides, by the enormous amount of labor employed in transforming the golden-domed city into a fairy scene from the *Arabian Nights*, by the unwonted number of the distinguished guests gathered together from the furthest ends of the earth, by the brilliant military reviews already announced, the splendid concerts and serenades, the gratuitous theatrical representations, the Lucullan banquets to princes and rulers, the generous largesse to the poor and needy and the endless round of routs, balls, receptions, religious ceremonies and civil pageants all crowded within that short space, the impending Coronation bids fair to eclipse

assuming the crown an
Patriarch Euphemius, susp
of secret sympathy for
made the recital of the c
sable part of the ceremo

IN THE FIFTH

This was in the fift
years elapsed before
Church to anoint th
throne with holy oil.
but modified by sin
coronation, and the
were officially inve
of rulers by a s
nounced by an a
they put on a ma
and a curious hat,
sugarloaf, which is
The first coronatio
from the last years
and it is a curious
solemnly, if simpl
and ruled, and his
by motives of su
tates of reason, dis
and ceremonies whi
of power.

The coronation r
very simple indeed,
of thanksgiving to t
of God and to P
The

lamentable f
Prince who
Russia.

CORONATI

The corona
called in ques
tinople on th
tions from th
Empire and
the entire c
adopted by t
served down
instead of re
from his peo
popular holic
robes and r
chain of the
ancient cost
too who, ins
first donne

which is of a charming magenta hue surpassing in richness the artful color of the

city is no mere official capital like St. Petersburg, nor a historic shrine like Kieff,

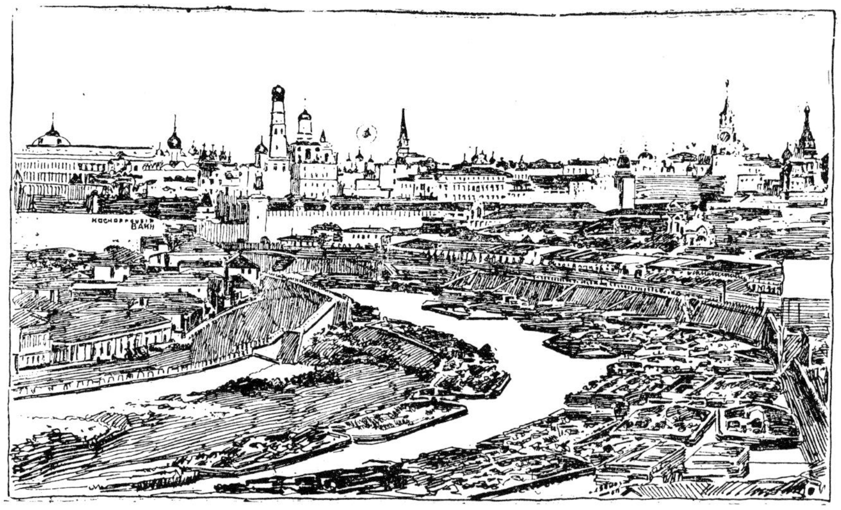

GENERAL VIEW OF MOSCOW.

Tyrians. His breast is liberally covered with gold lace and on his head he wears something like the headgear of the Scots Greys, on which a golden eagle is plainly visible.

THE SERENADE.

20 a serenade will be given in sky Park by the Russian Musical of Moscow, the Philh of the Im

the mother of Russian cities. It is the hub of the whole Empire, the heart of Holy Russia, whose loud beatings are now distinctly audible to natives and foreigners alike.

Moscow is the seat of that indefinable something, be it religious fanaticism or political faith, which during many momen of the nation's history has nding as th

A HERALD.

a
of
ands
entire
or say
ntre of
whether
iable fact
ent fever
nd hence-

REMONY.

tudy in this
of a simple
ent. For it
and more
eat Russian
d republics
gorod, and
veen those
ardom of
sugarloaf
was for
of the
own in
will

hat
would easily ... a time. No one man, even were he able, like Sir Boyle Roche's bird, to be in two places at one time, can hope to take part

TSARINA'S NEW CROWN.

in or even witness half of the sights and scenes that will be unfolded to the delighted gaze of the Muscovites and foreigners, and the most gifted contemporary chronicler must condescend to imitate old Homer and ...isodes of the

Pala
on the
days,
quaintl
the ci
and s
and th
cerem
on Tu
they w
lets to
his wife
carefull
most sa

On
ceremo
foreign
wonder
Orthodo
seem i
day, wh
standar
emblem
blessed
will t
compa
guard
the

wi
ac
Ro
is
Or
pa
ce
an
ne
th
th
in
th

fe
of
an
th
wh
th
ov
br
bo
bu
da
wa
so
all
ba
to

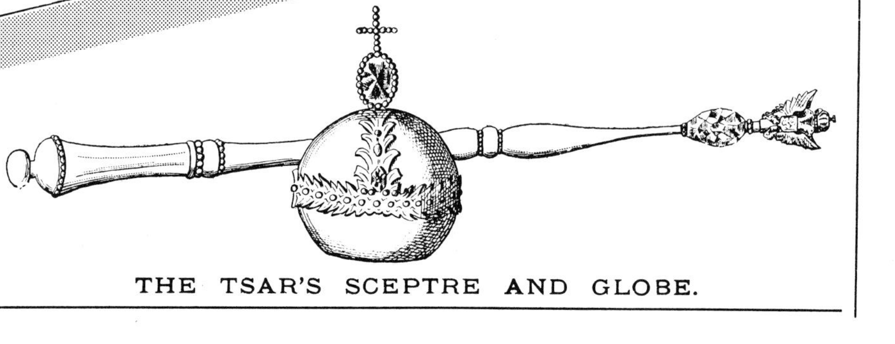

THE TSAR'S SCEPTRE AND GLOBE.

YORK HE

ESDAY, MAY 19, 1896. SIX PAGES.

CORDIAL MUSCOVITE WELCOME.

The Tsar and Tsaritsa Acclaimed on Their Arrival by Crowds of Loyal Subjects.

WAITED HOURS IN A TORRENT.

Wretched Weather Could Not Dampen their Enthusiasm for their Sovereigns.

THEIR MAJESTIES AT PETROVSKY.

Vivid Picture of the Scene at the Station by the Pen of Sir E Arnold.

LI-HUNG-CHANG'S WELCOME.

[BY THE HERALD'S SPECIAL WIRE.]

LONDON, May 19.—Both Dr. Dillon and Sir Edwin Arnold contribute telegraphic despatches this morning from Moscow to the *Daily Telegraph*. The former gives a vivid picture of Moscow as it appeared yesterday, the first day of the coronation celebration, while Sir Edwin Arnold describes the arrival of their Imperial Majesties at the ancient capital of the Tsars. Dr. Dillon's despatch runs as follows:—

MOSCOW, May 18.—The festivities of the Imperial Coronation begin, as they end, with a birthday, this being the anniversary of the birth of the Tsar and June 6 that of the Tsaritsa.

For days past the weather has been superlatively disagreeable, and telegrams have kept pouring in from all parts of Central Russia announcing heavy falls of snow, unparalleled frosts, deluges of rain and piercing Polar winds. Foreign visitors to Moscow who came here under the impression that, if not precisely summer heat, at least spring zephyrs might be reasonably hoped for, are now wistfully longing for their fur coats and winter clothing. But rain has so long been dominant that Russian weather prophets confidently predicted an end to its reign and the advent of fine balmy weather before the beginning of the fêtes.

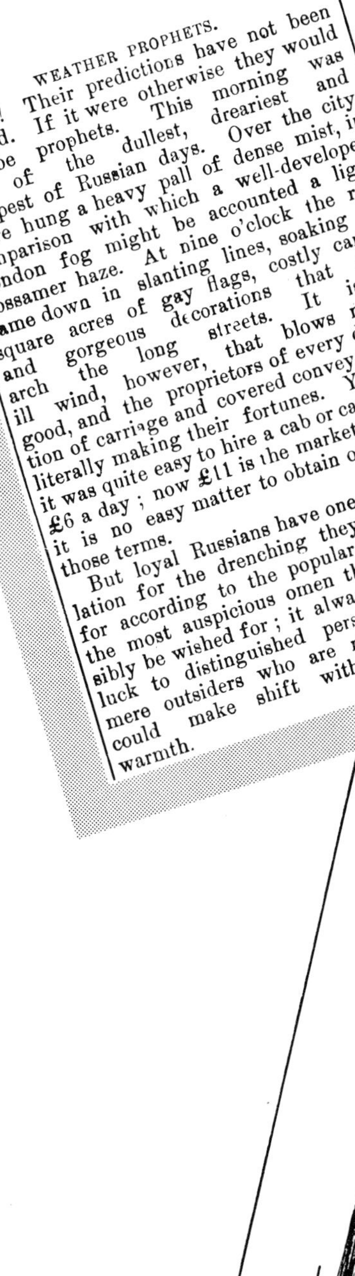

WEATHER PROPHETS.

Alas! Their predictions have not been fulfilled. If it were otherwise they would not be prophets. This morning was one of the dullest, dreariest and dampest of Russian days. Over the city there hung a heavy pall of dense mist, in comparison with which a well-developed London fog might be accounted a light gossamer haze. At nine o'clock the rain came down in slanting lines, soaking the square acres of gay flags, costly carpets and gorgeous decorations that overarch the long streets. It is an ill wind, however, that blows nobody good, and the proprietors of every description of carriage and covered conveyance are literally making their fortunes. Yesterday it was quite easy to hire a cab or carriage for £6 a day; now £11 is the market price and it is no easy matter to obtain one even on those terms.

But loyal Russians have one solid consolation for the drenching they are getting, for according to the popular belief rain is the most auspicious omen that could possibly be wished for; it always brings good luck to distinguished personages. Still, mere outsiders who are not superstitious could make shift with sunshine and warmth.

THE DUKE OF CONNAUGHT ARRIVES.

[SPECIAL DESPATCH TO THE HERALD.]

ST. PETERSBURG, May 18.—The Duke of Connaught and suite arrived at Cronstadt at seven o'clock this morning aboard the Royal yacht. His Royal Highness starts at seven this evening for Moscow.

The Empress Marie Feodorovna arrives here to-morrow morning and leaves in the evening for Moscow.

BIRTHDAY SERVICE IN PARIS.

A solemn service was celebrated yesterday morning, says the *Journal des Débats*, at the Russian church in the rue Daru in honor of the twenty-eighth birthday of the Emperor of Russia.

The President of the Republic was represented by the chief of his Civil Cabinet and two officers of his Military Household. M. Hanotaux, Minister of Foreign Affairs, wore on his coat the Grand Cordon of the Order of Alexander Nevsky.

st him writ large
luced an ancient

his divan would
esting-place in an
Russia it is used in
it will be until it is
d then it will un-
vay to the second-

H CLOCK.

hand side of the
alls of which are
with stucco work of
, facing the entrance
sees a magnificent
a marble, represent-
hydra.

noticed a very old
arked the minutes
Turkey was a
and Nicholas I.
ll the Russias.
se, you notice
ases of jasper,
l artistic fire-
ooms we enter
study of the
the former
prevailing
that of
cious hall
inst.

camp which will be inspected by their Majesties to-morrow.

SIR EDWIN ARNOLD'S ACCOUNT.

The following is Sir Edwin Arnold's description, telegraphed last evening, of the reception of the Tsar and Tsaritsa:—

MOSCOW, May 18.—Up to a late hour this morning some uncertainty prevailed in Moscow as to the particular station of the St. Petersburg Railway at which their Imperial Majesties would descend. The original arrangements were, however, more or less adhered to as ordered. In the vicinity of the Smolenski station, which is just outside the rampart of the city and no long distance away from the Petrovsky Palace, much festal preparation had been made and the interior was fitted up with every sign of ardent loyalty and warmest welcome, the occasion being doubly propitious both as the birthday of the Tsar and as that of his safe arrival at the outskirts of his inland capital. The platforms were covered with scarlet cloth, with a special way leading to the Imperial carriages. The station roof and ironwork were also freely draped with banners and pennons, and a brilliant throng, notwithstanding very unfavorable weather, awaited either within the station or in its precincts the much-longed-for signalling of the Royal train. It had been ordained in the high and mysterious bureau of the Arch Grand Master of Ceremonies, where these matters are ... how the special functions ... discharged. All the ... Moscow

their brown cloak
trickling down t
In the city, fa
everywhere susp
public building,
running colors i
It was one o
days, to be co
specimen that F
England. Yet t
equinox as it co
inclined to think
horses positively
courier Daniel
dered his wa
over such stor
terrify London c
at last, as the pri
with me, howeve
personages of M
sight of the Roy

THE AUG

It appeared
shunted into a si
and Empress u
night journey fr
albeit expected a
past five before t
alongside the sca

I wish I could
quate idea of th
tacle presented
to meet and gree
Never were su
uniforms seen t
except in Russia.

In most coun
crowd presents
... or blue, w

THE RED GATE, MOSCOW.

ENTERING MOSCOW TO-DAY.

The Tsar and Tsaritsa to Pass the Gates of Their Ancient Capital.

SPLENDOR OF THE DECORATIONS.

Designed by Seven Russian Artists—Fine Weather Not Wanting.

CLASSIFICATION OF NOTABILITIES.

Order of Precedence Definitely Settled by the Ceremonial Committee.

KHAN AND EMIR AT THE PALACE.

Rivalry Between the Rulers of Khiva and Bokhara Over Their Audience of the Tsar.

DRESSES AND COSTUMES TO BE WORN

[BY THE HERALD'S SPECIAL WIRE.]

LONDON, May 21.—The following despatch from Dr. E. J. Dillon, giving an interesting picture of Moscow on the eve of the Imperial entry into the town, was received last night and appears in this morning's *Daily Telegraph*:—

MOSCOW, May 20.—To-morrow their Imperial Majesties will make their solemn entry into Moscow between living walls of gorgeously - dressed troops, of cavalry and infantry, and hundreds of thousands of their loyal and curious subjects, some of whom have, to my own knowledge, pilgrimaged over a thousand miles on foot, with nothing but a capacious wallet and a stout long staff, in order to catch a glimpse of the Tsar and help to make a Russian holiday.

To-day the work of preparing the city is being hurried on to its conclusion. Enormous double-headed eagles, large enough to shelter a rhinoceros, are being gilded or painted; the flags ruined by the unceasing rain are being replaced by new ones; parts of certain streets along the line of the procession are being literally roofed over with garlands and festoons of every shade of green; and tens of thousands of little lamps of all the hues of the rainbow are being lighted in daylight to test the efficacy of the arrangements, this being the first time that electric light has been used at an illumination.

...for whose ...y adapted. ...ess when ...at it must ...aracterizes

...CIAL

...the wearer ...my meaning ...The maids ...at the Court ...Feodorovna, ...e who wait ...r in dresses ...ourt of the ...are robed ...match. ...s Court ...berry, ...g are ...s of ...long ...ds in ..., the ...the ...and ...ives, ...er is

...Ambassador has been received with so much distinction as the Representative of France, General de Boisdeffre, who was welcomed on arrival by the commander-in-chief of the Russian forces, the Grand Duke Vladimir.

LATER.

The weather has at last cleared up, the wind fallen, the clouds drifted away, unbarring the gates of light, and the sun, gorgeous and genial as in midsummer sheds floods of dazzling light, upon the fairy city, which reflects his image in millions of colored glass facets. The effect of this sudden change in the weather is indescribable, for it is the instantaneous change of two seasons: winter has gone and summer come almost in the twinkling of an eye. The very physiognomy of the streets has undergone a complete change.

A DECREASE OF BULK.

Peasants, artisans, merchants and pleasure-hunters, who an hour ago were wrapped up in heavy coats and ambled awkwardly along in high goloshes, are now lining the streets in the lightest of summer clothing, and owing to the vast decrease of bulk a thousand men have become as five hundred. Omnibuses and trams can now hold 30 per cent. more passengers than this morning, but unfortunately there is practically no demand for the increased accommodation. Indeed, omnibuses and droshkys are becoming useless. The public thoroughfares are blocked with carriages drawn by two, three, or four horses, and all the available spaces between them are occupied by men, women and children heedless of danger, if only they may move about and enjoy this glorious May evening after their own fashion.

All Moscow has turned out of doors in holiday attire. The shops are shut, crowds are chatting, laughing, criticizing the great ones, and the rich, golden rays of the setting sun light up one of the rarest and most marvellous scenes of human enjoyment that could well be conceived.

...south place is ...f the Duke of ...ing Princess ... way down, ...e. This order ...of the guests ...ge or modifi- ...The knowledge ...mmutable as the ...sians does not ...people from ...t for a brief ...ious incident ... the Emir of ...va should be ...sented to the ...st eleven and ...Emir being *...ersona grata* in ...atter, however, ...n on his rival, ...sky Palace long ...under the im- ..."first come, ...owed by the ...perial palace, ...tal's chagrin ...compelled to ...te-chamber, ...easant time ...and con- ...and his ... ...of

...passionate ...shopping which in England is reserved for ladies. His food differs in nowise from that of his suite, and one of the ever-recurring dishes consists

...calls it, long and high, ... On five occasions the nati... obligatory, on three the high long robes, and on eight the low dresses which give almost as great a scope to nature as to art.

HOUSE OCCUPIED BY THE UNITED STATES SPECIAL EMBASSY.

of cakes fried in the fat of rams, and known ... the vernacular as ...giv Pantagruel ...

It is no easy matter to describe the Russian national costume, which to eyes unspoiled by the everlasting black and sad gray ...loved of the West is pretty, tasteful ...

Alexander ... Cambridge recei... ...cross, as did also Princesses Victoria and Maud of Wales, under the late Tsar, Alexander III.

At all great ceremonies, such as the coronation itself and the Imperial banquet, the national costume is obligatory. The long and high dress may be of any cut that pleases its fair wearer or commends itself to Worth, and they are to be worn at the reception of the Ambassadors and the consecration of the Imperial Standard. As to color each lady is free to follow the promptings of her own æsthetic sense, which it need hardly be remarked is highly developed because unhampered by absurd prejudices among the fair subjects of the Tsar. Usually, however, many of the Court ladies imitate their immediate mistress and array themselves in robes of the color of her Court.

CONCERNING DÉCOLLETÉE.

Concerning the low-necked dress, which will be frequently worn during the coming festivities, it would be superfluous to say anything but this, that they have nothing superfluous about them. The costumes of the men naturally shrink into insignificance when compared with those of their wives and sisters. The coats of the highest Court officials are, to be sure, covered with heavy embroidery in gold and gold covered in turn with gems, jewels and decorations for signal merit, but the cut is always the same, and they look nearly as much alike as two drops of water.

Her Majesty the Dowager Empress has arrived at the railway station, wh... was receiv... Tsarits...

...on the P... entertai... Krüger ... these ... prese... it. ... crisis, ... generous ... play fast ... pal captiv... shrewd. T... his virtue a... a sore whic... peace, or... Africa ... Mr. K... the n... be se... the m... conne... under... which... somet... Gray ...

TI...

The ... mary o... The ... of the ... Fami...

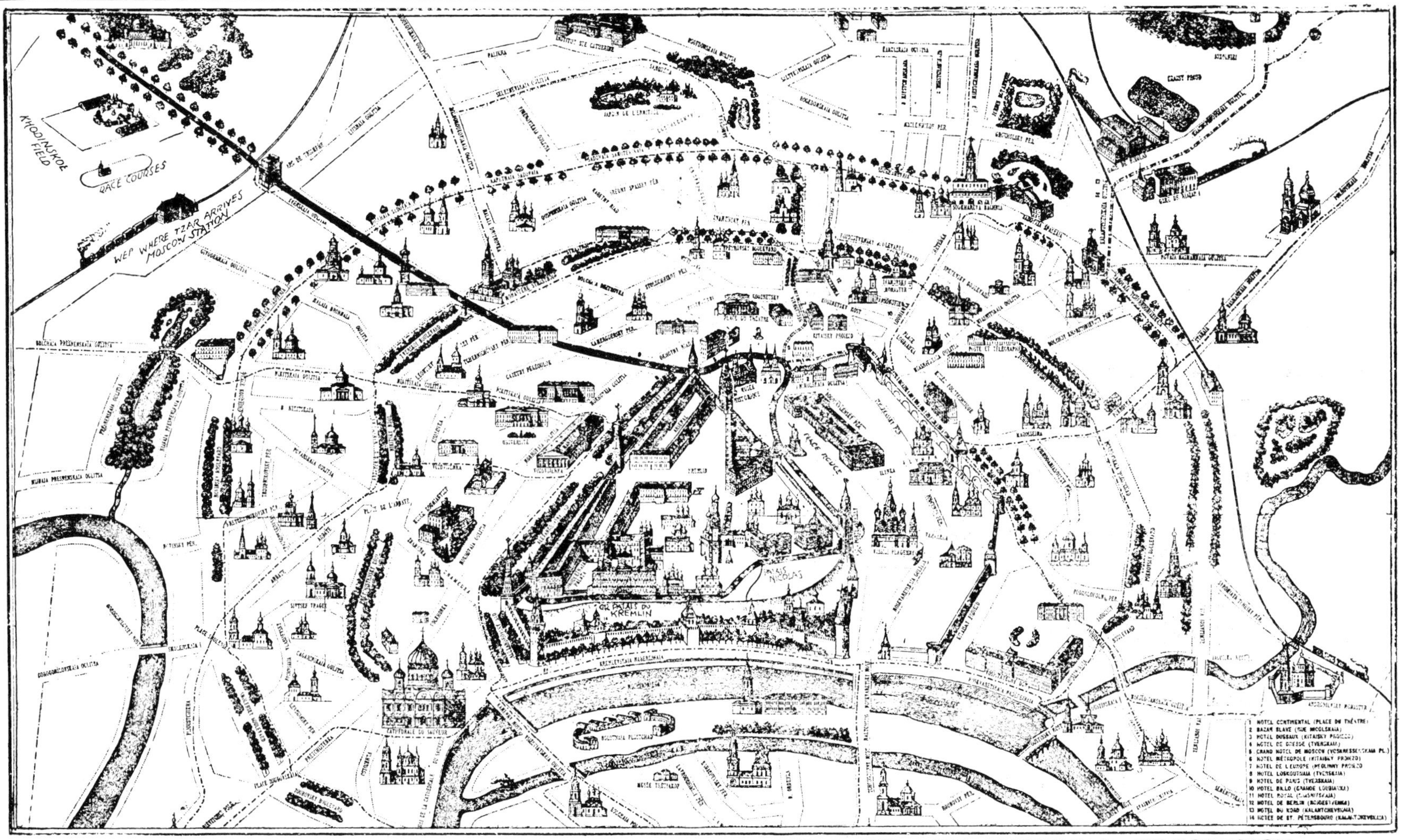

PLAN OF MOSCOW SHOWING THE ROUTE FOLLOWED BY THE IMPERIAL PROCESSION.

Nicholas II. and His Consort Pass from the Petrovsky to the Kremlin.

[BY THE HERALD'S SPECIAL WIRE.]

LONDON, May 22.—The imposing spectacle of the state entry of the Tsar and Tsaritsa into Moscow yesterday is described by Sir Edwin Arnold, whose despatch appears in the *Daily Telegraph* as follows :—

Moscow, May 21.—Early this morning nine guns fired from the Khodynsky camp aroused all who were not already on foot in the expectant city of Moscow, and gave the signal for the troops to take up positions carefully prepared for them beforehand.

The solemn entry of the Sovereigns into Moscow was about to take place, for the oft-mentioned Petrovsky Palace, where the Tsar had passed the vigil of his coronation, stands outside the ramparts. The great bell of the Assumption took up the warning from the big guns, and shortly afterwards there was to be seen gathering round the palace gates the chosen dignitaries who would have places in the state carriages, outriders, pursuivants and equerries with generals' aides-de-camp, generals of the suite, Emperor's aides-de-camp and officers attached to the persons of the grand dukes and foreign princes.

...unced ...trous ...mong ...scow, ...ntless ... eager ... that ...hes. ...onders ...erever ...p their ...loscow ...ussian ...ivities ... again ...eror's ...aught

... Krasnaya Ploshchad (the great and famous Red Square).

In one respect this great historical Red Square of Moscow is indeed transformed this morning, for not only is it metamorphosed in a general wild flutter of banners and streamers with double-headed golden eagles everywhere glittering, with tall masts rising wreathed in evergreens and garlands, and with artistic tribunes and trophies erected on every vantage ground, but along both sides of the great area immense grand stands draped in cloths of red and white and blue have been erected, capable of accommodating many thousands of spectators. And those are crowded to the last seat this morning with people of both sexes dressed in their very best and finest, as if it were an opera night and not a cold and doubtful Moscow morning.

Nine large tribunes have been reared on either side of the broad sanded roadway, ... each of ...

thr... "N... foo... at a... in a... the... splen... in fr...

Th... gen... fin... th... a... w... we... ser... bin... rod... bri...

PARIS DECORATED.

French and Russian Flags Displayed in Honor of the Coronation.

French and Russian flags made their appearance in the streets of Paris yesterday and will doubtless be more numerous still to-day in honor of the coronation of the Tsar.

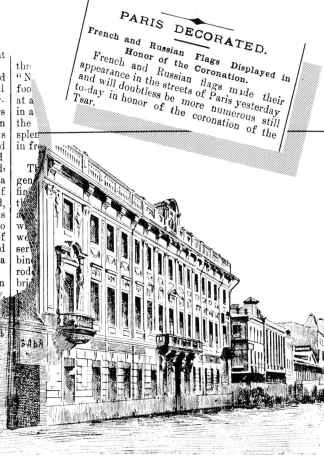

MANSION OF THE BRITISH EMBASSY, MOSCOW.

influence thus naturally disseminated—an influence so welcome and honored every- ...

as well as indecorous, not to make mention of this small but most momentous personage, whose smile was charming.

were... mus... Gua... duri... Quee... ciate... were...

Th... were... nize... Soci... the... larg... 611... clas... mar... judg... arri... spec...

T... exa... vete... were... and... hibi... mad... the... were... burg...

T... Cha... *Star*... Quee... larg...

CORONATION PAGEANT AT MOSCOW.

Display of Splendor and Magnificence that Baffles All Attempts to Describe It.

SCENE IN THE CATHEDRAL.

Course of the Imperial Cortège and Reception by the Clergy.

TWO HISTORIC THRONES.

Procession of the Dowager Empress and Her Ladies of Honor.

THE PROFESSION OF FAITH.

Nicholas II. Erect, a Solitary Man, with All Russia Kneeling at His Feet.

CROWNED WITH HIS OWN HANDS.

[BY THE HERALD'S SPECIAL WIRE.]

LONDON, May 27.—The splendid ceremony of the coronation of the Tsar is brilliantly described in a despatch from Sir Edwin Arnold which appears in the *Daily Telegraph* this morning. This striking report of a great and impressive event reads as follows :—

MOSCOW, May 26.—I have been standing since six o'clock this morning in the sacred and wonderful little church upon which the hearts and minds of one hundred millions of Russian people have been ardently concentrated, I have seen the Tsar and the Tsaritsa crowned amid such opulence of pageantry, such glory of surroundings, such startling signs of power and greatness and, it must be also added, of popularity, as with amazement fill the observer. And I have just returned through a vast, delighted, good-tempered and excited crowd, which thronged the thoroughfares with countless thousands, and made the air resound with their continuous huzzas of joy, because they had beheld with me their sovereign, crowned and anointed, stand bowing to them all at the top of a beautiful staircase, his diamond crown upon his brow, and side by side with him their Empress, also wearing her diamond coronet, and also bowing gracious thanks to Moscow from her lord's side.

But these, for all their enthusiasm, have not been present through every stage of the splendid and touching ceremony in the Uspensky Sobor. They have not stood, forgetting all fatigue, under the influences of passing scenes of state magnificence and ecclesiastical display in that strange and fascinating interior, its golden mysterious ornaments lighted up by glittering sunshine, its saints and angels dimmed from view by ascend-

ıe sheen of
d solemnity
chief per-
uperb Impe-

those seven
o the thrones
ne Uspensky
ith any suffi-
d description
miration and
ch so extra-
nge it.

e Empire
of the
not a
se privi-
Assump-
t and took

al shortly
by virtue
crown
had the
even at
s were
ely to
nto the
f was
ding at
great
plendid
hedral
pt for
colored
a few
giving
nts. The
ome time
Imperial
or the use

iew under
py which
of high
n as the
d. More
ful, it is
f ivory,
bearing
sides and
. At

an Imperial sacrament between the throne and the people, prefaced by long prayers, by fasting and seclusion, performed in the most holy of all the Russian shrines, and sacred virtue of the blessed elements and historical symbols.

USHERING IN THE GREAT DAY.

At seven o'clock this morning a salvo of

THE TSAR CROWNS HIMSELF

with the Tsar himself for the first and ... t himself receiving from ...

twenty-one cannon, rolling the thunder of its loud *réveillé* over the golden-domed city, has proclaimed that ... momentous day ...

THE SUPREME MOMENT.

Their Majesties enter the holy precincts together, and both those august heads are very reverently bowed before the sacred doors and the hallowed images painted upon them, in the hushed awe-stricken silence of the thronged cathedral. Then slowly rising to his full height, the young Emperor mounts the steps of the draped platform in the nave, and takes his seat upon the principal throne, the Empress seating herself on the other. By His Majesty's side the archbishops, archimandrites and officiating clergy range themselves in two rows between the estrade and the holy doors, while the choir intone, in solemn Gregorian manner, the psalm "Misericordiam et judicium cantabo tibit Domine." The chosen assistants of Their Majesties group themselves in a picturesque band on either side of the thrones, but behind them, while the Civil Governor of Moscow, with two other great officers of state, attends to unroll beneath the feet of their Majesties, at a given moment, the velvet carpet and pathway of cloth of gold, by which they will presently descend. Behind and between the Royal chairs stands the commander of the silver-eagled regiment, his sabre bared and gleaming, his helmet doffed. The personages elected to uphold the shoulder lappets and trains of the Imperial purple mantles are in their places, and four high dames of honor stand below ready to ascend when the time comes to affix the diamond coronet fitly upon the head of the Tsaritsa and to adjust the folds of her mantle.

THE TSAR CROWNS HIMSELF.

Then His Majesty commands, in a gentle, but clear voice, that the crown be brought to him, which he receives and with his own hands places upon his head, the same high ecclesiastic as before pronouncing an appropriate benediction. In like manner he receives from the proper officers, first the sceptre, taking this in his right hand, and next the orb of gold, taking this in his left hand. And being thus equipped in the full and complete dignity of the sovereign garments and signs of the Imperial power, we behold him sit for a brief space, silent, majestic, self-crowned, alone again upon his throne.

With exquisite softness of voice and gesture the Emperor called to him his Empress. A passing tremor seemed to me to shake the fair, tall form which rose obedient to the summons, but with all dignity and grace Alexandra Feodorovna upstood from her throne, and, sinking on her knee before her august lord, a golden-fringed pillow having been placed for her, she made obeisance before him, a sight as touching as majestic, her long hair loose upon her white neck, her splendid garments trailing in sheeny glory down the scarlet stairway, her ungloved hands meekly clasped, every inch a queen though not yet crowned.

other disti
fullest unif
tenue, almo
with stars
and jewelec
parterre of a
sadors-Extra
Plenipotentia
their wives,
Corps Diplo
attend som
full glory
Palace at
certain amo
their places i

MILITARY A

A good wh
palace had be
of soldiers
nadiers of
stationed
while alon
were detach
of cavalry.
Great Palace
Empress we
white and
along its m
Throne Roo
silver-crested
Swiatiya Se
military sch
gorgeous wi
silk and gold

Everywher
was to be wi
dotal element
four officers
been posted
form of the
silver helmet
officers with
northward a
sacred fane.
for the pres
Imperial Ma
brated, the
ciated being
the rhetoric
to the beards
jeweled fron
mitres with
They have be
are gone to
Marie Feodo

THE TSAR CROWNING THE TSARITSA.

CORONATION OF THE EMPRESS.

The Emperor, with slow, deliberate movements, now raises the Imperial diadem from his own brows and lightly lays it on the uncovered head, afterwards replacing it upon his own. Then they bring him a little diamond diadem especially fashioned for the Empress, and taking this with both hands, His Majesty himself places it upon the head of the kneeling Empress. In like manner His Majesty receives and puts upon his fair consort the Imperial purple mantle, lined with the whitest ermine and the diamond collar of St. Andrew with its azure sash, and all these sovereign trappings having been heedfully adjusted and fixed in their due propriety by the great ladies-in-waiting, the ceremonial portion of the function is finished. Nicholas II. is Tsar and Alexandra Feodorovna is Tsaritsa—he, by the Grace of God, self-crowned, and she, by the grace of Heaven through him, and the choir takes from an archpriest's lips the chant: "Lord preserve the Emperor, Lord preserve the Empress," followed by the rolling, sonorous refrain "Ad Multos Annos"—for many years—and the air outside, apprised by the signal of the grand event which has been concluded, suddenly rocks and splits, shudders and is convulsed with the ringing of a thousand bells and the thunderous congratulations of one hundred and one guns, hoarsely repeating with the bells and military music and the shouts of the people, "Lord preserve the Emperor and the Empress."

The ceremony of the holy chrism was finally performed in the sanctuary of the Eucharist before the Imperial cortège returned to the palace.

IN AMERICA.

Service in New York—Great Fête at the Russian Embassy.

[BY COMMERCIAL CABLE TO THE HERALD.]

NEW YORK, May 26.—A high mass in honor of the coronation of the Tsar was celebrated this morning in the Russian Chapel in Second-avenue.

In Washington arrangements have been completed at the Russian Embassy for a celebration to-night in honor of the coronation. A grand display of fireworks will take place at the country seat of Mr. John McLane Bauvoir, a few miles from the city, a banquet will be given at the Embassy and other preparations have been made to make the fête as attractive as possible.

The President, the members of the Cabinet, the Diplomatic Corps and all fashionable Washington have been invited.

KAISER'S GOOD WISHES.

William II. Congratulates the Tsar and Tsaritsa on their Coronation.

["FIGARO" TELEGRAM.]

BERLIN, May 26.—On the occasion of the coronation of the Tsar, the Emperor passed in review the regiments of which the Tsar and Tsaritsa are honorary chiefs.

At the dinner which took place in honor of the Sovereigns, the Emperor pronounced a speech in which he declared that the other nations represented at Moscow, and especially the German nation, shared in the joy of the Russian people. His Majesty then expressed his good wishes for the prosperity of the Tsar and the Tsaritsa.

The Emperor terminated his speech by a triple "Hurrah," in which those present heartily joined.

THE TSARITSA IN HER CORONATION ROBES.

SIXTY YEARS OF REIGN COMPLETED.

FIRST DAY OF THE JUBILEE CELEBRATIONS.

TUESDAY, JUNE 22 1897.

... hearty manner characteristic of him, the toast of the evening: "Her Majesty the Queen, God bless her!"

At the first allusion during his excellent

Her Majesty Queen Victoria Reached Her Diamond Jubilee This Morning

AT TWELVE MINUTES PAST TWO

Lords and Commons to Attend Special Services To-day at Westminster Abbey and St. Margaret's.

MORE ROYAL GUESTS.

Distinguished Visitors Have to Face Rough Weather in the English Channel.

TROOPS IN THE EAST END.

[BY THE HERALD'S SPECIAL WIRE.]

LONDON, June 20.—The Queen completed her reign of sixty years at twelve minutes past two o'clock this morning.

London at Fever Heat of Excitement, but Perfect Order Everywhere Prevails.

AT PLACES OF WORSHIP.

Lords and Commons Attend Special Services at Westminster—Judges Go to St. Paul's.

DISTINGUISHED VISITORS.

Gigantic Religious Gathering of Troops, Volunteers and Civilians at Woolwich.

SERVICES IN PARIS CHURCHES.

[BY THE HERALD'S SPECIAL WIRE.]

LONDON, June 21.—Yesterday was really the opening day of the Jubilee celebrations. It was Accession Day, and the event was observed in most places of worship as a day of general thanksgiving.

In London the affair had a spectacular element, a large number of members of Parliament, headed by the Serjeant-at-Arms and the Speaker, attending the service at St. Margaret's, Westminster. The Lord Chancellor and House of Lords attended Westminster Abbey, and the judges, with a considerable body of barristers, went to St. Paul's.

The services at these three places attracted a much larger crowd than was able to find admittance, and a great number of people had to be content with witnessing the arrival and departure of the distinguished persons outside.

those alrea... rived on ... severe wea... Grand D... Calais ir... of Opor... reache... cial ste... the Pa... of Bava... Prince ... Envoy ... panied ... General ... reached ... traveled on ... cess Aribe... The Pri... senting th... ceived a c... Victoria ... Ruspoli p... magnifice... received. represent... attaché, evening ... zam, t... Persia, Other ... Genera'... represe... repres... The ... had be... barke... yeste... Vice-... Comm... staff. Schar... Empi... Lond... Satelli... pier. arrived ... was me... Connaug... The L... the Mar... sents t... Sunda... to th... the ... met

THE QUEEN ARRIVES IN LONDON

Her Majesty, Looking in the Best of Health, Receives a Tremendous Ovation.

AT BUCKINGHAM PALACE.

Glorious Scenes at the State Luncheon and the Royal Reception in the Evening.

LIST OF JUBILEE HONORS.

No Surprises, No Startling Distinctions, but Many Well-known Men Honored by the Queen.

THE CELEBRATION IN PARIS.

Fourteen Hundred Members of the English Colony to be Entertained To-day.

OPINIONS OF THE FRENCH PRESS.

[BY THE HERALD'S SPECIAL WIRE.]

LONDON, June 22.—The Queen arrived in London yesterday and drove to Buckingham Palace amid such a scene of enthusiasm as surely no monarch could desire to see excelled.

...el ... de ... in- ... vard ... Mr. ... puty- ... Henry ... Mar- ... e and ... ntesse ... Com- ... Prin- ... sse de ... Cour- ... onstiers- ... Premier,

AT THE KAISERHOF.

Sir Frank Lascelles Presides Over the Celebration Dinner—Unbounded Loyalty.

[FROM OUR SPECIAL CORRESPONDENT.]

BERLIN, June 18.—The Diamond Jubilee of Her Britannic Majesty was worthily celebrated in Berlin on Wednesday evening at the Kaiserhof by a gathering of fully four hundred ladies and gentlemen, for the most part English, presided over by the British Ambassador, Sir Frank Lascelles, who wore over his Diplomatic uniform the red ribbon of the Bath with the star of that high Order.

on ... exag... of pu... during ... no sm... fluence ... whose ... of ... the t... It ha... own ... dred ... the r... All ... filled ... cess ... come

AT MELBOURNE.

["MORNING POST" CABLEGRAM.]

MELBOURNE, June 20.—A military church parade was held here to-day to celebrate the Queen's Jubilee. Tuesday and Saturday next will be observed as public holidays.

VALETTA "EN FETE."

["MORNING POST" TELEGRAM.]

MALTA, June 20.—The town of Valetta is to-day *en fête* in honor of the Queen's Jubilee. A procession marched through the streets, the national anthem being played as the Queen's statue was passed.

AGED SIX.

Princess of
lled with the
proceeded to
The flagship
ain left the
Her Majesty
later, and
uchess of

although
m con-
ors on
eption
nt to
there
ador
irt ;
the
ve

Volunteers and
Open-Air

IAL WIRE.]

anniversary of
ys the *Daily*
oolwich yes-
Volunteers
pulation as-
on on the
bilee service
impressive

was the largest
n the history of
played on the
er likely to be

Gentlemen Ca-
Academy, the
3rd Dragoon
Regiment, the
rdnance Corps,
. The whole
Major-General
the district,
service.
ery and Lincoln
cal portion of
arranged for
Paul's being
blic. Cavaliere
"Loyal
llery

FATHER COOKE'S DISCOURSE.

After the First Gospel the Very Rev.

Millage, R. V. C. Mooney, Miss Seward, Mrs. Noyes, Miss Scott, Mme. Pinget, Mlle.

THE QUEEN AT THE AGE OF 27.

Father Osmund Cooke delivered a discourse on the event of the day. He said that the Queen's Jubilee was not only memorable, but unprecedented and unique in history, both ancient and modern. Her Majesty ... any of her

de Cuadra, Mlle. Malempré, the Marquis de Ganay, Mr. Santos Suarez, Mr., Mrs. and Miss Hyland, Mr. E. J. Bowden, Mr. F. Ayrton, the Misses Murphy, Mi... Mr. E. B. Patrick, Mrs ... Mme. Mi...

and the busts of
German Emperor, we
able and animated fa

The Ambassador,
lish pastor, Mr. F
General of Great B
States, and Mr. Da
ladies, presided over
the others sat the S
Lord Gough, Lord
head, Mr. Cecil S
Seymour.

The American Am
and his secretaries w
unfortunately preven

"THE QUEEN, G

The health of the
posed by Sir Frank
received with appla
offered, in the refined
ner characteristic o
evening : "Her Ma
bless her !"

At the first allusi
speech to the perso
whole assembly ros
accord and interru
most enthusiastic a
for fully a minute, to
fold energy as the to
the band of the 1st D
of Great Britain an
ing up "God Save th
of which were sung
pany.

The Ambassador's
style, terse, brief and
Laughter and applause
tion of Disraeli to
Majesty "was the be
ever knew."

Other toasts follow
the Ambassador him
reception of which co
in doubt in regard to
which he enjoys
countrymen in Berlin
follows :—

Potage t
Saumon du Rhi
Salade de
Roastbeef garn
Riz de veau
Selle de
Riz à l'I
Glace à
Australian apple

The excellent mu
1st Dragoons was m
positions
lar

GREATEST PAGEANT ON RECORD.

The Scene in London on Jubilee Day Magnificent Beyond Description.

ENTHUSIASM UNBOUNDED.

The Whole "Almanach de Gotha" Represented in the Procession.

NOT A HITCH OR ACCIDENT.

Celebrations by British Residents in the Leading Capitals of Europe.

DECORATIONS IN PARIS.

All the Leading Tradesmen Close Their Shops in Honor of the Occasion.

MONSTER DINNER AT SAINT-CLOUD

[BY THE HERALD'S SPECIAL WIRE.]

LONDON, June 22 (8 p.m.).

TO THE EDITOR OF THE HERALD :—

"The greatest pageant the world has ever seen" passed from lip to lip as the representatives of every part of the earth came cavalcading along Piccadilly as a preliminary to the appearance of the central figures of the fête.

UNRIVALLED SCENES OF ENTHUSIASM.

Thousands Upon Thousands of People Cheer Until They Are Hoarse and Everything Passes Off Well.

[BY THE HERALD'S SPECIAL WIRE.]

LONDON, June 23.—The great day of the celebrations has passed in a series of scenes of enthusiasm such as London has never before witnessed and is not likely to soon see again.

The absolute devotion of the people to the Royal House, expressed at times in outbursts of the wildest excitement, has been almost indescribable. Thousands of people do not seem to have slept for hours.

All through Monday night the streets of London were filled with a wild singing, cheering, enthusiastic mass of people. All day yesterday they kept their places or merely moved from one scene of interest to another. Throughout last night again the thoroughfares were crowded, and this morning they are crowded still, thousands and thousands of men and women moving along in a dense mass, cheering themselves hoarse before national mottoes marked out in brilliant electric lamps from the principal buildings of the city and, at times, bursting wildly into patriotic songs.

At two o'clock this morning it would take a man several minutes to fight his way across Fleet-street.

THE STRIKING FEATURE.

The intense enthusiasm of the people has been the striking feature of the events of the day, and, with this extraordinary demonstration on record, many years must pass before Republicanism, which some years ago was a small element in English politics, can speak of a propaganda without exciting ridicule.

Everything went as grandly as the occasion demanded. The sun shone at the moment when the Queen looked upon her people. The organization of the procession was absolutely perfect, such as befitted a celebration of the greatest organization of Imperial Government that the world has ever known, and nothing in the great pageant itself was more splendid and impressive than the marvellous self-organization of the crowd which lined the long route.

THE NEW YORK

WHOLE NO: 22.665. EUROPEAN EDITION—PARIS. SUNDAY, SEPTEMBER 11. 1898.—WITH S

THE EMPRESS OF AUSTRIA

Her Majesty Stabbed to the Heart by an Italian Anarchist as She Was Walking from Her Hotel to the Steamboat Pier at Geneva.

HER DEATH MUST HAVE BEEN PAINLESS.

One Blow Only Was Struck—The Empress Fell, but Rose Again and Managed to Walk on to the Steamer Before She Fainted.

CARRIED ON A LITTER TO THE HOTEL BEAU RIVAGE

Every Effort Made to Restore Animation, but in Vain—The Empress Breathed Her Last as She Was Laid on the Bed in Her Room.

LUCCHENI, THE ASSASSIN, ARRESTED.

GENEVA, Saturday.—The Empress of Austria was assassinated this afternoon by an Italian Anarchist.

Her Majesty left the Hotel Beau Rivage between twelve and one o'clock, and was walking to the steamer landing stage, when a man suddenly struck her to the heart with a stiletto.

She was first taken on board a steamer and then conveyed on an improvised litter to the Hotel Beau Rivage.

The assassin is an Italian, and is said to be an Anarchist.—Reuter.

DETAILS OF THE CRIME.

BERNE, Saturday, 5.30 p.m.—Later details regarding the assassination of the Empress of Austria show that Her Majesty was just leaving the Hotel Beau Rivage for the steamboat landing when a man stepped up and struck her a violent blow, knocking her down. Her Majesty rose almost immediately and went on board the steamer, where, however, she at once fell in a fainting condition.

The captain of the steamer did not wish to put off from the quay, but did so at the request of the Empress' suite, no apprehension being then entertained that Her Majesty had been seriously hurt. The steamer, however, turned back before reaching the open lake, as the Empress still remained unconscious. Her Majesty was carried into the Hotel Beau Rivage on a stretcher. She died shortly afterwards. It was found that she had been stabbed in the region of the heart.

PORTRAIT OF THE EMPRESS.

path which ru
a few paces fi
a man, clad as
forward, struc
away. His
that it was a
merely a blo
woman who
The Empre
Her servant
and two lad
move the d
Majesty, w
her wound,
suffering,
went on.
on board t
while a me
M. Teisset,
ried her int
scious.
So little wa
appreciated,
of the captai
board, the
up the la
cleared t
to put a
stage, it
drop of b
from the
who had st
stabbed he
The grea
board. Ev
At last the
was convey
just left.
at that m

a ruffian at a
way.
uttering a cry.
ped to raise her,
d a brush to re-
ess. Then Her
ng conscious of
lm and scarcely
her heart and
r, had she got
he reeled, and
mont-Ferrand,
rms and car-
came uncon-

the incident
he hesitation
ny doctor on
, and headed
ver, had she
me necessary
the landing
red that one
the corsage
. The man
ad evidently

revailed on
assistance.
the Empress
hich she had
ess was dead
ell; her body
either a com-
even a sigh.

THE NEWS IN VIENNA.

Intense Grief and Indignation—Thousands of People in the Streets.

VIENNA, Saturday, 8 p.m.—The news of the assassination of the Empress of Austria became known here between five and six o'clock this evening, and spread like wildfire throughout the city, producing an effect akin to stupefaction mingled with a feeling of profound grief. The feeling was one of intense indignation at such an appalling and unprovoked crime.

The streets immediately filled with thousands of people, and in many places became quite impassable to vehicles. All the newspapers issued special editions with the intelligence, which seemed to many incredible, until the special edition of the semi-official "Wiener Abendpost" appeared with the confirmation. The journals all paid a warm tribute to the noble qualities of the head and heart of the late Empress. They were passed from hand to hand in the streets, and groups of people were to be seen on all sides gathered round someone who read the news aloud.

The performances in the Court theatres and in the Jubilee Exhibition were immediately cancelled.

Profound grief is everywhere apparent.—Reuter.

HERALD.

MENT. PARIS & DEPARTMENTS, 25 c.; LONDON, 2½d

ASSASSINATED

NTION.

th the Object
a High

nmediately after
assassin, the offi-
secutions went to
"service d'ordre"
f the Hotel Beau
ndous crowd had

refully explored
ty with the ob-
used by the

ve inquiries

BREAKING THE NEWS.

Count Goluchowski Conveyed It to the Emperor at Schoenbrunn.

VIENNA, Saturday.—When the news reached Vienna the Ministers were assembled in Council. Count Goluchowski at once hastened to Schoenbrunn, where the Emperor was stopping, and begged the aide-de-camp to introduce him at once into His Majesty's presence. The Emperor, who burst into sobs on hearing the news, immediately returned to Vienna.

The Archduke Louis, the Emperor's brother, was at the Exhibition. Herr von Kilmansegg, the Governor, at once went to fetch him and brought him to the Hofburg, where he joined the Emperor.

THURSDAY. APRIL 5, 1900.

ATTEMPT ON THE LIFE OF THE PRINCE OF WALES.

TWO SHOTS FIRED AT H.R.H. IN BRUSSELS.

A Youth Springs on the Footboard of the Royal Carriage and Discharges a Revolver at Him Through the Window.

BOTH SHOTS FAIL TO STRIKE.

The Would-be Assassin Is Arrested and Declares that He Wanted to Kill the Prince for Having Caused Thousands to Die in South Africa.

[SPECIAL TO THE HERALD.]

BRUSSELS, Wednesday.—The greatest consternation was caused here to-day by an attempt on the life of the Prince of Wales.

His Royal Highness, accompanied by the Princess of Wales and their suites, arrived in the Belgian capital at 4.45, coming from Calais, and en route for Copenhagen, via Cologne. While waiting for the Cologne express to be made up the Royal carriage was placed in a siding of the Gare du Nord. The Princess of Wales and the ladies of her suite remained in the carriage and partook of refreshment. The Prince of Wales, accompanied by two secretaries, walked up and down the platform in conversation with them.

student
rev
Si
ir
th
acti
whic
hand,
fired a
nant p
police
mistak
severe
Decl
I
ma
o

Roy. H

Meanwhile the Royal carriage had been attached to the Cologne express. A few minutes before the departure of the train, at 5.15 p.m., the Prince of Wales re-entered the Royal carriage. At this instant a youth, who looked about sixteen years of age, crossed the platform, jumped on to the footboard of the carriage, and fired two shots with a revolver in the direction of the Prince of Wales.

Preparing to Fire Again.

He was preparing to fire again when the stationmaster knocked up his arm, and the revolver fell to the ground. He was immediately seized and conducted to one of the waiting-rooms, where he was kept in custody.

The stationmaster then returned to the Royal carriage to assure himself that no harm had happened to any of the occupants. He found that the bullets had gone through the window on the opposite side of the carriage. The Prince of Wales, who had shown the greatest calmness and self-control throughout, asked the stationmaster if the would-be assassin had been arrested, and on receiving a reply in the affirmative the train steamed off to Cologne.

The prisoner was conducted to the nearest police station, where he was put through an examination. He stated that his name was Jean Baptiste Sipido, that he was fifteen and a half years of age, and was a tinsmith's apprentice.

He stated that he was not an anarchist, that he had thoroughly premeditated his crime, and that he desired to kill the Prince of Wales because he was the heir-apparent of a country that was killing so many thousand people in South Africa. He expressed regret that he had not succeeded in killing the Prince of Wales.

Inspired by Socialists.

It is supposed that he conceived the first idea of his crime at a meeting of Socialists held yesterday, at which several of the speakers denounced the British

counselled. I
meeting last
to-day. He i
a rather tho
The Sipido
many years i
was born he
descent. Si
Central Pris
It is believ
M. Picard,
fence. It is
employment
Socialist Ma

ANO

The Woul
Stuff

BRUSSELS,
the revolver
step of the
the Prince o
gentleman,
Thrusting t
the door, S
direction of
no one. He
when the st
and struck
stant two r
pido down.
and taken o
inspector.
the confusio
named Van
and assaulte
Sipido w

PRINCESSE HÉLÈNE'S WEDDING TROUSSEAU

Description of the Bridal Dress—White Satin Trimmed with Orange Blossom.

COURT ROBE AND MANTLE.

Latest Fashions Seen at Longchamp Races—Some Charming Toilettes.

[LETTRE D'UN VIEUX PARISIEN.]

DEAR MADAM,—About ten days hence will take place at Kingston-on-Thames the marriage of Princess Hélène of Orleans with the Duke of Aosta, nephew of the King of Italy.

ployed by
l permissior

As I thought you would take an interest in what has been made for the Princess's trousseau, and in her dresses, I went to see

PRINCESSE HÉLÈNE D'ORLÉANS.

the principal things ordered for the wedding at various establishments in Paris.

vith
iite

lawn, covert
a cuirass, anc

boulevard Haussmann. The train is composed of wide pleats and is lined with white moiré, trimmed underneath with a wide ruche, forming a *balayeuse.*

The body is slightly gathered in the middle in front and quite close fitting behind. Two pleats at the back entirely conceal the fastenings. The waistband, worn high, is of white satin, formed of three folds, drawn close to the figure and ends under the seams beneath the arms. The neck trimming is made of three frills of satin, with a small bunch of orange blossom on the left side. There is a similar bunch at the waist. The sleeves are puffed, but not to exaggeration. You can see that all this is extremely simple, and is only relieved from the point of view of elegance by a lace veil which extends from the head to the end of the train. According to the custom with princesses the face is left uncovered. This veil was made by Lefebure, boulevard Poissonnière, who allowed me to

ribbon and
diamonds.
A red satin
cascade of m
same color.
A dress of
broidery on t
A Court dr
fronts of wh
folds in a wa
A Court dr
A dinner dr
style, with fic
lace and buc
dinner dress c
dress, straw c
lace.
At Doucet'
dress which h
is very simple
pale blue satin
necked, with
mousseline de

I can give you some particulars of the jewelry presented by the Duke of Aosta to his bride.

The ring is of massive gold, in which a skilful Italian jeweler has set a large sapphire and a large brilliant. There is a necklace of one row of thirty-two large pearls, and another composed of eleven rows of pearls from the Ponte Vecchio at Florence, the great pearl market of Italy. A body trimming is of nut and pear-shaped pearls and diamonds.

de s
and t
Albert
black cre
trimmed w
and white a
Among th
Otero in a wh
ing one immen
white aigrette
Mme. Pie
the body tr
forming a
sleeves. l
border entire
roses.
Mme. Pre
large bunche
colors, and
and peonies.
There is
tume desig
of which a
It is of
formed in
which st
flaps at
I ma
were se
by Mll
is of la
twisted
given b
reeds and
Anothe
with rose
aigrette.
Capucin
of the F

F. de Rose

WEDDING DRESS OF THE PRINCESSE HÉLÈNE D'ORLÉANS.

make a drawing of the Princess's dress, and the permission was readily given when Mme. Garnier knew that it was for a *primeur* for the HERALD. You, therefore, will see it under two different aspects. The claim of this costume is its extreme simplicity. It is of white satin, perfectly plain, and is composed of 27 mètres of satin at 2fr. a mètre. The Princess is very tall early six feet in fact, and the *fourreau*

dress is of stuff embroidered on a granite ground trimmed with black faille ribbons.

The Court dress and mantle, which will be worn by the new Duchess when she is presented to the Queen of England, and afterwards when presented to the King and Queen of Italy, are by Worth. The is made of twe

flounces of white lace. Rice straw hat, trimmed with a tuft of white feathers, bows of lace and Paul Néron roses.

Among other dresses which I Longchamp

Pretty Pa

At the Capucines sunshade One

Empress Alexandra's Charming Idea of Resuscitating the Glories of Old Muscovy.

A REVELATION OF WEALTH.

Millions of Roubles' Worth of Jewels Worn at Old-Time Social Function.

ST. PETERSBURG, Thursday.

BY far the most original and interesting function yet known in this most brilliant of Courts has been the much-talked-of Boyard costume fête and ball, which took place at that part of the Winter Palace technically known as the Hermitage.

The highest expectations had been aroused concerning the richness and brilliancy of the entertainment. Society had talked of it for months as the "clou" of the season. Costumiers and dressmakers had been engaged for weeks and weeks, day and night, creating robes and costumes of such richness as they had never thought of before. It was almost like a coronation. The richest of the jewels of the Imperial Court, the rare old stones which for centuries have been treasured up in the palaces of Moscow; family jewels of the most ancient and representative houses in Russia; jewels ancient and modern were drawn upon to give yet further brilliancy to the already rich costumes, of the rarest brocades and cloths of gold.

The famous looms of Moscow had been busy for months and months preparing for this function those heavy and rich gold and silver tissues for which they are noted the world over. It was as though the olden days of the Boyards, with all their elegance and riches, had returned for this out-and-out Russian entertainment, in which all that was most picturesque and luxurious of the old Russian times was to figure.

Rare Jewels.

Towards the last week, hundreds upon hundreds of skilled workmen and women were kept hard at it for such long hours that they were almost dead from exhaustion, sewing the rarest and finest jewels on to costumes where silver and gold played a principal part.

wife, who were represented by the Emperor and Empress.

Expectations Realized.

Much had been expected of the Boyard fête. Let it be stated here that those expectations were realized to their utmost and most optimistic degree. Such was the success that to-day all kind of talk goes about of the Boyard dress being adopted for Court purposes, and of several of the heavier liveries which were brought in during the periods of German influence being abolished in favor of the more picturesque style of Russian dress as so well shown in the Boyard entertainment.

Those who saw the procession talk enthusiastically of its glories as one of the most beautiful sights possible to witness. It was a revelation, according to them, of the vast wealth which is to be found in this country, so often thought to be so extremely poor.

On the floor of the ballroom, as the guests looked round upon the gorgeous scene, jewels such as never h…

ried in his
sceptre. The
broché in gol
stood out an
It was trimm
shouba.

Next to th
able costume
Duchess Vla
picturesque t
of red cloth o
Duchess stoo
note of color
torical pictur
The huge sle
with the tin
with the tr
broidered in
highly effect
sign of a gra
cloth of gold.
beauty that
first time sto
beautiful disp
gold collar.
small …

The entrance to the Hermitage

The Empress.

"The Empress!" went up the hushed exclamation. And with it a suppressed murmur of admiration. A wondrous sight indeed it was that met the eyes of that gold, silver and jewel-bedecked audience. A vision of loveliness and splendor, a picture of silver and white studded with a perfect constellation of gems, pearls, precious stones, which had taken weeks of work from hundreds of expert hands to fix and to fashion. All real, every stone! Surmounting all a great mitre, on the beautifully-poised head, a mass of great dimonds, emeralds, rubies, the pick of the most valuable of the jewels of the Imperial Court.

"A Byzantine Madonna come down out of an ikon," was the impression the Empress made upon one of the most artistically-minded of the guests. And there Her Imperial Majesty paused for a second or two, smiling and so happy looking in all her glory, in all that brocade and silver, that constellation of jewels shining with prodigious effect upon the silver brocade as a silver sea studded with stars and phosphorescent light.

The Boyard Costume Fete

St Petersburg

A Boyard

A falconer

A Falconer

Streltzy costume

RECENT PORTRAIT OF HER MAJESTY QUEEN VICTORIA.

EW YORK HERALD.

-PARIS, WEDNESDAY, JANUARY 23, 1901.—TWELVE PAGES. PARIS, 15c.; LONDON, 2d.; DEPARTMENTS, 20c.

PASSES AWAY AT OSBORNE HOUSE.

End Came at Half-Past Six, Peacefully, Surrounded by Her Children.

GLOOM AT OSBORNE, SORROW AT COWES.

Kaiser William, the Prince of Wales, Duke of Argyll and Duchess of York Present.

SOME EARLY MORNING FEARS.

When She Was Thought to Be Dying, She Rallied and Recognized Bystanders.

DIED LIKE THE SETTING SUN.

OSBORNE HOUSE,
ISLE OF WIGHT,
Jan. 22, 1901.

OFFICIAL BULLETIN, 7.8 P.M.

HER MAJESTY THE QUEEN BREATHED HER LAST AT 6.30 P.M. SURROUNDED BY HER CHILDREN AND GRANDCHILDREN.

(Signed)
JAMES REID, M.D.
R. DOUGLAS POWELL, M.D.
THOMAS BARLOW, M.D.

BULLETINS OF THE DAY.

The Prince of Wales Announces His Mother's Death to the Lord Mayor of London.

[BY THE HERALD'S SPECIAL WIRE.]

LONDON, Wednesday.—The momentous bulletin came in the form of the following telegram to the Lord Mayor from the Prince of Wales:—

OSBORNE HOUSE, Tuesday, 6.45 p.m.—My beloved mother, the Queen, has just passed away, surrounded by her children and grandchildren.—ALBERT EDWARD.

An earlier message to the Lord Mayor from the Prince of Wales, says:—

OSBORNE, 4 p.m.—My painful duty obliges me to inform you that the life of the beloved Queen is in the greatest danger.—ALBERT EDWARD.

The Lord Mayor, shortly after the receipt of the telegram from the Prince of Wales, forwarded the following to His Royal Highness:—

"I have received Your Royal Highness's sad intimation with profound grief, which is shared by the citizens of London, who still pray that, under Divine Providence, the irreparable loss to Her Majesty's devoted family and loyal subjects throughout the Empire may still be averted. Will Your Royal Highness be pleased to accept this heartfelt expression of deep and sincere sympathy.—LORD MAYOR OF LONDON."

The following are the early medical bulletins:—

OSBORNE, 8 a.m.—The Queen this morning shows signs of diminishing strength, and Her Majesty's condition again assumes a more serious aspect.

JAMES REID, M.D.
R. DOUGLAS POWELL, M.D.
THOMAS BARLOW, M.D.

OSBORNE HOUSE, 12 o'clock.—There is no change for the worse in the Queen's condition since this morning's bulletin. Her Majesty has recognized several members of the Royal Family who are here. The Queen is now asleep.

JAMES REID, M.D.
R. DOUGLAS POWELL, M.D.
THOMAS BARLOW, M.D.

OSBORNE HOUSE, 4 p.m.—The Queen is slowly sinking.

JAMES REID, M.D.
R. DOUGLAS POWELL, M.D.
THOMAS BARLOW, M.D.

...thout suf- ... her mental ... breath after ... faces around ... icians real- ... g to stave ... went to ... t the end ... -four hours ... by artificial ... al family re- ... ey quickly ... rne had ... g and ... rs.

gaze slowly ... one to the oth... evident recognition and farewell.

Died in Her Sleep.

A quarter of an hour later the sovereign's clear eyes became silent. A mist fell over them and the lids closed. Death sealed them later. For the sovereign died in her sleep; she died without suffering, or pains, or throe. The heart beats gradually became weaker, scarcely perceptible, the breathing grew more labored.

At last, at half-past six in the evening, the heart stopped beating. All was over. Sir James Reid stood up, and with a strong voice uttered: "The Queen is dead."

And almost inaudibly, for the last time, the Bishop of Winchester murmured:—

"God save the Queen!"—Matin.

In the ... upplement to the ... ed this morning ...

A move... It nume... lence... ily ... fror... col... inf... th... th... an... em... the... fold... At... begai... they... burst... Royal... person... her as ...

AS SHE HAD WISHED.

Surrounded by Her Children and Grandchildren the Queen Passed Into Peaceful Slumber.

COWES, Tuesday.—It is all over. The tension is relaxed. The great Queen is at peace.

The news came, not with the pomp and circumstance of a State announcement, but rather with a hush of sorrow.

The Queen is dead. Cowes is hushed and silent. The gloom at the gates has spread over the town.

There are no demonstrations of emotion in the streets. The entrances to Osborne House are deserted. Cowes is mourning in silence.

Funeral Arrangements.

With regard to the funeral, it is understood that there will be a procession in state through the streets of London before and after the lying in state in St. Paul's. It is also expected that as many of the reigning Sovereigns of Europe as can will be present.

There will be the German Emperor, of course. The Tsar of Russia and the King of Greece, the King of Italy and the King of the Belgians are already among those mentioned as being almost sure to be present.

Impressive Ceremonies Before the Privy Council in St. James's Palace.

THE NEW YORK

WHOLE NO.: 23,530. EUROPEAN EDITION—PARIS, THURSDAY, JANUARY 24, 1901.—EIGHT

KING EDWARD THE SEVENTH T

THE NEW KING MAKES A SPEECH.

Tells the Councillors He Will Do His Utmost to be Worthy of His Great Position.

WHY HE IS NOT ALBERT I.

Desire to Leave Memory of His Father's Name Exclusive Treasure of His Mother.

SCENES IN HOUSE OF COMMONS.

[BY THE HERALD'S SPECIAL WIRE.]

LONDON, Thursday.—The urgent claims of State leave no interval for the indulgence of private grief upon those closely associated with the Throne. It was therefore necessary for His Majesty, the King, accompanied by the members of the Royal Family and others, to leave Osborne for London yesterday morning.

A Day of Anguish at Osborne—A Day of Royal Peace and Rest.

A SACRED SILENCE IS OBSERVED.

Stillness is Ruffled only by the King's Hurried Departure for London.

MINUTE GUNS AT NOON.

The Dead Queen Lies in the Simple Majesty of Her Womanhood.

...ce-
nected
... Lon-
...ilway;
... Rear-
...Brand;
...vill, Mr.
...Macrae,
...tended
...y. The
...ricaded
...n of the
...ie press
...ons, was
...
..., 12.55,
...station
...andstill
...rectors
...oor of
... any
... across
...owed by
...olford.
...who had
...ud hur-
...d along
... drove
... Marl-
...arden
...y was
...aptain
... in St.
...o'clock.
...ame as
...reached
...e were:
...d Rosc-
... Henry
...n, Lord
...bourne,
... of Cov-
...Spencer,
...ach, Mr.
..., Sir W.
...the Lord
...ke of De-
... L. Jack-
...a, Lord
...e, Mr.
...Earl

...F. Jeune, ... Goschen, Lord Lansdowne and Mr. J. W. Lowther.

THE PRIVY COUNCIL.

The Press Association has been favored with the following particulars of what transpired on this interesting occasion. The King was in a separate apartment from the various members of the Privy Council. To the latter the Duke of Devonshire made the formal communication of the death of Queen Victoria and of the succession to the Throne of her son, the Prince of Wales.

The Royal dukes, with certain Lords of the Council, were then directed to repair to the King's presence to acquaint him with the terms of the Lord President's statement.

Shortly afterwards His Majesty entered the room in which the councillors were assembled, and from the Throne delivered a brief address. The King's speech was spoken without notes, and created a fine impression. At the outset His Majesty's voice was broken with emotion, but it gathered strength as he went on, and the speech is described as admirable in tone and touching in its dignity and pathos.

His Majesty said he had decided to assume the title of King Edward VII., in accordance with the wish of his beloved mother, who, His Majesty said, united the virtues of supreme domestic guide with the affection and patriotism of a wise and peace-loving monarch. He had a respectful desire to leave the memory of his father's name, Albert, the exclusive treasure of his beloved mother. Notwithstanding his personal desire he could not hope to do justice to the renown and virtues associated with Prince Albert's name. He would do his utmost to be worthy of his great position.

Then came the Lord Chancellor's important duty. Lord Halsbury had to administer the formal oath to the new King. By this oath His Majesty bound himself to govern the kingdom according to its laws and customs, and, after declaring his sense of the high office he assumed, the King had to proceed to express his firm reliance upon the wisdom of Parliament and the loyalty and affection of his people.

The Cabi... ...dvanced to

and s...
observe...
Councillors...
The King...
was then ...
the King...
Council t...
"London...
ly statec...
in the pr...
of Grea...
of India...
the Duk...
the Duk...
the Arc...
Chancel...
represe...
When...
for the r...
crowd w...
cheered...
called ou...
live King...

Simple b... Tal...

[BY...
LONDO...
terest att...
ment yest...
death of...
her succe...
did, the c...
ed of all...
ordinary...
Shortly...
cellor, att...
all the la...
the Chan...
was alre...
peers b...
of taki...
sovere...
A...
mour...
Pray...
cellor...
taken ...
he again...
swearin...
The...
Hou...

MOURNING TO LAST A YEAR.

Official Instructions for Deep Mourning for Six Months and Half-Mourning an Additional Six Months.

[BY THE HERALD'S SPECIAL WIRE.]

LONDON, Thursday.—A second supplement extraordinary to the "London Gazette" was issued this morning, as under:

Lord Chamberlain's Office, Jan. 24, 1901.

Orders for the Court to go into mourning, for her late Most Gracious Majesty Queen Victoria, of blessed memory, viz.,

Ladies to wear black dresses, trimmed with crape, and black shoes and gloves, black fans, feathers and ornaments;

Gentlemen to wear black Court dress, with black swords and buckles.

Mourning to commence from the date of this order.

The Court to change mourning on Wednesday, July 24 next, viz.:—

Ladies to wear black dresses with colored ribbons, flowers, feathers and ornaments, or gray or white dresses with black ribbons, flowers, feathers and ornaments;

Gentlemen to continue the same mourning; and,

On Friday, January 24 next, the Court to go out of mourning.

THE ARRANGEMENTS.

"How long the Queen will lie at Osborne no one can say. The King returns to-day, and he will then decide. Yesterday, however, carpenters, working as swiftly and as silently as best they might, were preparing the Queen's dining room to receive the late Queen's body. There she may lie for a week, or till such time as she is borne to Windsor.

"Then, as befits a mistress of the seas, Her Majesty will, on her last crossing of the Solent, be guarded by one of the greatest fleets that ever gathered at one time. Her Majesty's bodyguard of Grenadiers came to Osborne to-day to keep watch and ward, and orders have been given for the Channel Squadron to assemble at Spithead as soon as possible."

EDWARD VII., KING OF ENGLAND.

(From a portrait painted by Mr. Julian Story and reproduced by his permission.)

WEATHER IS BLAMED FOR DEATH OF KING

Miserable Climatic Conditions Accentuated Bronchial Trouble, Inducing Spasms of Coughing.

HEART AFFECTION FOLLOWS.

Once Crisis Seemed Safely Passed by, Renewed Paroxysm Has Fatal Termination.

(BY TELEPHONE TO THE HERALD.)

LONDON, Sunday.—The following statement given to a correspondent of "Lloyd's Weekly" yesterday may be taken as an authentic account of King Edward's illness and of his sudden death :—

To the physicians in attendance, the death of the King came with some amount of surprise, for on Friday afternoon His Majesty seemed very much better. The only cause for anxiety—and that was a very real one—were unexpected severe coughing spasms which threw an enormous strain upon the heart of the Royal patient and the blood-vessels pasing from it to the brain.

On Wednesday the bronchial trouble became a little more marked, and there were added to it violent paroxysms of coughing. Seeing there was a considerable amount of catarrh His Majesty's throat specialist, Dr. St. Clair Thomson, was summoned. The climatic conditions of Thursday were exceedingly unfavorable for such a complaint, in that the weather during the past week has been of the worst possible kind for anybody suffering from bronchial troubles. Indeed, it may be said that the fatal termination of the King's illness was due to the climatic conditions which have lately existed.

During Friday evening the spasms of coughing became more frequent. A tremendous strain was thrown upon the heart, which immediately became the cause of chief anxiety. It was feared that death might occur at any moment from one of these attacks, so severe were they. What prompted the alarming bulletin issued on Friday morning were these violent accesses of coughing.

Shows Improvement.

As noon approached the coughing became less frequent, and in the afternoon His Majesty appeared so much better that he was able to sit up and take tea with various members of the Royal family.

His Majesty's condition had so much improved that as a matter of fact the fear of a fatal termination of the illness was no longer entertained, but during the early evening symptoms of heart failure developed, and when the last consultation was held so rapid had been the change that a fatal end seemed inevitable; the 6.30 p.m. bulletin recording that His Majesty's condition was critical.

There was no abatement of the symptoms after that. Edward VII. gradually got worse. The paroxysms of coughing again grew more frequent, and as had been feared death speedily followed.

His Majesty remained conscious practically to the end and was able to converse with those around him up to within a short time of his death.

The direct cause of death was heart failure following upon frequent paroxysms of coughing. His Majesty was suffering slightly from pneumonia supervening upon bronchitis.

... Graham ... fixed for Thursday at the Ritz Hotel.

An Affable Guest.

In the last twenty-four hours much has been written and said of the general grief and consternation at the death of the King, but to that more circumscribed circle which came into personal contact with him the loss is that of a most valued friend. The various hostesses whose frequent guest he was always welcomed the prospect of a visit from King Edward, and many are the reminiscences of his affability.

Dinner parties at which he was a guest meant less a carefully-selected menu than a carefully-chosen list of kindred spirits. In fact, so little did he care for the quality of the dinner that a story is told how one evening, on leaving the house of an Anglo-American hostess, whose menu had been so strikingly bad that her guests had commented on it among themselves, His Majesty remarked to his gentleman-in-waiting: "What a delightful little dinner?" He may have merely referred to the company invited to meet him; it certainly could not have been the comestibles.

Sympathies at ...

... at Aldershot ... noted that His Majesty looked pale and seemed in pain. As soon as he returned to London Sir Francis Laking was sent

... problem ... closing up of the ... followed the visit of Ge... De Wet and the constit... Transvaal and Orange ...

But it is in the domain ... politics that King Edward specially deserved

... first visit, they ... to receive the visit ... Archduke Friedrich, who came as representative of the Austrian Emperor to return King Edward's visit to Vienna.

A few days later the first official visit

thing could be learned from ... Court. There was nothing that King Edward so much objected to having publicly discussed as his physical condition, and he always imposed the greatest discretion on this point on his medical attendants.

KING EDWARD VII. THE PRINCE OF WALES AND PRINCE EDWARD

KING EDWARD, MUCH TRAVELLED MONARCH, A GREAT STATESMAN

As Prince of Wales, Visited United States, Canada, India and Nearly All Courts of Europe—Was Artisan of "Entente Cordiale" with France and Good Understanding with Russia.

Edward VII., King of Great Britain and Ireland and of the British Dominions beyond the Seas, Defender of the Faith, Emperor of India, was born at Buckingham Palace on November 9, 1841, the eldest son of the late Queen Victoria and Prince Albert of Saxe-Coburg-Gotha, Prince Consort.

His early education was entrusted to the Rev. Henry M. Birch, Rector of Prestwich; Mr. Gibbs, barrister-at-law; the Rev. C. F. Tarver and Mr. H. W. Fisher. His university studies were carried out first at Edinburgh, where he studied one session, and afterwards at Oxford, where one of his principal tutors was the famous Canon Kingsley, the author of "Westward Ho!" "Alton Locke" and other works. In spite of the canon's advanced political views (he was a strong partisan of the Chartists) the then Prince of Wales and he always remained warm friends.

Early Travels.

His school and university education finished, by the desire of Queen Victoria he made a series of voyages extending over nearly three years. These gave His Royal Highness a taste for travel, which never deserted him up to the last years of his life, and which laid the foundation for that marvellous knowledge of foreign countries and foreign affairs which was one of his characteristic features. In this study of men and things he was helped by his wonderful powers as a linguist.

As a young man he spoke perfectly French, German and Italian. His first journey, made when he was eighteen years of age, was to Italy. A year later he visited the United States and Canada.

Visits European Courts.

A year later he made a tour in Germany and visited the various Courts. In 1862 he visited Austria, Egypt, Turkey and Greece, and in June of the same year he was received by Napoleon III. at Fontainebleau, and three months later by Duke Christian Frederick of Schleswig-Holstein, who subsequently, when King of Denmark, became his father-in law. It was on the occasion of this visit that he first met the Princess Alexandra, who afterwards became his consort.

In February, 1863, he took his seat in the House of Lords as Duke of Cornwall in the peerage of England. In the peerage of Scotland he was given the titles of Duke of Rothesay, Baron Renfrew and Lord of the Isles, and Earl of Dublin and Carrick in that of Ireland.

Engagement Is Announced.

In the beginning of 1863 the engagement of the Prince of Wales to Princess Alexandra of Denmark was announced, and in the month of March Her Royal Highness arrived in London, where she was given an enthusiastic reception. On March 10 the marriage was celebrated with great pomp at Windsor Castle.

Aft… the death of the Prince Consort …

the visits he paid to P… Exhibition was open … which he received … general atten… tinued up … the great …

In 1883 … wedding … cess of … cess of … Berlin. … sion by … most cor… this occa… Field Ma… been hon… Hussars.

In Ire…

Two … Prince … first m… family … given … Then, i… Wales a… Paris F… same … marri… to P… of th…

At … relatio… his Im… This w… result c… ing the … In the … tion t… paid … coinc… end … mai…

Rela…

Tho… fected, … were r… diality … orient… good … "ent… the … co…

O… tribu… visit … death … III. O… journ… young … There … mor… dat… iste… pir…

ga… m… peo… flue… two …

In … cam… of … the … the … cir… o…

… of making automobile excursions, frequently travelling between London and Windsor by road.

King Edward had ever a warm place in his heart for France and the French people. As Prince of Wales, he was a frequent visitor to Paris, and after he became King hardly a year passed in which he did not visit some part of the country. In Paris he was particularly popular and was looked upon by people of all shades of political opinion as typical of what a Monarch should be.

The … of Europe …

…een …xtend… …l steam … famous … many … pride. …ing in …er in … dur… …stin… …his …

KING EDWARD LIVED LIFE OF AN ENGLISH GENTLEMAN

He Shared His People's Occupations and Sports, and Endeared Himself to Them by Democratic Ways, While All the Time Remaining "Every Inch a King."

King Edward held in a peculiar degree the love and esteem of his people. A thorough, even a typical, Englishman, he was at the same time a citizen of the world. He had seen men and countries; he could express himself in many foreign tongues; he had studied colonial problems on the spot. Throughout his career he was noteworthy for his wide, practical knowledge of the world, with the resulting broad, sympathetic outlook. His tact was proverbial.

To all Englishmen the King was a familiar figure, for he lived much in the public eye, and had ever a profound repugnance for secrecy or the undue safeguarding of his movements. He took part in all such pursuits as engross his people, and had performed all the civic duties which fall to the lot of patriots. There was nothing affecting the welfare of the State which was alien to him, while he was indefatigable in organizing enterprises to which he had given approval.

As Prince of Wales, he exhibited a keen and intelligent interest in that pressing problem of modern life—the housing of the masses; while what the hospitals of London owe to King Edward's Fund, which he personally organized and pushed on, is incalculable. The international exhibitions which in London, Paris and elsewhere have done so much to encourage commercial reciprocity and to discover the achievements of the nations had no more zealous patron than King Edward VII., for he was above all an earnest apostle of peace. In another sphere, musicians never appealed to him in vain, and … utmost for the caus… tion.

His Love of …

But, abo… self to Engl… At Sandringha… life of a count… ed nothing wh… country life. He once … in a speech as a "farmer on a s… scale," which was but a modest figure of speech, for he was one of the most successful breeders of stock in Great Br… tain, and animals of hi… always promi…

… impressed all who saw him as being "every inch a King." Queen Victoria, who disliked public functions, had allowed the outward and visible signs of the Sovereign's formal supremacy in the State to become scanty or obliterated. King Edward, on the other hand, at once reverted to the practice of her predecessors and never failed to keep alive the impression that the motive power of the machine of State resides in the Sovereign.

Fond of a Joke.

Personally the King was not only a genial man, but he was also many-sided. Fond of a joke, he was at the same time a shrewd man of business. His knowledge of politics and people, not only of his own country, but of many others as well, was more complete than that of any statesman of his day. Nor could anyone be in his society for half an hour without discovering this. Men bitterly opposed to the whole system of government of which he was the head have borne witness not only to his "bonhomie" but to the shrewdness of his estimate of men and affairs.

His knowledge of human nature almost approached genius. His blue eyes so seldom deceived him that the late Lord Randolph Churchill used to say he would have made a splendid judge—no evidence would have deceived him. He also had a great memory.

Sandringham, the country home of King Edward is typical of his tastes. This is no stately palace where comfort is of secondary consideration to splendor; it was designed not for show, but for use. In every detail it was eloquent of simple taste and refined domesticity. The tablet above the door bearing the inscripti… "This house was built by Albe… Prince of Wales…

… and head keeper. He … of time for reading when … study in the country. His … subject was history, and … ably knew more abou…

…ath …and

ers of running them they were quickly set at rest. King Edward showed himself a ruler of unusual wisdom, knowledge of statecraft and full of innate tact and diplomacy.

The first problem that faced …

THE NEW YOR

PRICE: PARIS and FRANCE, 15 Centimes.
ABROAD. 25 Centimes.

EUROPEAN EDITION—PARIS.—FRIDAY, JUNE

The Coronation

PICTURES OF THE PR
TAKEN FROM TRAFALGA

K HERALD.

11.—TWELVE PAGES. NO. 27.332.

King George V

SSION
QUARE.

Thousands of Loyal Subjects Cheer King George, His Queen and Royal Children, as They Proceed to Westminster Abbey, the Central Figures of the Most Superb Pageant London Has Seen for Many Years.

[BY THE HERALD'S SPECIAL WIRE.]

LONDON, Friday.—Amid the tumultous cheers of thousands and thousands of his loyal subjects King George V. with his Queen passed yesterday from Buckingham Palace to Westminster Abbey for the solemn ceremony of Coronation. The Royal procession was a superb spectacle, and it was touching to witness the enthusiasm with which the children of the King and Queen were greeted by the huge crowds who lined the route.

The service in the historic Abbey, hallowed by the associations of generations, was of the most impressive character.

CEREMONY IN ABBEY IS IMPRESSIVE AND BEAUTIFUL.

Great Throng Looks on With Patriotic and Religious Awe.

[BY THE HERALD'S SPECIAL WIRE.]

LONDON, Friday.—That one supreme hour of glory and solemnity in every English reign came to George V. yesterday, when he was crowned in Westminster Abbey with the most profuse magnificence, and was acclaimed King by millions of his loyal subjects on his return journey to Buckingham Palace.

It was a leaden day with a lowering sky, but leaden days and lowering skies, so long as there is little rain, mean good luck in London. There was only the suggestion of showers at intervals, and these drove no one indoors and produced few umbrellas, while the sun shone at intervals.

No untoward incidents marked the climax of the great desires of the United Kingdom and the Overseas Dominions.

Everything moved with nicety under the arrangements of the Duke of Norfolk, the Earl Marshal. There was no flaw in the handling of the troops or the police by Lord Kitchener, Knight of St. Patrick since Tuesday. So last night all hats were off and only good wishes expressed for England's young and vigorous King and but regard and homage for his gracious Queen.

No scene of such splendor or signi-

THE NEW YORK HERALD.

COMPLETE NUMBER 12 PAGES. EUROPEAN EDITION—PARIS, SATURDAY, APRIL 16, 1904. COMPLETE NUMBER 12 PAGES.

3 Lifestyle

AT THE TURN OF THE CENTURY, Paris was definitely the center of the Western world; on April 15, 1900, the Universal Exhibition was opened by President Emile Loubet, in evening dress and wearing the grand ribbon of the Legion of Honor. It was a most brilliant fête, amid the acclamations of 14,000 people, including the élite of France and representatives from the whole of the civilized world. Royal visits were expected – the Prince of Wales, the Kings of Sweden and Norway, the Shah of Persia, the King of Greece, the Prince Royal of Denmark. By the time the exhibition closed on November 12, with a signal gun booming out from the Eiffel Tower, about 50 million people had visited it.

Viewed from the Pont de l'Alma, the exhibition was a sea of towers and minarets and gorgeously decorated buildings with gilded domes. Altogether, there were 100,000 names in the printed list of exhibitors, which came to 30 volumes. The 101 pavilions were crowded even if, as the *Herald* noted, the pleasure was spoiled by heat and dust. The most popular installation in the whole Exhibition was the moving sidewalk. Another hit was the Russian pavilion, full of stuffed polar bears, beautiful furs, sledge dogs, a model of an ice-breaking ship, and, all alone in a room, a magnificent jeweled map of France, which was to go to the Louvre.

Other notable contributors were Queen Victoria, who lent two portraits by Hoppner, and J. Pierpont Morgan, who also lent some Romneys to the British Pavilion. The latter, which was supposed to be an old house, was compared by Mark Twain, with typical wit, to Wagner's music: "Better than it sounds."

Popular Paris

"The French love a pageant," the *Herald* pointed out in 1906, "and the more democratic a nation becomes, the more ruling passion there is for 'panem and circenses'."

The 1870 war had put an end to Opera balls and masquerading, but with the gradual recovery of France's prosperity, Paris sprang up again and the Parisians were determined to revive their wonderful popular fêtes. One of the most successful was the carnival "Boeuf Gras," successfully restored in 1896 after a lapse of 27 years. Said to equal the most brilliant fêtes during the period of the Empire, it lasted three days, with a carnival king and satellites parading on the Champs Elysées. Some 1,770 square meters of Paris were covered with confetti. Confetti-throwing was "hard and hot work" and revelers had to wear protective garb. The allotted time for this enjoyable activity was three hours, which the *Herald* correspondent found too long.

The 1896 Boeuf Gras appeared four times, Saturday night at the Opera ball and Sunday, Monday and Tuesday in the streets. Everyone, from the president of the Republic to street scavengers, turned out to see and be seen.

The procession started at the Palais de l'Industrie, on the Champs Elysées, and included a tambour major in the traditional bearskin, a corps of 50 drummers and buglers in the uniforms of the First Empire, a band of musicians and one float harking back to the Boeuf Gras of 1844. The Boeuf Gras that followed this float stood contentedly, a fine animal viewing crowds from a gilded pen. Six gray horses drew the hero of the carnival. There were more floats, including the "Char de la Bergerie," dedicated to Watteau.

The "Char de l'Alimentation" was a work of art. On two great peacock pastries rose, in the form of an arch, two huge lobsters whose claws supported as perfect a dish of fruit as one could hope to see. In the arch were cool-looking ices and around the whole were immense bottles of champagne. Young girls in white dresses, trimmed with blue ribbons, invited all to eat, drink and be merry.

Fifty pastrycooks followed, some carrying huge ices and chocolate pyramids. A "chef de cuisine" of mammoth proportions divided his attention between two enormous pots, in which rabbits refused to be cooked and from which, very much alive, they were trying to escape. A smart crack with the ladle, however, was sufficient to keep them stewing.

The procession ended with King Carnival, young, handsome and dainty in blue silk, in a chariot of clouds, holding golden reins and controlling four prancing steeds – not unlike Neptune ruling the waves. Jesters in green and yellow caps and bells danced about. Men in bathtubs with pigs' heads on, great cabbages and pumpkins featured a world gone mad in vegetables.

The geography of Paris was somewhat different then from what we know today. During the 20th century the city has moved westwards toward Auteuil and Passy which, at the turn of the century, were obscure villages. Belle Epoque Paris was known for its Boulevards, and street life, a substitute for today's indoor entertainments, gravitated to them – from Boulevard Montmartre to the Madeleine. This is where rich and poor mingled, and around the rue de la Paix and the Opéra famous "boulevardiers" would stroll among *midinettes* or "rats de l'Opéra."

Families also promenaded along the Boulevards, which were especially animated on Christmas days. In Place de la Madeleine, street vendors sold songs, or rather a song. One man played the air on the violin, another sang it, while a third sold copies with the words. The crowds formed a circle and, song in hand, caught the tune and joined in the chorus.

In 1897, the songs in vogue were a pot-pourri of the military and the risqué, what with "Les Soldats de Sambre et Meuse", "Looping the Loop" and "Viens Poupoule."

Café-concerts and "bals musettes" were very popular, and so were street singers – although the latter were reportedly "beginning to abuse." Censorship made life difficult for the owners of 214 café-concerts – a platform for sentimental, patriotic, rustic, spicy and ribald songs.

Statistics showed that in 1895, an average of 600 songs, ballads, rondeaux, monologues, etc., were deposited monthly at the censor's office. The latter had to make sure that the piece submitted was not offensive to public morals. Political songs also were examined with great care.

In 1900, a "rollickingly jovial" New Year's Eve heralded a new century. Hotels, bars and restaurants were crammed with people commencing the celebration. Restaurants along the Boulevards were crowded "until the wee sma' hours." Smart crowds gathered at the Ritz, the Chatham and at all kinds of English-sounding restaurants – Henry's, William's, Benson's, as well, of course, as Maxim's.

Henry's had a buffet supper for all hands and a separate room for ladies. Maxim's had 250 seats booked up and 250 more waiting. The proceedings were said to be both hilarious and peaceful.

The Champs Elysées

Building activity was as intense in Paris during the Belle Epoque as it is in New York City today. Baron Haussmann had accomplished the basic street layout of the city during the 1870s but its modern appearance was being fashioned during the two decades before the outbreak of World War I.

In 1898 the *Herald* announced "Champs Elysées Improvement." The stalls on both sides of the great thoroughfare, at which toys and sweets were sold, were going to be replaced by octagonal kiosks where flowers, refreshment, tobacco and newspapers could be bought. A writer in *Le Temps* called it "the commencement of the end for the Champs Elysées," noting that "boys and girls will renounce their former amusements and thanks to the goods in the kiosks, will be introduced to the charm of the 'petit verre,' nicotine and politics."

The Champs Elysées stirred all kinds of wild projects, including turning the section between the Rond Point and the Etoile into a hippodrome, which involved uprooting trees and making the open space smaller. Fortunately, nothing came of this. Another plan to line the Champs Elysées with a hundred statues of great men was also abortive. Antonin Proust declared the idea "hideous," and Emile Zola, who said that in principle he liked statues, also spoke against it because he could not see how one could gather a hundred masterpieces.

New white stone apartment houses kept rising on the Champs Elysées, causing as radical a transformation in *la vie Parisienne* as the changes carried out under Haussmann. Families, who had hitherto considered an hôtel in the French sense of the word as a private house as a *sine qua non* of elegant living, were moving to apartment houses or flats. The reasons? Lower rents, fewer taxes and more comfort. All rooms were on one floor, which meant no more running up and down stairs to wash hands before dinner, not to mention hot and cold water on tap at any hour of day or night, dumbwaiters, "vide-ordures" and even "monte-lettres," which saved the servants' time.

This new departure was reported to be due to the influence of English and American families who made Paris their place of residence, and architects readily admitted that they learned a lot from the Anglo-Saxons' demand for comfort.

The luxury of this era was mind-boggling. In 1904, an Indian prince ordered solid silver bedroom furniture from Sheffield, at an astounding cost. The bedstead, described as "a wonderful work of art," was decorated with soothing silver figures representing guardian angels at each corner.

In the same year the Travelers Club was inaugurated in Paris in the celebrated hôtel of La Paiva. It had been built during the Second Empire at a cost of several million francs by the Marquise Paiva, described as "a famous chatelaine, who had entertained kings and emperors" – a polite way of referring to a *cortisane extraordinaire*. Her wonderful bedroom, with a multitude of lights, was famous, as was her marble bathroom, with a solid silver bath sunk into the floor, and gold water taps studded with turquoises, rubies and other precious stones. The onyx grand staircase itself had cost over a million francs.

The affluent classes were discovering the palace-type grand hotels. The Paris Ritz, Claridge's of London, the Grand Hotel in Rome and Shepheard's in Cairo were all built during these years. In 1895, Countess Grey laid the foundation stone of the new Claridge's in Brook Street, on the site of the old one – "a time-honored hostelry which was connected with everything that was expensive, smart and ultra-fashionable." The Ritz opened in Paris in 1898, and its unique appointments, long terraces, lovely gardens and fountains soon drew crowned heads and princes of all nations, as well as rich Americans, who appreciated its elegance and privacy. Charles Ritz also had an accomplished chef, Escoffier; both of them had been responsible for making the London Savoy an outstanding success.

By Belle Epoque standards, however, cuisine was losing ground. In 1899, "Great Chefs Gathered at the Second International Culinary Salon" declared that dining had become a lost art because society was too busy to dine at regular hours, or worse, took meals in too great a hurry to properly appreciate the arts of the table.

The Salon's presidents were two imposing gentlemen, clad in full evening wear and loaded with jewels and gold chains. "People don't know how to eat, now," said President Docquet, the chef of Baronne de Hirsch, and formerly in the service of the Prince of Wales.

"Formerly, dinner was one of the chief events in life," added the second president, chef of Baronne Alphonse de Rothschild. "Now, they bolt their food, in a hurry to go to the theatre or a party. At Baron Alphonse de Rothschild, the 15 courses go through in 40 minutes."

Docquet sighed over the days when 10 pounds of beef, a capon, four partridges and half a ham were cheerfully sacrificed to make a sauce.

But there was no way to turn the culinary clock back. Around 1906, dining in Paris became distinctly simpler. Menus were shorter. There was a reaction against elaborate sauces and vegetable purees became a forerunner of the Nouvelle Cuisine of today.

London society, too, was changing; there were fewer balls and dances, and not so many heavy dinner parties at home. In London, as in Paris, restaurant life affected home life. Simpler and lighter restaurant menus killed the old-fashioned dinner party with its dozen different courses and half-a-dozen wines.

The closing in 1910 of the Café de Paris on the Boulevard des Italiens, celebrated by Meilhac and Halévy in *La Vie Parisienne*, announced the virtual end of the Belle Epoque. The restaurant had been launched by the famous Rothschild chef, Dugléré, who once had around the same table three emperors, four Russian grand dukes and a dozen princes. This champagne-only, fifty-year-old landmark had seen all kinds of "imperial orgies," held not in *cabinets particuliers*, which were considered too small and banal, but in *caves* – elegant catacombs decorated with wrought-iron vines and illuminated grapes.

The *Herald* also registered the beginnings of the sidewalk café – explaining that "a café evolved into a brasserie when braseros were put on Boulevard cafés' terraces, enabling Parisians to stay out" even in cold weather. This new trend, which took shape around 1900, coincided with the Parisians' growing taste for the outdoors, which made them reject "musty old cafés."

In 1904 changes were taking place on ocean liners, whose owners called on Charles Ritz and the management of the Carlton in London to devise an "à la carte" system. In America, as in Europe, the "à la carte" system had become the fashion. M. Autor, manager of the Carlton, said he believed Americans especially would take to the idea of having whatever they wanted direct from the grill, at practically any hour of the day. The American "drugstore" concept was not far behind.

The mode of life aboard trains was also changing in 1895 with the introduction of dining and sleeping cars. A Salon Restaurant was added to the Trouville Express, which left from the Gare Saint-Lazare. The

Herald also announced the inauguration in that year of a new de luxe train called "The Calais Engadine Express."

Daily columns in the *Herald*, headlined "Salons," kept readers informed about this most important facet of Belle Epoque life. The season started in January when people returned from Christmas celebrations and hunting seasons in their châteaux. The hôtels' shutters were reopened, and concierges, in their employers' liveries, were at the doors.

The salons gave an accurate idea of who was who in the Belle Epoque and of how people entertained themselves. Ladies had their *day*: Monday, for example, was claimed by the Comtesse de Castellane, Tuesday by Madeleine Lemaire, Wednesday the Duchesse of Bisaccia, Thursday the Comtesse d'Haussonville and Friday the Comtesse de Pourtalès. There was a constant round of musicales, five o'clocks, dancing lessons, charity bazaars and amateur theater. The level of taste and quality was considerable and important artists paid great attention to the leading hostesses, who acted as influential patrons of the arts.

At a soirée given by Comtesse Greffulhe for the King of Sweden – at which she wore red velvet trimmed with sable – an actor named Silvain recited verses composed by the King himself. The Duchesse d'Uzès had admirable musicales in her salon, featuring works by Massenet, Gounod and Grieg on the program, "and the hostess sang most delightfully." The Princesse de Polignac's equally memorable salon once had the violin virtuoso Georges Enesco paying a Fauré sonata, accompanied by the composer. After one splendid dinner in 1908, the Princesse, according to the *Herald*, also introduced Paris society to the art of Aubrey Beardsley, still unknown in France. When Baron and Baronne Henri de Rothschild entertained in the outdoors theater of their avenue Gabriel hôtel, they thought nothing of hiring the whole orchestra and ballet from the Opéra.

The "Salons" column also offered ample descriptions of luxurious weddings and spectacular gift lists.

Baronne Nathaniel de Rothschild gave a regal present to her future daughter-in-law, Mlle de Weisweiller: a necklace of exceptional and enormous rubies which she had collected one by one over thirty years.

When a nephew of King Umberto of Italy married in 1895, the King gave him a villa near Turin and four magnificent saddle horses; the Pope sent a sacred relic studded with diamonds and the Comtesse de Paris a collection of jewels, including two black pearls, a diamond crescent, a carriage rug, an English pony cart with pony, and two shawls, including one that had belonged to the Duchesse de Montpensier.

Lord Carnarvon, 29, owner of the most magnificent estate in England, Highclere Castle, gave his bride a diamond crown, a diamond tiara, emeralds, a pearl and diamond necklace, a ruby and sapphire bangle, an emerald and diamond ring, diamond dress ornaments and a quantity of superb and valuable lace.

*

Proustian Paris

A Proustian Paris also emerged from the *Herald*'s pages, with its central characters, Baron de Charlus (Robert de Montesquiou in real life) and Duchesse de Guermantes (Comtesse Greffulhe) described in full Belle Epoque splendor.

Proust himself once appeared in the *Herald*'s pages, giving a "most elegant and witty" dinner party in his apartment on the rue de Courcelles. Among the guests were Prince and Princesse Edmond de Polignac, Comte Henri de Ségur, Léon and Lucien Daudet.

The Comtesse Greffulhe was portrayed parading a pair of lion cubs, drawing a little cart filled with lilies and roses into her salons – or giving a "Bal Blanc" for her daughter's début, in her rue d'Astorg house full of precious woodworks and tapestries, the garden lit with Chinese lanterns. A great music fan, the Comtesse frequently sponsored prestigious events. At a concert she organized in 1906 with the Russian Ambassador and M. Diaghilev at the Grand Palais, the program included works by Tchaikovsky, Rimsky-Korsakov and Borodin.

Aesthete Montesquiou was described walking his white Russian wolfhound, the dog wearing a turquoise necklace – in the Allée des Acacias. Or staying an extra month at the Château de Fresne to put the last touches to a new volume of verses, that would be read a month later by Coquelin *cadet* in the salon of Madeleine Lemaire.

There is a physical description of Montesquiou as well, giving one of his famous lectures on the respective talents of the caricaturists Sem and Roubille. A lot of Tout-Parisians, all victims of Sem's sharp pen, attended, including the diminutive painter Boldini. Defined as "a master of courteous perfidy," Montesquiou, svelte and elegant in his morning coat, with violets in his buttonhole, appeared on the stage. Behind him was a sumptuous tapestry in pale greens, in front of him an easel holding the text of his address. He gave his lecture with exquisite art, underlining all its points with very few gestures. When he felt applause coming, like all seasoned lecturers, he picked up his glass and drank – slowly.

His house, the famous Pavillon des Muses, included a magnificent marble tub that had belonged to Madame Pompadour. The "delicate poet" once hosted a charity bazaar and the proceedings were an excellent example of Belle Epoque refinement. The entrance on rue Charles Lafitte was framed with antique tapestries, big Oriental rugs were spread under the tables where tea was served, vases were filled with rare flowers and Japanese dwarf trees mixed with simple rose bushes in bloom. A gypsy orchestra played waltzes and a little Chinaman handed roses to the ladies.

This exquisite Parisian failed to make much of an impression in America, when he went there in 1903 to lecture on Versailles. "America treated me and my lectures lightly," he said, with a shrug of his shoulders. "But that is because they did not understand me."

*

One curious aspect of the Belle Epoque lifestyle was the amount of attention given to the subject of dogs. Everybody had a luxury dog. A regular *Herald* column, "Kennel," kept readers informed about dog shows and the popularity of bull terriers versus pomeranians. Edward VII's mistress Lillie Langtry had all her poodles clipped to read L.L. In 1908, the 53rd dog exhibition at the Crystal Palace in London attracted 3,800 dogs of the highest standard. Queen Alexandra won four First Prizes with her basset hounds. Prize dogs, the *Herald* noted, "bring 40 pounds an ounce or more than twice the price of gold."

During a dinner party in London, a poodle devoured a square yard of a guest's dress. "The dress had cost between 40 and 50 pounds," the *Herald* noted, adding "The dog is still living."

Fashion for dogs filled page after page. In Paris, the "Dog Chauffeur" was equipped with goggles to follow his mistress in her auto. A Palais Royal shop offered canine wardrobes almost as extensive as their mistresses', including shirts of every kind, coats with fur trimmings, waterproof coats, toilettes for riding, visiting, receiving, yachting and other fashionable "ings."

The wife of a khedive ordered a dog overcoat with broad revers of emerald velvet and a lace jabot. The Grand Duke Michael of Russia ordered for his fox-terrier a collar with coral and another with turquoises. There was even a trousseau for a dog's wedding – the fantasy of an English lady, this one.

In 1909, the Paris Dog Show was evicted from the Tuileries Gardens. "A terrible blow," said the Comte de Bagneux, as this was the most important dog show in France.

As for the demi-monde of this period, the *Herald* tells us remarkably little. But there were occasional transparent stories which referred to "demi-mondaines" or "professional beauties." The rivalry between two of them, Liane de Pougy and La Belle Otero, was famous. Liane de Pougy made headlines when she tried to commit suicide with laudanum – but was promptly revived.

The *Herald* tells us of one instance in the casino at Nice when tables and chairs were moved back and Otero executed a "pas de seul" à l'Espagnol. De Pougy was eclipsed as she had to sit still and be pretty.

Of the two, Otero was the more flamboyant. "La Otero's jewelry is not quite as profuse as a week or two ago," the *Herald* wrote in 1895, "she having been politely requested by the authorities not to make quite such a lavish display." But a few days later, at a Monte Carlo dress ball, La Otero was astoundingly got up – in lovely white satin, with hand-painted violets on the bodice and tufts of artificial flowers strewn over the chiffon sleeves.

A lawsuit to try to evict Otero from her apartment reads like a Belle Epoque vaudeville. Her landlord, a Mr. Bittner, claimed that in bringing a music-hall star like Mlle Otero to the house, Mr. Bulpett (her lover) ceased to inhabit it "bourgeoisement" as his contract obliged him to do. The landlord requested her expulsion, giving a long list of grievances, including the fact that "Otero receives a large number of people; crowds form on the pavement opposite whenever she appears on the balcony, there is a constant procession of pianists, singers, dancing masters, etc., also tumultuous scenes that end up at the Commissariat of Police."

In the end, "Pretty Mlle Otero Cannot Be Evicted," the *Herald* told its readers after the court decreed that there was insufficient evidence to prove that Otero was a sub-tenant of Mr. Bulpett. The latter was declared free at his own risk and peril to bring anyone to live with him, for the court had no jurisdiction over such guests.

In 1896, Otero was in the news again, this time because the Spanish dancer, in Paris with an authentic Russian prince, was selling her "effects" at the Salle Drouot – after which she declared that she was definitely leaving Paris for St. Petersburg. The sale drew a crowd, but there was nothing remarkable being offered – just the conventional upholsterer's furniture in gilt wood and brocaded silk, and a billiard table with the crest of La Belle Otero, surmounted by a count's coronet.

The demi-mondaine world, fancy as it seemed to be, was apparently not a patch on what it had once been. The Belle Epoque cocottes could not compete with the "cortisanes" of the Second Empire, such as the Comtesse de Castiglione, whose property sale was reported by the *Herald* in 1901. This noted mistress of Napoleon III was prudishly described as "a professional beauty who had had such a reputation under the Empire."

The sale of her jewelry alone took three days. She had rented no fewer than five apartments, all crammed with treasures. The one on rue de Castiglione contained more than fifty chased silver and gold-mounted fans which she carried when attending fêtes in the Tuileries Gardens. One chest was full of furs, another full of lace; there was one pawn ticket for jewels on which 18,000 francs had been lent, one famous pearl necklace worth 250,000 francs, silver, dresses, Dresden china and an incredible number of Louis XV sunshades with ivory and gold handles enriched with precious stones.

Other objects of special interest were several strings of pearls, including a five-row example containing 279 beautiful pearls and estimated at 120,000 francs. The most interesting item, according to the *Herald*, was a small ball program, of tortoiseshell set in gold, in which was a miniature of King Victor Emmanuel. Upon one of the ivory tablets could be read with difficulty these words in the handwriting of the "Re Galantuomo": "Alla bellissima Nacchia, il povero padrone."

"What this program contained, when it was presented by the 'poor king,' it would be interesting to know," the *Herald* mused.

*

Life in the Belle Epoque had its dangers. Duels took place frequently — often when somebody wrote something that somebody else did not like, such as when the playwright Francis de Croisset provoked Léon Parsons, theater critic of *Le Petit Sou* (in 1901) for having referred to his work as a "muflerie littéraire." Parsons refused the challenge.

The *Herald* described not only the duels but the way the duellists were dressed. For instance, when Prince Henri of France fought a duel with the Count of Turin (nephew of the King of Italy), the latter wore a black frock coat and a white waistcoat and he had his trousers turned up "à l'Anglaise" upon patent leather shoes. He also wore a straw hat. Prince Henri wore a blue serge suit with a white waistcoat, a straw hat and tanned shoes. The Prince was badly wounded in the abdomen. "But he'll live," the *Herald* noted laconically, adding that the Kaiser had congratulated the Count of Turin.

In November 1904, there were three duels in a single day. The ultimate in gallantry was probably a letter from Count Cavalotti, "a poet and a politician," who died in a duel. On the morning before he met his fate he wrote to his wife the Countess: "I am going to fight today, consequently I am not sure that I shall be able to come and see you this evening. But I am so anxious to come that I will do my best to strike some good blows and not receive any."

Ultimately, a new society was formed to suppress duelling. "Calling a man a coward is not enough reason," a front page story read. "A man who refuses to fight is worthy of the highest esteem."

Not only duels, but "crimes passionels" were also part of everyday life. In 1904, Emma Georgina, Countess of Ravensworth (and twice married, the first time in 1872), married her coachman. The groom was a smart, handsome man of about 28, who had been in the Countess's service for four months. Once a coachman, always a coachman. After the wedding, the groom lived in the mews and resumed his former duties, but only for a week.

The Princess of Caraman-Chimay, née Ward and from Chicago, created an even bigger scandal when she eloped in 1897 with a gypsy named Rigo, also known as her "Hungarian enslaver." The latter had lived near the Château of Chimay for weeks and the Princess had come to him in her emblazoned carriage in the sight of all. The couple left for Paris. When asked if she had no regrets for her children, the Princess answered: "It is too late to think of them. Let us face facts and have a good dinner on reaching Paris." This they did, going to both Paillard's and the Moulin Rouge.

The Princess later attempted a Folies-Bergère career that was nipped in the bud by the prefect of police. She ran into more notoriety when photographs of her in scanty costumes (by the photographer Reutlinger, who was supposed to give her a royalty of 25 per cent on all cards sold) went on sale on the Boulevards, and sold by the thousands.

Dancing was all the rage during the Belle Epoque, and in 1905 even the deck of a British warship, HMS *Drake*, was equipped with a dance floor for 600 people. Its "programme for the next two years includes visits to America, the West Coast of Africa and South America," the *Herald* explained, "and the officers and men of the Squadron will meet with lavish hospitality across the waters." The dance floor was to give them an opportunity of returning this hospitality, if not on the same extensive scale, at any rate in an adequate manner.

In a more classic vein, balls of all kinds – "White" or "Pink", "Fancy" or "Poudre" – still opened with old-fashioned, 18th-century quadrilles. Gypsy bands were on hand to play until the early hours of morning. Dinners were followed by "Tours de Valse" and suppers by cotillions. The latter, often termed "the business of the evening," were the pretext for much merriment.

St. Petersburg outshone every other city in 1903 with a famous Boyar Ball for which the treasures of the Boyar Sanctums were searched and the jewels as worn in Boyar times were brought from Moscow. They were seen for the first time out of their cases, adorning the costume of the Grand Duke Heir Apparent. One stone he wore was valued at about half a million rubles. The sensation of the evening undoubtedly was the Empress Alexandra. For ten days, and the greater part of ten nights, a small army of expert needlewomen had been engaged in sewing precious stones, pearls and diamonds onto the dress which the young Empress wore that evening.

At the last cotillion of the 1895 Bad Homburg season, 75 couples danced in a large suite of salons on the first floor of the Kurhaus, ablaze with hundreds of lights, flowers, beautiful dresses and diamonds. At the end, a bicycle composed entirely of flowers was wheeled into the room.

At a Pink Ball given in Florence by a Mrs. Labouchere, the men in the 26-couple cotillion wore "fracs rouges" (red evening jackets), which gave a peculiar brilliancy to the occasion. At a Venetian fête given on the Island of Puteaux, lit for the party by a double chain of Bengal lights, great carpets were spread on the lawn, seventy decorated boats paraded and the cotillion was gypsy – the guest of honor being the Grand Duchess Vladimir of Russia.

A somewhat bizarre cotillion at a London ball included a duel figure, with foils fitted with huge powder puffs. A cotillion on the banks of the Danube ended with Fortuna sitting at her wheel and presenting the women with green leather cigarette cases and the men with riding whips. At Shepheard's Hotel in Cairo, a cotillion included two young live camels, followed by a sleek little dun-colored donkey, with large side baskets filled with flowers, led into the room by Arabs in pink and lavender costumes. The picturesque procession made the tour of the Oriental salons, decorated with green palms and exotic flowers. In 1901, everybody in Paris society remembered the ball given the year before by Mme. Madeleine Lemaire, at which the Exposition Universelle furnished the theme for the costumes imposed on the guests. Then there was the ball, no less graceful, given by Mme. de Castellane at which each lady represented a flower.

To cope with all this action, the chic thing was to have one's own custom-made ballroom. In London, a Mrs. Adair had hers outfitted with pale reseda green brocade satin walls, a little minstrel gallery at one end and a fine parquet floor, always kept in excellent condition for dancing. A fancy ball she gave in 1903 was the most brilliant since the Devonshire House ball during the Diamond Jubilee in 1897, according to the *Herald*. That evening, a second band and a crowd of footmen, in Adair's brown-and-canary-yellow livery, were stationed in the hall under huge palm trees to welcome 400 guests, including the Prince and Princess of Wales.

Amid trails and festoons of smilax, dotted here and there with roses, Mrs. Adair stood – magnificent in a gorgeous Empire dress of yellow satin, the same she wore at the Great Durbar Ball in Calcutta. On her head blazed an Empire tiara of enormous emeralds and diamonds, with similar jewels around her neck, while ropes of pearls and masses of other jewels gleamed on the corsage of her dress.

The ball opened with a "Goddesses Quadrille," society girls representing Aurora, Diana, Flora, etc. After dinner, little plays and sketches from various music halls were given on a stage that Mrs. Adair had had erected in the ballroom, its proscenium draped with rose and ivory colored satin.

At Chatsworth, the splendid home of the Duke and Duchess of Devonshire, balls were held in the large dining hall. On one occasion there was music by a Hungarian band and bronze figures on each marble mantle holding a galaxy of electric lights. Supper took place under several trees, including a feathered bamboo, a high tree fern and a 20-foot high camellia bush, lighted by gaily colored electric globes.

In New York, Mrs. Cornelius Vanderbilt's $5-million house on Fifth Avenue, opened in 1895, had an immense gold-and-white ballroom in Louis XVI style, the largest private ballroom in the city. Its ceiling had been painted in Paris by M. Toudouze and represented thirty nymphs being wafted into space by zephyrs. In 1901, Mrs. William C. Whitney opened her grandiose new Fifth Avenue residence, which featured a marble staircase and a main hall whose ceiling came from the Barberini Palace in Florence. She also had a ballroom whose walls came from the Château of Phoebus d'Albert, near Bordeaux.

In Rome, Principe Doria gave a ball in 1906 for the wedding of his daughter, Donna d'Orietta, in the newly redecorated and enlarged ballroom of Palazzo Doria, whose center of attraction was a famous portrait of Pope Doria by Velasquez. The Palazzo was a magnificent suite of drawing rooms and galleries, in each of which a good-sized villa might have been built with ease. Donna d'Orietta, who was marrying Conte Febo Borromeo, was in the palest mauve chiffon, and wore a present from the groom: eight strands – or three yards – of large pearls and a diamond coronet. Her parents had given her, among other things, a Cartier all-round diamond crown. For this wedding, which absorbed Roman society for weeks, Worth did the wedding dress in a cloth of silver, with a long trailing skirt trimmed with eight flounces of chiffon.

Princess Metternich's ball at the Redoutensaal – a vast hall arranged differently each year – was an annual red-letter event in Viennese society. In 1909 the hall was a submarine scene, featuring a series of grottoes with coral formations, seaweed effects and strange sea monsters. A forest of water plants floated in a sunken sailing ship. The guests were offered a variety of fish and crustacea.

The Princess wore a diadem and a dress of heliotrope brocade, its corsage embroidered with fins. A Princess Clementine was dressed as a piece of coral. Others wore fish scales, mussels as well as sea roses, water roses, pearl crowns and big chains of real pearls hanging from hair to waist.

The balls given by Countess Kleinmichel, a leader of St. Petersburg society, were also famous. At one in 1897, she posted at the entrance a Swiss of prodigious size, in gold-striped uniform and holding a halberd. Eight *valets de pied* in wigs helped guests take off their fur coats and cloaks. Charles, a famous coiffeur dressed as the Barber of Seville, was on hand to attend to the coiffures of the ladies.

The famous house on the Sergievskaya Road was built in Greek Revival style. The atrium and beautiful double staircase had, on each side and facing each other, colossal men from the Chevaliers de la Garde dressed as Venetian Negroes in the time of the Doges – their faces blackened, their huge turbans surmounted by peacock feathers, and each of them bearing a long-handled, picturesque Venetian lantern.

At the top of the first flight of stairs, four knights in full armor were wearing blue velvet jackets embossed with the arms of the hostess. With a trumpet fanfare they saluted the arrival of members of the Imperial family. The fanfare was echoed by a herald in armor on the floor above, astride a richly caparisoned horse – life-size but stuffed. He held a red banner reading "Bonne Année." At the top of the stairs, the Countess and her daughters were in Henri III costumes with ruche collars and perfect coiffures. There were lots of Louis XV soubrettes, Alsatians and Russians of the 17th century.

One room was arranged as a winter garden and that was where the Imperial family took tea in one corner. In the library, the hostess's famous Dresden collection was displayed on a horseshoe table. A huge fireplace at the end of the room had been fitted with a vast block of ice, through which shone colored lights, magnified by the ice. Diminutive turbaned Negroes were serving drinks at a buffet for over 500 guests. Negroes also acted as pages behind the Countess. Mazurkas were played in the big ballroom. Supper was served at 2:30, a choir of gypsies sang and there was a very lively cotillion at breakfast time.

BUYING FLOWERS FOR THE EASTER SEASON IN TWENTY-THIRD STREET.

NEW YORK HERALD'S 19

January

SUN.	MON.	TUE.	WED.	THU.	FRI.	SAT.
	1	2	3	4	5	6
7	8	9	10	11	12	13
14	15	16	17	18	19	20
21	22	23	24	25	26	27
28	29	30	31			

February

SUN.	MON.	TUE.	WED.	THU.	FRI.	SAT.
				1	2	3
4	5	6	7	8	9	10
11	12	13	14	15	16	17
18	19	20	21	22	23	24
25	26	27	28			

March

SUN.	MON.	TUE.	WED.	THU.	FRI.	SAT.
				1	2	3
4	5	6	7	8	9	10
11	12	13	14	15	16	17
18	19	20	21	22	23	24
25	26	27	28	29	30	31

April

SUN.	MON.	TUE.	WED.	THU.	FRI.	SAT.
1	2	3	4	5	6	7
8	9	10	11	12	13	14
15	16	17	18	19	20	21
22	23	24	25	26	27	28
29	30					

May

SUN.	MON.	TUE.	WED.	THU.	FRI.	SAT.
		1	2	3	4	5
6	7	8	9	10	11	12
13	14	15	16	17	18	19
20	21	22	23	24	25	26
27	28	29	30	31		

June

SUN.	MON.	TUE.	WED.	THU.	FRI.
					1
3	4	5	6	7	8
10	11	12	13	14	15
17	18	19	20	21	22
24	25	26	27	28	29

THE NEW YORK HERALD, (EUROPEAN EDITION), SUNDAY, DECEMBER 17, 1905.

July

SUN.	MON.	TUE.	WED.	THU.	FRI.	SAT.
1	2	3	4	5	6	7
8	9	10	11	12	13	14
15	16	17	18	19	20	21
22	23	24	25	26	27	28
29	30	31				

August.

SUN.	MON.	TUE.	WED.	THU.	FRI.	SAT.
			1	2	3	4
5	6	7	8	9	10	11
12	13	14	15	16	17	18
19	20	21	22	23	24	25
26	27	28	29	30	31	

September

SUN.	MON.	TUE.	WED.	THU.	FRI.	SAT.
						1
2	3	4	5	6	7	8
9	10	11	12	13	14	15
16	17	18	19	20	21	22
23	24	25	26	27	28	29
30						

October

SUN.	MON.	TUE.	WED.	THU.	FRI.	SAT.
	1	2	3	4	5	6
7	8	9	10	11	12	13
14	15	16	17	18	19	20
21	22	23	24	25	26	27
28	29	30	31			

November

SUN.	MON.	TUE.	WED.	THU.	FRI.	SAT.
				1	2	3
4	5	6	7	8	9	10
11	12	13	14	15	16	17
18	19	20	21	22	23	24
25	26	27	28	29	30	

December

SUN.	MON.	TUE.	WED.	THU.	FRI.	SAT.
						1
2	3	4	5	6	7	8
9	10	11	12	13	14	15
16	17	18	19	20	21	22
23	24	25	26	27	28	29
30	31					

GRAND LAC, BO

DE BOULOGNE.

FASHION SUPPLEMENT.

THE NEW YORK HERALD.

PARIS. SUNDAY. MAY 29. 1910.

LE MATIN AUX ACACIAS. ❊ MORNING SCENE IN THE BOIS.

By L. SABATTIER.

AU PESAGE A LONGCHAMPS ❊ THE PESAGE AT LONGCHAMPS.

By L. SABATTIER.

TINTING THE EASTER EGG.

In Cairo, society also went dancing-mad with "Tours de Valse," small dances, large dances, balls, cotillions, dancing dervishes and the belly dance. At a Grand Khedive ball, the marble and crystal halls of the two-winged Abdeen Palace were a fairytale scene with 1,500 guests, who danced until 3 a.m. Iron braziers, several feet tall, stood two or three yards from each other, blazing like torches. The light was reflected by the carriage windows and on the buttons and side arms of the military police, who stood almost shoulder to shoulder all the way from Opera Square to the square in front of the palace, with another row mounted on snow-white Arab horses.

In 1903, all of Europe seemed to be dancing, with a two-page spread in the *Herald* recording a "Bal Poudre" in Dublin; a ball given by Baron and Baroness Baracco Doria in Naples; a ball at the Villa de Buisson – where the library was completely dismantled and turned into a ballroom – in Pau; a ball given by Contessa Papadopoli at the Venice Opera House for her daughter's wedding; and a ball at Palazzo Borea, in San Remo.

They danced and danced until they dropped – sometimes literally. A wealthy brewer from Poona, India, a Mr. H.G. Meakin who also owned the Indian *Times*, felt ill during a pause in the dancing at the Kursalon in Karlsbad, and sat down to rest. As the *Herald* matter-of-factly put it: "On a friend addressing him and receiving no answer, it was discovered that he was dead."

COMEDY OF ERRORS.

A Faithless Husband Takes Advantage of His Wife's Supposed Absence.

GIVES FRIEND HIS LATCHKEY.

When the Latter Arrives at the House He Is Arrested as a Burglar.

M. Desroussins is married to a jealous wife, whose jealousy, however, says the "Journal," is not unjustified. A couple of days ago she informed him she was going to Dieppe and would not return till Saturday.

This her husband regarded as three days of liberty. In the course of the afternoon he looked up his friend, M. Larplanchet, and invited him to go for a little excursion to Montmartre the same evening. They began their expedition by an excellent dinner in a restaurant on the boulevards, after which they proceeded to scale the heights of Montmartre. Here they made the acquaintance of two amiable young ladies. The companion of M. Desroussins was indeed so amiable that he announced to his friend his intention of not tearing himself away from her.

M. Larplanchet, who lived at some distance from the "sacred mountain," had no desire to return home. Knowing that Mme. Desroussins had left for Dieppe, M. Desroussins proposed to his friend that he and the lady who had so far shared his fortunes should take up their quarters for the night in his apartment in the rue Manuel. This proposition was accepted, and M. Larplanchet and his companion, armed with Desroussins' key, proceeded to that address.

When they arrived at rue Manuel they found some difficulty in opening the door. Hardly, however, had they accomplished this, than they were horrified to find Mme. Desroussins armed with a lamp and somewhat scantily clothed. The latter had changed her mind about going to Dieppe and had been waiting up for the arrival of her faithless husband. Seeing a couple of strangers open the door with a latchkey she proceeded to shriek for assistance with all the strength of her lungs. The other tenants of the house were speedily alarmed. The concierge closed the street door, and M. Larplanchet and his lady friend were arrested as burglars and taken to the police station. Here the matter was explained.

When, however, M. Desroussins, returned home, it was only to be informed by his indignant wife that she was returning to her mother, and that his next news from her would be an invitation to attend the Divorce Court.

the Divorce Court.

A Faithless Husband

A DESPAIRING LOVER.

Senorita Otero States what Her Relations Were with M. Chrétien.

LOVE AT FIRST SIGHT.

He Encloses Ten Thousand Francs in An Invitation to Supper.

A number of fresh details are forthcoming regarding the suicide of the young man named Chrétien who shot himself on Monday in the Bois de Boulogne because, as he stated, Senorita Otero, the Spanish dancer at present performing at the Folies-Bergère, had refused to accept his advances.

Senorita Otero has given particulars of her relations with the unfortunate young man to a reporter of the *Temps*. She states that some time ago she received, after her performance at the theatre, a visiting-card inviting her to supper with Chrétien. She sent back a reply by the *huissier* of the Folies-Bergère to the effect that as she did not know the writer, she could not accept his invitation. A few minutes later she received a letter repeating the invitation and enclosing 10,000fr. in bank notes. These she also returned.

After this Chrétien laid siege to her hotel in the rue Pierre-Charron, sending her messages that if he was not received he would commit suicide. Senorita Otero accorded him one single interview in presence of several witnesses at which she informed him of the hopelessness of the efforts he was making to gain her affections.

In spite of this communication Chrétien continued to send her letters and to call at her house. His letters remained without reply and at each of his visits he was informed that Senorita Otero could not receive him. This so affected him that he resolved to commit suicide. On Monday afternoon he addressed a letter to her in which he declared his intention of putting an end to his life.

Two hours later he put his resolve into execution by shooting himself in a cab in the Bois de Boulogne.

"LA BELLE OTERO" AND HER CREDITORS.

Curious Reception Accorded to Her Linendraper by Her Friends.

"La belle Otero," the Spanish dancer of the Folies-Bergère, is again supplying material for the *chronique scandaleuse* of the French press.

According to the *Temps* a M. Capdeville, a linendraper in the boulevard Haussmann, has lodged a complaint against her with the Commissary of Police of the quartier des Bassins.

M. Capdeville states that Mlle. Otero owed him 500fr. and that in spite of repeated applications he could not obtain payment. He informed her that on the day of the Grand Prix he would make another application for the sum due. On the afternoon of Sunday M. Capdeville met Mlle. Otero in the *pesage* at Longchamp and demanded payment of his account. He was requested to send his wife to her house the following day at two o'clock.

Having heard, however, that Mlle. Otero intended to give his wife a bad reception M. Capdeville determined to accompany her. When they arrived at the house they were shown into the dining-room, where they found Mlle. Otero, her secretary, a dancer, a singer and two other persons.

A BATTLE ROYAL.

As soon as they had entered the room the secretary came forward and informed M. Capdeville that he had written Mlle. Otero an insolent letter, for which he would have to ask pardon on his knees. At the same moment Mlle. Otero seized a decanter and hurled it at him. M. Capdeville seized another to return the compliment, when he was seized by the persons present by the arms and legs and thrown down. Mlle. Otero, he maintains, kept screaming, "Kill him! kill him!"

Mme. Capdeville terrified broke a window and shrieked for help. After a struggle which lasted fully ten minutes, M. Capdeville and his wife managed to escape from the house. The former maintains that during the struggle Mlle. Otero armed herself with a revolver and closed the door of the room to prevent the egress of himself and Mme. Capdeville.

Mlle. Otero on her side states that M. Capdeville's account was disgracefully overcharged and that he had wearied her with constant application for payment. On Sunday morning she declared M. Capdeville had sent her an insulting letter, in which he declared that he would publicly climb into her carriage at Longchamp and would refuse to get down till he was paid. He had at the same time called her a *saltimbanque*.

When M. Capdeville called he made a movement as if he would assault her. It was then her friends interfered and seized him to prevent his doing so.

LOVER SHOT, SHOOTS BACK.

Lively Revolver Encounter in the Street Between M. Périer and His Wife's Friend.

HUSBAND BACK TOO SOON.

Matrimonial Complications in which an Argentine Engineer and a Jewelry Agent Figure.

M. Henri Périer peppered his wife's lover, M. Carassalle, with a revolver, in front of the latter's residence, on Thursday evening, as the guilty couple came out. M. Carassalle first took to flight, then drew out a revolver himself and emptied it at the outraged husband, Mme. Périer meanwhile throwing herself between the two. Fortunately, no one was seriously wounded.

The story of the matrimonial complications which led up to this unique episode would require a three-volume novel. They may be briefly summed up as follows—and the salient theme around which they revolve is the extraordinary confidence placed by M. Périer in his wife's veracity. M. Henri Périer, says the "Figaro," is an engineer doing business at Buenos Ayres, aged forty-four, who came to Paris for the Exhibition. He took up his residence with his wife, Mme. Adrienne Périer, aged thirty, and their three children, in a dainty apartment at 5 rue Vignon.

Husband's Friend.

Mme. Périer left the Argentine Republic with her children last February. Her husband having some business to settle followed some time later. On landing at Marseilles the young wife met a compatriot and friend of her husband's, M. Carassalle, who is an agent in jewelry, and who was also proceeding to Paris. M. Carassalle, a bachelor of forty-eight, paid such assiduous attention to his friend's wife that he succeeded in capturing her heart.

When M. Périer reached Paris he noticed a change in his wife. He noticed, also, that she was absent quite frequently from their home. One day suspicion arose in his mind, and he followed her, and discovered that her destination was M. Carassalle's residence, No. 3 rue Boissière.

He taxed her very severely with her conduct when she came home, but Mme. Périer successfully "bluffed" him with the remark, "Why, it's only natural that I should go to see him. He was most kind to me when I was alone in Paris." So infatuated was the engineer that he believed her.

At the beginning of August M. Périer left with his children for a change of air at Neuchatel, his wife remaining behind on some pretext or other. But once away his suspicions again got the better of him, and he returned unexpectedly. The house was empty. Mme. Périer entered at eleven o'clock in the evening. She had been dining with her husband's friend, but nevertheless managed to convince M. Périer that all was correct.

On September 4 M. Périer again left for Neuchatel, where the children had remained. His wife accompanied him to the station, and insisted that he should let her know by telegram as soon as he had arrived. Her insistence only had the effect of again rousing her husband's suspicion. He sent the telegram from Pontarlier, "Journey quite safe. Thousand kisses," and straightway took the train back to Paris. It was evening when he reached the rue Vignon, and he again found his wife out.

Two Shadows.

Then he wended his way to the rue Boissière, hid under a convenient gateway, and watched his friend's windows, where he could see two shadows reflected.

Towards ten o'clock the door of No. 5 opened, and Mme. Périer appeared hanging on M. Carassalle's arm. The engineer, mad with jealousy, rushed up to the couple, brandishing a revolver. "You wretch," he shouted to the jewelry agent. "I am going to kill you," and he accompanied the words by emptying the five chambers of his revolver. M. Carassalle was hit in the left hip and in the chest. He bolted down the street calling loudly for help, but nobody came. He then turned round, drew a revolver and emptied five barrels almost point blank at M. Périer, wounding him in the chest.

The shots and the cries of the distracted lady finally brought the police on the scene. M. Périer's wound having been dressed at the Beaujon Hospital, he was conveyed to his home. M. Carassalle is also being attended at his residence. The authorities have the case in hand.

GER[...]

Mr. Edo[...] gistica[...]

LESSONS

Ideal Refor[...] Which O[...] Va[...]

M. Edoua[...] Marine, cont[...] articles to t[...] navy, summin[...] marineamt[...] The ar[...] columns[...] deals mos[...] in which[...] navy has[...] thods. Th[...] matters tec[...] man system[...] board the I[...] He says: [...] by each bat[...] slightly larg[...] have placed [...] Foudre. Thes[...] of twelve knot[...] ed to be lowe[...] battle is pendi[...] moment. No [...] France, nor, I [...] serves attention. [...] fore ourselves, th[...] of fast torpedo-[...] accompany the s[...] given up this i[...] whether the G[...] problem is no[...]

Teutonic Meth[...]

Discussing th[...] zation of the G[...] which dates b[...] month, M. I[...] praise of the[...] vision of la[...] methods w[...] energy.

He adm[...] navy has [...] the fact [...] tion, fre[...] For this[...] study of[...] importan[...] Up to [...] tion, th[...]

[...]MER.

High Tem-[...]enced in

[...] THE HERALD.]

The compilation [...]his is the hottest [...]erature was three [...] mean for that [...]ds were broken. [...]nest August re-[...]

[...]or June, July [...]g. Cent. The [...] been exceeded [...]the average was

[...]AL CRISIS.

[...]nthracite Coal [...]ylvania Go[...] [...]e.

[...]TO THE HERALD.]

[...].—Though lack-[...] the support of [...] numbers of the [...] Pennsylvania [...]ecert the col-[...] [...]standstill, and [...] orders. The [...]c of discussion. [...]loat that operators [...] down all the col-[...] [...]n Sunday. This [...]mpossible for the [...] strength, and [...] to terms with-[...] [...]ed to make a [...] differences by

mous and [...] fleet in bein[...] tion, known [...] mando and [...] ganization wa[...] der Golz in [...] realized what [...] ing to create [...] of the fleet in [...] struction, or, [...] fleet from the [...] and the fleet [...] same hands wit[...] simple days of [...] former now rec[...] less complicati[...] effective and a [...] tive division.

In the Arsen[...]

"Germany e[...] in the higher [...] is more import[...] first of all tr[...] will see it at [...] Such a distri[...] when everythi[...] is singularly d[...] of France, [...] have to be ren[...] centuries, in[...] rangements, b[...] However adi[...] tained by Ad[...] have been, the [...] when that exce[...] placed on the [...] organization re[...] M. Lockroy, wa[...] tween the two [...] friction had ari[...] To do away w[...] kommando was [...] placed under [...] Kaiser, repres[...] in the same [...] personal swa[...] nical branch, [...] istence. But [...] drawbacks be [...] rangement, t[...] changes will [...] ceasing effort[...] Lockroy attrib[...] of the German[...]

ECCLESIA[...]

Italian Bishop[...]

AN UNFAITHFUL EMPLOYÉ.

M. Georges G——, an employé at the branch of the Comptoir National d'Escompte in the boulevard Montparnasse, has stolen 15,000fr. and disappeared with his mistress, whom he had installed in an apartment on the boulevard Edgar Quinet. The *Temps* states that M. G——, who is a married man with a family, decamped with the money after being sent to the Bourse to sell some securities.

[...]owever, [...] they acc[...]ished [...]an they were horrified to find Mme. Desroussins armed with a lamp and somewhat scantily clothed. The latter had changed her mind about

RISK IN
RSE TRADE.

akes Riding in
ticable — Great
rness Horses.

.Y OPTIMISTIC.

ver, Takes Gloomy
for Decline of
biles.

little change in the ne past seven days, brisk, the mild wea- the Bois still prac- for harness horses rope continues, and nt moment, is the

y purposes Messrs. have done little. ring on our dull ad of the firm yes- that officers, who, y short of cash, are ents that they will best girls' in a few ill not be until they w Year's festivities emselves together' m again. That is, some good-natured that sort to make a mount for their sometimes happens. few days we have horse, an English officer at Saumur. everal good animals not complain. On the thoroughbreds, idamus and Octo- ribed in last Thurs- the two American hich we have had nder our price. have a smart bay- 70cm., a remarkable ask 2,500fr., and a unter, or carriage whose price is 3,000 s specialty there is with high

New Duel Figure in Cotillons in England.

The Looking-glass Method of Choosing Partners in the Coming Winter Dances in England.

Foils Used Fitted with Huge Powder-Puffs Instead of the Usual Button.

(From the "Daily Mail.")

The cotillon is likely to be as much in favor as ever at the smart dances of the coming winter, and many young matrons and men are qualifying for the proud position of leaders.

To be a good leader of cotillon is to write one's self down a very gifted person, for the position demands plenty of invention, an infinite amount of spirit, and that quality of good generalship that inspires others to follow one's lead right through.

Some novel methods of choosing partners are likely to be seen. The ordeal of the sheet proved a favorite method last season. A big sheet is hung down the room dividing the men from the women. At a given signal each man places the first finger of his right hand over the sheet and the ladies then choose their partners according to whichever finger pleases them most.

Another way of taking partners is by the sign of the paper bag. Each man and woman before entering the ballroom is given an enormous paper bag large enough to put right over the head and to drop as far as the waist. Every bag is named in pairs; two are labelled tea, two more sugar, a third pair rice, a fourth soda, and so on, running through the whole of a ... store. Enveloped in th... th only their eyes ... not be recognized, ... the ballroom until ... bearing the labels

...he dancers were ...ent colored rib- ... of reins. One ... the room, and ...en men. The ...elves, according to the color of the reins they had held, and danced off.

New duel figure in the cotillon. The sham swords are fitted with powder puffs.

One more famous and critical manner of choice is that of the mirror. A certain small number of pretty girls seat themselves with looking-glasses in their hands. Behind them, so that their faces are revealed in the mirror, file the men. Until she sees the face of her own squire in the glass, the girl who is making her choice wipes the face off the glass with her handkerchief, and the discarded partner kneels on the bare boards behind her. Sometimes a long row of men marks dear Lady Disdain's difficulty to please herself; but when she is satisfied, up spring the rejected ones and dance off with other unmated women.

At one big party a duel figure was danced, or, rather, fought, with sham foils, each one of which was fitted with a huge powder-puff instead of the regulation button. As may be imagined, the result of this encounter was a very harmless but most amusing fight. Another effective figure hinged upon the war in the East, and all kinds of Japanese kimonos were worn.

AMERICAN
IN PA

Commercial Pr
Guyot, of Par
in Unit

PLANNING BIG

Would Concentrate
of America
Old

(From the NEW

Declaring that " tection has now re in the United Sta one of the leading Europe, and for t Public Works in F Board of Trade a New York a plan velopment of Ame and Europe genera at greater length the details of the

"I represent an dicate," he said, " ganize in the heart tinent an America the home of which Palais Royal in Pa project before the ington. It has be by both the Secret Secretary of Comm we are authorized dially sympathize general policy whi signed to carry ou

"In 1896-97 the to this country w they have now rea exports from the U are more than $ $6,000,000 worth tured articles were ing 1900—the yea the figures reached day they stand a And yet your Co plain that your m ing, as regards Eu spasmodic, irregula

Knows America.

M. Guyot has Roosevelt since co a short time ago. White House, has drew Carnegie, bre and now, as he ex dorf-Astoria, he be something of Ame American affairs.

Describing the Royal project, M.

"The proposal w commercial world has been suggeste which the great bu their sales by mea which establishes various States. T United States coul serving his individ tion or a central a would have branche The proposal is sim advice so familiar American Consuls.

FIRST COURT BALL OF THE YEAR AT VIENNA

Brilliant Scene in the Salle de Redoute at the Hofburg.

THE EMPEROR PRESENT.

...the Hall, Lead-

listen to what Mr. Edwin ... of coaching in ... had more

two o'clock precisely. On Saturday at the Tattersall Français, Neuilly establishment, there will be a sale of bloodstock, of which the particulars will be published in these columns to-morrow.

...IT IS SETTLED.

...ed in Stubborn ... Thousands ...rts.

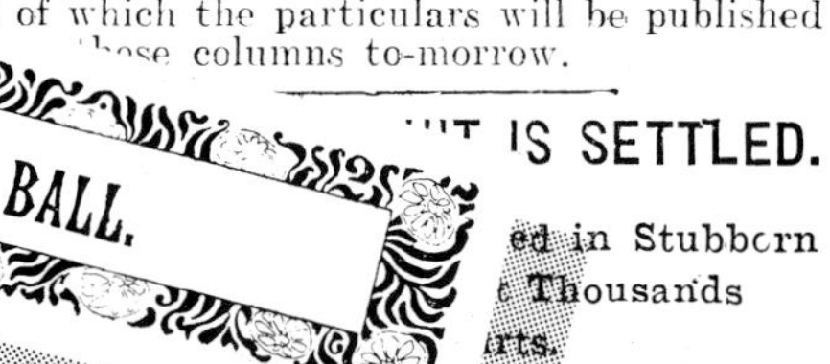

VIENNA'S GREAT HOFBURG BALL.

"I assert," ... trade is as bad as it ... corn chandlers, the harness-makers ... they will tell you that they can barely make a living—and I am only speaking

MRS. B. MARTIN'S COSTUME BALL.

"The Most Sumptuous, Brilliant and Costly Function Ever Seen in America."

GORGEOUS AND MONARCHIST.

Descriptive of Historic Costumes in which New York Society Ladies Appeared.

["DAILY TELEGRAPH" CABLEGRAM.]

NEW YORK, Feb. 11.—All authorities agree in declaring that last night's ball was the most sumptuous, brilliant and costly function ever seen in America. It will be classed with the Schermerhorn ball, given fifty years ago, the great dance held in honor of the Prince of Wales, and the Vanderbilt ball, the latest and most successful function of the kind; but it eclipses all these memories.

The scene within the ballroom was dazzling. The white and gold panels of the Waldorf Hotel gleamed through ancient

MISS KATE BRICE AS MARIE ANTIONETTE.

tapestries, foliage plants and tropica flowers, and the broad wall mirrors se back in electric rays reflections of beau and wealth and of historic characters radiant attires that seemed to have tra ferred New York to Versailles.

costume ball, wore a Merveilleuse dress of white moiré, sprayed with small baskets of pink roses, which were divided by narrow stripes of pink satin. With this costume went an enormous bonnet, with poke crown and brim of grass-green chiffon, decked with clusters of pink roses.

Mr. Belmont's costume was of Henri IV. period. Over a dress of black velvet he wore a full suit of armor inlaid with gold, and valued at £2,000. He also wore the Order of Saint Esprit in jewels, together with a jeweled sword.

Mrs. William Allen, as Peg Woffington, appeared in Pompadour silk, with a Watteau train of white gauze, and corsage trimmed with ropes of pearls.

Mrs. James Beekman, as Lady Teazle, was in a rich brocade dress which was once worn by an ancestress.

Mrs. Henry Burnett also wore an old ancestral petticoat of satin as the Marquise de Suffern.

Sir Bache Cunard belonged to the Court of Louis XVI., while Lady Cunard, in a superb costume, was the Duchesse de Destantes.

Miss Edith Devereux Clapp personified the Duchess of Devonshire with powdered wig and curls and costly jewels.

Miss Annie Morgan's Pocahontas costume attracted much attention. It was made by Indians, of real leather, with a war bonnet and mocassins correct in every detail.

Mrs. Stuyvesant Fish as Marie Antoinette had a bodice lined with diamonds, a pearl necklace, and gems in her hair.

Mrs. Katherine Duer, another Antoinette, had powdered hair, in which was a diamond aigrette.

Mrs. George de Forrest, as Titian's daughter, wore a splendid costume of pale blue velvet, on which hung a trained mantle of cloth of gold, the whole set off with clasps, and a tiara and a necklace of diamonds and ropes of pearls.

Mrs. W. Sherman was similarly resplendent with diamonds and was in a pink satin costume.

Miss Evelyn Sloane, as Juliet, in a dress of white brocade, had her waist embroidered with pearls and a small jeweled cap over her hair, which was entwined with pearls.

Mr. Belmont Tiffany was a Knight Templar and Mrs. Tiffany the Marquise de Polign...

Miss ... Puritan maide... pleate... on he...

A... the... fied...

J... Ge... St... M... V... s...

MR. J. BLAGDEN, JR., IN COSTUME.

LADY WARWICK'S BALL.

Ancient Glories of the French Court Revived in the Famous English Castle.

COSTUMES OF LOUIS XV AN...

The Historic Halls Shine... Blaze of Electric Light... Fancy Dresses.

[FROM OUR SPECIAL CORRESPONDENT.]

WARWICK, Feb. 4.—The Countess of Warwick's great *bal poudré* took place on Friday night and was an enormous success. No fashionable event for some time has created so much interest. Dressmakers and hairdressers have been at their wits' end. M. Emile of Conduit-street had forty heads to do in the Castle alone, to say nothing of others in houses in the neighborhood. Seven men were sent to the Castle on Saturday, four of whom arrived expressly from Paris on Friday, so as to get over the *mal de mer* in time, as the patron said. Everyone was *poudré* and the costumes were of the time of Louis XV. and Louis XVI., the beautiful hostess appearing as the unfortunate Queen Marie Antoinette. No smart young man in London considered himself in the swim if he could not show his invitation to this unique function. Moustaches had to be sacrificed, but this was willingly done in many cases.

Lady Warwick had as many visitors staying in the castle as it could comfortably hold. There were: Prince Francis of Teck, Prince and Princess Henry of Pless, and pretty little Miss Cornwallis West, M. de Soveral, Count Deym, Mrs. Arthur Paget, Lord Chesterfield, Lor... Grey de Wilton, the Duchess of Sutherlan... Lady Westmorland and Lady Ange... Erskine, Lord and Lady Rosslyn, Miss Nayl... Lady Feo Sturt, Lady Norreys, Lady Cair... Mr. Cecil Foley, Mr. O. de Murietta, Mrs. Menz... and Miss Muriel Wilson, Lord Richard Nevil...

tables and in the ... there were ... table for the Queen and her *entourage*.

The strawberries, apricots, grapes and pineapples were all sent from Trentham, which belongs to Lady Warwick's brother-in-law. Here is some of the *menu*: Filets de saumon, consommé de volaille, côtelettes d'agneau, suprême de faisans, poulets Médicis, asperges d'Argenteuil, petits poussins au cresson, sandwiches varié, Macédoine de fruits au champagne, pâtisseries assorties, fraises.

Out of the hall leads the red drawing-room or ...room, which look...d magnificent in a blaze ...nd lounges wer...

LADY WARWICK'S COSTUME.

WARWICK CASTLE.

the Duke of Manchester, the Earl of Lonsdale, ... the Earl of Bradford and ...

DIPLOMATIC BALL IN BERLIN.

Brilliant Function at the British Embassy—Many Royal Princes

STATE BALL AT THE ITALIAN COURT.

King Humbert and Queen Margharita Preside Over a Brilliant Function.

Sign... Bülo... Bild... Mar... tess... Mo... Oli... Vi... we... ne... Sa... P... C... T...

BRILLIANT SCENE IN THE SALLE DES FÊTES.

M. Emile Loubet, President of the Republic, Formally Declares the Exposition Open Amid the Acclamations of a Vast and Enthusiastic Assemblage.

SUPERB SPECTACLE IN THE GROUNDS.

Official Party Traverses the Champ de Mars and, Saluted by a Salvo of a Hundred Guns, the President Returns to the Elysée.

A FRENCH VIEW.

M. J. Cornély, writing in this morning's "Figaro," says: "The Exhibition will not be a pledge of national peace only; it will also be a guarantee of international peace. When, to-morrow, men assembled from all parts of the world begin to walk through these gardens, these monuments, these marvels, they will understand that nations were not sent into the world to kill, but to help one another; and that since all men are sons of the same father they should behave as brothers."

THE NEW YORK

EUROPEAN EDITION—PARIS, SUNDAY, APRIL 15, 1900.—48 P

WHOLE NO.: 23,246

UNIVERSAL EXHIBITION OPENED

e furthest advanced due to private enter- s, the Swiss Panorama, he Tour du Monde, the Tableaux-Vivants, the Topsy Guillaume, the hundred and one

cannon ... Then, as the Seine toward III., the Pre the Nations s

The request of the authori... was well carried out in the more central quarters, the scene round the Opera being perhaps the most striking. In the more outlying districts less enthusiasm was shown.

Popular Inauguration To-Day.

It is to-day, however, that the more popular inauguration will take place, when the Exhibition will throw open its doors to the general public. It is expected that every means of locomotion will be put to a severe test.

Regulations for Admission.

Admission to the Exhibition will be entirely by ticket. No money is taken at the doors. All round the doors and in the nearest cafés dealers in tickets will be found. The face value of the tickets is 1fr., but their market value at present is from 60 to 75 centimes.

NOTICE.

To-day's Easter number of the HERALD consists of 48 pages. It is sold at the usual price of the Sunday issue—viz., 25 centimes.

of Ministe Secretary barieu. A received Commerc Presiden Presiden eral Co General Presiden the Salle

Mme. Lo

Mme. I with the spicuous specially the Presi China colored Ve the same c aigrette.

Imagine area, cover 130 feet h of sixte others. glass, an ings co

THE CELESTIAL GLOBE.

ERALD.

PARIS & DEPARTMENTS, 25c.; LONDON, 2½d.

N SOLEMN STATE.

LA PARISIENNE

ENGLISH CORDIALITY.

London Papers Speak Most Enthusiastically of the Exhibition.

[BY THE HERALD'S SPECIAL WIRE.]

LONDON, Saturday.—All the morning papers have leaders on the opening of the Paris Exhibition. The "Daily Telegraph" says: "The last Exhibition was followed by the Cronstadt fêtes, which showed that the isolation of the Republic was at an end and signalled the 'rapprochement' between Paris and St. Petersburg. So far as the Exhibition is the festival of the prosperity of France and the peace of Europe, no country will have a more generous interest than England in its success."

The "Daily Mail" says: "If the Exhibition of 1900 brings France and England closer together, it will have been well worth holding. We want to realize that many of the causes of common distrust are groundless or could easily be removed. Let us be friends, not for the sake of ourselves alone, but for all that the world holds most dear."

AMERICA'S HOMAGE.

The "Figaro" this morning, as its leading "echo," says:—

"To-day when the President of the Republic, inaugurating the Exposition, passes before the American sections, and before the national flag of the United States, a delicate attention will be shown him.

"The American Guard, of about sixty men, will salute him with the French flag, thus symbolizing the union of the two great Republics. Is not this attention on the part of the Americans worth calling attention to?"

UNVEILING GLORIES OF ARABIAN NIGHTS.

What Was Proudly Announced as the Synthesis of the Century Receives Its Consecration—One of France's Most Brilliant Fêtes.

FOURTEEN THOUSAND PEOPLE THERE.

Elite of France and Representatives of the Civilized World Form an Audience Worthy of the Occasion and the Scene.

"The Exhibition of 1900," wrote M. Jules Roche, Minister of Commerce, in 1894, in the decree which ordered its organization, "will constitute the synthesis and will determine the philosophy of the nineteenth century."

The great work thus proudly announced saw its realization yesterday, and received its consecration at one of the most brilliant fêtes in the history of the Third Republic.

Nothing was wanting to give brilliancy to the scene. From the earliest hour in the morning the sun was shining in an almost cloudless sky. The whole city was early afoot, and thousands of people kept pouring in a steady stream towards the Champ de Mars. On all sides nothing was heard but the music of the various regiments marching to the Exhibition ground to form the President's guard.

Marvellous Beauty.

Viewed from the Pont de l'Alma the scene was one of marvellous beauty, a realization of the glories of the "Arabian Nights." On every side rise palaces of marvellous beauty. Up towards Nôtre Dame the eye is fascinated by the rue des Nations, that product of the friendly rivalry of the nations.

Beyond this lies the double line of palaces flanking the Esplanade des Invalides, and connected with the Champs Elysées by the monumental Alexandre III. bridge.

The eye meets nothing but a sea of towers and minarets, gorgeous decorations and gilded domes.

On the right bank rises the picturesque group of buildings forming the restoration of Old Paris and the splendid conservatories of the Palace of Horticulture.

Down stream is the magnificent sweep of the Trocadéro, with the rushing waters of its fountain glittering in the sun. Facing this is the double line of palaces of the Champ de Mars, culminating in the grandiose façade of the Salle des Fêtes, the "clou" of the whole Exhibition.

For the President.

Such was the sight that met the eyes of M. Loubet when he drove yesterday, escorted by a squadron of Cuirassiers, from his palace to the Champ de Mars.

The scene in the avenue de la Motte Piquet was a most striking one. As far as the eye could reach it was a mass of cabs and carriages. Ministers of State, Ambassadors, high functionaries, Academicians, generals, Deputies, Senators, and all that Paris counts in the way of social eminence were pouring towards the entrance to the Galerie des Machines. Every decoration and every order in Europe was to be seen, Russian "boyards" elbowed Hungarian magnates, and Turkish fezes contrasted with Cossack astrakhan caps.

Punctually to the minute the command "Présentez armes!" a roll on the drums, and the strains of the "Marseillaise" announced the arrival of the President of the Republic and the members of the Cabinet.

One by one the five magnificent gala carriages discharged their occupants, and, escorted by M. Millerand, Minister of Commerce, and M. Picard, Commissary-General of the Exhibition, M. Loubet entered the Salle des Fêtes.

Salle des Fetes.

The grandiose building will undoubtedly attract greater admiration than any other palace in the World's Fair of 1900, and will be a triumph and a monument of

THE NEW YORK HERALD, PARIS, SUN

SOME NOTABLE BUILDINGS

...., 1900.—EASTER NUMBER.

OF THE PARIS EXPOSITION.

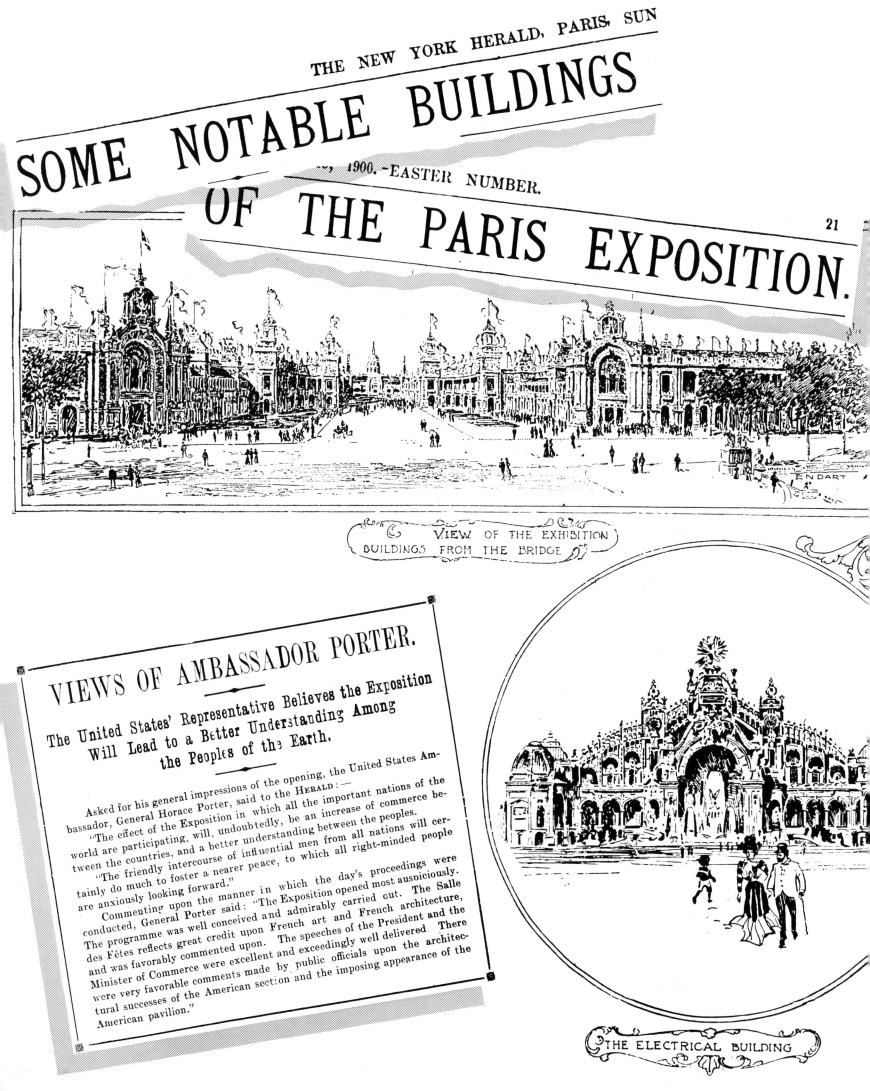

VIEW OF THE EXHIBITION BUILDINGS FROM THE BRIDGE

VIEWS OF AMBASSADOR PORTER.

The United States' Representative Believes the Exposition Will Lead to a Better Understanding Among the Peoples of the Earth.

Asked for his general impressions of the opening, the United States Ambassador, General Horace Porter, said to the HERALD:—

"The effect of the Exposition in which all the important nations of the world are participating, will, undoubtedly, be an increase of commerce between the countries, and a better understanding between the peoples.

"The friendly intercourse of influential men from all nations will certainly do much to foster a nearer peace, to which all right-minded people are anxiously looking forward."

Commenting upon the manner in which the day's proceedings were conducted, General Porter said: "The Exposition opened most auspiciously. The programme was well conceived and admirably carried out. The Salle des Fêtes reflects great credit upon French art and French architecture, and was favorably commented upon. The speeches of the President and the Minister of Commerce were excellent and exceedingly well delivered. There were very favorable comments made by public officials upon the architectural successes of the American section and the imposing appearance of the American pavilion."

THE ELECTRICAL BUILDING

A Few of the Principal Sights in the Great World's Fair Which is Opened to Visitors To-day.
BRITISH SHOW AT EXPOSITION.
Old English Manor House, Furnished with Modern Luxury, on the Seine's Banks.
LOAN COLLECTION OF ART.
Colonial Exhibits in the Trocadero Gardens Larger Than Those of Any Other Power.

PLACE DE LA CONCORDE ENTRANCE

BRIDGE OF ALEXANDER III

Society Notes and News from Europear

BIARRITZ.

Two Capital Runs with the Hounds, One Fox Escaping Each Day.

HALF-HIDDEN BOULDER TRAPS.

Field Led at Clinking Pace Over Nasty Country in the Direction of Cambo.

BIARRITZ, Wednesday.—We have had two capital days with the hounds. On Saturday, in ideal weather, the fixture was at Saint-Pée-sur-Nivelle (18kil.), a lovely spot near the Spanish frontier, and in spite of the distance a good number turned out.

Our first fox was not much of a flyer, and soon met with his doom. Hounds soon got on another, who evidently knew what was up, for off he went like a greyhound at a clinking pace, up hill and down dale, through woods, over half-hidden boulders —such frequent traps for the unwary— leading us into as nasty a piece of country as could possibly be imagined in the direction of Espelette and Cambo. The scent was a burning one, but evidently Mast... Reynard gave us the slip near... place and got awa... caped, for...

DINARD.

Many Visitors Arrive for Easter Holidays and Spring Meeting at the Golf Club.

CONCERT AT THE NEW CLUB.

Given in Aid of the Hospital Attracts a Large and Fashionable Crowd.

DINARD, Wednesday.—Dinard is filling up very rapidly for Easter; indeed, it has never been very empty since the summer season, for now so many people take houses for the whole winter. But a great influx of visitors is expected for the week after next, the spring golf meeting being the great attraction.

The Grand Casino is to be opened at Easter. This is an innovation that may not be a success, but M. Bertrand, the director, deserves credit f... energy in making the... Tzigane... promise...

ROME.

Spring Has Set In with a Cloudless Sky and Delicious Atmosphere.

KING AND QUEEN'S HOLIDAY.

They Go Quietly to Monte Christo in Their Auto and Steam Yacht.

ROME, Wednesday.—Spring has now set in. The sky is cloudless and the air soft and delicious to breathe. If you drive outside the gates you will see all the undulating ground enamelled with daisies and other wild flowers. A walk in the Borghese Villa in the morning is delightfully invigorating, though you must not expect to meet many people there at th... time.

The King and Queen the other... drove quietly to their new Vi...

MONTREUX.

Place Filled with Visitors, Enjoying the Brilliant, Sunny, Early Spring Weather.

OUTDOOR SPORTS INDULGED IN.

At Clay-Pigeon Shooting, Mr. Hawker Carries Off the Prize from Geneva Visitors.

MONTREUX, Thursday.—The brilliant, sunny weather is making the early spring a delight here. The place is filled with visitors, and lawn tennis, golf and boating are all liberally indulged in. The spring golf competition takes place on April 11 and the following days, and is expected to be full of interest. The lawn tennis...

POSTAGE
Abroad.
France.
6
18
36
70

broad.
France.
5
10
20

RK HERALD
de l'Opéra,

ndertake to
nications.

lway and
TWENTY-
STREETS,
, 81 FLEET-
ies of the
n, W.C.
ition of
regular

arge at
ute cir-

advertise-
ale, at the
rtisements
rent Bros.,

ERALD will
Indépendance

OOMS.

reedner Bank,
strasse.
and U.S. Vice

ruhl.
an Navigation
tel Kaiserhof.
a, oppos. to the
nstrasse.
strasse.
Campo S.S.
church).

GER CIRCU-
EWSPAPER
TINENT.

. No. 135

ST.

s.—12 to 4
days, 1fr.
5

Saturdays of
Prefect of the
aya.
by permission

WEATHER IN PARIS.

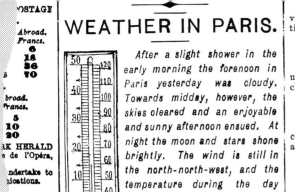

After a slight shower in the early morning the forenoon in Paris yesterday was cloudy. Towards midday, however, the skies cleared and an enjoyable and sunny afternoon ensued. At night the moon and stars shone brightly. The wind is still in the north-north-west, and the temperature during the day ranged from a minimum of 3deg. to a maximum of 15deg. Cent. The barometer stood steadily at 771mm.

At four o'clock this morning the HERALD'S thermometer registered 6deg. Cent. It was fine.

FINE.

The weather forecast for Paris to-day gives changeable winds, westerly predominant, fair generally, and rather milder.

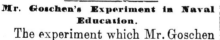

Mr. Goschen's Experiment in Naval Education.

The experiment which Mr. Goschen foreshadowed in his speech ... time back is ...

... enjoy a ...

... conditions of entry to the ... published ...

blackmailing gang which has been victimizing people of position there for a long time past.

Finance. FROM various causes the stock markets in New York, London and Paris yesterday showed an easier undertone, without, however, any marked declines in prices of leading factors.

To Athens. ACCORDING to the information of our special correspondent in Salonica, the Turks mean to proceed as far as Athens before coming to an arrangement for concluding a treaty of peace.

Kempton Park. THE Kempton Park "Jubilee" meeting opened yesterday, the Prince of Wales being present. This afternoon the Jubilee Stakes, one of the most valuable events of the English racing year, will be decided.

Cuba. FROM a Cabinet Minister our Washington correspondent learns that the President's expected Message to Congress about Cuba merely contemplates relief for destitute Americans there, and that he is entirely opposed to intervention.

Uniforms. SOME Americans seem to be attaching a great deal of importance to the wearing of uniforms and decorations, to judge from the quarrel that is going on over the style of those worn by some of the American representatives at the coronation of the Tsar in Moscow.

COURT AND SOCIETY.

The Duke and Duchess of Marlborough Among the Guests at the Queen's Dinner Party.

[BY THE HERALD'S SPECIAL WIRE.]

LONDON, May 15.—The *Daily Telegraph* contains the following items of Court and fashionable news:—

The Queen's dinner party at Windsor Castle last night included the Duke and Duchess of Marlborough, the Marquis and Marchioness of Tweeddale and Lord Lister. Her Majesty's guests remained at the palace.

The Duke of Cambridge has intimated to Sir Donald Currie, Chairman of the South African dinner committee, that he will preside at the annual dinner to be held at the Hotel Métropole on Saturday, June 19.

The Bishop of Hull has so far recovered from his recent illness as to be able to leave Scarborough for London on his way to the Italian lakes.

Earl and Countess Stanhope and the Ladies Stanhope have arrived at 20 Grosvenor-place from Chevening, Sevenoaks.

The Duchess of ...

... -street from ...

... Winfield Bonser, Chief Justice of Ceylon, has arrived at 58 Maddox-street for the season.

Colonel and Mrs. Houston Boswall Preston, have arrived at Bel... Grosvenor-gardens.

Globe, th... placed ... vessels i... A Sh... *Standard* issued c... at Chat... torpedo ... the wint... Sheerness there bei... for naval ... cannot be... The Sa... terday fr... port-guard... been refitte... tion on Ju... The *St.* ... Wye, store... Chatham, w... The Lord... ralty have ... Greenwich B... Among the... under the wi... and a freeho... the will of that town. ... the benefit of men of the n... The follo... nounced at Staff Cap... Assistant ... dated May Staff Su... Wildfire, a... date Marc... Chief ... T. P. Ja... June 8; additiona... Chope, ... to the Sturgeon, Gibson ... tional, fo... Wildfire, T. Steam, the Jupite... broke, addi... April 22. Assistant the Victory, Jason, to date Barracouta; ... neer A. W. M... Chief Gun... additional, for all to d...

... cruiser coaling. well o...

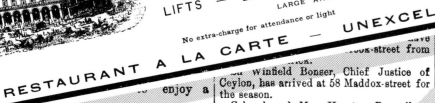

nental weather reports:—

BADEN-BADEN.—Lovely morning; 8deg. Cent.
BOULOGNE.—Fine; 9deg. Cent.
DIEPPE.—Clear sky; 9deg. Cent.
OSTEND.—Clear sky; 9deg. Cent.
ROUEN.—Fine; 9.5deg. Cent.

PERSONAL INTELLIGENCE

FRANCE.

Lady Falmouth has arrived in Paris and is at the Hotel du Jardin des Tuileries.

Professor and Mrs. Y. L. Morin, of Montreal, have arrived in Paris and are at the Hotel Saint-Pétersbourg.

Mr. O. Q. van Swinderen and family, who have been stopping at the Hotel de Calais, have left Paris for Arcachon.

The Fate of Ixion.

"The decree," announced the messenger of Jupiter, "is that you shall be bound for ever to the wheel!"

"W—Which make?" asked Ixion, anxiously.—*Puck.*

Mrs. Rudd Taylor and the Misses Rudd Taylor have arrived in Paris from Rome and are stopping at the Hotel d'Iéna.

M. Guido Hulse, the Ottoman Consul at Dresden, has arrived with his family at the Hotel Château Durieux, Aix-les-Bains.

Prince Obolensky and Princess Obolensky, *née* de Mingrélie, have arrived after their wedding at the Hotel de La Trémoille.

Mrs. J. Phillip Smith, of New York, and Miss Anita Gonzalez Smith have taken apartments at the Hotel de La Trémoïlle.

When?

The horseless carriage having been successfully introduced into Paris, now the inhabitants of the gay capital wonder when they shall have horseless beef.—Salt Lake *Herald.*

And dogless sausage.—Chicago *Tribune.*

And legless ballets.—Cleveland *Plain Dealer.*

Sir Henry and Lady Roscoe, of Manchester, and the Right Hon. Thomas Sinclair and family, of Belfast, have arrived in Paris and are at the Hotel de l'Athénée.

Among the latest arrivals at the Hotel de l'Athénée are Mr. and Mrs. F. W. ... and family, Dr. and M... New York ...

... singing of ... the last act of "Tann... by the Comtesse Miranda, better known as Christine Nilsson. Among the guests were: Mme. Hegemann, Mr. and Mrs. Bradley Martin, Mme. Luckemeyer, Sir George Beaumont and the Comtesse de Reban.

THE "FIGARO'S" LE MONDE ET LA VILLE.

La princesse Radziwill, que l'impératrice d'Allemagne avait envoyée à Paris pour la représenter à la cérémonie de Notre-Dame, a dîné, jeudi soir, chez la comtesse de Beau-

APARTMENT-HOUSES VERSUS "HOTELS."

Radical Transformation in "la Vie Parisienne"—Flats Preferred to Separate Houses.

A QUESTION OF CONVENIENCE.

Less Taxes, More Comfort and a Variety of Other Advantages in Their Favor.

HOW THE RENTS RANGE.

During the Last Twenty Years "Loyers" in Fashionable Quarters Have Nearly Doubled.

INCREASED VALUE OF LAND.

La mode n'est plus aux hôtels !

Like the heroes of Balaclava, to right and to left of you, before and behind you—everywhere you see prodigious buildings springing into existence, striking the eye with their new white stone and elaborate ornamentation. They are the apartment houses that are causing as radical a transformation in *la vie parisienne* as the improvements effected by that potent magician Baron Haussmann made in the material aspect of the city.

Reference has already been made in the editorial columns of the HERALD to this new departure. Families who heretofore have considered an "hôtel"—in the French sense of the word—as a *sine qua non* of existence are now transferring their Lares and Penates to apartment houses—to "flats." Only the other day a case was mentioned where a lady of the first rank in Parisian society had taken a flat in one of the new apartment houses erected in the avenue des Champs-Elysées.

For a change so radical as this there must be valid reasons.

"Reasons!" exclaimed Mr. Thomas Sprent, of the well-known firm of Sprent Brothers, rue de Rivoli, when questioned on the subject, "the reasons are obvious.

"To begin with, you have less taxes to pay in a flat, at least, as a general rule. If you are living in an *hôtel* you have probably ground rent, whereas, occupying a flat you have only the furniture tax and about 5 per cent. on your rent to pay for the carpets, heating apparatus and other general 'charges.'

"Secondly, in an apartment you have the very appreciable advantages of being on one floor—there is no running up and down stairs, no necessity to mount a flight of stairs in order to wash your hands before dinner. In these days little things like that count.

"Besides, the ideas that now govern the builders of apartment houses are those of utility and saving of labor. The modern apartment houses are designed with a view to what is most practical and most rapid. Not to speak of the hot and cold water that is on tap at any hour of the day and night, there are numberless other conveniences in the nature of dumb-waiters, *vide-ordures*

same ground for 400fr. a mètre—that is, for 2,400,000fr. Killian told me of this himself, so I can swear to it," said Mr. Sprent, emphatically.

"Again, in the month of January some ten years ago, a certain tract of land in the avenue Montaigne, at the corner of the

Bérenger, the Senator, has the *entresol*, for which he pays 28,000fr.

"Each apartment in this house comprises an antechamber and *galerie*, two salons, billiard-room, eight bedrooms, six cabinets de toilette, bathroom, five water-closets, dining-room, office de salle à manger, ser-

APARTMENT HOUSE IN THE CHAMPS-ÉLYSÉES.

avenue de l'Alma, was sold for 225fr. a mètre. In April of the same year, not six months afterwards, the same property was resold for 650fr. a mètre.

"These, of course, are isolated cases and are not to be met with every day.

"As a general rule, while the value of real estate in the centre of Paris has decreased, or at least remained stationary, the price of land in the western quarters, in " Champs-Elysées and Etoile quarter especia has continually and remarkably increas At the present time you can take 2,000f mètre as the maximum price in the aver des Champs-Elysées. In the avenue du B de Boulogne 1,000fr. a mètre will in all p bability be paid before long. On the oth hand, the Plaine Monceau is suffering a se back which, however, is slight and w doubtless not be lasting.

"Contrast with this the case of a lanc owner in the rue Montmartre, who, s recently as 1892, wanted to sell his property He could not obtain 1,200fr. a mètre for it and rather than sell at that price decided to pull down the existing building and rebuild at his own cost. I scarcely think it would be an exaggeration to say that real estate in this quarter of Paris has fallen 30 per cent. in value during the last thirty years."

"To resume, Mr. Sprent, your argument is that the rents now charged in the new apartment houses are simply an outcome of the increase in the value of land and the extra expense entailed in fitting the new houses with the most modern improvements?"

"Exactly so."

"Another question! How do the rents of these modern flats range?"

"Well, let us take two houses in the avenue des Champs-Elysées as instances—No. 82, to begin with, as it is perhaps the finest apartment house in Paris. There are only four floors, including the entresol, above the rez-de-chaussée. The *distribution* of all is the same, the sole difference being the height of the ceiling. With the lifts at the disposal of the tenants, and the *ascenseurs de service*, the *monte-lettres*, the *monte-charges*, &c., the disadvantages of upper floors are minimized. Consequently there

vants' hall, kitchen, washroom, linen rooms, servants' rooms, cellars and stables and coachhouse. Each apartment has both gas and electric light, hot and cold water, steam-heating apparatus, lifts, electric bells, telephone and dumb-waiters. The height of the apartments range from 4 mètres 40 on the

firs[...] case of the *rez-de-chaussée* and fourth floor."

A plan of the interior arrangement of the apartments in this house is given with this article. So with the yet uncompleted house bearing the number 104 avenue

on the rue Washington, the rents are follows:—

	Francs
Entresol	26.500
First floor	28.000
Second floor	25.000
Third floor	23.000
Fourth floor	21.000
Rez-de-chaussée	25.000

Then the apartments to the right, as y look at the house from the Palais de l' dustrie side of the avenue, are of somew less rent, as follows:—

	Francs.
Rez-de-chaussée	10.000
Entresol	25.000
First floor	26.000
Second floor	23.500
Third floor	21.500
Fourth floor	19.500

Finally, the apartments looking over rue Washington only have a much lo rental, the *loyers* ranging from 6,000fr. 8,000fr.

But these prices, it may be stated, susceptible of reduction. In fact, as M Sprent, from whom the above details w obtained, told me, a very considerable red tion can be obtained if one only knows h to go about it.

"And how is that, Mr. Sprent?"

"By going to a respectable house age The insurance companies generally 3,000fr. to 4,000fr. more on the rents th they are willing to accept. I can give y a recent instance in point. A lady came us about an apartment in one of these n apartment houses. The company wan 25,000fr. per annum, dating from January next. We got the apartment for her 24,000fr. a year from April 1, and givi our client the facility of entering i possession on January 1.

"That, as you see, means [...] 8,000fr."

No. 104 AVENUE DES CHAMPS-ÉLYSÉES.

PARIS CHURCH NOTES.

At Holy Trinity, the American Episcop Church, the Rev. Dr. Morgan, rector, w assisted yesterday by the Rev. Richa Hayward and Dr. Tuttle-Smith, of N

FRANCE.

BAGNÈRES de Bigorre.—Hotel de Londres splend. sit. Open the whole year

BIARRITZ. HOTEL D'ANGLETERRE. First class. 200 rooms, 80 sunny apartments. Full south facing the sea. The best situated. The most comfortable and the most popular. (Marcel CAMPAGNE, prop.)

DIJON. Renowned railway BUFFET. All trains fr. & to the South, Italy & Geneva stop here.

FONTAINEBLEAU.—APPARTEMENTS MEUBLES avec pension, française, confortable ; renseignements à Paris. De la Bretonnerie, 165 boulevard Haussmann.

PAU. JOHN JARVIS, Chemist, 20 RUE SERVIEZ. Highly recommended

PAU.
HOTEL GASSION.
Lift. A. Meilon, prop., Hotel d'Angleterre, Cauterets.

GERMANY.

AIX-LA-CHAPELLE.—Hotel Gd. Monarque First-rate hotel. Reasonable terms.

BADEN-BADEN.
HOTEL MINERVA.
Excellent new first-class hotel. Lift. Lichtenthaler Allee. Park.

BADEN-BADEN.—HOTEL VICTORIA. First-class. Princ. frequented by Americans and English. Lift.

BADEN-BADEN. HOLLAND HOTEL. Large park, 2 lifts. Pension

BADEN-BADEN.—HOTEL DE FRANCE. First-class. Lift. Ref. Mark Twain. Arrangement for long stay.

BADEN-BADEN. HOTEL DE RUSSIE. 1st cl. On Prom. Gard. Lift.

BADEN-BADEN. HOTEL MESSMER And three Villas. Finest situation near the Casino. Highly recommended.

BAD GASTEIN. HOTEL STRAUBINGER FIRST CLASS HOTEL WITH EVERY MODERN COMFORT. Favorite residence of English and Americans.

BAD NAUHEIM HOTEL AUGUSTA VICTORIA Splendid new building, finest situation opposite the Baths and Sprudel

BERLIN.—GRAND HOTEL DE ROME 39 Unter den Linden. First-class family house. Old reputation. ADOLF MUHLING, Proprietor.

BERLIN. HAVANA CIGARS 12 Unter den Linden. **R. F. LIEDTCKE.**

BERLIN. HOTEL BRISTOL. 5 Unter den Linden. First-class aristocratic family house. C. UHL, Prop.

BERLIN. HOTEL DU NORD, 32 U. d Linden. Highly patr. by Americans

BERLIN. Hotel "The Reichshof," 70a Wilhelmst., close Unter den Linden, British Embassy and Reichstag. Most elegant home for families Arrangements made. Inclu. terms. L. SCHWARZ, prop

BERLIN PENSION KAHRN. 97 Zimmerstrasse. Fav. American home. (Close Wilhelmstr.

BERLIN. VICTORIA HOTEL. U. d. Linden. Cheapest first-class house.

BERLIN.—WESTMINSTER HOTEL, 17, 18 Unter den Linden. Finest situation. Highest American comforts.

SAVOY HOTEL Newest most accomplished hotel establishment. Latest American comforts. Friedrichstr. Close "Unter den Linden." **BERLIN.**

BREMEN. CENTRAL HOTEL, Only first-class hotel opp. the Station

BONN. GRAND HOTEL ROYAL, First-class Hotel, With Large Garden on the Rhine.

BONN. HOTEL SCHOMBARDT. (Formerly HOTEL BELLEVUE.) Favorite summer residence in finest sit on banks of Rhine. C. SCHOMBARDT, also prop. of the Golden Star Hotel.

CASSEL. HOTEL PRINZ FRIEDRICH WILHELM. Close railway station.

BOARD AND LODGING WITH HIGHLY RESPECTable family; lessons in painting, German and ...

GERMANY.

COLOGNE—DOM HOTEL
First class. Facing the cathedral and station. Rebuilt in latest American style.

COLOGNE HOTEL DU NORD, Facing Cathedral and Railway Station.

COLOGNE. HOTEL ERNST. Nearest the station, opposite the cathedral. Old first class family hotel.

COLOGNE. HOTEL GROSSER KURFURST FIRST-CLASS HOUSE. Facing the Cathedral and railway station.

DRESDEN.—HOTEL DE ROME. Central, comf., quiet, family home.

EMS.—HOTEL D'ANGLETERRE—Finest sit Chief resort of English and Ameri. F. SCHMITT.

FRANCFORT-O. M. THE SWAN HOTEL. Hotel where Bismarck and J. Favre settled the Treaty of Peace 1871.

FRANCFORT S.—M. Hotel Continent... First-class. Electr... Opp. Central Station. Pat. by Amer. and Eng...

FRANCFORT S.—M. Hotel Na... First... Opp. and nearest Central Station. Highly...

FREIBURG (BADEN) HOTEL... First-class Fa... Near the Station. All modern comfor... and terrace. Chiefly frequented by Ame... visitors. F. HA...

HAMBURG. HAMBURG... The newest and...

HAMBUR...
HOTEL DE L'EUROP...
The only English Hotel in ... Recently rebuilt and refurnished. La... English improvements. Magnificent... facing the Alsterbass... Patronised by all Imperial and...

HAMBURG. HAMM... Elegant first-cla... American comforts. Rooms from...

HAMB...
STREIT'S
Oldest first-class hotel of ... looking the Alsterbassin. All... FRITZ SCHULTE, Manager.

HAMBURG. VICT... FIRST-C...

HANNOVER — PENSION... 11 Höltstrasse. Excelle...

HAN...
CONTINENT...
Finest situation. Orig... and refurnished with ever... high and airy rooms, with... Favorite residence of Amer...

HEIDELBERG. HO... Firs...

HOMBURG. VICT... and VILLA'S, HELENA, BEATRICE, with private ... Mountains. Patronized by H... Best stag shooting and tro...

KISSINGEN.

MUNICH. ...

M...
HOTEL
First-class, best p...

MUNICH.—H... Hotel. Hydraulic elevato...

MUNICH. HOTE... railway s...

MUNICH—HOTEL LEINFELDER,

GERMANY.

NURNBERG. Hotel Bayerischerhof. First-class Largely patronised by American...

NURNBERG. Hotel Strauss. 1st-cl. fa... hotel. Elec. light. G. Tod...

NURNBERG. Wurttemberger... 1st-Class AMERICAN... Left hand of the Station.

STUTTGART. HOTEL VICTORIA. New. F... Lift. Electric light. C. Reiniger, pr. Railway...

TRIBERG.—BLACK FORE... SCHWARZWALD Favored residence of Americans. Univer...

TRIBERG (BLACK FORES... 2.300ft. above sea le... Atmosphere rich in OZONE. Wonderful results i... exhaust... mucous membrane ... class famil...

VIENNA. ... First-class and best situ... by English and American visitors.

...48 Chaussée d'Antin

...GE, ELECTRICITY.—M. ORCIER (Diplomé) faubourg Saint Honoré. Daily, 2 to 6. Visits ... morning by appointment.

...E. LACHAPELLE, QUALIFIED MIDWIFE 27, rue Mont Thabor, re...ves patients from 2 to 5 p.m. She may be consulted in cases of disease, sterility, or expected confinement.

RUTH MITCHELL'S
BREAKFAST ROOMS,
26 Avenue de l'Opéra, Paris.
Corn beef hash
Codfish balls
Hominy waffles
Corn bread, doughnuts
Chicken à la crème
Scones, egg noggs
Lemon squash
Strawberry short cake
Cream cod on toast
Coffee or chocolate cakes
Cocoanut cake
Cold slaw and
Every kind of pie

51 Bd. Haussmann, Opp. the "Printemps,"
NEAPOLITAN MANDOLINES, MUSIC.
Lessons at all prices. Pianos to let. English spoken

...er, and ...ntinued re...ception was ...it: Marchesa Onofrio, Donna Passari, Prin... Marchesa Antici-Aquara. ...ake place shortly ...Acqua Santa, ...offered a prize ...iety at the res...el—that is, not ...nows something ...aught sight of ...who looks like ...and Marchesa ...Pecoul, Lady ...Potocka and ...r less smart. ...ced for Easter, ...gin afresh, or, ...ntinued, since ...ng Holy Week. ...Starles of Prussia ...h her suite, and ...de Londres. ...s Schoenfeld are ...u Quirinal. ...lolleurs de West-...same hotel. ...Minister of Hol-...just arrived in ...post was at ...s one of the ...He is stop-...Signor Mar-...tel by Signor ...sa di Rudini's ...ng her numerous ...ontessa Pasolini, ...esa Casati, Com-...sa Orlandini and ...ENCE. ...l at the ...o., Flo-...simir de R. ...: Mr. Dane ...; Miss M. L. ...E. A. Loomis, ...Cleveland; Mr. ...New York; Mrs. ...Smith and Miss ...Mlle. Decombes, ...Gaily, Kansas; Miss ...Mr. Sebastian B. ...James, Boston; ...U.S.A.; the Rev. ...ttile Smith, New ...Baltimore; ...Jackson, U.S.A.; ...and Mr. F. H. ...Higinbotham, New York; Mr. ...Henry Purdy, ...ston.

ANNOUNCEMENTS.

ANNOUNCEMENTS.

AIX-LES-BAINS.
REGINA HOTEL BERNASCO...
The most modern and elegant hotel, in unique situation, with its immense terraces and gard...

CAP MARTIN HOTEL. BETWEEN MENTON & MONTE C... Offering every modern comfort. Finest situa... the Riviera. Electric trams to Menton and ... Carlo; station close to Hotel. Address MAN... CAP MARTIN HOTEL, near MENTON.

CANNES. BEAU-SITE. FIRST-CLA... HOTEL.
Best situation. Nearest Golf course. Famous Tennis Courts and Garde...

CANNES. GRAND HOTEL.
Formerly Manager Grand Hotel Monte Carlo and Gen. Manage... of Savoy and Claridge's Hotels, London. H. Menge, Prop.

MONTE CARLO. HOTEL VICTORIA
Entirely renovated. Suites of apartments with bath room and toilette. Ve. REY, Prop.

CAUX s.-Territet-Montreux Lake of Geneva. **Palace & Grand Hotel.**
Finest and best establishment. Spl. position and view of the Alps. Full South. Heated throughout by steam. Concerts. Grand Balls. Magnificent hall and festival room. Spec. suit. for Amer. & Engl. families.

FLORENCE. Gd. Hotel de la Ville
First class throughout, with every modern comfort. Apartments with private bath rooms. Restaurant Français. AUTENRIETH, Prop.

NAPLES. GRAND EDEN HOTEL
Magnificent garden. Tennis. Steam heating all through. Most central position with splendid view.
Only Hotel with Accommodation for Automobiles.

NAPLES GRAND HOTEL DU VESUVE.
First class. Splendid situation. Apartments and bedrooms with private bathrooms. Latest comfort. STEAM HEATING. O. AND G. FIORENTINO, Props.

ROME. Bertolini's Splendid Hotel.
CORSO UMBERTO I. Modern. 1st class establishment. Largest and finest Italian Restaurant. Select French Restaurant. Open January 1, 1904 A. BERTOLINI & Co.

Varallo Sesia GRAND HOTEL.
(NOVARE, ITALY.)
FIRST-CLASS.
An Alpine health resort about 1,500ft. above sea level. Splendid situation. Beautiful garden and park. Latest comfort. English church and physician. OPEN APRIL 15.

MRS. LANGTRY'S NEW LONDON PLAYHOUSE.

The Imperial to Be Opened To-morrow with a Romantic Drama of the Period Preceding the French Revolution, Entitled "A Royal Necklace"—Peculiarities of the New Place of Amusement.

SCHEME OF DECORATION AND ILLUMINATION.

LONDON, Saturday.—For many years people would not accept Mrs. Langtry, work as she would—and how she did work her intimate friends know only too well—as a serious actress. It was more or less widely conceived in the public mind that she was more of a beautiful woman made to wear lovely dresses, with superb grace, than anything else. They could not realize, especially in England, that this idol of so many London seasons should take up the hard work of the stage, go in for it thoroughly, and become in the truest sense of the word an actress—an artiste.

How surprised those very people would be if they could see Mrs. Langtry, as I have seen her to-day, combining in herself with zeal and energy and capacity the multitudinous duties of chief actress in a specially written historical play, directing on and off the stage, and at the same time taking upon her shoulders all the responsibilities of managership.

Not a Dummy Manager.

Nor is she playing at this managership. Every single detail entailed in her dual part as actress and manageress she attends to herself. But that is not all. It is she who gives the ideas, makes the suggestions, scrutinizes critically the plans of the architect, holds solemn council with the electrical engineer as to the artistic arrangement of the lights, engages the actors and actresses, runs over to Paris to superintend the details of all the costumes, not only her own but those of every woman and man in the piece, talks solid business with her manager and gives instructions everywhere. There is nothing of the dummy manageress or pampered actress about Mrs. Langtry. She is just as exacting, just as much absolute mistress of her own theatre, as her friend Sarah Bernhardt is of hers in Paris.

Mrs. Langtry is looking slim, and I might almost say better than she has ever looked in her life. Hard work and keen interest in what she is doing has made her feel as well as she looks. Her eyes are bright, her body is in fine training, she looks and feels alert. She is radiant!

"When is your new piece coming out?"

"On April 22," replied Mrs. Langtry. "But I must rub wood!" And she began rubbing her palm against the edge of the chair so as to break the spell. Then she resumed:—

"At all events, my contractors have assured me that I may absolutely count upon that date for the first night of 'A Royal Necklace.'"

Mrs. Langtry's new theatre is the Imperial, which some of us who have long memories may remember in olden days as a very poor kind of a theatre. People always wondered why it existed as a theatre. It was too small and too inconvenient. Someone said it would have made a good place for holding prize fights. None ever suggested its fitness for marble with which the inside of the house is lined."

"What are the characteristic peculiarities of the theatre?"

Full of New Ideas.

"It is full of new ideas," replied Mrs. Langtry, "but the boxes, perhaps, are the most remarkable. They go right up to the top of the house—a sort of Napoleonic dais with canopy. The effect is charming!"

"Where did you get such an idea as that?"

"Curious as it may sound, it comes from a theatre in which I played in Toledo, Ohio. I saw such boxes there, and they looked so beautiful that I said to myself that if ever I built a theatre I would have just such boxes. The tops are like the pictures of the canopies of Napoleon's thrones.

"There are but two large boxes. Each has a retiring room, each a private entrance. There are two other boxes in the house, and they are above and behind the dress circle. Over these the most ludicrous mistakes have been published. In making out the plans, I said these should be called the 'morning boxes.' By that I meant they should be for people who were up in town for the day from the country, or for some other reason did not care to dress in evening costume. Well, the country was full of mourning just at that time, and there have been endless paragraphs of a morbid tendency, talking of the strange idea of having 'mourning boxes,' and so forth.

"My stalls have been built with the idea of comfort. They have six inches between them more than those of any other house in London. They are upholstered in buttercup-yellow.

"There are no tableau curtains, but a great drop curtain, like a huge festoon blind of green velvet, but with a very high border on which are embroidered gold sphinxes and swans, very decorative, the eyes represented being made of jewels. This embroidery is of solid gold, and when the curtain goes up it remains visible as an overhead decoration.

"In front of the proscenium, the high altar of the theatre, is a marble pediment with pedestals of chipolene marble on black marble bases. The capitals are formed of large bronze eagles with outspread wings.

Invisible Lighting.

"The lighting of the theatre is invisible. The house is flooded with light in the same way as the House of Commons. In the lighting I have specially thought of the ladies, and the whole light passes through amber, so that there will be a soft golden light throughout the house. Around the dress circle there are handsome bronze torches with amber flame-shades.

"On each side of the proscenium is a large bronze tripod, standing upon a marble pedestal, headed by amber flame-lights. In fact, the whole house is flooded with a golden light, just sufficiently tinted to

MRS. LANGTRY DIVORCED.

She Obtains a Decree in a California Court, Her Husband Not Opposing.

[CENTRAL NEWS CABLEGRAM.]

LAKEPORT, CAL., May 14.—Mrs. Lily Langtry obtained her divorce in the Courts here to-day on the evidence of witnesses from London.

MRS. LANGTRY.

There was no opposition to the suit and Mr. Langtry did not appear.

MRS. LANGTRY'S AMERICAN RESIDENCE.

Mrs. Langtry, on her first visit to California, some years ago leased a cosy cottage on Liberty Heights, at the Mission, in San Francisco, and took up her residence there with a view to becoming a legal resident, in order to obtain a divorce.

BOURSE.

Friday.	Saturday.
102.47	102.47
100.70	100 80
105.40	105 47
23 15	...
89.30	89 40
18.80	19 30
61 50	61.95
105.55	105.75
103.90	104.00
105 00	105.30
101.50	101.90
103.75	103.20
520.00	524.00
563.00	567.00
698 00	706 00
770 00	771.00
3,175 00	3,190.00
512.00	515 00
675 00	677 00
76 00	78 75
357 00	356 00
257.50	255 00

VISITORS IN PARIS.

The following visitors have been registered at the NEW YORK HERALD Office, 49 avenue de l'Opéra :—

Baron, B., of New York ; Grand Hotel.
McCready, R. H., of New York ; Continental.
Hardy, Mrs. F. G., of New York ; 85 rue La Boétie.
Hayslip, Mrs. N. A., of New York ; 85 rue La Boétie.
Monahan, John W., of New York ; Binda.
Perkins, Frederick W., of Chicago ; Binda.
Damson, Edwin, of East Orange ; Hotel Continental.
Grégoire, P. S. and Mrs., of Lowell, Mass. ; Hotel de Bretagne.
James, Mrs. C. P., of Chicago ; 3 square du Roule.
Philbin, Miss, of New York ; Athénée.
Spacks, Mrs. John and Miss M. K., of New York ; Hotel Balzac.
Spain, William J., of New York ; Continental.
Thompson, Fanchon H., of Chicago ; 3 square du Roule.
Adams, Miss M. E., of New York ; Hotel Continental.
Bryan, Miss M. E., of New York.
Cambon, Miss K., of New York ; Continental.
Dickie, Miss Florence M., of New York.
Deacon, W. H., of New York ; Continental.
Ganaon, Mrs. N. S., of New York ; Hotel Continental.
Just, C. and Mrs., of New York ; Continental.
Leazenbee, Mrs. Mary J., of New York.
Lindheim, R., of New York.

VISITORS IN NICE.

The following visitors have been registered at the NEW YORK HERALD Office, 1 place Masséna, Nice :—

Boardman, Rev. Dr. and Mrs., of New York ; Hotel International.

HER STAGE CAREER NIPPED IN THE BUD.

"Miss Ward" Warned that She Must Not Create a Scandal at the Folies-Bergère.

M. LÉPINE'S WISE ADVICE.

The Ex-Princess May Accept an Engagement for the Belle-Alliance in Berlin.

Notwithstanding the publication of Dr. Deschamps' despatch to M. Marchand, manager of the Folies-Bergère, certifying that Miss Clara Ward, ex-Princesse de Caraman-Chimay, is suffering from influenza with complications, the public fail to be convinced that this is the real reason for her non-appearance on the music-hall stage. The fact of the matter is that the Prefect of Police has placed a veto upon her public appearance.

M. Lépine has informed a representative of the *Temps* that the performances at which Miss Ward would have appeared would most certainly have been disorderly.

A WARM RECEPTION PREPARED.

"I know that many people intended to go to the music-hall to protest against the appearance of the ex-princess by whistling and throwing all kinds of objects at her. I could not tolerate such a scandal. I therefore informed M. Marchand that if he gave these performances he did so at his own risk. 'If these disorders occur,' I said to him, 'I shall close your establishment.' This doubtless made M. Marchand reflect.

"There then remained certain questions to be settled between the parties interested, but I can tell you that Miss Ward and M. Marchand are now both free from any engagements they may have made."

According to the *Gaulois*, the ex-princess called upon M. Lépine at six o'clock on Wednesday evening. She was preceded by a quarter of an hour by M. Marchand. Miss Ward was the first to be received. The Prefect of Police pointed out to her the very serious reasons which were against her exhibiting herself in public. As the *débutante* did not appear to see these reasons and made out she had the right to appear on the stage, the Prefect gave her to understand that he did not wish to take any official measure before the performance, but if it was the occasion for a scandal, and he considered this as absolutely certain, he would be under the cruel necessity of closing the music-hall and requesting her to leave France—a step which he begged her not to oblige him to take.

M. LÉPINE GIVES HER ADVICE.

Then M. Lépine laid stress in a friendly, almost paternal way upon certain questions of a private nature. So eloquent and persuasive was he that at half-past six o'clock Miss Ward was convinced. She gave her word there and then not to appear on the stage in Paris.

After leaving M. Lépine's office the ex-princess proceeded to her hotel, where she shortly received a visit from Dr. Deschamps. She had no need to act the part of a sick person in order to explain to the public her decision not to appear at the Folies-Bergère, because she was really unwell. Her medical adviser saw at once that she was suffering from influenza with pulmonary complications and that she was in a feverish state.

Dr. Deschamps gave her the following prescription: "To be taken two or three times a day, two to three dessert spoonfuls of the following mixture, diluted in a glass of decoction of mallow: Acetate of ammoniac, 15gr.; tincture of aconite, 20 drops; sirop of codeine, 100gr; orange-flower water, 40gr."

Miss Ward has not yet decided whether she will remain in Paris or return to Berlin, where she has received the offer of a brilliant engagement from the Belle-Alliance, one of the leading music-halls there.

Though the ex-princess will not be seen at the Folies-Bergère there is every probability that photographs representing her in the scanty costume made specially for her *début* by the Maison Landolf will shortly be sold upon the boulevards. The *Gaulois* states that she was yesterday to sit for her portrait at the studio of one of the large Paris photographers.

THE PRINCESSE DE CHIMAY.

ALD.

; LONDON, 2d.; DEPARTMENTS, 20c.

DUCHESSE DE SAGAN'S FÊTE.

Talleyrand-et-Sagan Mansion Opens To-morrow and Wednesday in the Cause of Charity.

RARE TREAT FOR THE PUBLIC.

Brilliant Matinee Under Royal Patronage and a Rich and Varied Programme.

If the sun will only shine. . . .

Yes, that is all that is needed. If the sun will only be kind to-morrow afternoon and on Wednesday, the fête to be given in the stately Talleyrand-et-Sagan mansion, in the rue Saint-Dominique—modestly numbered 57, though the "porte cochère" itself is as big as a good-sized house—is infallibly one of the most successful social functions of the season.

All Paris knows the residence of the Duchesse de Talleyrand-et-Sagan.

It is there that some of the most brilliant entertainments of these latter years have been given. It is there that the Prince and Princess of Wales were the guests of honor at one of the duchesse's receptions. It is there that a magnificent ball was given for the Duchesse d'Aoste.

Every Parisian knows these things, knows that the monumental building was erected in the first quarter of the present century by the Dutch banker, Mr. Hope, who spent something like six million francs upon it—an enormous sum, considering the greater purchasing value of money at that period.

THE TWENTIETH PARIS DOG SHOW.

Twelve Hundred Entries at the Great Exhibition Which Will Open To-day.

IN THE TUILERIES GARDENS

Twenty-four Packs of Hounds of Various Breeds in the Kennels.

FINE ENGLISH BLOODHOUNDS

The Finest Collection Both for Number and Quality Ever Seen in France.

THE ARRANGEMENTS UNEQUALLED.

Remarkable Exhibition of Sporting Pictures by Eminent French Artists.

JUDGING TAKES PLACE TO-DAY.

Like the prologue to some engrossing spectacle the Twentieth Exposition Canine opened yesterday.

It was really but the prologue. Not until to-day does the serious interest of the exhibition begin. A mass of details have to be disposed of always before the real opening. Yesterday only saw the "kings of the kennel" received, inspected, approved and installed in the quarters to be their homes until Tuesday. To-day the juries begin the work of adjudging the awards; to-day all the animals will have arrived; to-day, then, the exposition will be fairly launched.

Kings they were, indeed, some of the superb creatures that ran the gauntlet of the examining committee yesterday.

Oh, that committee! Veterinary surgeons whose eyes no beauty of form could close to defective characteristics! But majestic St. Bernards and Newfoundlands, impertinent fox-terriers, full of "devilment" . . . and bark; forbidding bulldogs, animals you may not love but whom you feel forced to respect; graceful profiled collies with their look of supernatural intelligence; toy spaniels that made you long to pet them; Bordeaux dogs with their look of careworn indifference, gentle-eyed bloodhounds, filed past all day long, beginning at half-past eight and continuing until dusk.

And all day long the din increased!

All day long the Terrasse de l'Orangerie du Jardin des Tuileries resounded with the music of dogs giving tongue. At times it swelled to a mighty chorus with the deep baying of hounds and the shrill yapping of fox-terriers as bass and soprano; then it would sink to the fretful solo of some whimpering pet, while, all the time, the *cors de chasse* sounded their most inspiring *fanfares.*

A BRILLIANT OPENING.

But the quasi-opening, it is true, and yet what a success! Seven hundred and forty harriers and bloodhounds have been sent to this year's exposition. These belong to the Marquis de Lespinay, M. A. de Bégarry, M. Edmond Maurice, Dr. Caillot, the Marquis de Lestrade, Comte de Maleissye, who has a pack of twelve Norman crossbreds, among whom are some superb animals; as well as a pack of twenty English foxhounds; M. Henri Penin, and Mr. Hubert Courteney, who sends a pack of eight bloodhounds, beauties, in their ranks being the great Rollick, winner of forty first and second prizes since 1892, among them being prizes won in Liverpool, at the Agricultural Hall, London; Edinburgh, Cambridge, Manchester, Glasgow, Dublin and most of the big English cities. He is indeed a magnificent brute, with a dewlap half a foot long, a deeply corrugated front, and as solidly set up on his legs as a colossus. In the same pack is his perhaps greater son Rameses. He is only two years old the 28th of this month, and is already the holder of nine first prizes and *prix d'honneur*, having borne off four this very year.

SCENES AT THE PARIS DOG SHOW.

M. Le Coulteulx de Caumont has on exhibition a pack of ten English foxhounds. MM. Daniel and Marcel Haentjens have a pack of fifteen very handsome beagles, while M. Arillard has a pack of twelve of the same breed, and M. Camille Breton also sends a pack of eight.

Then there are packs of bassets and briquets and griffons. No wonder the old arrangements of the society were found inadequate. Consequently everything has been renewed. The packs are now housed in big, roomy, pine-wood kennels, railed round on three sides, so that they can be closely inspected; the toy dogs have been supplied with raised cages, cosily fitted up and curtained off so as to protect the delicate pets from draught, and the other dogs have comfortably constructed compartments in which they seemed to quickly find themselves at home.

ARRIVAL OF THE DOGS.

It was half-past eight when the dogs [illegible] facing the place de la Concorde, the Blenheims and Skyes on the same line, but further to the north, while the St. Bernards, Newfoundlands, setters, &c., are in the long-covered gallery running parallel to the quai des Tuileries. The arrangement is very convenient. The dogs can easily be compared with others of the same breed and it would perhaps have been impossible to place them in a better order.

In the early morning but few people were present—naturally, as the exposition only really opened at four o'clock. Of course the Prince de Wagram, the enthusiastic president of the society, was one of the first to arrive. And later, among the members of the committee to put in an appearance, beside Comte G. de Torcy, the honorary vice-president; Vicomte de Montsaulnin, and M. Léon d'Halloy, vice-presidents, were: Vicomte d'Auchald, Comte Geoffroy d'Andigné, Comte A. de Bagneux, Comte René de Beaumont—who exhibits, by the way, in the picture exhibition a spirited and well painted "Hallali!" in water-colors, the subject being treated in a manner full of life and action—General de Biré, M. Paul Caillard, Baron de Carayon-Latour, Comte de Danal, Comte d'Elva, M. Fessart, the Duc de Gramont, the Marquis de L'Aigle, the Duc [illegible]

factory kind if it is true that in muc[h] counsel lieth wisdom. Each group of dog[s] has some half-dozen judges, all connoisseur[s] of accepted authority, to decide upon th[e] awards.

For the house and sheep dogs, includin[g] the St. Bernard and Newfoundland, th[e] judges are M. Emmanuel Boulet, M. A Touchard, M. H. Ménous de Corre, Mr. Joh[n] Proctor, M. de Boiville and Mr. George R Krehl, the editor of the *Stock-keeper*, a[n] authority upon dogs whose word carrie[s] convincing weight, and a man with th[e] pedigree of every famous horse and do[g] at his tongue's end. I may say that M[r.] Krehl has offered two prizes of 125fr. eac[h] to be awarded: to the finest French pet o[r] house dog of a French owner, and for th[e] finest setter or pointer either of French o[r] English breed, but also of French ownership.

The judges in the second class, viz terriers used in hunting, are: Mr. Kreh[l] and Mr. Proctor. French hounds will b[e] judged by Comte G. de Montesquieu, M Ballu de Passay, M. Paul de Rozier, M Raoul Treuilles and Comte Elie de Vézins while the crossbred hounds will be adjudicated on by Comte d'Andigné, M. G. de l[a] Chapelle, M. G. Chevallereau, Vicomte d[e] [illegible]

achts; Comte de ... e Montsaulnin, Mme. A. ... Vicomtesse de Dam... omtesse de Martel, Vicomtesse de Dam... ierre, Marquis de Roger, Mme. de Sousy,

INTERESTED AND INTERESTING VISITORS.

d by an 800

rning out some the Electromo- ous garage is ntaigne, also Champs-Ely- lso at Leval- ructs exceed- ughams, the o open car- letting-out sily able to radius of es around

writer had pany, the there is a ric carriage l improve- in the bat- ually becom- ce developed chanism, too, week or so I a new inven- ng out, and n not only in plosion motor

ng daily. We ges at prices and 17,000fr., to Prince de , Comte de sey, Comte sul-General; York; Mr. M. Fernand M. Blumen- a; M. José E. Fischhof, Penha, M. Mme. Mar- nau-Varilla, and Duc de

n we have at ist—the price per month, in- he driver—are M. de Lagrave, , Mme. Wibaux, aurice Bunau-Va- e de Montsaulnin, Dr. Doyen, Comte J. B. Thompson, Porgès, Princesse Comte de Lévis- ejeune. n day and night, eeping vehicles is price of electricity t. Quite a num- eople keep their , among them be- M. Ph. de Bunau- M. E. Fischhof, Kirschein, M. ne and Mme.

establishments in their own country.

For your information, circular letters of credit, which we issue here to our clients, give the facility of cashing them

credit companies not in relations with them cannot be aware.

On the other hand, you may be sure if Americans have experienced difficulty in

the questio... direct tax... promise on... following

A. Com... comprise (... reduction ... remission ... discharge ... dressed to ... three mon... schedules, ... double ass... pires at th... time when ... notificatio... the receive... disputed. ... for modera... unforeseen ... in a fortn... events in ... cated are r...

B. Dema... tion, if th... or above ... stamped p... the appli... founded, ... persons co... to mentio... penalty o... amount of ... or, in the ... from the ... article in ... tribution" ... the claim ... the reason ... based mus...

C. I ma... duction m... or formal... clarations. ... ceived at ... ment in w... is issued, ... the public ... after a su... is not im... grounded, ... who is al... make his ... form. As ... "réclamati... payers mu... in support...

D. The ... deliver on... inscribed ... to his "con... from the ... cost of eac... ing the s... When the ... extract is ... ceivers fo... as many ... contributi...

E. In ... indicate ... in matter... moment I...

THE COMING DOG.

Mr. St. Loe Strachey, in his interesting introduction to *Dog Stories*, a collection republished from the *Spectator*, gives as his opinion that the inference to be drawn from some of these stories is that "it becomes very difficult to doubt that dogs may learn the first principles of the science of language." One dog story proves nothing, but the following gives scope for deductions: "The Italian dog, which did the narrator a service by fetching him cigars, demanded payment in the shape of a penny, and then used that penny by exchanging it for a loaf, was far advanced in the practice of political economy. He not only understood and acted on an implied, but realized the great fact at the back of currency. 'What are guineas,' said Horne Tooke, 'but tickets for sheep and oxen?' The Italian dog did not, like a savage, say, 'What is the use of copper to me, I cannot eat it?' Instead, he perceived that the piece of copper was a ticket for bread. . . . Again, the Glasgow story shows that a dog can learn to realize that a halfpenny will buy not merely one thing but several things—in fact, that the great advantage of exchange by currency over barter is that it gives you a choice."

Then Mr. Strachey becomes prophetic. How little more is wanted to convert a dog capable of thus much reasoning into a free agent! "If a dog can exchange his faculty for cigar-carrying or his tricks against halfpence, why should he not exchange useful services, such as guarding a house or herding sheep, and so become self-supporting? Imagine a collie paid by the day, and, when his work was over, receiving twopence and going off to buy his supper! But the vista opened is too far-reaching. One sees down it dogs paid by the hour and by the piece, and then dogs asking for better pay and shorter hours, and, finally, dogs on strike and dog 'blacklegs' or free dogs."

When that day comes why not provide the canine world with a new religion and a new set of commandments, beginning "Thou shalt not strike"?—*Daily Graphic.*

Dainty Toilettes for Dogs.

HOW DOGS ARE BEING DRESSED THIS YEAR.

(From the London "Daily Mail.")

"Lucky dog" is an expression which might well be applied to the animal of to-day, if indeed its wealth of possession is appreciated by the canine owner. The latest innovation this season is a collar made of soft glove kid. This is seen in a variety of colors scarlet, palest gray, tan, or mauve; but a very delicate shade of turquoise blue, which makes a charming contrast to the white or tawny silky coats of the small wearers, is the most popular shade.

A quaint notion, now all the rage, is an exact imitation of a man's linen stand-up collar with a little bow tie, all made in celluloid. The collars are somewhat Christy Minstrel in style, and are generally striped blue, white, or red and white with ties to match the color.

The coat, or rather the coats, are an important consideration. In Paris these coats are this year generally bordered with the fashionable dull gold or silver galon, and are frequently made of material to match the dress of the dog's mistress. Many ladies take a delight in making these small canine garments themselves, and put the finest stitchery into them. They are wadded and lined with the soft silk, and invariably possess a tiny patch pocket, put on either close to the shoulder or to one side of the back. From this protrudes a diminutive handkerchief of cambric, edged with lace or daintily hemstitched.

The fashionable boot is a high Wellington affair, made of india-rubber and laced up the back. This idea really is practical, and appeals to most dog owners during bad weather. Another kind of boot is like a miniature sponge bag, or one of those little sachets for a powder-puff, and a funny sight is a group of little dogs all with their paws tied up in these.

Even that weapon of chastisement, the whip, is made into a thing of beauty, with a handle of carved horn or of chased gold or silver.

PASSING BEFORE THE COMMITTEE.

HIS DOG DIED OF "ENNUI."

M. Vaughan, the manager of the *Intransigeant*, was sentenced to a fine of 5fr. on Saturday by the Eleventh Chamber of the Correctional Court for having infringed the sanitary laws regarding animals in not taking immediately to the Institut Pasteur his dog, which a servant had stated was mad.

M. Vaughan's defence was curious. "My dog," he said, "died at the Institut Pasteur, not of rabies, but of *ennui*. The poor animal has been the victim of a judicial error."

M. ... by the ... ment ... of De... the A... by Mr...

M. ... after ... object... tion w... by M... client

DE ROTHSCHILD'S NEW STEAM YACHT ATMAH.

NEW PALATIAL STEAM YACHT.

The Atmah, Just Built for Baron Edmond de Rothschild, Makes Her Trials on the Clyde.

LARGEST YACHT IN EUROPE.

Interior Chiefly Designed by the Owner—The Hull by Mr. G. L. Watson.

The trial trips of the steam yacht Atmah, which has just been built for Baron Edmond de Rothschild by the Fairfield Shipbuilding Company, were conducted on the Clyde on Wednesday and Thursday last.

The Atmah is the largest private yacht in European waters, and is only exceeded in dimensions by some two American yachts—Mr. Vanderbilt's Valiant and Mr. Robert Goelet's Nahma.

The leading dimensions of the Atmah are as follows: Length on load water line, 280ft.; extreme breadth, 34ft. 2in.; depth, moulded, 21ft. 3in.; tonnage, Thames measurement, 1,650 tons.

She is propelled by two sets of triple expansion engines, each having four cylinders, of a respective diameter of 20½in., 34in., and two, each of 37in., by a common stroke of 27in. Steam is supplied at 160lb. by two return tube boilers.

SEVERAL NOVEL FEATURES.

The Atmah presents several novel features in design and arrangement, having been planned in a large measure by her owner. Mr. G. L. Watson is generally ... wide form, though modified

THE OWNER'S APARTMENTS.

The engines and boilers occupy the middle of the ship, and immediately forward of these are the owner's own apartments. These consist of a spacious deck sleeping cabin, with bath-room and lavatory opening from the same, while the stateroom opens into a large deck saloon, occupying the entire fore end of the deckhouse, and from the after end of it the main staircase leads down to the apartments on the cabin deck.

These apartments consist of a drawing-room, occupying the whole width of the ship; of a stateroom for the baron and baroness, from which open lavatories and bath-rooms.

The fore end of the vessel is devoted to staterooms, of which there are five, for guests. All of the rooms are large and airy, while forward of these again is very generous accommodation for servants. In the extreme fore end are the stewards and cooks.

On the main deck, and under a raised forecastle, are rooms for the carpenter, boatswain and quartermasters, a hospital for any sick hands, and a bakery for baking bread, with the usual lamp rooms and other offices.

THE YACHT'S TRIALS.

On Wednesday morning the Atmah proceeded down the river from the builder's yard, and at Gourock picked up a small party of those more immediately interested in the trials.

A preliminary run was made down the ... and afterwards the coal trials were ... tinuing all through Wed... strike of the ...

KING LEOPOLD BUYS THE MARGARITA.

Mr. A. J. Drexel's Yacht Personally Inspected by His Majesty Before the Purchase Was Made.

[BY THE HERALD'S SPECIAL WIRE.]

LONDON, Monday.—Mr. A. J. Drexel has sold his yacht the Margarita.

The ostensible purchaser was Williamson Johnston, of this city, but the yacht was bought, it is hinted, for the King of the Belgians.

His Majesty personally inspected the boat, and all the trials were carried on under the direct supervision of the Belgian Minister of Marine.

The Margarita will be known as the Alberta in future. The price paid was £70,000.

It is said Mr. Drexel intends to build a new vessel to replace the Margarita, of somewhat larger dimensions and of greater speed.

DIEPPE REGATTA.

... Programme Drawn Up By ... Voile de Dieppe.

ALD'S
DVICE.

Letters of
Cover All
tany.

ECT TAXES.

Those Who
mplaints as
utions."

ERALD:—
," in the HERALD,
.)
te the following
ittany, and has
ricans:—
to Americans,
he offices of the
Bank of France,
etc. But there
etters of credit
these establish-
n only be cashed
n those letters.
of them are dis-
they present the
es of the banks,
cause the letters
ere or Morbihan.
be able to get
Quimper, Lori-
en compelled
urs

Most Powerful Racing Machine Built in America.

NEW AMERICAN 100 H. P. RACER.

(From the NEW YORK HERALD.)

What is regarded as the most powerful racing automobile ever constructed in the United States has been completed for and delivered to the Central Automobile Company, of New York. It is an eight-cylinder machine of 100 horse-power under brake test, but capable of much higher development. In appearance it is not unlike the Winton Bullets, though it is longer of base, of lower build and of greater apparent power.

It has direct drive, spiral spring suspension, radiator and double pan cooler, four carburators and eight spark plugs. The wheel base is 120in. and the length over all 13ft. The machine weighs 2,600 pounds and escapes the ground by only six inches. It was constructed in the shops of the Buffum Manufacturing Company, at Abington, Mass.

The huge racer will be entered in all open competitions on road or track and in all time trials to which it is eligible in the Eastern States. It will be driven by Lafayette Markle for the Central Company. Though not entered for a place on the American team in the International Cup race, it may be placed at the disposal of the Automobile Club of America should that be desired. Though no actual test of its speed has yet been made, it is expected it will be capable of a rate of nearly ninety miles an hour on a straightaway course. It is to be named the Central Greyhound.

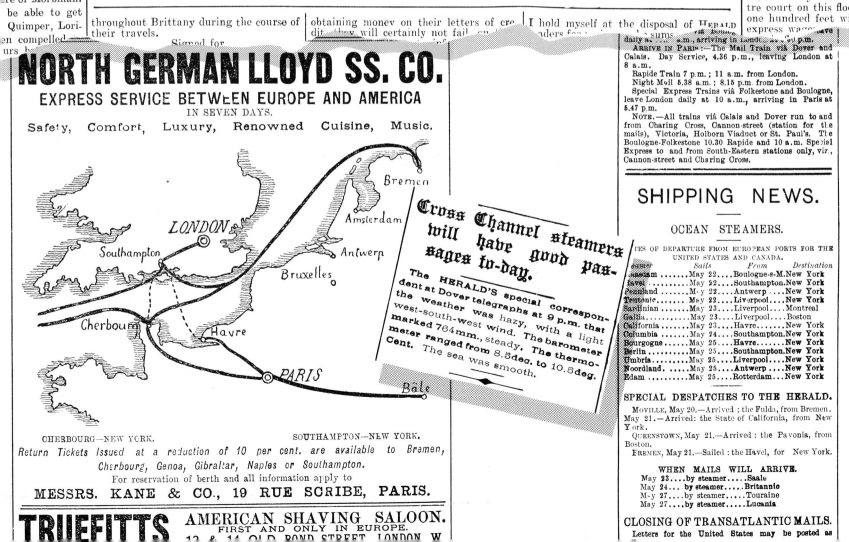

throughout Brittany during the course of their travels.

Signed for

obtaining money on their letters of credit they will certainly not fail

I hold myself at the disposal of HERALD readers

third street and a res
Madison avenue. New
awarded the contract fo
work to be done on the
minal of the New York
on the site of the pres
Station, in Forty-secon

Mr. Warren will wo
with Reed and Stem, a
at No. 5 East Forty-sec
will have personal and c
artistic features of t
which, if the promise
one of the greatest ar
structures of its kind

Mr. Warren was fortu
award, because several
firms entered the conte
were McKim, Mead and
Burnham and Co., of N
Samuel Heckel, Jr., of
plans submitted by Re
Mr. Warren were appro
of the railroad company
in charge. Mr. Warren
he could not yet give o
of the work he propose
road officials were also

In general, however,
made indicate that in
ture and in accommoda
tion will probably be
the great buildings no
but of Europe as well.
stories high. All offic
lunch and baggage roo
from the ground floor,
voted to the tracks,
feet below the street

The second floor is
the north end at grad
fifth street viaduct an
which is to come down
the railroad yards. A
tre court on this floor
one hundred feet wide
express wagons

Cross Channel steamers will have good passages to-day.

The HERALD'S special correspondent at Dover telegraphs at 9 p.m. that the weather was hazy, with a light west-south-west wind. The barometer marked 764mm., steady. The thermometer ranged from 8.5deg. to 10.5deg. Cent. The sea was smooth.

daily at ... a.m., arriving in London ... p.m.

ARRIVE IN PARIS:—The Mail Train viâ Dover and Calais. Day Service, 4.36 p.m., leaving London at 8 a.m.

Rapide Train 7 p.m.; 11 a.m. from London.

Night Mail 5.38 a.m.; 8.15 p.m. from London.

Special Express Trains viâ Folkestone and Boulogne, leave London daily at 10 a.m., arriving in Paris at 5.47 p.m.

NOTE.—All trains viâ Calais and Dover run to and from Charing Cross, Cannon-street (station for the mails), Victoria, Holborn Viaduct or St. Paul's. The Boulogne-Folkestone 10.30 Rapide and 10 a.m. Special Express to and from South-Eastern stations only, viz., Cannon-street and Charing Cross.

SHIPPING NEWS.

OCEAN STEAMERS.

(DA)TES OF DEPARTURE FROM EUROPEAN PORTS FOR THE UNITED STATES AND CANADA.

Steamer	Sails	From	Destination
Rhaetia	May 22	Boulogne-s-M.	New York
Havel	May 22	Southampton.	New York
Zeeland	May 22	Antwerp	New York
Teutonic	May 22	Liverpool	New York
Sardinian	May 23	Liverpool	Montreal
Gallia	May 23	Liverpool	Boston
California	May 23	Havre	New York
Columbia	May 24	Southampton.	New York
Bourgogne	May 25	Havre	New York
Berlin	May 25	Southampton.	New York
Umbria	May 25	Liverpool	New York
Noordland	May 25	Antwerp	New York
Edam	May 25	Rotterdam	New York

SPECIAL DESPATCHES TO THE HERALD.

MOVILLE, May 20.—Arrived; the Fulda, from Bremen. May 21.—Arrived: the State of California, from New York.

QUEENSTOWN, May 21.—Arrived: the Pavonia, from Boston.

BREMEN, May 21.—Sailed: the Havel, for New York.

WHEN MAILS WILL ARRIVE.

May 23....by steamer.....Saale
May 24....by steamer.....Britannic
May 27....by steamer.....Touraine
May 27....by steamer.....Lucania

CLOSING OF TRANSATLANTIC MAILS.

Letters for the United States may be posted as

THE NEW YORK HERALD.

COMPLETE NUMBER 12 PAGES. EUROPEAN EDITION—PARIS, SATURDAY, APRIL 16, 1904. COMPLETE NUMBER 12 PAGES.

4 Fashion

IF WE THINK FASHION IS IMPORTANT TODAY, it hardly compares to what went on during the Belle Epoque. In 1901, 60,000 people were engaged in the dressmaking trade in Paris. They worked for 2,500 firms (as against 223 in 1850), of which 200 were of real importance. The annual turnover was 250 million francs. The glove industry alone employed 70,000 people in 1906, and in 1911, 300 million birds a year were killed in the interest of fashion. A grim figure which, even in those insouciant days, made ecologists begin to worry.

Fashion was a ritual. The *Herald* commented in 1903 that "In past days, no woman would have been ashamed to wear a dress a second year or last year's hat. Nowadays, they won't wear them more than three or four times."

Society women changed at least four times a day and traveled with a maid and several trunks. The maid was essential to arrange Madame's voluminous hair – combining several handy postiches, such as "Pouf Printania" and "Pouf Imperial" (available at chic hairdressers like Autard at 30 francs apiece) – or handing her a peignoir when she stepped out of the sea in a white mohair, black-braid trimmed bathing costume as well as hat, shoes and stockings. For even going to the beach was a fashion event, with every accessory, including hats and stockings, especially designed.

In 1906, seventeen trunks were not considered excessive when traveling, what with morning toilettes, tennis toilettes, afternoon toilettes for visits or excursions, dinner toilettes, theater, concert or soirée toilettes – not to speak of indoor robes of varying degrees of elegance, plus hats, parasols, ruches and boas, fans, gloves and shoes of all kinds.

So furious was women's love for fashion that in 1908 they could not resist the hobble skirt, even if they had to be lifted by their escorts into their autos – a fact that left the American Ladies Tailors' Association "stricken," and unanimously determined that such a fashion would not find favor in America.

The "Daily Life of the Paris Woman of Fashion" was rigidly Proustian, with daily outings in the Bois – riding, driving or on foot – a 2 o'clock so-called "breakfast," followed by dressmaker, milliner and such, ending with tea at some fashionable resort between 4 and 5. Then, from 5 to 7, calls to make or receive. After that, dinner in town followed by a theater or soirée.

The two high points of the Parisienne's day were the promenade in the Bois and the tea hour, the latter imported from England and a great success, as was everything with a British accent.

The Bois was a sort of social parade ground, and in summer the Bagatelle Polo Ground was a charming place for fashionable gatherings. Society women met, admired, criticized and gossiped amid perfect surroundings and had tea to the strains of a melodious orchestra.

The tea hour had started at home, but then went public. By 1905 various tea rooms had opened, and this coincided with women's desire to get out of the house. But before that, in January 1903, "the home month par excellence," the *Herald* described a classic tea party as known in France, with dainty and varied tea services, tea tables adorned like altars, profuse floral decorations, lights skillfully arranged to set off the dresses of the callers, seats well grouped to facilitate conversation.

The "toilettes de reception" were borrowed from the 18th-century Watteau style with ivory muslin, velvet and brocade insertions of Alençon lace. The "pretty gourmandes" ate "enticing chatteries" (sweets) of French cookery – cakes, bonbons, glazed fruit, almond paste, custards, meringues, and dainty sandwiches of foie gras and jam. Around that time, pictures of women at the races began to appear more frequently in the *Herald*, and the result of all these "chatteries" was, unfortunately, an undeniable dumpiness.

New tea rooms, with such exquisitely vintage names as Colombin, Rumpelmayer and the Elysée Palace, seemed to be opening every week in 1905. The Ritz, another elegant landmark, is still with us. Everybody drank tea, or pretended to. Between two fittings, two visits, you saw exquisite toilettes, furs from all over and daytime jewels. Daytime jewels made a distinct difference between society women and demi-mondaines. A "Vieux Parisien" once told the *Herald*: "It is a mistake for a woman of the world to wear even a plain row of pearls in the daytime as many demi-mondaines do."

Haute couture

The *Herald* described in detail the beginnings of a unique phenomenon, the Paris "Grande Couture" (or today's Haute Couture) and its founding fathers, Worth, Paquin, Doucet, Redfern, *et al.*

There was no romanticizing in those days. Fashion houses, located on the rue de la Paix, were bluntly called "Dressmaking Establishments" and the men who ran them were, quite plainly, tailors and dressmakers.

From 1901 till 1914, the *Herald* ran fashion supplements at least twice a month, and specially lavish ones appeared for Christmas and Easter. These were beautifully illustrated by notable artists of the day, mostly sketches at first, then photographs by the likes of Nadar and Reutlinger.

Some of the art came from the couturiers themselves, who were fully aware of the *Herald*'s affluent clientele.

Then as now, Paris always welcomed and assimilated foreign talent, which partly accounts for its strength. This century's fashion has been shaped by, among others, a Spaniard, Cristobal Balenciaga, two Italians, Pierre Cardin and Elsa Schiaparelli, a German, Karl Lagerfeld, and a Japanese, Kenzo Takada. They are all the successors of an illustrious Englishman, Gaston Worth, who can be credited with starting the whole magic world of Paris couture.

The son of an impoverished solicitor, Worth went to work at 13 as an apprentice at the Edgar and Swan emporium in London. Seven years later he went to Paris where he worked for Gagelin, a firm famous for silks. He stayed there twelve years.

At this time, there was no fashion house in Paris that both made and sold material, the *Herald* noted, unknowingly pinpointing the debut of couture; this combining of the two branches struck Worth as a good idea. Having obtained permission from his principals to try it, he began with cloaks, and a train that he designed gained a medal in 1855.

When the firm later refused him a partnership, Worth opened his own house, employing fifty people. At his death, in 1895, which was recorded as "The Biggest News of the Day," Worth employed 1,200 people turning out between 6,000 or 7,000 dresses and from 2,000 to 4,000 cloaks every year.

Worth prided himself on the fact that his house set no overall trends "because my clientele looks for individual 'toilettes,'" and that he was quite expensive. "We make a lot of Court dresses and are working right now on a dress for the next Drawing Room – entirely made of Argentan lace, and the lace alone is worth 25,000 francs," he once told the *Herald*.

He influenced jewelry through his son-in-law, Louis Cartier, the artistic director of the firm whose name has become legend. In a 1904 interview, Cartier credited Worth with "giving me excellent advice and helping me visualize jewels as ornaments. My great preoccupation," Cartier said, "is to find the becoming side of jewels, and I must say that in this respect, I have been aptly advised by my father-in-law, M. Worth."

Another fashion legend, Paul Poiret, also filled a good number of *Herald* columns. On March 22, 1904, the paper ran its first Poiret interview, in which the flamboyant designer described lavishly embroidered mandarin's coats, which seemed to herald the Ballets Russes, with whom Poiret's clothes later became so strongly identified.

In another interview, Poiret talked about America and American women. In 1913, just after his first trip across the Atlantic to give several lectures on "La Mode Feminine," Poiret noted that the "women of America dress too soberly." Then as today, couturiers traveled a great deal, and in three weeks Poiret visited seven major cities.

Though he found American men stern and "devoid of fancy," he described the American woman as "charming, but she should prove it. She reappears in my memory dressed in black satin, with a black velvet hat.

This extreme sobriety in dress betrays the influence of the clergy. Even in the street, all the crowd is serious. Each one runs to his business without looking out for other distraction. But all that is unimportant, as the country is the most curious, novel and attractive of all the countries I have seen. I shall go back."

Other designers such as Redfern, Paquin, Martial et Armand were also mentioned in the *Herald* at regular intervals. But Chanel, who started her career around the same time, is remarkably absent, except for one puzzling *Herald* story. On November 19, 1905, the paper ran a page about furs – nothing much, just a series of paragraphs describing several houses, including one by the name of Chanel.

This is all the more intriguing as practically every biography of Chanel has her starting her career with a hat shop in Deauville around 1912, by courtesy of her lover 'Boy Capel.' But in the *Herald*, a good seven years earlier, there is a short report which reads: "At Chanel's, quantities of pretty fantasies, lots of mixed furs, otter and ermine, breitschwanz and ermine etc. Muffs are still flat and soft."

The last sentence, "They must accompany the movement of the woman without hindering her in any way," sounds so familiar that it might have been a direct quote from the famous fashion liberator, the great Coco herself.

At that period there were no fashion shows as we know them today, with collections paraded the year around on live mannequins. How did women know what was in fashion? They depended on a few specialized magazines, such as *Femina*, *Chiffons*, and *L'Art et la Mode*. But the theater, where actresses were only too happy to promote the latest styles from Paris couturiers, was a major source of information.

"Each new play awakens the curiosity of all smart women," the *Herald* wrote in 1905. "After the first question – 'Is it good?' – one asks: 'Are the dresses pretty?'" Or, in the words of Worth, who created for Eleonora Duse "manteaux de chambre" that were later used by elegant women as indoor coats: "The theater is one of the most active agents in the propagation of fashion. By her personal charm, a popular and graceful actress may contribute to the adoption of an ordinary idea."

Paquin, who triumphed with a dress in the Directoire style, was the dressmaker whose creations caused the greatest sensation. He gave the keynote to fashion. "In fact," the *Herald* noted, "one cannot go to a couturier of second importance without being told, 'This is a Paquin model.'"

Well aware of his fame, the designer once told the *Herald*: "One makes fake Paquins as one makes fake Old Masters' paintings."

Actresses were not bashful about advertising perfumes as well, and (in a 1902 supplement) both Sarah Bernhardt and Jane Hading often sang the praises of Lenthéric's perfumes.

Aside from famous actresses, women also took their cue from royal figures whose likes and dislikes in fashion were as important as royal verdicts. If Edward VII was a sartorial dandy, his wife – the stately, swan-necked Queen Alexandra – was no less an influence. She reportedly set the vogue for choker necklaces, as confirmed in a 1903 story reporting that in London, instead of wearing pearls or diamonds around the neck, some of the smartest women were wearing a very narrow band of black velvet from which hung the most beautiful pearls and diamonds.

Redfern, who catered to every court in Europe, claimed that Alexandra also influenced the "Tailor Mades" – or today's tailored suit – which were perceived as a sign of woman's emancipation, one result of the invention of the steam engine, the bicycle and electricity. In 1901, he declared: "Twenty years ago we opened our Paris house, and from that date, the Redfern 'Tailor Mades' have been the talk of the town. Her Gracious Majesty, when she was Princess of Wales, started the fashion of what are now called 'tailor-mades,' her splendid figure showing a good fit to perfection."

Unlike Queen Victoria, Alexandra had a great objection to "crape," and was given the credit for lightening up mourning, which, in 1904, was not so severe as it had been fifteen or twenty years before.

Society women also eagerly eyed and copied each other. In Paris, the "toilettes" of the eminently elegant Comtesse Greffulhe were constantly in the news. When her daughter married the Duc de Guiche at the Madeleine, the Comtesse wore a 72-pound dress of gold and silver, with a long train edged with sable, and a big brown tulle hat circled with paradise feathers. Gabriel Fauré was at the organ, playing a "Tantum Ergo" he had composed for the occasion and dedicated to the Comtesse. Among the wedding gifts were three rows of large diamonds from the mother of the bride and a fan, painted by the Comte de Montesquiou.

In London, Lady Algernon Gordon was designated the best-dressed woman by the *Herald*, which noted in 1901 that she was the first woman to have appeared in London with her hair "waved."

Although the demi-mondaines played an important part in Belle Epoque fashions, there is remarkably little written about them, and what there is comes out in a discreet filigree. Actually, the demi-mondaines' display of jewelry was blatantly extravagant. Otero thought nothing of wearing an entire stomacher of diamonds and emeralds as well as "the most magnificent sable coat I have ever beheld and which must be worth 2,000 pounds if a penny," the *Herald*'s reporter wrote in 1895. The costume included a toque "which seems nearly half a yard across the front, composed of large pink and red poppies, white chiffon and jet beetles' wings."

Women seemed to run into all kinds of trouble paying their bills, if indeed they paid at all. Judging from the *Herald*'s matter-of-fact reporting, this was a light offence which society took in its indulgent stride – the way we would regard a traffic ticket today. So it did not matter that the offenders were quite famous figures and that, after Feydeau-like rows, Sarah Bernhardt, La Belle Otero and other actresses ended up in court over unpaid dressmakers' bills.

Liane de Pougy was sued by the department store Bon Marché in 1900 for an alleged debt of 858 francs for articles supplied to her in 1889. Otero was worse. "She is as well-known at the Palais de Justice as she is at the Folies Bergère," the *Herald* noted. "A few days ago, she was sued by her groom and yesterday by her milliner." The original price of a magnificent white dress embroidered with waterlilies and yokes in silver, and in which she hoped to win First Prize at the annual carnival, was 3,565 francs.

There was no end of haggling. In 1900, Otero had her dressmaker's bill reduced by 500 francs by a Paris court. Another time, she questioned a lace bill from a tradesman by the name of Capdeville. Declaring his charges "extortionate," Otero paid as much of the bill as she thought reasonable, and informed the merchant that he would have to wait for the rest. He wrote back insulting letters, threatening to jump into her carriage; and indeed he accosted Otero in the enclosure at Longchamp race course on Grand Prix day, demanding payment of his bill. Otero told him to send his wife to see her the next day. Capdeville and his wife were shown into Otero's dining room, where she was with a friend who spoke French with an English accent, her secretary, her dancing teacher as well as her dressmaker. There was a lively scene and Otero was said to have thrown a water decanter at the tradesman's head. Capdeville sued for assault.

Socialites were just as bad. In 1900, Mrs. Howard Gould had similar problems with her dressmaker. The latter told the court that in an effort to resemble Mrs. Langtry (King Edward VII's mistress) Mrs. Gould would often change to a new style of corsets after her dresses were finished, and as a result the waists would not fit.

"If we can get her to try one or two of these dresses in court, we shall be able to show the jury the justice of our claims," the dressmaker argued.

Mrs. Gould's lawyer said his client would not try on any dresses in court.

The Corset

A Belle Epoque woman was a complex and elaborate edifice built upon the corset – "the soul of the toilette" – the very basis of the silhouette, giving it shape and allure. A famous establishment at 19, Boulevard Haussmann, Margaine-Lacroix, described this in an ad (on September 21, 1900) for "La Brassière Sylphide," which gave one the fashionable carriage of the day and that pretty forward movement which characterized the elegant Parisian.

Full-page ads were also taken by a Mme. C. Guillot, "La Reine du Corset," to explain "How to Obtain a Good Figure" and "How To Keep It." Her corsets included the "Mystère" and the "Calice" – both with slender or rounded hips – and the Sheath-Corset Combination, inspired by fashion and athleticism. Besides being absolutely the latest thing, the latter was said to be highly hygienic. And while "Maison de la Valtière" claimed to hold the record for the lightness of corsets, Mme. Desbruères advertised "Grand Corset Louis XV," "The Fourreau, fitting the bust like a glove," and the "Corset de la Faculté" of silk satin brocade and Pompadour embroidery, which cost 200 francs, including suspenders.

No doubt in an effort to reassure the reader, the *Herald* ran a full page (in its April 8, 1906 supplement) showing "The History of the Corset. Instruments of Torture Compared with the Modern Corset."

Even men wore corsets. "Otherwise, how would one see in London's streets men with such thin and elegant waists?" the *Herald* asked in 1906.

As early as 1899, American women were waging war on the corset, forming a "Good Health Club" and arguing that corsets were the cause of fainting in public. In Leeds in 1904, a group of men formed a club and swore never to marry a woman wearing a corset. In 1900, even the French were discovering that it was immensely difficult to reconcile the rules of impeccable aesthetics with those of absolute hygiene. The corset was causing ravages to the female organism but, as the *Herald* noted: "One might as well preach in the desert."

The corset, however, did show signs of improving, and "Le Bien Etre," by Mme. Cadolle, had a straight busk, with the bust occupying its normal, natural place. Reportedly inspired by the Ancients, it supported the chest and hips separately by an ingenious combination and connected the two parts by the back, allowing for the curve of the hips.

In the end, it was all a question of cut, technique – and money; and well-to-do women were simply supposed to change their corset every time they changed their dress.

Accessories

If corsets were the foundation on which fashion was built, accessories provided layer upon layer of most important touches. Underpinnings were incredibly frothy and elaborate. Trousseaux, such as that of the future Marquise de M. – whose husband was the bearer of one of the greatest names in France – included four dozen day chemises, divided as follows: one dozen very plain, of the finest cambric, edged with English embroidery and very perfectly fitting, four dozen pairs of drawers, three dozen night chemises, all of different shapes, 24 petticoats, four dozen white cambric handkerchiefs and, lastly, an indefinite quantity of fancy handkerchiefs "about the size of your hand, that can be hidden in a glove at a ball or in the purse when making calls – just an atom of lawn delightfully embroidered and edged with priceless lace."

Hats and gloves, which no lady would have been caught dead without, filled page after page of the *Herald*. Hats were "smart," "stylish," or just "fashionable" and certainly complicated – such as one of wheaten matted straw, trimmed with application lace, a coq de roche, and snuff-colored velvet. The fate of old hats was simple: "A Chic Woman Cannot Wear Last Year's Hats!"

Hats for the theater were a red-hot issue. Every so often, there was a big campaign to force women to wear smaller bonnets. In 1908, "London Women Accept Edict on Theater Hats" – and finally removed their chapeaux without demur for a matinee of *The Belle of Brittany* at the Queen's Theater . . . except for one who, pleading in anxious tones, said that her shady flower garden had curls attached to it. She had to leave with her escort.

In Paris, women were less docile. In 1897, the composer Camille Saint-Saens railed against insensitive Frenchwomen who "go to the theater not to see but to be seen."

Veils and hatpins also followed fashion which, in 1906, called for charming voilettes in delicately tinted tulle and embroidery. There were also very pretty and practical platinum hairpins, very small and ornamented with diamonds and other stones. Hatpins were extremely varied, ranging from tortoise-shell to pink quartz, cut crystal set with real stones, pearls and diamond dust setting. By 1911, these long, dangerous hairpins were no longer necessary since the wearing of false hair had gone out of fashion.

Gloves were another essential accessory. In 1906, the Louvre department store alone sold more than five million pairs of gloves. Yet trade was already reported down.

We are not likely to see again the likes of the article on gloves which appeared in the Fashion Supplement of June 30, 1901. Stating that there were "gloves and gloves," the *Herald* described white kid gloves or white suede gloves for afternoon wear and for paying visits. Traveling, riding, driving – all called for different gloves, except that the latter could also be worn for tennis or croquet. Lastly, the "Gant de Saxe" was preferred for the country or the seaside.

In 1906, wood-colored gloves enjoyed a revival because, no matter how many extra pairs one carried along, it was hard to return home impeccable after a couple of hours shopping. "It is a false economy to buy cheap gloves," the *Herald* warned sternly. "They cannot wear and never look nice. Nothing looks worse than a torn glove or a glove with a button off. It can only be compared in abomination with a veil with a hole in it."

Parisian women had the reputation of possessing a fairy-like tread, which enabled them to confront quagmires of city mud without soiling their boots. Though all but hidden, shoes and stockings were essential in a fashionable wardrobe. Feet had erotic connotations and nothing was considered more sensually exciting than the sight of pretty feet, which were exposed automatically when a woman in the street cunningly lifted up her frilly, sweeping petticoats, showing a pair of neat ankles.

Fashion in shoes was amply recorded. The fashion prediction for winter 1902 was a return to Louis XV heels, even for boots, which, for daywear, were preferred to shoes with ribbons. The foot was supported better, particularly with high heels, and there was less danger of sprains. Close rows of buttons were abandoned to the export trade. The majority of boots were of dull kid, with patent leather toe-caps, with small patterns and seams.

Patent leather was going out of style, to be replaced by black satin, embroidered and ornamented with black pearls. Satin was preferred to velvet which had the disadvantage of making the feet appear larger. For the evening, shoes to match the color of the dress (a pretty idea revived by Christian Dior in 1947) were greatly in vogue. Certain old fabrics, Louis XV lampas among others, made very attractive evening or house shoes.

Stockings lost their uniformity and were frankly "fantaisistes," and assorted to suit the color of the shoes. With black satin slippers, however, they were very elaborate; in silk, embroidered with flower designs, done with open work or ornamented with incrustations of white or black lace – and a far cry from today's practical but oh! so ugly pantyhose.

In 1908, Americans were invading the market with practical shoes based on anatomy. Americans also brought along the so-called American pocketbook of soft leather embroidered with silver, marking the end of the dainty net purse. Black was the favorite color, with gunmetal fastening, sprinkled with tiny pearls – "and a charming fashion for semi-mourning."

Fashion is always a clue to lifestyle and we can tell a good deal about the way Belle Epoque women lived from the way they dressed. Just as in the 18th century women moved and sat in a particular way because of their wide panniered skirts, Belle Epoque women, their bodies constricted in stiffly elaborate toilettes, walked about more slowly and pompously than our jeans generation. There was also a whole set of precious movements which disappeared at the same time as parasols, fans and lorgnettes.

Here and there, we find traces of these different attitudes. Describing opera glasses, a luxurious bibelot made of mother of pearl, enamel, tortoiseshell, porcelain, gold or silver, the *Herald* wrote in 1905, "By affixing a handle of the same material, which is most practical, the charming, impertinent movement of the lorgnette may be obtained."

Coquettish women also used frivolous parasols, foamy concoctions made of taffeta or *mousseline de soie*, trimmed with ruches or headed with comet ribbon. A highly improbable novelty consisted of sunshades covered with tufts of artificial flowers or with branches of fruit trees, and ornamented with long strawberry runners or branches of cherry with fruit and flowers. A bit much, even for the *Herald* reporter, who expressed doubt that this fashion would find much favor "for it makes the sunshade very inconvenient to carry when closed."

Coquetry aside, nature took its toll. Women, ensnared in tightly constricting corsets, were apt to have vapors and to faint – which made fans a practical as well as ornamental part of their paraphernalia. The choice was immense, including "Les Mouettes" of Japanese paper, costing eight francs, and "Les Geraniums" at the same price. There were fans for all occasions – for resorts, they were made of bone, which was less fragile than tortoiseshell, and black tulle. Others, for autos, were of hand-painted linen or beige taffeta. In 1904 Empire-style small gauze fans, embroidered with gold or sequins, were extremely practical because they were small and went with every dress. This same year, there were predictions that the next hunting season would revive fans made of pheasant feathers.

Fans also figured prominently among chic wedding presents. Queen Margherita of Italy gave a real lace one mounted on tortoiseshell to Donna d'Orietta upon her marriage to Conte Febo Borromeo in 1906.

Some women were real experts. "Spanish women know how to use them best," the *Herald* wrote, adding that "The other night at Covent Garden, a professional beauty, sitting at the front of a box, had the wise coquettishness to hold her big red feather fan behind her head, making a halo to her superb and dark-haired beauty."

Jewelry changed according to seasons and circumstances. Summer meant no diamonds and other precious stones, but baroque pearls and enamels. Women did not deprive themselves of jewels because they changed their residence or mode of life, but they were supposed to replace them as they did their dresses. Pearls, less gaudy and more discreet than diamonds, were very much in favor. In 1906, short sleeves were reported to be bringing back the vogue of bracelets, and introducing a novelty – "the most desirable watch bracelet – pretty, neat and very convenient for the wearer who during a tiresome call does not dare look at her watch. But through a graceful and natural inclination of the head, she can easily perceive that her time of trial will soon be over."

When women were in full fig, they added a last touch: flowers in their corsages, orchids on fancy occasions but most generally roses – an expensive habit since these had to be replaced every couple of hours. At a Drawing Room given by Queen Victoria in 1898, pink roses were worn not only by ladies in their carriages but also by dignified coachmen and footmen, sitting on the box seats.

Fashion and Sports

Sports ultimately dealt a fatal blow to the frills and furbelows of the Belle Epoque. "Sporting tastes have so invaded modern society," the *Herald* wrote in 1902, "that a fashion paper dealing exclusively with sporting costumes might sustain the interest of its weekly readers from one end of the year to the other."

Every month had its favorite pastime: cycling, golf, lawn tennis, archery, yachting, walking, ballooning, automobiling, shooting, riding and driving, the races, fishing, swimming and skating, the latter sometimes practised by Spanish ladies to an accompaniment of castanets.

American women were always the most adventurous. The first sign of undressing on a beach came from Baltimore, "where it's said that fashion next summer will kindly permit ladies at seaside resorts to bathe without stockings."

In 1908, "Mondaine on Wheels" revealed that another "go-ahead American has enabled us femmes du monde to cycle out in the open when she ventured out in the Bois one morning, little caring if she might be taken for a demi-mondaine or not."

Analyzing the bicycle's impact, reporter Georges Frost (whose name was beginning to make an impression in the *Herald*'s usually anonymous pages) noted that dressing the part was capital. "Just call on any lady in Paris. There are ten chances to one that you will see on the mantelpiece her photograph taken in cycling costume. She is proud of it."

Frost also wrote about cycling up the Champs Elysées one morning when he saw, emerging from a porte cochère, the young Comtesse de X, one of the best "amazons" in Paris. While the liveried footman held the portal ajar, she pushed her machine onto the roadway, wearing a canotier hat, a white veil, a tight-fitting gray tweed jacket, knickerbocker trousers and brown leather shoes.

"I expressed surprise at her allowing Sultan, her favorite horse, to remain idle," Frost wrote. "'I want du nouveau,' she replied with a laugh." First stop was at a flower shop where Frost noted with admiration: "She jumped off unconcernedly on the left side, right foot over left, nor would she accept any assistance to remount. 'You see how convenient it is,' she remarked. 'I can select my own flowers instead of sending my maître d'hôtel.'"

The Comtesse had a "rendezvous" at the gate of the Bois with friends, all very distingué. Out of five men, four were "décorés" (decorations were very important during the military-minded and honor-conscious Belle Epoque) and one of them was a white-haired general. The women, of the highest aristocracy, were all married save two: a girl from Boston and one from New York. 'Bonjour' was no sooner said than they headed for the Allée des Acacias where "a delightful morning smell of acacias blended with that peculiar smell of wealth and fashion."

To Frost's question: "Do you consider that a woman looks graceful on a bicycle?" the general replied: "Ma foi, a pretty woman is a pretty woman wherever she is and whatever she does." (Not everybody felt the same way. In a *Herald* cartoon, one woman asked another: "How do you like your new cycling costume, Daisy?" – "I don't like it a bit. Why, there isn't a single thing about it to make a man turn and look a second time.")

The group went to La Cascade, had a peep at the polo grounds, halted at the Chalet du Cygne for refreshments, then to the home of the Comtesse "who invited us to lunch 'sans façons,' dressed just as we were" – an important breakthrough and a sign that, thanks to sport, people were beginning to discover the meaning of the word relax.

The "Femme-Chauffeur" soon stole the show and the *Herald* kept coming up with exciting fashion news. In 1900, it was charming automobile mantles in waterproof materials, nothing to do with the Indian rubber garments which were "odious." In 1901, the "practically invisible Mask for Chauffeuses" spared women the necessity of wearing the terrible goggles which male automobilists affected – and which caused many members of the fair sex to decline using the vehicle of the future.

By 1904, things were definitely improving, as an article on driving coats remarked: "How they've changed! We used to be bundled up. Now coats are elegant as well as comfortable." In 1906, the *Herald* felt able to announce that "Beauty is Possible in Auto Attire."

By 1913, the culture of the modern woman was not considered complete unless she proved herself an expert in one or more sports. The latest, and most dangerous, was aviation, "which makes the greatest demands on one's courage, but it has not frightened a few women who like to share the danger with some capable pilot. In this case, a special costume is indispensable and of course, it must be eminently practical (a new word in the fashion vocabulary) and no attention at all must be paid to any consideration of vanity." This "practical" outfit included a protective helmet, a coat of soft leather lined with swansdown, flannel or fur, wide culottes and boots or leggings.

The ancestor of the sweater-girl of the 1950s was wearing woolen sweaters clinging to the figure for many sports. These were used not only by women aviators, for whom they replaced the corset, but also by winter-sport fanatics who went in for skiing and bobsledding.

It is a difficult thing to decide what will be the fashion for ladies' dresses in Paris. It varies more often than the weather itself. A well-known painter whose name I forget, who was once ordered to draw the fashion of each country, represented a Parisienne in the costume of Eve, with the materials for a dress under her arm. "It is impossible," he said, "to give an idea of the fashion in Paris, for it changes continually." It is, therefore, difficult at the present moment to decide on a lasting fashion for this charming but changeable daughter of Eve. The most enterprising designers of costumes, however, do not hesitate to attempt to foresee her caprice in "creating" a number of masterpieces.

The HERALD to-day devotes a whole page to the reproduction of some *modèles* of costumes and to the description of others.

I will begin with some morning dresses.

A handsome morning dress has the skirt in blue serge trimmed with circular stripes to the waist. The corsage, in blue taffeta of the same shade as the skirt, is covered with white lace (the model which I saw had splendid *point à l'aiguille*), with bunches of ribbon in black satin on the front; cravate in pleated black mousseline de soie, and the sleeves matching the skirt. The belt is in black satin, trimmed at the ends with pleats of mousseline de soie.

To impart variety to this costume, a corsage in cornflower blue entirely in black mousselin de soie may be worn. For a *petit déjeuner*, such as are often given in spring, the cravate may be replaced by a cornflower-blue collier with a large bouquet at the belt.

The hat to be worn with this costume is in green straw, with cornflower-blue trimming, with old lace *en aigrette*, and with a crown of cornflowers.

The sunshade should be very simple without flounces of any sort, but it ought to be in harmony with the costume. The handle ought to be in iris wood. The sweet and penetrating odor of this wood is very charming.

Gloves are still worn in light colors, white is somewhat out of favor and may be replaced by maize or cream color.

A STRIKING COSTUME.

Another morning dress is one in almost white beige. The skirt is completely circular with a hole in the centre to fit the waist, with *piqûres* a centimètre apart right down to the knee as sole trimming.

green and pink glacé
skirt of black taffetas,
form (without diminu
of Chantilly to the hei
The redingote cross
corsage is *fuyante* on
somewhat the Directo
are flat. A Marie
without ends, is at
the front of the c
green mousseline c
brings out the arm

The hat for thi
trimmed with ca
there bunches
The Gismonda h
the face disappe
veil.

Here is anothe
well with this co

It is a round
farini, the front
form of a sabot.
very effective, th
ears of corn rai
the sabot, a

THE FASHION IN CAPES.

Little capes in cloth, silk and lace will be much worn this year. I have just seen a very pretty one in light pearl gray cloth lined with white taffetas having as its only ornament a large capuchon which could easily cover two heads. This capuchon is gathered in large deep pleats lined with white silk, and is fastened in front with a large bow of white satin and white satin ribbons.

Young lady's
with yellow

surrounds the c
a somewhat lar

THE PROS

The modern
month of Feb
morning and eve
The old French
thing, but add
somewhat rococco
greatest hopes of
the sun.

Si Février e
Croyez bien
Que pour cet
Pâques aura

Let us, therefore, pr
full confidence in th
ancestors.

Taffetas glacée will

For morning wear, dresses of self-colored cloth embroidered in the same shade are the proper thing. English cloths, and especially Scotch, in the tailor-made style, will be very popular. For convenience, small capes will still be worn, because of the large sleeves, which are still in fashion, for if they are not actually pretty, they are becoming. Short women should, however, be careful not to wear them too large.

The last visit I paid was to Doucet, the famous dressmaker. He showed me some very pretty dresses. Here are some of them:—

Fistly, a morning dress, skirt in navy blue lainage piqué with white. Body of the same; on the front an *entourage* of écru batiste trimmed with old guipure lace. Both dress and corsage are embroidered with narrow braid of various shades.

A princesse dress of water-green satin, corsage trimmed with guipure and strass buttons on the left side. Sleeves of silk muslin, a bow of pink ribbon and a large bunch of roses and violets on the left side.

A dress for the theatre is of pink broché, with bows of Louis XVI. ribbons spangled with silver and muslin roses embroidered in relief. This dress is made for Mlle. Sybil

jet over a claret ground; waistband, and a bow of the same color on the left side.

BOOTS AND SHOES.

Before concluding, I should like to call your attention to a detail which in my eyes appears to be of the highest importance—I mean boots and gloves. A pretty woman can better do without a new dress than neglect that part of her toilette, for however simple her dress may be, if she is well gloved and well shod, she is always more elegant to our critical taste, than another, however well-dressed she may be, who neglects these details.

Here is a word of advice: never hesitate to advise your shoemaker to make your boots long and narrow, a well-made boot should give the foot the effect of length and not of width.

I cannot understand the fashion adopted by all the shoemakers, of putting such a quantity of buttons on ladies' boots. The bad makers sometimes go to the extent of fourteen buttons and even beyond. The best never exceed nine and are often below that number. In my opinion eight are quite sufficient.

I like boots somewhat in the English style, of calf, with toe-piece. They can be

DURING THE BALL.

Drawn by Fournery. (Lent by the "Grand Monde.")

THE GREAT DRESSMAKERS OF PARIS.

The Leaders of Fashion and their Latest Creations.

inlaid in the cloth in scollops. The body is a blouse and trimmed in the same manner. The sleeve is tight, trimmed in the same way; at the top is a falling drapery of cloth. The waistband is of gray satin. The ... by Carlier.

BEER.

... to be worn when visiting, is of ... with narrow ...

taffetas. The lappels open over a chemisette of frilled lawn. The sleeves are half length, draped with flat pleats. The waistband is wide in front and narrow behind. The hat is made by Drouard.

ROUFF.

This dress is ...

and double breasted and has large lappels of white satin covered with spangles. Behind the neck is a high collar of white satin also spangled. The neck is trimmed with white satin surmounted with a ruche of ... de soie. The sleeves ...

The body is soft with a wide-draped waistband of blue and white linen as wide in front as behind. The upper part of the body is formed of a yoke of blue and white ... velvet ... is trimmed with ... navy-blue ...

... neglects these details.

Here is a word of advice: never hesitate to advise your shoemaker to make your boots long and narrow, a well-made boot should give the foot the effect of length and not of width.

SUMMER FASHION

AU BON MA

PARIS.

MAISON ARISTIDE BOUCICAUT.

The BON MARCHÉ always endeavors to offer the Latest Novelties in Dress Fabrics of eve Goods, produced in their own Workrooms, and of which the High Fini employed leave nothing to be desired.

The persistent cold weather so unwilling to leave us until we find ourselves so far advanced in the year has certainly put all Dressmakers, Milliners and Tailors into a dilemma as to what extent the summer Fashions would be influenced thereby. The success of many of the very early styles has in consequence been completely sacrificed, but now that the milder season has really declared itself, and that Paris promises to look as charming as ever under the kind influence of May sunshine, which brings with it long vistas of Boulevards and Avenues bordered with blossoming chestnuts, the city is beginning to fill with visitors, and everyone is beginning to search for those pretty and becoming combinations of Dress that only Parisian Artists can produce. The most attractive centre, where the largest variety of the most stylish and fashionable productions are to be found, is certainly the Grands Magasins du BON MARCHÉ. A most elaborate and interesting display on a very extensive scale is to be made by this Establishment on Monday, May 6, and following days, which will include all the Season's Latest Novelties in Ladies' Costumes, Mantles, Millinery, Jackets, Capes, Tea-Gowns, Robes de Chambre, Trousseaux, Children's Costumes, &c. We feel sure that the readers of the HERALD'S Supplement, who are for the most part assiduous customers of the BON MARCHE, and well acquainted with their magnificent premises and innumerable resources, will be pleased to be initiated beforehand as to what has been prepared for this brilliant display. The few drawings of to-day's supplement have been chosen so as to give some previous idea of a few of the styles in each of the above-named departments, but a personal visit will satisfy the reader that many more equally interesting remain to increase the variety of choice.

A pretty Costume on the first figure, marked 78fr., is made in either black or cream Alpaca with very full sleeves, a silk velvet collar and gros-grain belt with a metal buckle, very full godet skirt. A Foulard Dress at 95fr., white designs on navy ground. The bodice is trimmed with a pretty Cream lace insertion, and the collar and belt are of satin ribbon with a full godet skirt. A pretty écru Lawn Dress, with the blouse waist in colored spots and satin ribbon trimmings on the sleeves and at the waist, price 59fr. Another Elegant Lawn Dress in small designs, at 78fr., with a very full skirt and bodice trimmings of lace and check ribbon trimmings. A stylish Blouse on the end figure, at 29fr., is made of Oriental Crépon, with very full sleeves and satin ribbon trimmings.

1895.

RCHE.

PARIS.

Description; also in all kinds of Made-up
nd Quality of all Materials

The Children's and Young Ladies' Department will offer particular attraction not only by the taste displayed in the composition of the various Costumes and Mantles exposed, but also in the great variety offered for all ages from four to sixteen years old. A Child's Costume, as on the first figure in the drawing, is made in fancy pique, a pretty, new material, with a deep frill collar of embroidery and insertion to match, price from 23fr. to 37fr., according to age. Taking the others as they follow, a Cotton Crepon Dress in blue and white, pink and white or mauve and white, prettily trimmed with embroidery, is made in all sizes, from 11fr. 50c. to 23fr., according to size. The Embroidery Dress is made in either white or cream, and also in pompadour colors, trimmed the same way with pretty bows of ribbon, for children from three to eleven years, and varies according to size, 37fr. to 55fr. The Sailor Suit is made with a pleated serge skirt and a blouse bodice with a double linen collar prettily embroidered for children from four to fourteen, and ranging from 21fr. to 39fr., according to size. A pretty Cotton Crépon Dress behind with colored spots on white grounds and a pretty frill of embroidery to match, from four to fourteen years, also, and varying accordingly, from 18fr. 50c. to 35fr. The other Costume at the side is made of a very narrow striped woollen material in a variety of colorings, with a cream serge blouse, from five to thirteen years, and varying in price from 23fr. to 39fr. accordingly. The pretty Child's Frock is of printed batiste, trimmed with embroidery, and is made only in small sizes, from two to five years, price 9fr. 75c. A Sailor Suit is made in navy, cream or red serge, with a blue linen front, from five to thirteen years, and varying in price from 18fr. 50c. to 29fr. Another Stylish ... on the back figure ... in M...

DESCRIPTION OF THE HEADDRESSES.

It should be understood that our mode of procedure is quite different from those adopted hitherto.

HEADDRESS NO. 1.

The engraving "Coiffure No. 1" represents the head of a young woman who lost to complete the head dressing, which is very becoming, either the accessory No. 1 or No. 2, which is placed on the top of the head as is shown. This coiffure may also

NO. 4.—DINNER DRESS FOR LADIES, MADE UP WITH THE LAURENCY LOW FRONT AND ACCESSORY NO. 3.

her front hair after an attack of typhoid fever. Any lady in the same position, or one who has not lost her hair but wishes her hair dressed in the same style, has but be worn by a person who has entirely lost her hair; but in such a case, instead of using the accessories above named, a transformation (wig) of a very light texture is

ART IN

AND TH

Headdre

MAISON CRO

9 RUE

That hairdressing is an art has been recognise ing the women whose heads they dressed, have maintai

But although it may be possible for a lady to d to fever or illness, from becoming partially bald, or bec invented in 1867, the year of the great Exhibition, by M hair, waved in such a manner that the illusion may be

That this object has been attained, and the tit that our readers, having seen the engravings we submit

pearance, may make their minds easy. They have an extensive choice among these coiffures, all of which (like all the articles we make) are made of natural waved hair, and fit so perfectly that no one can perceive that any addition has been made to the hair of the wearer.

COIFFURE NO. 4.

With this and the following coiffures, we enter into another category.

Having shown how young women can

Accessory No. 7.—New model in hair, turned up over the forehead; used in Coiffure No. 11 *(45fr.).*

dress their hair themselves, the next thing is to show how middle-aged and elderly ladies can make up their coiffure in the

HAIRDRESSING

MAKING OF POSTICHES.

es, Wigs and False Hair from the

AT, LAURENCY & GAISSAD,

U 4 SEPTEMBRE, PARIS.

ll times, and many of those such as Lefèvre, Léonard, Croisat and others, who have excelled in the art of embellish-e well-deserved reputation of artists.

ner own hair and bring it into harmony with her features, it very often happens that, either from paucity of hair due ashion demands it, she may need the addition of those charming small *postiches*, in natural wavy hair, which were rency, the well-known *coiffeur posticheur*, whose one object has been to bring them to perfection, using only natural ete and that the addition made to the hair to have it well dressed cannot be perceived.

his article, "L'Art dans la Coiffure et la Fabrication des Postiches," is well deserved is our belief, and we trust eir notice and read the explanations which accompany them will agree with us.

...older and a little balder, is made with a postiche called *Dessus de Tête*, larger than the last (as the space requiring to be covered is larger), also set in Alençon point hair tulle, the price of which is 140fr., with the addition of Chignon No. 4, the price of which varies from 45fr. upwards.

COIFFURE NO. 6.

This coiffure, which resembles in style Nos. 1, 2 and 3, already described, is one of

Accessory No. 1. New and elegant chignon used in the latest style of hairdressing. With a branch and curled ends it costs 30fr.

the most becoming produced for many years. Here is a description of it, by Claire de Chanchenay, in her fashion notes:

...remark because it is a fact that no matter what the talent of a fashionable hairdresser may be, the fashion, with few exceptions, is not set by him, but from the information daily furnished by ladies who visit our showrooms. For instance, it would be easy to give a name to each of the coiffures in this number. We have selected as models those of our most elegant customers who wear them regularly. Our readers can satisfy themselves by a glance at the various faces, of different ages, that they are not merely fancy drawings, but the features of living persons, whose coiffure has been sketched. This Coiffure No. 4, for a middle-aged lady beginning to become bald, is made with a descending waved front called the "Laurency," set upon Alençon point tulle, the price of which is 100fr., with the addition of accessory No. 3—a twist with curled ends—the price of which is 45fr.

FROM THE "MODE ILLUSTRÉE."

TO OUR READERS.

In our programme of the new organization of the *Mode Illustrée*, after enumerating its contents in the way of useful and pleasant work, such as: dresses, millinery, tapestry, &c., we have repeatedly said that we should like to teach mothers, aunts and elder sisters the art of dressing their own hair and that of younger members of their family. We have applied to M. Camille, of the firm of Croizat, Laurency and Gaissad, 9 rue du Quatre-Septembre, for professional lessons in hairdressing with illustrations to complete the explanations, and we know that our subscribers have profited and will profit by these good lessons.

The firm in question, which was founded by Croizat in 1820 and which is the only one that has been recommended for thirty-eight years by the *Mode Illustrée*, publishes all its creations in the text of the journal. also *L'Etude*, containing seventy engravings, which treats of all degrees of baldness at all ages and affords information in dressing one's own hair.

EMMELINE RAYMOND.

NO. 20.—UNDULATING PIN.

Specimen of the Croisat waving pin used in Coiffures 3, 10 and 12. Five pins in box, 1fr. 50c. if bought at shop; 1fr. 75c. by post.

The Croisat waving fluid, indispensable to obtain a satisfactory result without curling tongs. Price 3fr. per bottle. Sent to any address in France for 3fr. 85c.

Accessory No. 2, used in making up Coiffures Nos. 1 *and* 6. *Price, from* 15 *to* 20*fr.*

Accessory No. 3.—*Used in making up Coiffure No.* 4 (45*fr.*).

HAIR AND POSTICHES.

(From the Figaro.)

The firm Croisat Laurency and Gaissad is, to our knowledge, the oldest in Paris; it was founded in 1820 by Croisat. Its object, continued by Laurency and by the present manager, Camille Croisat, has always been to maintain the reputation of a *maison de confiance*. It is also without a rival as regards the workmanship and quality of its productions. The postiches, mounted on Alençon point tulle, in which only natural waved hair is used, last twice as long as those made on Chantilly tulle, and will bear without uncurling water, perspiration and the sea air. It is for these reasons that the firm has obtained numerous recompenses at various exhibitions, and the favor of being recommended by the *Figaro*

Accessory No. 4.—*Used in Coiffure No.* 5. (*Price* 45*fr.*)

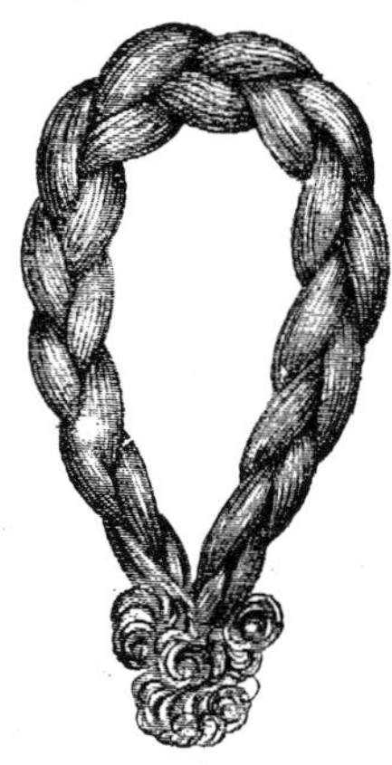

Accessory No. 5.—*A postiche composed of three unequal branches with curled ends used in Coiffure No.* 8. *Length* 60 *to* 65 *centimètres.* (*Price* 40*fr.*)

NO. 6.—COIFFURE BAIN-DE-MER, STYLED "REINE A LA MODE."

NO. 11.—NEW COIFFURE.

(1830 *style*) *is made with a* 1830 *roll, price* 45*fr.*

MATERIALS USED FOR LADIES' HAIRDRESSING.

LATEST FASHIONS IN LADIES' HATS.

Diminution in Size but Bright Colors Still the Order of the Day.

ARTIFICIAL FLOWERS.

Dresses Worn at the Omnium Club's Meeting—Costumes at Recent Weddings.

[LETTRE D'UN VIEUX PARISIEN.]

DEAR MADAM,—Certain symptoms allow me to inform you that it will not be long before we see a change in the fashion in hats and, considering the expanse of most of them, this change cannot but bring about a diminution in their volume. Indeed, it is difficult to go out on foot with the forms now being worn. In modern broughams, which are so little like the *carrosses* and *berlines* of former days, they are inconvenient, and in open carriages the wind, which gains a purchase on their large wings, often causes the hat

DRESS OF THE PRINCESSE DE CHIMAY IN THE BOIS DE BOULOGNE IN THE MORNING.
Drawn from an instantaneous photograph by Comte C. de Mazibourg.

to be displaced, if not carried away. Hats, then, are to become less voluminous, but be reassured they will remain as brilliant, as elegant and as flowery as in the past. They will have less expanse, that is all.

I am glad that this little evolution will affect neither their colors nor ornaments, for I certainly find the hats of to-day very pretty and I congratulate myself on a fashion which has replaced dull and sombre tints on ladies' heads by the brightness and color of the most brilliant flowers and most attractive taffetas.

I am not one of those who protest so ... little ...

lution that the great reform which replaced the *coiffure en cheveux* by hats for town wear and walking dress was effected.

The *Journal des Modes de Paris* of 1785 contains the following advertisements :—

At Mademoiselle Fredin's, modiste, at the sign of the Golden Scarf, rue de la Ferronnerie, will be found hats on which is represented a vessel fully rigged and its guns ready for action. This is called the "Chapeau Amiral"

At Mme Quentin's, rue de Cléry, may be seen

POLIGNAC HAT.

a puff hat with military trophies. The standards and kettledrums on the front give a very pleasing effect.

It was at that period that straw hats, imported from Italy, began to come into fashion. Since then, though the style of ornament has changed, hats have always been the favorite coiffure for ladies out of doors, and to-day they play a very important part in dress.

I have consulted some of the leading milliners in Paris as to changes that are likely to be made. They all agree that the tendency is towards the old styles, but none of them has yet attempted to carry it into practice and in all my rambles I have seen nothing which will justify me in saying: "This is to be the fashion to-morrow."

In the meantime I have seen some very pretty creations, and you will find in the columns of the HERALD to-day some of the designs which appeared to me to be the prettiest and most interesting.

I will begin by describing those which I prefer myself, for if I were to speak of all I have seen the page would be filled and the whole paper would not suffice to give merely the names of the modistes of Paris.

At Berthe and Virot's, in a splendid set of rooms, 5 mètres high, on the first floor in the place Vendôme, elaborately decorated in the style of the Restoration, I saw some charming designs, as original as they were in good taste. I have selected two, sketches ...ich you can see for yourself.

...f mauve tulle or

of the same material behind, tufts of white roses as cache-peigne.

The other is of fine straw, Louis XVI. style, turned up behind, with two rosettes of black satin. Bows of the same kind in front, with tufts of feathers. At the nape of the neck black satin and crêpeline.

At Mme. Virot's, rue de la Paix, where there is always an excellent choice of hats of every description, I especially noticed a kind of capote-cap, styled the Capote-Katia, which is very pretty. It is of white lace over a pink transparency, with two high wings of pink taffetas plaited.

I afterwards went to Esther Meyer's, rue Royale ; the show rooms in the Louis XVI. style are very lofty and handsome. I did not see a very great variety, but this sometimes happens even with the best millinery houses. Here is a description of two designs which I considered the best.

One is a white straw hat with black feathers and orange bows, trimmed with old strass buttons. The other, also, is of white straw, bordered with black velvet and a large bow leaving the chignon uncovered.

At Mme. Marguerite's, 35 avenue de l'Opéra, I saw a hat of écru lace in the form of a beretta, with pink cache-peigne and large wings of black feathers, made for the Princesse de Lucinge. Also a black rough straw hat trimmed with black and white tulle poppies and a bow of green and yellow shot mousseline de soie. All the above-named houses turn out very pretty things, but not everyone can afford to pay their prices. There are other houses where pretty things can also be obtained much cheaper. For instance, I have seen some very stylish hats at a small millinery establishment, that of Mme. Saillard, rue St. Honoré. I cannot remember the number, but it is near the rue Royale. One of the designs I saw was a capote of white rice straw with two immense pansies of jet and a black aigrette.

PINS FOR HATS.

While speaking of hats, it may interest you to have some particulars respecting hat-pins. What I prefer are quite plain, or with a small pear-shaped pearl head with a serpent turned around it. In gold heads some very elegant things are made combined with precious stones, but as nothing

The yellow Marshal Niel roses and the r... dodendrons are especially admirable as p... fect imitations. Mme. Lespiaut has enab... me to call your attention to an interest... novelty : real green leaves are now used a... are perfectly preserved by a new process ...

Mme. Lespiaut, who now makes v... pretty hats, showed me a toque made ... rhododendrons and violets, *violine* ...

HAT MADE FOR MME. ALBERT MENIER.

mauve, with an aigrette and bow of aub... gine taffetas, which is intended for t... Duchess of Leuchtenberg.

She also showed me a hat of mauve w... a large butterfly knot in taffetas change... and white and mauve rhododendrons wh... Mme. de Ganay is to wear to-day (Sunda... with a large peony in her corsage. Nothi... can be more beautiful than the peonies ... all shades which were shown me. The b... roses and sweet pinks are also very s... cessful.

Before closing this budget of inform... tion, I thought I would go to the fount... head, and therefore called on M. R. ... l'Isle, president of the Chambre Syndic... of Flower and Feather Makers. He w...

HAT WORN BY MLLE. DE MALAKOFF.

Gelot
Berthe
Fernande Fournier
Lody
Lewis
Maison Moderne

MAISON POUYANNE,

4 Rue de la Paix, Paris.

LARGE STRAW CAPELINE, DRAPERY OF MUSLIN EMBROIDERED WITH STRAW FLOWERS WHITE FEATHERS.

TOQUE OF STRAW AND PINK MUSLIN, TRIMMED WITH FLOWERS AND MUSLIN.

HAT OF WHEATEN NATTED STRAW, TRIMMED WITH APPLICATION LACE, A COQ DE ROCHE, AND SNUFF-COLORED VELVET.

LATEST NOVELTIES IN FASHIONS.

Taste for Bright Colors Spreading Daily—Some of Doucet's Newest Creations.

DESIGNED FOR THE "HERALD."

Capotes Quite Superseded by Toques—What will be Worn by "Mondaines"

DEAR MADAM,—It is somewhat difficult to surmise what surprises fashion may have in store for us, but it seems to me that a taste for the bright and showy is gaining ground daily. Whether this is a matter for complaint I know not. I only state the fact without expressing an opinion.

MANTLES.

The *cache-poussière* is very convenient for excursions, traveling and driving out, but should not be worn in the streets, as it is not graceful and hides the dress too much. It can be made of alpaca, glacé taffetas or pongee, or better than either, of Silesian. There is nothing new in the shapes this year.

Large mantles with wide sleeves and cape falling to the waist are also worn. They can be made of surah taffetas or droguet. Lastly comes the jacket, which is now worn very short, with undulating basques scarcely 25 centimètres broad. The fronts are worn with silk flaps, but the sacque paletot has gone quite out of fashion. Capes will always be worn because they can be so easily put on over balloon sleeves.

There is another style of jacket which I ought not to forget to mention because it is very convenient to wear over the corsage blouse. The body is of cloth with flat pleats in the Watteau style falling over an inset of silk. The sleeves are very large. Then there is a cape in the form of a fichu, lightly crossed over the chest.

Another shape is also very pretty. The back and front are formed of two pieces alike, falling below the waist in the form of a herald's dalmatica. These two pieces are joined by *barettes* which hook under the arms, leaving the body of the sleeve free. They are trimmed round the neck with a large ruche of silk muslin. This mantle can be made in embossed velvet braided with gold or embroidery, or of brocaded damask. Many capes are also made of cloth braided, with a small braid set upright.

I have seen this style of braiding used for corsages at John Hendry's, rue Auber. At this establishment I also saw some bright drab dresses slashed with silk, which pleased me much.

As regards materials the fashion appears to have set in for crépons and glacé taffetas. Self-colored crépons cost from 1fr. 25c. to 6fr. per mètre, and fancy crépons from 6fr. to 11fr. Taffetas cost from 2fr. 90c. to 5fr. 90c., the first plain, the second brocaded. Taffetas with printed patterns are also very effective and also certain moires shot with silver.

HAT FROM THE MAISON LEWIS.

Among the Milliners.

Certainly the reign of the small and elegant capote is over. Not a single milliner leaves you the slightest doubt on that point. "We don't make them any more" I was told at Virot's, "except for old women." The capote is dead and the toque has taken its place. They are entirely made of flowers as the capotes were, and there is really little difference between the two styles. The show-rooms of Virot, 12 rue de la Paix, and of all the leading milliners are regular flower gardens.

I noticed a charming toque in green straw, surrounded with five large bunches of violets, forming a garland, from the midst, of which rises a light aigrette of feathers. This has been chosen by the new Comtesse de Castellane, who has just arrived at the Hotel Bristol from New York.

Another that I noticed was equally pretty. It was also of straw and trimmed with large pansies with bright green spangles and surmounted by an aigrette of black feathers. This has been copied from the one worn by Mlle. Bartet in "Le Pardon." Another is of Italian straw, rather thicker, and a corner turned up behind with a large bow of lace and ribbon on one side and bunches of large pansies on the other.

HAT FROM THE MAISON LEWIS.

THE

adour bou-
n trimmed
ross and an
he wings,
e trimmed

l'Opéra, I
. One of
with shot
tterns and
kind of
gauze,
. maroon
xed with

had never
d original
ave straw,
t and two
d poppies
of black
d with
n one
nother
e hat
ruby-
of shot
e Ven-
les, but
crinoline
broidered
black bird

covered
ouis XVI.
as. Black
eigne. A
nother of
ts in front
d pansies
tte, is also
of *violine*
nd violine
bow of the

skirt, and with the body of the bolero form over a silk chemisette of Scotch green tartan. The sleeves, of the same material, are very wide. The front opens over a blouse of embroidered lawn. The waistcoat is trimmed with large strass buttons.

I also noticed a pretty silk muslin cape in accordion pleats, over a transparency of tender blue, with an inset striped with blue and gold braid and an entre-deux of black puffed silk muslin. A jet and chenille trimming is laid on the inset, ending in a jet medallion. I consider this little garment extremely elegant.

M. Henri Creed, 25 rue de la Paix, showed me all his models. I shall leave to another time a description of the riding and cycling habits, of which he makes a specialty, and speak only of ordinary dress. "The costumes I am making at the

extremely elegant, was made for La Otero, the Spanish dancer. It is of pink satin, covered with orange silk muslin and trimmed with three entre-deux of écru guipure. The sleeves, which are long, are of moiré taffetas, pearl-gray in color, with large bunches of mauve flowers woven in the texture.

What will be Worn.

Skirts will be plain and self-colored, and the bodies very much trimmed.

High-waisted corselets, draped and ending just below the chest, will be very fashionable.

Vests without sleeves will be worn so as not to tumble the sleeves of the corsage.

Artificial flowers will be generally worn, and—what is a real innovation—will be used to trim day dresses.

DRESS IN TAFFETAS IN CHANGING MAUVE, COPIED FROM THE ORIGINAL AT DOUCET'S.

present moment," he said, "are almost in all cases of self-colored materials, for large checks and stripes have gone out of fashion. In one class of dress the prevailing taste lies in the quiet color of materials, but perfection in the cut. There is a dress, for instance, which I have just made for one of your fair countrywomen, a member of the Vanderbilt family, and which, as you see, is of plain electric blue. The skirt, cut on the cross, measures about 5m. 50cm. round the bottom, the vest is in

They will be worn round the neck and on the corsage in large bunches passed under the waistband or pinned to the shoulder.

For little girls large capes and long skirts with short waists in the Kate Greenaway style will be the principal wear.

The varieties of ribbons, this year are endless: they include every variety of Scotch tartan in bright or dark; plain satin woven with Pompadour bouquets; taffetas glacés or quilled, and gauze woven with bunches of flowers.

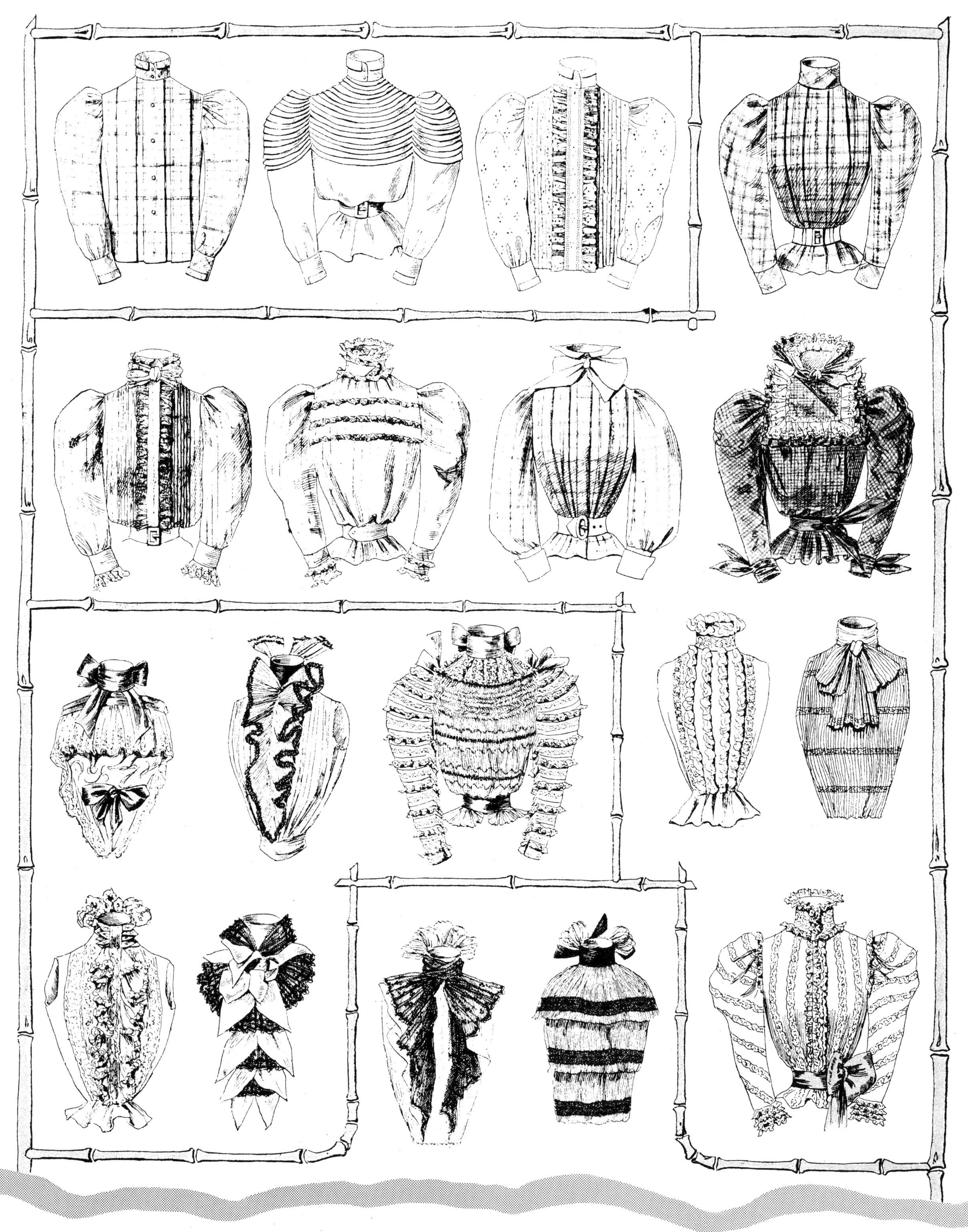

BLOUSES AND FRONTS OF CORSAGES.

DRESS OF CERISE SHOT TAFFETAS.

DRESS AT THE SEASIDE.

Newest Creations in the Way of Bathing Costumes for Adults and Children.

THE INEVITABLE KODAK.

How to Set off Charms that Nature Has Bestowed and Create Those Which She Has Refused.

In these days when amateur photographers swarm everywhere and when the click of the indiscreet apparatus takes one by surprise, on the plain, in the valley, on the mountain, it is necessary, more than ever, for women of fashion, to watch over their reputation for style.

The bathing hour at the fashionable seaside resorts is, above all others, the most critical. At that moment the kodak rages. "Kind friends," "the family," and even unknown persons are seized with an acute attack of instantaneous photographing, and women, delivered over to the tender mercies of these maniacs of the "dark room," have no retort and no defence but their beauty.

Ah! our grandmothers vaunted the grace with which they draped themselves in their Indian cashmeres. How much more difficult is it to enter or leave the water, to put on or take off with dignity the peignoir held up by one's maid! These are trying moments in the existence of woman of fashion, and ... confiden...

adorable model in black and white; t... shaped skirt trimmed round the botto... with a broad bias of white cloth; a ve... short bolero incrusted on a white blou... corsage, a white shawl collar fastened wi... a red regatta tie over a red, low-cut fro... with a black anchor in relief embroider... upon it.

To wear these costumes with comfort, ... is indispensable to have a waistband c... set of strong linen, very slightly stiffene... which supports the back and gives a cur... to the loins. Women have lost the norm... equilibrium of their bodies since the a... cestral custom of wearing corsets came i... and their outlines would be lacking ... firmness and curve if they did not reso... to them.

In the same way, flat shoes, the antiq... cothurnum of white linen rolled round t... leg in bandelettes, is equally embarrassin... owing to the habit of wearing high hee... intended to increase the height. One ... two thicknesses of felt fixed in the interi... of the sandal will obviate this inconver... ence, and allow the step its noble ar... rhythmical movement. Lastly, need w... sacrifice our pretty waved hair, whi... forms an aureole round our features ar... a pleasing nimbus to which all eyes a... accustomed? A fringe of curled hair wi... adapt itself to the interior of our select... coiffure and preserve intact the habitu... harmony of the face. The hair is car... fully enveloped in an indiarubber cap, ar... the illusion is complete, and at the sam... time hygiene is assured.

The coiffures are varied and charming... there is the large Greenaway capote, i... ruby tissues printed with flowers an... edged with lace or embroidery, or th... shape of straw known as "baigneuse," di... creetly trimmed with a light-colored c... black taffetas bow, and strings to match... or the classic cap of some bright material... or the beretta; or the silk handkerchie... draped "en marmotte," which is very be... coming with the addition of a few frizzes...

The mantle-shaped peignoir is one o... the most useful, and at the same time on... of the most comfortable of garments. I... is surmounted by a gathered hood. Whe... made of white Pyrénées cloth lined wit... pink or pale blue, it is very pleasing in ef... fect; those made of a spongy tissue i... ...lers are al...

COSTUMES FOR LITTLE GIRLS.

...deformed, ex... ...iticisms of the ... eover that the ... ...he accessori...

coming combinations are produced. The drawers are knickerbockers, and the skirt, attached to the corsage and shaped, ...

What a delight for the dear little victims of city promenades; the joy of complete freedom supplements in a large degree the strengthening virtues of the salt air. Their new and brief liberty must not be curbed, and they should be dressed in garments suited to their sports. Woollen costumes are the best to protect the dear little ones from the damp of the sands; and for children of both sexes at an early age I should recommend jerseys composed of knickerbockers and a tight fitting or bloused shirt with a navy collar, blue or white, and a Genoese cap of the same material. Thus dressed children are adorable; they should have woollen stockings and canvas shoes with rubber soles and cork soles inside them, so as to avoid the unpleasant stickiness of indiarubber alone.

When one gives way to the fancy for more luxurious dress, it is well to make use of large waterproofed silk knickerbockers over everything, drawn in at the knees; in this manner the dress is kept dry up to the waist; somewhat at the expense of grace, I must admit, but in certain cases it may be dispensed with.

Woollen costumes with long waists and short skirts and pleats are the most con...

Muslin baby hats are extremely becoming for the river and the garden, but remember they must be put on with care and over a well-coiffée head. Somehow one's hair is not always well coiffé in the country, and on this point let me give you a word of advice. Nowadays, hairdressing accessories are so numerous that it is really laziness on the part of the woman without a maid who is not bien coiffée. She can take lessons if she likes, or she can leave town with her hair well waved and spend an extra five or ten minutes each day in waving it herself.

Perfectly splendid for country wear are those coarse burnt or even black rush straws, trimmed with bows of bright-colored foulard in all shades or striped fancy ribbons. I think I have told you before that these bows can be picked up ready-made.

DRESSES FOR TROUVILLE.

(From the "Queen.")

Red surah, printed black, trimmed white muslin bands embroidered red, and cut out in vandykes, along which run frills of white muslin, embroidered red like the turned down collar. Blouse and deep flounce in muslin or cambric, spotted red. Chapeau Marquis, with turned-up brim in beige straw, with tufts of poppies, cluster of pink ribbon loops, and grenadine draperies.

Blouse in white and partly tucked ...

GROUP OF COSTUMES FOR SEA BATHING.

MODES DE

Tailleur
de Sa Majesté le Roi
Alphonse XIII
Roi d'Espagne.

THE PREMIER HOUSE
IN PARIS.

KRI

23 RUE

INTEMPS

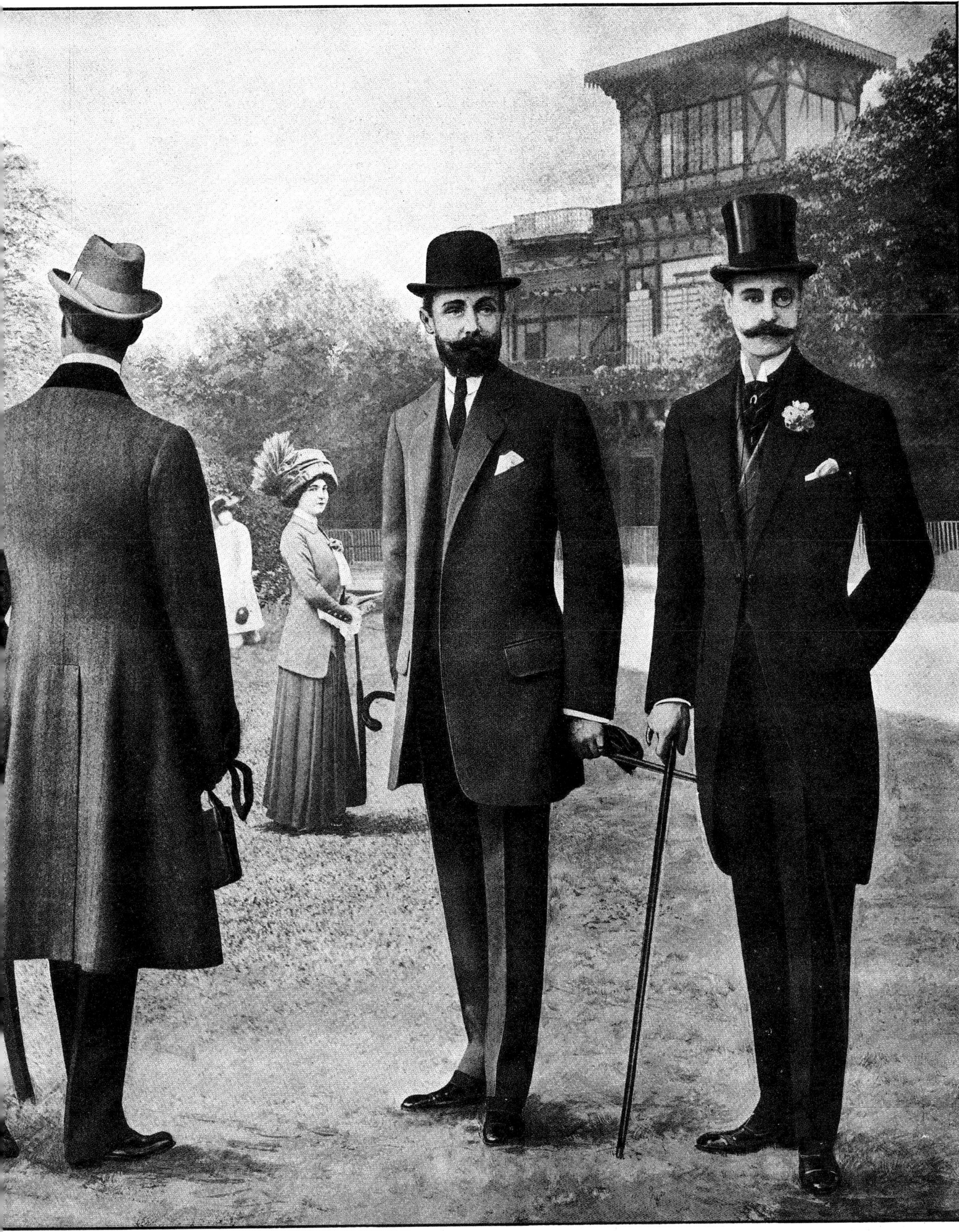

GCK

OYALE

AMERICAN TAILOR
IN PARIS:

Tailleur
de Sa Majesté le Roi
Manuel II
Roi de Portugal.

LATEST DETAILS OF PARIS FASHIONS.

In a "Lettre d'un Vieux Parisien," Ladies will Find Valuable Information.

ORIGINAL "HERALD" DESIGNS.

Costumes Specially "Created" for Riding, Cycling, Yachting and Sport Generally.

Since you would like to have an opinion on the best style of costume for the bicycle, I should certainly recommend you, from a practical point of view—after all the most important consideration in matters athletic—to choose the broad and baggy knicker-bocker. A short skirt accordeon-pleated is perhaps more elegant and decidedly more graceful when off the machine; but, while riding, it is very much in the way and often a source of danger from its liability to get

DRESS FOR MOUNTAIN CLIMBING.
Produced by Viola.

entangled in the wheels. The boléro jacket is not always graceful, and for women of a certain embonpoint it even looks ridiculous. I would, therefore, recommend the adoption of a jacket reaching below the waist. It is like a smoking jacket, which may be fastened by a single button in front or open with large revers on a waistcoat of similar material or of white piqué.

For slim women a short jacket with small basques à godets is more becoming.

In the selection of a cloth I am in favor of the whip-cord for country excursions and plain woollens for ordinary rides. It is also handy to have a costume of silver gray alpaca for the hot weather.

the dress.
ppique I noticed two
ne of them was of
and mordoré, entirely
a large bouquet behind
white faille in front.
of coarse green straw
k quilled tulle and high

stitched, and waistcoat of lavender blue linen, with white spots.

"HERALD" SPECIALTIES.

Original Designs for Riding, Cycling, Tennis and Yachting.

For an elegant woman a riding habit ought always to be des'gned in the most correct style. Corsets can be worn or not; they can be replaced by a crinoline waist-band in three pieces, confining the waist, kept together by small bands of white leather. This waistband is fastened in front with three buckles with leather straps. A *maillot* of black silk from head to foot and small patent leather boots made by a good shoemaker. So much for underwear.

The skirt is of black silk, rather thick, and the jacket very simple, with sleeves like those of a man's coat, opening in front so as to lighten the figure with a small white point. Cravat of black satin and chemisette of very fine batiste with linen collar. The hat, to be really elegant, should always be high crowned, except when taking an early morning ride. White gloves with heavy black stitching and a very simple, but well-chosen riding whip. Saddle and bridle should be as light as possible. It is best to go to saddlers of well-deserved reputation and be guided by their experience, for a good seat often depends on the saddle and bridle.

Tennis Costumes.

A neat costume is of tartan wool, very bright and half-length, cut in dog-tooth pattern over a skirt of white taffetas. Blouse of the same material: the front entirely made of separate flaps, showing the blouse of white taffetas at every movement. Neck trimmed with lilies of the valley and orange bow, chemisette sleeves. Hat of white esparto or Panama; large tartan bow very high up on the chignon, and several tufts of lilies of the valley with orange velvet bows in front.

Yachting Costume.

... jersey of navy blue silk, ... with wide pleats. ... navy

in front over a white wool chemisette, with collar turned down; sleeves of mordoré cloth, showing the white wristband of the chemisette. Hat of mordoré cloth, trimmed with undressed leather and kid cockade of the same shade; traveling boots of undressed leather, Scotch plaid stockings, marron and beige.

Cycling Costume.

Small princess dress of white cloth with the seams piped, scolloped in squares over

CYCLING COSTUME.
Specially designed for the HERALD.

an orange silk jersey. Hat of white cloth with wild-duck wing; stockings forming socks of large-ribbed white wool, and orange at the upper part.

Another costume is of écru mohair, the skirt pleated; the body made of lace in- ... and blue satin ribbon, sleeves of ... without sleeves, which ... Hat of ... ie side.

LATEST FASHIONS IN MOURNING.

Monastic Severity No Longer the Mode —Etiquette and Duration of Mourning.

SOME NEW CREATIONS.

Description of a Wedding Trousseau—What Will Be Most Worn This Season.

[LETTRE D'UN VIEUX PARISIEN.]

DEAR MADAME—I now redeem my promise to give some details respecting the duration of mourning, and the way in which it should be worn by ladies.

All dresses for deep mourning are in black lainage and English crape d... first period and bl...

MOURNING DRESS.

Mourning for a grandfather, a grand- ...brother or sister, brother-in-law or ...ix months: the first ...dead and

WALKING DRESS.

By the firm of Aine.

WIDOWS' MOURNING.

Widows' mourning, the longest of all, should be worn for a year and six weeks. Some even prolong the period to eighteen months. In the first case, lainage is worn during the first six months with crape; during the next six months silk and lace, and during the last six months half-mourning materials. In the second case deep mourning, woollen fabrics and crape are worn for a year, silk and lace for three months, and half-mourning for three months.

At the beginning of mourning a long dress should be worn in the house with headdress of crape. The English widow's cap with a small white diadem is in favor just now. Trimmings of white batiste are also worn on the sleeves and at the neck.

Mme. BELLANGER - Corsets Stella

47 Boulevard Haussmann. **Telephone 162.18.**

Mme. Bellanger is universally known as the corsetière of the great majority of the ladies of foreign courts and of French ladies residing abroad. By sending her models to all parts of the world, she gives the dominant note of the lines in fashion. Those ladies unable to come to Paris have recourse to her catalogue and correspondence. Mme. Bellanger personally attends to all letters and gives instructions for the proper execution of the orders received.

Being the corsetière of almost all American ladies resident in Paris, she endeavors to oblige them in every way. She reminds them that her corsets are to give proper support to the organs, particularly at a period when sports are so much in vogue. Quite straight, 20 centimètres, 17fr. 90c.; 24 centimètres, 25fr.; the same, 28 centimètres, with arched front, 30fr. May be worn with or without the corset without inconvenience.

No. 225 is a "gaine" or tight-fitting garment, interwoven with elastic forming a sheath, intended to replace the corset, and with its supple, flowing lines, gives the illusion the wearer is without corset. The present "chic" styles require precisely such light, undulating lines without the aid of the corset. This model is here represented with a busk,

No. 223.

No. 225.

made to measure at very reasonable prices and ... herself. Ladies disliking to order with- ... best shapes are offered the advan- ... before ordering. Some ... corset which is ... than

but may be made without it, and may have an opening or lacing at the back with or without whalebone, as required. All these models meet with equal success, and are well adapted for the present period of sports and automobilism, when ladies, while wishing to have good figures, also ... pliancy and ease, and they satisfy hygienic ... by giving the organs proper support. ... 35fr.; 35 centimètres, 45fr.; ... breast entirely ... very ... ong, ... s no

It will be welcome news to many a fair one to learn that the secret for obtaining a supple and lithe figure has at last been discovered. Corpulence can be reduced and the lines of the hips rendered slighter and more graceful through this wonderful discovery, and that without medical treatment whatever.

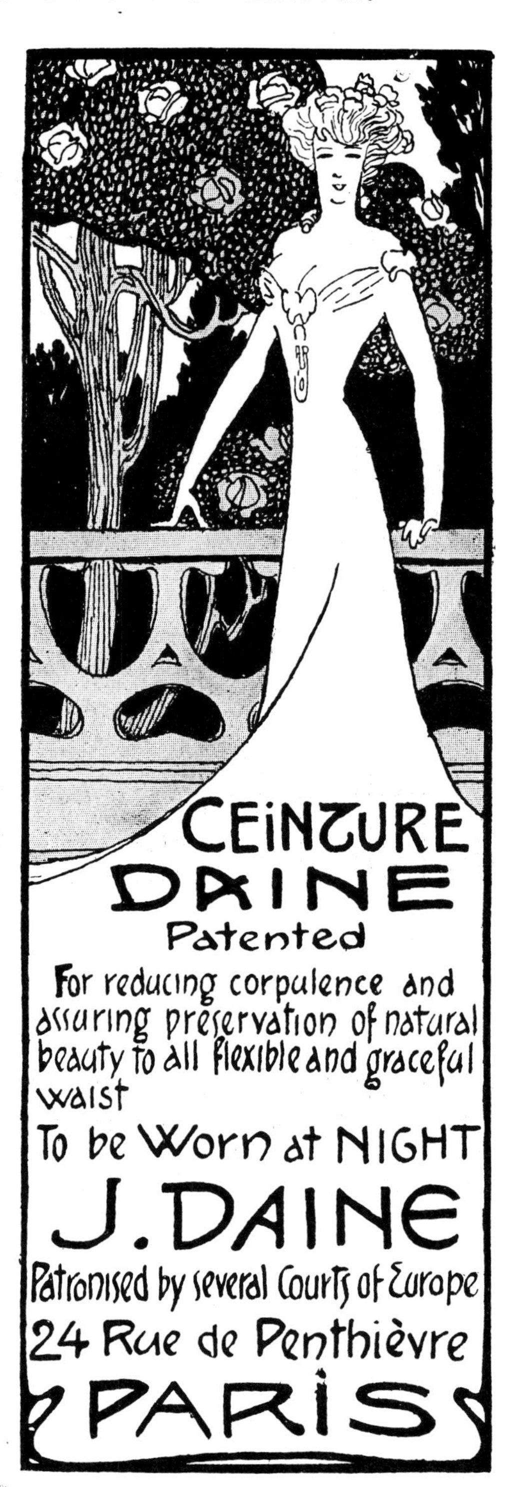

HE SMARTEST "STRAIGHT IN FRONT" CORSET.

GUILLOT & Co.

10 Rue de la Paix,

PARIS,

ustly enjoy the highest re-utation among ladies who are nxious about their beauty and ne suppleness of their waist. his establishment, whose orsets and Petticoats are eritable marvels of grace and ood taste, multiplies its crea-ons to satisfy the require-ents of its customers by the ontinual production of no-elties.

OODS SENT TO ANY PART OF THE WORLD.

A SMART CORSET

n best obtainable satin-coutil, white, eam, blue, pink, mauve, terra-cotta Nile, trimmed with beautiful lace.

BEST MAKE and FINISH from 45fr.

elivered in any part of the United ingdom carriage paid against cheque or postal order in favor of

GUILLOT & CO.,

For £1 18s. 6d.

With this Lovely Corset the Ideal Figure is obtained.

GUILLOT & Co.

10 Rue de la Paix,

PARIS.

Measurements Required to Execute Orders by Correspondence, to be taken over corset laced and worn

1. Size of Waist.
2 to 2. Length of Busk.
3. Measurement round the Chest.
4. Measurement round the Hips.
5 to 5 Under the Arms to Waist.

EVERY ATTENTION GIVEN TO ORDERS BY MAIL.

A SMART CORSET

In best obtainable satin-coutil, white, cream, blue, pink, mauve, terra-cotta or Nile, trimmed with beautiful lace.

BEST MAKE and FINISH from 45fr.

Delivered in any part of the United Kingdom carriage paid against cheque or postal order in favor of

GUILLOT & CO.,

A Costly Undertaking.

It is well to take a good look ahead when uying pretty lingerie. Its upkeep, the ecessary washing, the caprices of fashion, hich changes novelties to antiques almost efore one is aware of it, and the dyer's ills, all swell the monthly budget for the oilette to the point of bankruptcy.

I have seen silk chemises so tricked out real laces, ribbons and kni

OPENWORK EMBROIDERY UPON DAINTY LINGERIE.

Its Present Vogue Results Largely from the Terrible Costliness of Cleaning Lace.

TRUE STANDARD OF ELEGANCE.

(From "L'Art et la Mode.")

Openwork embroidery is very much in fashion for linen garments, and is so finely worked sometimes that it looks like real lace.

A few years ago, embroidery played a very important part in the make up of chemises and drawers; at present it is quite out of fashion, and lace is much preferred to it. Lace, however, is unfortunately very frail, very dear and costs a great deal for cleaning and keeping in order. So that it is only a few of the articles in a trousseau that can be decked out with Valenciennes, Malines, guipures, etc.

A Costly Undertaking.

It is well to take a good look ahead when buying pretty lingerie. Its upkeep, the necessary washing, the caprices of fashion, which changes novelties to antiques almost before one is aware of it, and the dyer's bills, all swell the monthly budget for the ... point of bankruptcy.

... and for all, for he charged 30fr. for each every time they passed through his hands. Millionaires can indulge in fancies of that sort, but not ordinary people.

In my opinion, the elegance of a chemise or pair of drawers consists more in the quality of the material employed and in the cut than in the knicknacks with which it can be overloaded. Night garments should be made very wide and flowing, to ensure a good night's rest; it is in bad taste to attend too much to their mere prettiness.

Straightcut drawers are preferred at the present day, and they are certainly more stylish than any other.

Taffeta Petticoats.

Petticoats are also included within the range of luxurious underwear. Lace ornamentation is no longer much used for petticoats; it was far too easily torn, and used to cause terrible falls when the heel caught in its meshes.

Taffeta petticoats in Pompadour patterns, well cut to the shape, and covered with rows of little flounces, set in wavy or straight lines, with a narrow velvet border above and below, are the most fashionable town wear just at present.

WHERE TO BUY REAL LACE.

The Venice lace manufacturers, Melville and Ziffer, who have obtained the Grand Prix at the St. Louis Exhibition, have a branch in Paris, 54 Faubourg St.-Honoré. —*(Communicated).*

A. MELLET, Gérant.

W YORK HERALD, PARIS, SUNDAY, OCTOBER 27. 1901.
LADIES' TAILOR.
LADIES' TAILOR.

HERALD, PARIS, SUNDAY. OCTOBER 27, 1901.
TURIERS.
LADIES' TAILORS.

THE NEW YORK HERALD.

COMPLETE NUMBER 12 PAGES. EUROPEAN EDITION—PARIS. SATURDAY, APRIL 16, 1904. COMPLETE NUMBER 12 PAGES.

5 Sports

SPORTS SHAPED THE WAY OF LIFE and the looks of the Belle Epoque; it also marked the eclipse of the boudoir.

Thanks to the *Herald*'s statistics, it is easy to follow the spectacular success of bicycles, cars and airplanes. In 1901, there were 839,856 bicycles in France or 21 machines per 1,000 inhabitants. It was estimated that there were 4,000,000 machines throughout the world.

In 1899, it took a little over 11 days to cover the 765 kilometers between Nice and Paris by car – at 12 miles an hour. By 1906, Duray, on a Dietrich machine, set a new 113-kilometer-an-hour record at the 600-kilometer "Circuit des Ardennes." Aviation was also making progress. In 1906, the Wrights, after declaring "The aeroplane problem is solved," flew a record flight of 24 miles, or a mile a minute. In 1911, the American Charles T. Weymann covered 150 kilometers in 1 hour, 11 minutes and 36 seconds in a monoplane race. After being cheered by 15,000 enthusiastic spectators, Weymann made a statement for the American public: "I have been called courageous, I'm really only adventurous."

As they learned to play golf and tennis, to swim and to ride, people changed and sportswear was invented. Women reaped the greatest advantage. It took years for the corset – which shaped women's bodies like a firm and splendid S – to unwind, but it finally did, and by 1910 the silhouette had straightened into a triumphant and liberated I.

This did not all happen overnight. Around 1895, ice-skating, a dainty sport which has become increasingly marginal in recent times, was still enormously popular. People gathered around the Horseshoe Pond in the Bois de Boulogne, where they exercised both their social and sporting prowess. One gets an idea of skating's importance in the life of the Belle Epoque from the *Herald*'s regularly and somewhat primly asking: "Ladies, have you all got your precious cards (pink this year) for Le Cercle des Patineurs? If not, it is high time to do so, you know how difficult they are to obtain, unless you are blessed with a friend at court."

The "Cercle des Patineurs" was "for the elite, including Lord Dufferin." His Lordship, a recognized eccentric, would put his skates on at the Embassy, then step out of the carriage, his blades locked in wooden blocks "which he took off himself."

Unlike skating, swimming was just beginning to revolutionize people's lives. Within easy reach of Paris, Trouville-Deauville became the chicest of all sea resorts. In 1909, the *Herald* reported that at Deauville –

"a very simple little beach" – some ladies drove to the beach in their bathing suits. Once they had finished swimming, they wrapped up in huge peignoirs, handed over by their maids, and came back to their villas. A ladies' orchestra played during the swim as well as during the 4 o'clock tea.

There was a continual coming and going between the two neighboring towns, visitors in Trouville going for walks in Deauville and the inhabitants of Deauville paying similar visits to Trouville. A large number went in carriages and in automobiles, and some even on horseback.

Yachts anchored in the harbor of Trouville included, on a sunny day in 1900, the *Alberta*, which belonged to the King of the Belgians. The King had lunch at the Hôtel de Paris, then went to the races. Among the habitués, the *Herald* listed the Duc de Grammont, the Marquis de Noailles and a Mr. Cromwell and family from New York. The chief point of rendezvous was the Rothschilds' stud farm at Meautry, a setting still used today for summer entertaining by Baron and Baronne Guy de Rothschild.

Evenings were spent at the casino, where actors from Paris, such as Marguerite Deval of the Mathurins, and Tarride from the Gymnase, performed. In August 1908, the *Herald*'s reporter noted a large number of light dresses, "many in dark yellow Irish and Cluny lace on a white background." Women were not afraid to wear all their jewels in public. "It seems quite natural that the women should be covered with pearls and diamonds during the day. The result is that their evening dresses positively blaze with gems."

Bicycling – or "La petite reine bicyclette" – made a huge impact because it reached down to the masses. Compared to walking, which was now looked upon as monotonous, cycling was declared a suitable sport for women and a good cure for nerves.

In 1895, cycling had caught on in Paris as *the* winter sport. Despite bitterly cold weather, on January 7th that year thousands of spectators witnessed the racing at the Vélodrome d'Hiver, and "entre nous, the attendance did not consist only of what racing scribes call 'oi polloi' but a goodly gathering of our leading turfistes, the Omnium Club's stand and reserved boxes being au complet."

The *Herald*'s famous Weather Girl, sketched by Henry Tenré, which appeared every day on Page Two, was now a pretty girl on a bicycle, either riding merrily away in the sunshine or fighting the elements. Useful hints to cyclists, often illustrated with sketches, became a regular *Herald* column. One of them bluntly advised "How to look awkward or nice on a wheel." Counsel for lady cyclists included the best method of sitting, the necessity for having a correctly adjusted machine, and even what to eat and drink when cycling. The advice ended with: "Study your instrument."

Cycling naturally led to cycling costumes. Wool was declared the only material that could be safely worn during "sustained open air exertion." The first trace of women wearing trousers appeared in the form of knickerbockers, which required the hand of a competent cycling tailor.

Bloomers were a controversial issue – whose charms were lost on some. On July 17, 1898, the *Herald* reported from Berlin: "A few days ago, a young lady called as a witness arrived at the court on her bicycle and gave her evidence wearing 'bloomers,' which brought upon her a stern reprimand from the presiding judge."

Another having problems over her bicycling was Princess Louise of Saxony, very much a New Woman, who, causing a "Tempest in a Dresden Vase," horrified her Royal mother-in-law by riding a bicycle. After her first ball, she said it would be the last because if she couldn't ride a bicycle, she wouldn't dance. The princess, who was pretty, young, good, gay and happy, was also wild, and sometimes drove like mad, until even a groom, perched behind her, dared to remonstrate.

Automobiles were having a spectacular success. In February 1895, the *Herald* recorded that Messrs. de Dion Bouton and Co. sent eighteen vehicles for the horseless carriage race from Paris to Bordeaux. By 1900, automobiles represented an enormous investment for the French who, that year, exported six million francs' worth – or nearly eight times as much as in 1898. As early as 1901, cars became a status symbol. The *Herald*, reporting on "A Bourgeois and his Auto," wrote that "Durand buys one. Madame Durand was humiliated. Dupont already had one."

In 1899, the trip between Nice and Paris by automobile – at 12 miles an hour – was declared better than by carriage, for "it would take three teams of horses to cover the same ground and also be more fatiguing." But the expense – 48 francs a day for motor naphtha, steline and automobiline, plus two servants going by rail each day with the luggage, which brought the total to about 100 francs – was considered excessive. Advice to car owners included such basics as: "Get a competent mechanic."

As people started traveling longer distances, they experienced dismal accommodations. The Touring Club de France fought to bring country inns up to hygienic requirements. In 1900, the Club listed a number of rules and brought out a specimen bedroom "which may be seen and studied in the health section of the Exhibition." The bedroom, it was decided, should have sunlight, simple furniture, light colors, a chimney and no hangings – only white muslin curtains. It was recommended that the bedstead be of painted iron and the night tables of metal – the same for the bidet. This decor is still to be found in many a French country inn.

The 12 miles an hour very soon became 61 kilometers an hour. On June 15, 1900, "French Team Wins International Automobile Cup" with a M. Charron covering 566 kilometers in 9 hours, 9 minutes and 49 seconds.

Improvements in production were moving fast as well. In April 1899, Comte de Dion was prosecuted for employing men beyond the legal hours. The facts were simple enough: "Automobilism is very much the fashion. The Puteaux factory received more orders than it can take so the comte asked his workers to work overtime."

In 1901, an entire page was devoted to "The Automobile and its Future," an exhibition at the Grand Palais which was attracting thousands of visitors. "The Exhibition is sure to become a permanent fixture in winter or early spring," the *Herald* predicted and it was indeed a great success.

Two years later, the circulation (traffic) Committee of the Paris Municipal Council submitted the speed question to a practical test, sending 22 autos on a trip extending over 15 kilometers, after which the automobilists easily convinced the City Fathers of the extreme facility with which autos can be maneuvered. It was decided that 20 to 25 kilometers an hour would not be dangerous.

On May 23rd of the same year, this so far carefree world suffered its first spectacular casualty. During the Paris-Madrid race, which drew about 250 competitors, a fatal accident killed Marcel Renault. It was he who, in 1898, had founded the Renault factory in Billancourt and placed on the market the Renault voiturette with the so-called Cardan system of transmission which he had designed in cooperation with his brothers.

By 1904, the Salon de l'Auto had become the greatest spectacle of the modern industry. France was able to provide 'de luxe' models of the latest type. Germany too, with Mercedes, was right up there. America managed to exhibit some cars despite the distance, but offered no competition to European manufacturers. The *Herald*, however, voiced a warning: "The special manner in which they [American cars] are constructed points to the fact that they will compete to some extent with autos made 'wholesale' or 'Bon marché.'" It took Henry Ford to do just that.

On April 26, 1905, the *Herald*, which had been sponsoring coaching trips, ran its first automobile trip to Versailles, in a 15 HP Panhard Levassor. The round trip cost 20 francs per person. The same year, Peter Lorillard Reynolds, the father of coaching in America, was ending his last 1,000-mile coaching tour. He now planned to buy a French auto.

In 1906, the Kaiser agreed to sponsor the Imperial Automobile Club, infusing new life into that institution. Before long, kings and emperors were acquiring all kinds of fancy, exclusive, custom-made cars. In 1906, Grand Duke Alexander of Russia's vast auto had novel coachwork. It included at the rear two seats back to back, protected by a hood, for servants. It was the first time such an arrangement had been made. The car did not travel at high speed, 40 kilometers an hour at most. The duke was going to use it first in Biarritz, then in Russia.

The *Herald* ran an ad in 1906 for "the most comfortable car in the world," a Lorraine-Dietrich limousine, belonging to the Countess of Warwick. It was divided into two compartments, with four seats that could be drawn together and turned into couches for repose. It also had two folding tables for games, meals or reading, electric lights, Vuitton drawers and bureaux – plus external space for holding playing cards, writing material, medicine chest, and, of all things, revolvers. There was also a washstand and a tap for water, a WC, a wardrobe, two drawers for table linen, a cupboard for photographic apparatus and a kitchen, also installed by Vuitton.

Autos were causing all kinds of problems, including "a knotty question" that was settled by the French Council of State, which declared autos to be of the masculine gender – and not feminine. The question of the horn was also raised, with Paul Meyer urging its suppression in big cities and arguing that if a chauffeur had nothing but his voice to warn other users of the road, he would be compelled to drive at moderate speed.

Another hassle was settled when the owner of a house in Parc Monceau went to court to prevent one of his tenants from bringing his car into the courtyard. He lost the case. The judge decided that automobiles had as much right to enter the courtyard as other carriages.

Fashion never lost its rights. In 1901, tailor-made costumes were numerous, with skirts topped by short boleros and large mantles of Russian ponyskin. A new windshield by Huillier, offered by the Mors Cie., promised to do away with the exquisite torture of the wind and goggles "which make one look like a beast of the Apocalypse."

Automobiles and elegance were bound to join hands. On November 9, 1900, at a great automobile fête with about 150 handsomely decorated vehicles, the sable-clad Baronne de Zuylen (wife of the Auto Club president), seated amid a mass of multi-colored dahlias, chrysanthemums and fern leaves, drove a 12 HP Panhard. Also familiar to Parisian gawkers was Mme. de Gaste, who appeared in her well-known car, the Walkyrie, smothered by chrysanthemums, pink carnations and white heather, while other women were drowned under rare orchids.

Lifestyle changed as, thanks to the all-powerful automobile, the distance between the rue de la Paix and the heights of Ville d'Avray or between the Place Vendôme and Versailles was abbreviated. Exciting lawn tennis matches were got up, dainty "gouters" organized, "sauteries champêtres" improvised, "and in the evening, everyone goes back to Paris, if so disposed. This is a picture of town and country life which is greatly appreciated at the moment both by hostesses and visitors."

It was not long before women drivers became an easy target, with headlines asking: "Is a woman to be trusted at the automobile steering wheel?" The prudent answer: "In the last 10 years, women's nerves have stiffened with tennis, golf, swimming, hunting, yachting and now automobiling. She has nerve and courage, she is ready and more women, even plucky society girls, are driving autos more today than ever before."

Other sports that came into their own during the Belle Epoque included polo, yachting, ballooning and flying. Flying is still a major and revolutionary force in our everyday lives, whereas polo, yachting and ballooning have remained rich men's sports.

Polo, which Gordon Bennett loved and which he introduced to America, came second after racing in 1905 and offered a good dose of snob appeal. "Polo is famous," the *Herald* wrote, "for its little breakfasts, dinners and above all, its five o'clocks." The season, then as today, ran in Paris from April 15 to July 13 and then moved on to Deauville.

At the turn of the century, yachting, or "Maritimo Villegature," was becoming more and more the fashion, causing another change in lifestyle and altering the summer social season. Instead of taking a villa or stopping at a hotel, people began to own or charter their own yachts. The reasons then were the same as today. The aim of those seeking "repose" was to get away as far as possible from the turmoil of busy life, its political incidents and all its worries.

Millionaires were fiercely competitive in the way they used their yachts. In 1900, Sir Thomas Lipton declared: "There is nothing I want more than that cup," and gave carte blanche to the builders of the *Shamrock II*, for "I am not even thinking of money in this case. What I want is the best possible boat." By 1903, Sir Thomas's dream came true as *Shamrock III* won the Lipton Cup hands down.

For kings and emperors, yacht-racing was a spectacular and prestigious issue. In 1904, with ideal weather at Cowes, Lord Ormond gave the signal for the start of the race for Emperor William's Cup. The King and Prince of Wales and the other men present wore the evening dress of the Royal Yacht squadron – a little dark-blue mess jacket trimmed with gold buttons, white waistcoats, black ties and trousers to match the jackets. Among the yachting novelties, several men were wearing evening dress waistcoat buttons and links made of cut crystal, upon which were enameled the pennant of the Royal Yacht Squadron.

At the beginning of the century, ballooning was declared here to stay and safer than riding in a tram. By 1908, balloon parties had become a favorite Sunday recreation and on April 11, 1910, for the first time in France, paying passengers ascended for short flights after preliminary tests at Pau.

The sport had a keen fan in publisher Gordon Bennett. Six years after launching the Gordon Bennett Cup race for automobiles – which became the French Grand Prix – he established the Gordon Bennett Cup International Balloon Race. In June 1906, 250,000 Parisians filled the Tuileries Gardens and lined the banks of the Seine to watch the ascent of sixteen gas-filled balloons from six countries. The race became an annual event until 1939 when it was dropped, only to be revived in 1979 in Los Angeles.

In June 1900, Jacques Balsan, starting from Paris in the *Saint Louis*, landed near the St. Petersburg railway station, after covering 2,000 kilometers. He and Godard together made the highest ascent of the

Exhibition contest, rising to 8,225 meters. The height record, however, according to the *Herald*, still belonged to Glaisher and Coxwell who soared to a height of 10,500 meters, narrowly escaping with their lives.

It was also in 1900 that Count Zeppelin's giant airship, the *Koenig Karl* – which was shaped like a German sausage and had taken two years to build – steered and moved against the wind. This most interesting trial of the big aerial wonder took place over Lake Constance.

In April 1903, the pilot Santos-Dumont was busy rigging up his airship No. 7 at Neuilly. Weather permitting, the famous aeronaut was to sail over the Bois de Boulogne the following week. And in May, he told the *Herald* of his experiment with No. 9: "I shall not try to make a speed record with it," he said. "It is a little toy which could not resist a moderate wind. It is useful to me for experiments."

Americans were getting into the act. On October 3, 1906, the "Coupe Internationale des Aeronautes" was won by the American Frank P. Lahm, who went from France to England and dropped near Chichester. In a London interview, he told the *Herald*: "This is my 15th ascent and the longest journey I have ever made in the air. Being American, I am sorry the balloon was not of American make."

On May 22, 1906, the *Herald* carried a picture of Louis Bleriot's new airplane, on which he was putting the finishing touches before trying to fly it on Lac d'Enghien. Bleriot was described as an inventor and a well-known constructor of headlights.

Three years later, on August 20, Bleriot made a record flight in a monoplane from near Etampes to outside Orléans, with only one stop. "The flight will make history in records of conquests of the air," the *Herald* wrote, following up with a poetic description. "It was a quarter to five in the gray of a dull sunrise that the aeroplane, a grayer shadow against the gray scheme of things, started across the plain after running 30 meters and flashing heavenward like an arrow. There was a burst of applause from the spectators watching the daring aviator. Suddenly, something went wrong as he was over Eure et Loir. He gently glided to earth. The peasants gaped as he repaired the damage and took off again." He had covered 47 kilometers in 56 minutes, 10 seconds.

For his feat, the first flight of 40 kilometers or more in a straight line, Bleriot won the Aero-Club de France's 14,000 francs prize. (In the same column, the *Herald* reported that the Wright brothers were having trouble at Fort Myer; after two attempts their airplane had succeeded in flying only the length of the parade ground.)

On August 24, 1909, the American Glenn H. Curtiss achieved the world's speed record at Rheims aerodrome, covering 10 kilometers in 8 minutes, 35$\frac{3}{5}$ seconds and beating the flight made by Bleriot earlier in the day. Curtiss's compatriots were wild with enthusiasm over the capture of the Coupe Internationale. A Mr. Herring, who was one of the builders of the prizewinning machine, commented: "I want to say that the *Herald* has done much toward bringing this victory to America. Not only has the *Herald* been the foremost champion of aeronautical development from the start, but it has had much to do with the success of this meeting at Rheims."

In 1910, Morane set a new world's height record. He reached 2,582 meters at a Deauville aviation meeting and said: "It is easy to rise high but it is another matter to descend safely."

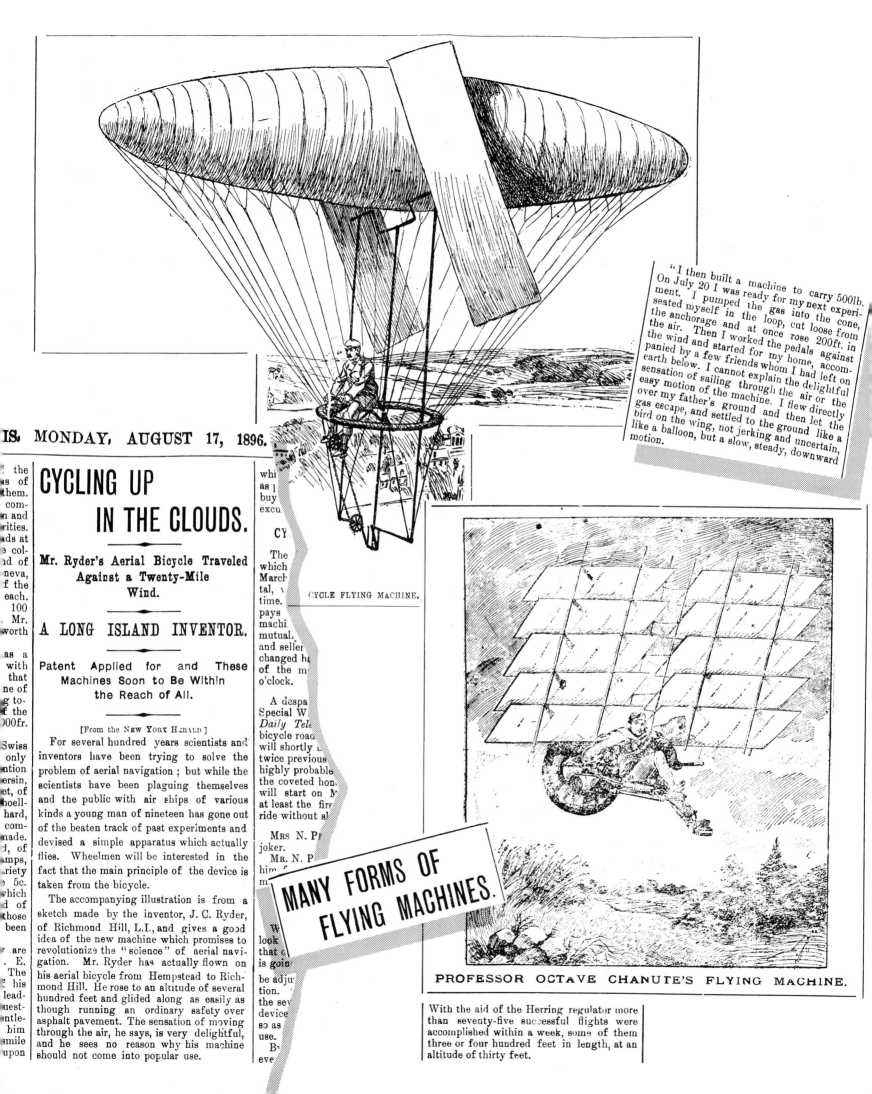

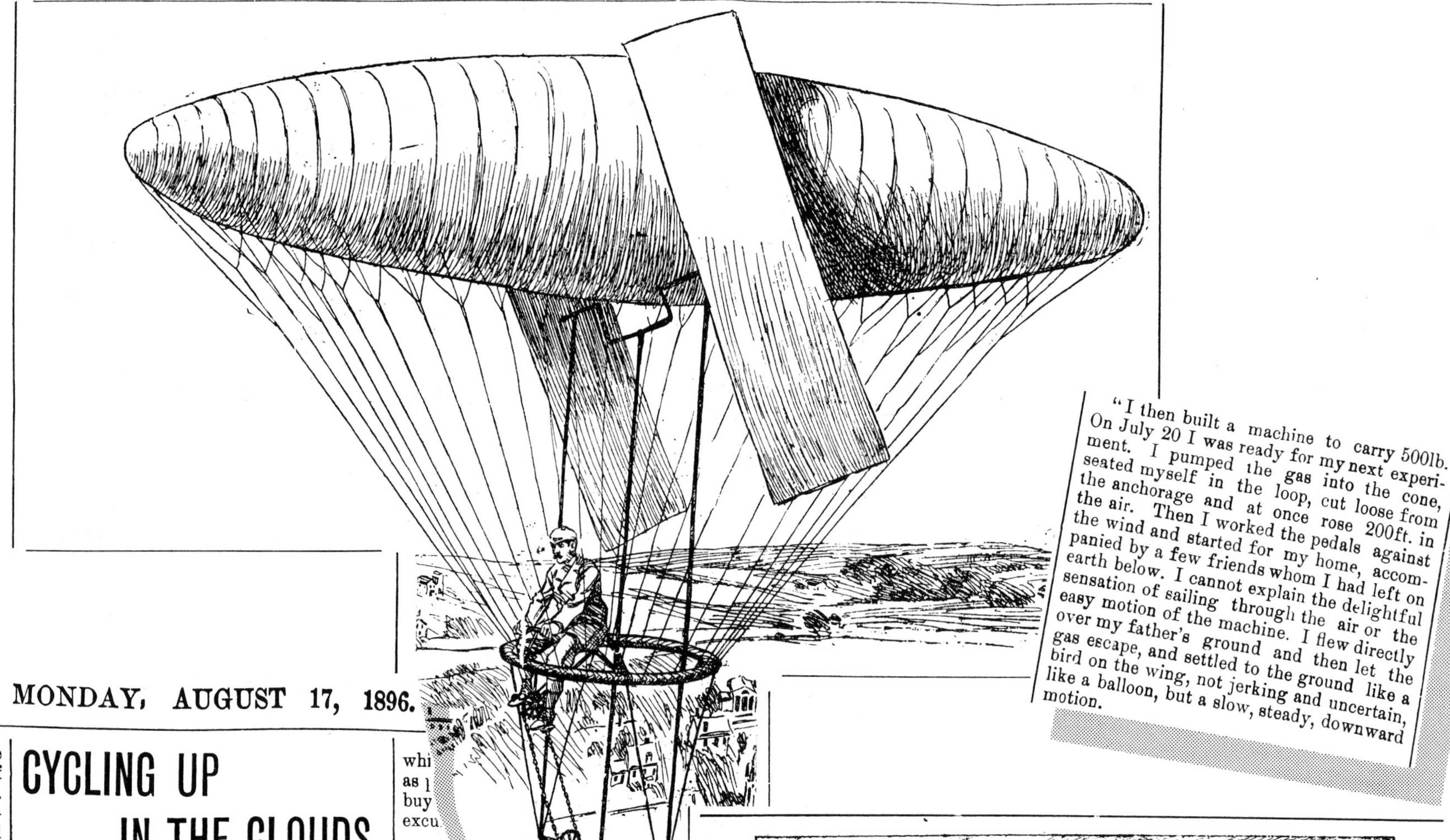

CYCLE FLYING MACHINE.

"I then built a machine to carry 500lb. On July 20 I was ready for my next experiment. I pumped the gas into the cone, seated myself in the loop, cut loose from the anchorage and at once rose 200ft. in the air. Then I worked the pedals against the wind and started for my home, accompanied by a few friends whom I had left on earth below. I cannot explain the delightful sensation of sailing through the air or the easy motion of the machine. I flew directly over my father's ground and then let the gas escape, and settled to the ground like a bird on the wing, not jerking and uncertain, like a balloon, but a slow, steady, downward motion.

MONDAY, AUGUST 17, 1896.

CYCLING UP IN THE CLOUDS.

Mr. Ryder's Aerial Bicycle Traveled Against a Twenty-Mile Wind.

A LONG ISLAND INVENTOR.

Patent Applied for and These Machines Soon to Be Within the Reach of All.

[From the NEW YORK HERALD]

For several hundred years scientists and inventors have been trying to solve the problem of aerial navigation; but while the scientists have been plaguing themselves and the public with air ships of various kinds a young man of nineteen has gone out of the beaten track of past experiments and devised a simple apparatus which actually flies. Wheelmen will be interested in the fact that the main principle of the device is taken from the bicycle.

The accompanying illustration is from a sketch made by the inventor, J. C. Ryder, of Richmond Hill, L.I., and gives a good idea of the new machine which promises to revolutionize the "science" of aerial navigation. Mr. Ryder has actually flown on his aerial bicycle from Hempstead to Richmond Hill. He rose to an altitude of several hundred feet and glided along as easily as though running an ordinary safety over asphalt pavement. The sensation of moving through the air, he says, is very delightful, and he sees no reason why his machine should not come into popular use.

MANY FORMS OF FLYING MACHINES.

PROFESSOR OCTAVE CHANUTE'S FLYING MACHINE.

With the aid of the Herring regulator more than seventy-five successful flights were accomplished within a week, some of them three or four hundred feet in length, at an altitude of thirty feet.

Outbreak of Invention in America Which May Rival the Bicycle Craze.

MANY PATENTS ALREADY FILED.

Some Have Succeeded Partially, but Most of Them Are in the "Model" Stage of Progress.

MR. FREYMANN'S ODD IDEA.

He Starts on a Bicycle, Others Adopt the Kite Principle, and Others the Balloon.

EXPLOSIVES AS A MOTIVE POWER

To judge from the newspapers that have recently arrived from the United States, the flying machine craze bids fair to soon eclipse the bicycle craze. Hundreds of flying machines are being experimented with in all parts of the country.

A FLYING BICYCLE.

Mr. Oscar Freymann is the inventor of a brand-new flying machine which has several

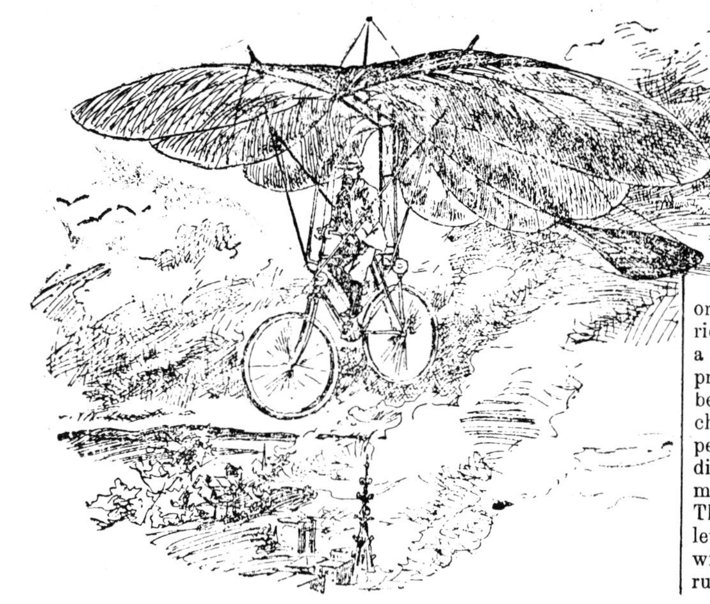

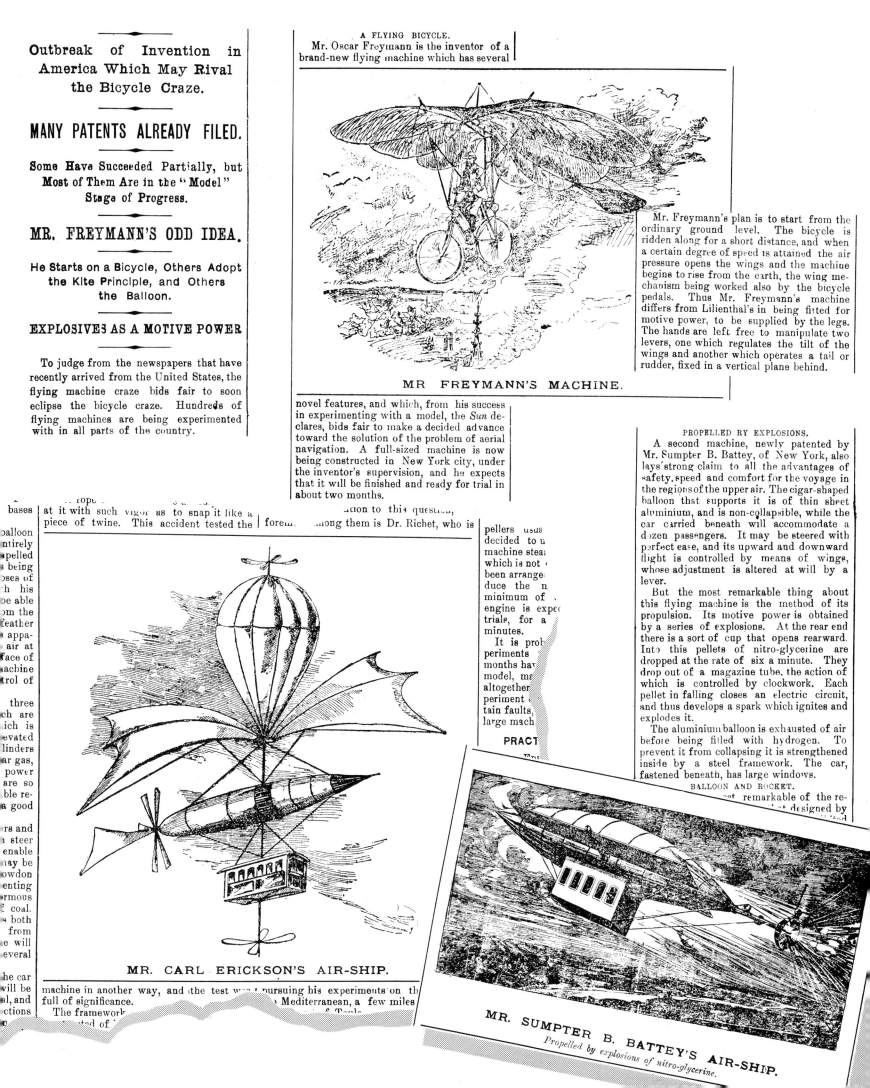

MR FREYMANN'S MACHINE.

novel features, and which, from his success in experimenting with a model, the *Sun* declares, bids fair to make a decided advance toward the solution of the problem of aerial navigation. A full-sized machine is now being constructed in New York city, under the inventor's supervision, and he expects that it will be finished and ready for trial in about two months.

Mr. Freymann's plan is to start from the ordinary ground level. The bicycle is ridden along for a short distance, and when a certain degree of speed is attained the air pressure opens the wings and the machine begins to rise from the earth, the wing mechanism being worked also by the bicycle pedals. Thus Mr. Freymann's machine differs from Lilienthal's in being fitted for motive power, to be supplied by the legs. The hands are left free to manipulate two levers, one which regulates the tilt of the wings and another which operates a tail or rudder, fixed in a vertical plane behind.

PROPELLED BY EXPLOSIONS.

A second machine, newly patented by Mr. Sumpter B. Battey, of New York, also lays strong claim to all the advantages of safety, speed and comfort for the voyage in the regions of the upper air. The cigar-shaped balloon that supports it is of thin sheet aluminium, and is non-collapsible, while the car carried beneath will accommodate a dozen passengers. It may be steered with perfect ease, and its upward and downward flight is controlled by means of wings, whose adjustment is altered at will by a lever.

But the most remarkable thing about this flying machine is the method of its propulsion. Its motive power is obtained by a series of explosions. At the rear end there is a sort of cup that opens rearward. Into this pellets of nitro-glycerine are dropped at the rate of six a minute. They drop out of a magazine tube, the action of which is controlled by clockwork. Each pellet in falling closes an electric circuit, and thus develops a spark which ignites and explodes it.

The aluminium balloon is exhausted of air before being filled with hydrogen. To prevent it from collapsing it is strengthened inside by a steel framework. The car, fastened beneath, has large windows.

BALLOON AND ROCKET.

... remarkable of the re... designed by ...

bases ... balloon ... ntirely ... pelled ... being ... ses of ... h his ... e able ... m the ... eather ... appa- ... air at ... face of ... achine ... trol of

three ... ch are ... ich is ... vated ... linders ... ar gas, ... power ... are so ... ble re- ... a good

rs and ... steer ... enable ... ay be ... owdon ... enting ... rmous ... coal. ... both ... from ... e will ... everal

he car ... vill be ... al, and ... ctions

... rope ... at it with such vigor as to snap it like a piece of twine. This accident tested the

MR. CARL ERICKSON'S AIR-SHIP.

machine in another way, and the test was ... full of significance.

The framework ... ...cted of ...

...tion to this question, ... foremost among them is Dr. Richet, who is ... pursuing his experiments on th... Mediterranean, a few miles ... of Toulo...

pellers usua... decided to u... machine stea... which is not ... been arrange... duce the n... minimum of ... engine is expe... trials, for a ... minutes.

It is prob... periments ... months hav... model, ma... altogether ... periment ... tain faults, ... large mach...

PRACT...

MR. SUMPTER B. BATTEY'S AIR-SHIP.

Propelled by explosions of nitro-glycerine.

NEW WRIGHT RECORDS MADE

"Herald" Correspondent Accompanies Aviator and Describes His Impressions of Travel in an Aeroplane.

FLIGHT OF NEARLY AN HOUR

With Passenger, American Inventor Makes a Remarkable Trip of Fifty-five Minutes.

[SPECIAL TO THE HERALD.]

LE MANS, Saturday.—I have had the good fortune at last to make an aeroplane flight with Mr. Wilbur Wright. It is true, it was only a short one of 3min. 21sec., but it was long enough to enable me to form an opinion as to what aeroplane travel is like. Furthermore, the flight, I presume, was more or less historical, since this is the first time on record that a newspaper correspondent has been carried through the air under such conditions.

It was a marvellous day and very shortly after eight o'clock this morning Mr. Wright commenced his series of flights. First of all he flew for 4min. 50sec., then for 9min. 31sec., and finally for a couple of minutes. Mr. Wright flew so low that he cut the heads off the long grass which covers a portion of the Auvours camp. But he was so far merely testing his new propellers and it was when he descended at about 10 a.m. that I was able to get a definite promise from him that I should be the first passenger of the day, no matter who might request to be taken for an aerial trip. Already I had his promise that the HERALD correspondent should be the first journalist he would take for a flight with him.

"Have You Made Your Will?"

At four o'clock Mr. Wright again went for a trial spin which lasted 18min. 24sec. Then the aeroplane was replaced on the starting rail and Mr. Wright having looked over all its parts carefully, and having examined the wires, head-piece, tail and levers, walked over to where I was standing and laughingly remarked: "Have you made your will?"

This I took to be Mr. Wright's invitation to take a seat in the aeroplane, and I at once climbed over the wires of the framework and got into the passenger's seat by the side of the motor. The seat is small and not over comfortable, but for the present Mr. Wright's aim is not to provide comfort, but to secure practical bird-like flight

When I was well seated, Mr. Wright pointed out a few details. First of all he told me to rest my feet firmly on a bar between two cords. Then I was to take care not to touch a cord crossing near my chest and which the operator strikes when he wishes to stop the motor. Another and important instruction was to force down a small catch on the magneto when he nudged my arm just before the start.

Final Preparation.

Everything was now ready for flight. The weights had been hoisted up into position and the rope attached to the frame. At a signal given by Mr. Wright two machinists set the motor revolving. Seated as I was by the side of the engine the noise was deafening. The sharp crackling of the open exhaust reminded me of a racing automobile getting up speed. As soon as the motor was fairly humming, Mr. Wright climbed into the seat by my side, and with his left hand gripped the lever controlling the head-piece. His right hand held the rope which controls the weights. He gave me the pre-arranged nudge, and I pressed down the catch on the magneto. The motor responded instantly and roared still louder.

"Now!" said Mr. Wright, and he let the weights drop. Good God, what a rush! I never felt any other sensation before like it, except once when dashing down a water chute. The sensation lasted just about a second, that is to say, until we had cleared the rail; then all real sensation ceased. Higher and higher we climbed, until we reached the turning at the eastern end of the field, and then, at an altitude of fift feet, we swept round the bend and began the straight run back of about a mile.

What Was Happening.

It was not until the aeroplane rounded the first corner that I was sufficiently accustomed to the novelty of the situation to take in all that was happening. Going down the straight, however, I got the impression I had been hoping for, and which I was sure would come, and that was the feeling of absolute security. We glided in the air. There was no shock of any kind, no vibration, and only the roar of the motor prevailed to keep in the mind the idea that this was really mechanical flight.

The most striking feature of the experience was that all impression of high speed disappeared as the machine progressed. Although we were rushing along through the air at more than 60 kilomètres an hour, all objects were so far away that they appeared to pass by slowly. Tufts of grass, pieces of paper, small trees and other objects stood out clearly between the bars, and even the groups of people lining the entire field looked small.

Personal Impressions.

Every now and then I could see enthusiasts waving their handkerchiefs. In the distance I noticed a horse galloping towards the middle of the camp. After taking the corner at the western end of the field, we must have risen to an altitude of 60ft., at least it seemed so. The starting pylon lay well beneath us as we passed by, and even the watch tower did not dominate us.

As we again left the crowd behind I began to watch Mr. Wilbur Wright. He sat calm and cool, his countenance showing no sign of anxiety or worry. Except in taking the turnings, he never used the levers which twist the wings. His left hand, however, was constantly at work with the headpiece. It was like a man playing billiards. He handled the lever lightly, even playfully. To each of his movements the machine responded instantly. He put the apparatus where he liked, so to speak. If he wanted to fly at an altitude of fifty feet, he placed the aeroplane at that altitude, just as a clever "chauffeur" would bring up an automobile on any indicated line upon the road. It was all so definite and so absolutely complete that the conviction, long since formed in my mind, became positive—viz., that this man is not making experiments, but real demonstrations of the art of flying.

MR. WRIGHT CREATES YET ANOTHER FLYING RECORD.

He Flies for Fifty-Five Minutes with a Passenger.

[SPECIAL TO THE HERALD.]

LE MANS, Saturday.—Mr. Wright made a further ascent this evening, M. Frantz-Reichel, of the "Figaro," this time being his passenger in what proved to be a record-breaking flight which lasted 55min. 31sec.

When the aeroplane got away after a false start the sun had already set, and for the most part of the time the machine was invisible. As it periodically came into line with the after-glow the spectators, however, obtained a remarkable view of this marvellous craft speeding steadily through the air far from the ground.

All records made by the French school of aviators with a passenger in their aeroplane are thus beaten by Mr. Wright with ease, and there is every reason to suppose that had daylight lasted Mr. Wright would have beaten his own record of an hour and a half.

When a descent was made shortly before seven o'clock it was quite dark, and Mr. Wright had to be guided home by a lantern which was hung on the starting pylon. As the descent was completed M. Frantz-Reichel kissed Mr. Wright in true French fashion, the American aviator submitting with goodwill to the ordeal.

Experience of a Lifetime.

M. Frantz-Reichel told me in a conversation that it was the most marvellous experience of his life. "I believe," he said, "that it would be a quite simple matter to drive an aeroplane," and he added: "If I had had a notebook with me I should have written half my story for the "Figaro." After the first half-hour the sensation became quite monotonous. There is no doubt Mr. Wright has solved the problem of mechanical flight."

It is calculated that during his flights this morning Mr. Wright attained a speed of over 74 kilomètres an hour with the wind and 54 kilomètres against the wind. The average speed was judged to be 61 kilomètres an hour. During the flight to-night with M. Frantz-Reichel an average speed of 60¼ kilomètres an hour was maintained. So far as could be estimated, the whole distance covered was 58 kilomètres. This flight will count as one of the two flights stipulated in the contract between the brothers Wright and M. Lazare Weiller.

Among those who witnessed to-day's experiments were: Major Baden-Powell, Mr. Moore Brabazon, Mr. and

that was the feeling of absolute security. We glided in the air. There was no shock of any kind, no vibration, and only the roar of the motor prevailed to keep in the mind the idea that this was really mechanical flight.

WHILE DOVER AND CALAIS STILL SLEEP, M. BLÉRIOT FLIES ACROSS THE CHANNEL

BIRD'S EYE VIEW OF DOVER & DISTRICTS.

SHAKESPEARE CLIFF.

MAP SHOWING COURSE OF AEROPLANE.

M. BLÉRIOT IN AEROPLANE GARB.

ASPECT OF BLERIOT MONOPLANE.

IN VIEW OF DOVER CLIFFS.

VIEW OF DOVER, SHOWING CASTLE.

Successful Trial Trip Over, He Leaves Les Baraques and Steers His Aeroplane Out to Sea.

JOURNEY OCCUPIES 37 MINUTES

His Arrival in England Is Reported to the Authorities by Stolid English Policeman.

[SPECIAL TO THE HERALD.]

CALAIS, Sunday.—The English Channel has been crossed by aeroplane, and the "Daily Mail" prize of £1,000 has been won. The hero of the exploit is M. Louis Blériot, a man who was yesterday hobbling about on crutches. The machine employed for the first aerial journey from France to England is the Blériot Monoplane No. XI, driven by a 20 horse-power Anzani motor.

M. Blériot started from Les Baraques, on the outskirts of Calais, this morning at 4.41 o'clock and a little more than half an hour later had descended in an

ago at Issy. He walked with considerable difficulty, but when in the aeroplane declared that his injured foot did not in any way handicap him.

POLICE CONSTABLE REPORTS M. BLERIOT'S ARRIVAL.

Aviator Stops Only Few Hours in England.

[SPECIAL TO THE HERALD.]

DOVER, Sunday.—Dover was taken too much by surprise at the arrival of M Blériot early this morning to display great excitement. The first person to sight the artificial bird from France was Police Constable Fleet, who at once reported the arrival to the authorities.

An automobile rushed up from the Lord Warden Hotel to the Castle, near

to-morrow for further official celebrations and rejoicings.

FLIGHT WAS MAGNIFICENT, BUT LANDING DIFFICULT.

M. Blériot Tells the "Herald" of His Impressions.

[SPECIAL TO THE HERALD.]

DOVER, Sunday.—M. Louis Blériot was radiant when the HERALD's correspondent interviewed him at Dover shortly after his successful trip across the English channel. He was wearing the ribbon of the Legion of Honor which had been conferred on him the previous day. He appeared to limp less than when I had seen him a couple of hours before at Calais.

"How was the trip made?" I asked.

died maps carefully, and had had the country described to me."

"Did your injured foot handicap you?"

"Not in the least; for the effort necessary to work the pedals was very slight, and after I landed I simply had to wait until an automobile arrived from Dover to take me down to the town."

MME. BLERIOT DESCRIBES TRIP ON BOARD DESTROYER.

Aeronaut Made Circle in Mid-Channel to Await Warship.

[SPECIAL TO THE HERALD.]

DOVER, Sunday.—Mme. Blériot, who followed her husband on the destroyer Escopette was wild with excitement at the success of the trip.

"But I can assure you," she said, "it was an anxious time, for the aeroplane got entirely out of our sight and we were more than half an hour without news.

COUNSEL FOR LADY CYCLISTS.

Instructions for Beginners by Miss Maria E. Ward—Many Practical Hints.

BEST METHOD OF SITTING.

Necessity for Having a Correctly Adjusted Machine—Hurry to Be Avoided.

STEERING AND PEDALLING.

Difficulties of Hill Climbing—What to Eat and Drink When Cycling.

STUDY YOUR INSTRUMENT.

[From the NEW YORK HERALD.]

Should ladies use the bicycle? That is a question which is now settled. Ladies do bike. Therefore they ought to bike. No lucid female mind can fail to see the absolute cogency of this logic. But if they bike, ladies ought to know how, when and under what conditions they should do so, how they should take the first steps, how they should choose a machine and learn to use it, what amount of exercise of this sort is useful, what injurious; what they should eat and drink, how they should dress, how they should keep their machine in good order.

MEMORANDA FOR BEGINNERS.

Here are Miss Ward's instructions as to what should be kept in mind when you are taking your first lessons: Attend to the bicycle and to nothing else. Don't attempt to talk, and look well ahead of the machine, certainly not less than twenty feet. Remember that the bicycle will go wherever the attention is directed.

In sitting upon the wheel the spinal column should maintain the same vertical plane that the rear wheel does, and should not bend laterally to balance in the usual manner. A new balance must be acquired, and other muscular combinations than those that are familiarly called upon. To wheel by rule is the better plan until the natural balance of the bicyclist is developed. Sit erect and sit still.

The bicycle must be kept from falling by a wiggling movement of the front wheel, conveyed by means of the handle bar. When moving the rapidly revolving wheels maintain the vertical plane by rotation, with but little assistance or correction from the handle bars.

HOW TO WHEEL A BICYCLE.

The "Art of Wheeling a Bicycle" receives a chapter to itself. It is explained that there are three very important methods of controlling the bicycle—namely, steering on the hands, guiding by foot pressure on the pedals, and guiding by the swaying of the body; and these methods may be used separately or in combination.

bt, an ken on, urn to nd sed ent

FOOD AND DRINK.

Even a bicycler must eat and drink. What to eat, what to drink and when to do each are important questions which Miss Ward answers with her usual good sense.

In warm weather, she says, it is permissible to drink water when wheeling; but it should be remembered that the bicyclist passes through all sorts of country, and the water may sometimes be anything but drinkable from a sanitary point of view, even causing typhoid and other fevers. Water that has been boiled is unpalatable, but it is safe; boiled and cooled, it may be rendered more palatable by shaking it or pouring it from one pitcher to another to mix air with it.

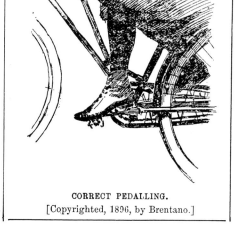

WHEELING FROM THE PEG, SHOWING INCLINATION OF THE WHEEL.
[Copyrighted, 1896, by Brentano.]

Ice in water is another source of danger.

Never prolong bicycle exercise without eating, and never work after a hearty meal; but the consumption of a couple of sandwiches at noon cannot be regarded as a serious meal; and it is often better to push on after a short halt, moving slowly, than to sit around on rocks or stumps to wait for a proper digestive period to elapse. It is well to have a small reserve supply of food, such as chocolate or beef tablets, to tide one over a prolonged period between meals. Milk and bread and cheese are good to take as an extra meal. Never work hungry if it can be avoided; the bicycle will lag, and the cyclist wonder at being weary. Keep up the food supply by all means, for fatigue sets in quickly with the desire for food, and the system quickly becomes enfeebled.

The amount of work different individuals can perform, of course, varies. Find out how much work you ought to do and do it. A physician is the only competent judge of your limitations. Never attempt any new form of exercise without being examined.

CORRECT PEDALLING.
[Copyrighted, 1896, by Brentano.]

...dvantages ...ed after the ...pt to resume it ...is necessary to ...for unless the the wheeler ...work. The ...ycle without ...his attention ...novice must ...machine.

...e too soon ...ar from the ...grasp the ...tion. The ...e pedals to ...ward, down,

...the other foot...

If the saddle is not right, dismount the wheeler in this way: Have the wheeler's feet firmly placed on both pedals, and see

BACK PEDALLING.
[Copyrighted, 1896, by Brentano.]

that the down pedal is on the side on which you are standing. Pull the machine a little to that side, and see that the foot is on the down pedal. Then direct the wheel...

it is necessary... propel or push... indeed, to ove... the bicycle an... friction, provi... of grades the... the infinite va... the muscular... respiration of...

The pedal i... adapted to th... many varietie... weights, patte... placed on the... is communica... bicycle forwa... dead centre, t... and continues... reached. No... just the right... too hard, the... too fast, and... down on the... weight press... enough...

PREPARING TO MOUNT, SHOWING INCLINATION.
[Copyrighted, 1896, by Brentano.]

THE NEW YORK HERALD, PARIS, WEDNESDAY, MAY 20, 1896. EIGHT PAGES.

uickly enough to enable you to know here to look and what to look for.

As soon as your teacher will allow it take e wheel for a little walk. This may seem ather an absurd proceeding, but it will as-st you greatly in learning the feel and ten-encies of the machine. Lead the bicycle bout carefully, holding the handles with oth hands and avoiding the revolving edals. Learn to stand it up, to turn it uickly and to back it in a limited space.

At first, in practising pedalling, the eight of the saddle should permit the ollow of the foot to rest firmly on the edal when the pedal is lowest. The ball f the foot only should press on the pedal. he foot should be made to follow the edal as early as possible. Point the toe ownward on the last half of the down troke, and keep pointing it until the pedal s at its lowest, following the pedal with he foot, and pointing downward until the edal is half way on the up stroke. This arries the crank past the dead centre.

INCORRECT POSITION—LEANING AGAINST THE INCLINATION.

[Copyrighted, 1896, by Brentano.]

To acquire a proper method, attention should be directed to each foot alternately.

To learn to balance, have the saddl as high as possible, so that foot just touches

ing power being centred in them. A learner always pushes too hard on the pedals. Learn to avoid this fault.

If out of breath wait until rested. Rest for a few minutes in any case, and look about and note the surface wheeled over. Then plan another spin of perhaps a few hundred feet. Fix upon an objective point, wheel to it and dismount. Rest thoroughly and mount again. Be careful to avoid becoming chilled while resting, stopping only long enough to restore the natural breathing and to look over the road.

HALF AN HOUR ENOUGH.

Half an hour of this kind of work at first every suitable day is enough. If you are need keep no one from attempting a moderately long run.

It is all important to get on the saddle quickly and easily and without necessity for readjustment. Therefore Miss Ward advises that if a skirt is worn, it should be arranged before placing the weight on the pedal, and the knee should be slightly bent when the pedal is lowest. The saddle should be the right height; handle bars should be a trifle high—that is, when the rider sits erect; the hands should rest easily and comfortably on the hand grips. Now the thing for the rider to do is to ride and hold on the handles. Don't let the wheel get away from you. To prevent an accident, should this happen, the

pedalling or simply by gravity in descending a grade. The use of the hands on the handle-bar is twofold for the inexperienced —for steering and for correcting undue pressure on the pedals. The hand opposite the pedal that receives too much pressure corrects the tendency of the bicycle by an extra pull on the handle-bars. This is very good exercise, but it is a useless expenditure of force and cannot be prolonged without great fatigue. It is the work of hill-climbing done on the level. The feet are on the pedals, and the natural tendency is to press equally at all times on both pedals and pull at the same time on both handles. One pedal must descend and the other pedal must ascend; they are attached to the same axle, which is turned by either pedal or both pedals. As the pedals are always on opposite sides of a circle, one is always coming up, and its upward tendency is resisted by any pressure, however slight. The lifting of the foot, therefore, from the ascending pedal means

TURNING BICYCLE OVER.

[Copyrighted, 1896, by Brentano.]

CORRECT POSITION—LEANING WITH THE WHEEL.

[Copyrighted, 1896, by Brentano.]

accustomed to be prolonged alf; or you

Two important points for the bicyclist to study are avoidance of road traffic and consideration of the surface ridden over. The law of the road applies to all traffic passing over the road; the law of mechanics to the surface of the road as it affects the bicycle and the cycler.

know how to come off the can step to the has time to fall. that is down

easy wheel is one of the hardest little or no

HILL CLIMBING—PUSHING CRANK OVER.

[Copyrighted, 1896, by Brentano.]

FOLLOWING THE PEDAL.

[Copyrighted, 1896, by Brentano.]

LIFTING.

[Copyrighted, 1896, by Brentano.]

COSTUMES FOR LADY CYCLISTS.

The Ladies' Tailors Say it is Quite Impossible to Create Striking Novelties.

DIVIDED SKIRTS ONLY WORN.

French Leaders of Society Follow the Example of Their Sisters in England.

NO OBJECTIONS TO THEM.

Costumiers Work on the Assumption that the Chains of Bicycles Are Boxed Up.

SPECIMENS OF WELL-MADE DRESS

Costumes Worn by Some of the Most Distinguished Members of the Rallye-Vélo.

VARIOUS STYLES OF HATS.

By no means the least important detail connected with bicycling is that of dress. "What should I wear when I go to the Bois?" is as natural a question as it is one absolutely necessary to solve.

(6) Costume like that generally worn by Princess Zurlo. The skirt is of black serge

No. 6.

with tabs and buttons up the sides. The body is like the skirt with pleats and a double row of buttons. Lavallière scarf; boating hat of black straw with black and white couteau feathers.

The most sedate cyclist looks foolish after endeavoring, in vain, to pump air into a tire which he did not know had punctured. —*Cycling*.

CYCLING'S EFFECTS AROUND PARIS.

Fifteen to Twenty Thousand Wheels Pass Suresnes on a Sunday.

2,000 ON A WEEK-DAY.

Cafés and Restaurants Do Not Benefit Much by Them, but the Trade Has Changed.

That lazy feeling that overcomes a bicyclist after a smart run in the glaring heat of July was accountable for the lounging about Suresnes the other day on the part of a HERALD Correspondent who had wheeled thither from Paris.

The place is interesting to a meditative bicyclist since some of the most important bicycling resorts about Paris are approached by that town, and one can get a good idea of Parisian bicycling from, say, the terrace of Picq's Café as anywhere and perhaps better. The Bois de Boulogne may attract the stylish cyclist, but the more serious wheelmen will be seen passing the bridge of Suresnes. For the most part they are clad in woollen "sweaters" and their manner is slightly different from that of the majority one meets in the Bois.

The stream of travelers begins moving over the bridge from about five o'clock in the morning and continues steadily all day, but the most important hours are between seven and eleven o'clock in the forenoon.

"How many pass here?" replied an official of the octroi, whose life has been spent at the Porte de Suresnes. "Well! I think you would be well within the mark if you were to state that on an average Sunday 15,000 pass through this gate. Some say 25,000, but that would be placing the number too high. On an ordinary week day I suppose the number would not be greater than 2,000 at the outside. But still even these figures are enormous. Of course any special attraction calls out great numbers, especially if the weather is at all good."

(2) Costume seen at Petit's. Divided skirt in bright drab lainage. White piqué bolero over a mauve lawn chemisette. Black scarf and Tyrolean hat of Java straw.

No. 2.

(5) Costume of Mme. Ferdinand Bischoffsheim. The skirt is of black serge; chemisette of small striped cambric; sailor's hat of striped linen; couteau hat and black veil.

No. 5.

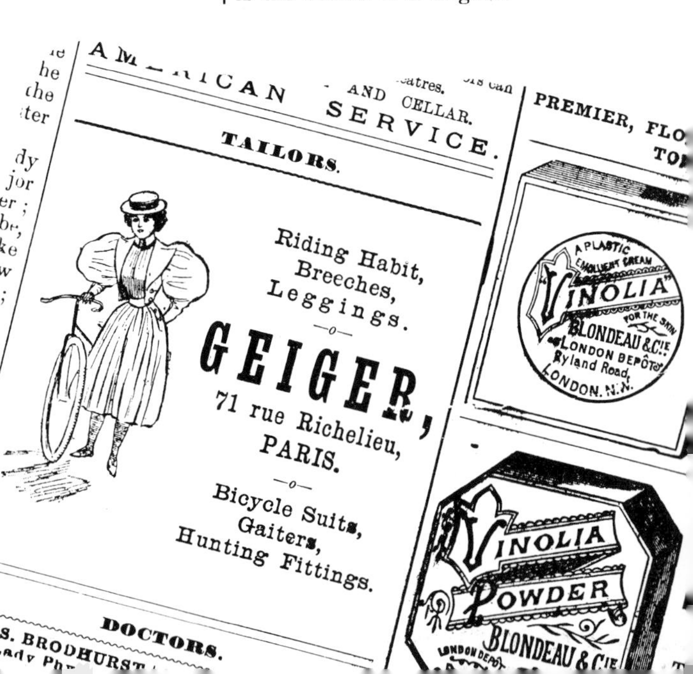

THE NEW YORK HERALD, PARIS, MONDAY, JULY 20, 1896. SIX PAGES.

CYCLING SCENES AT SURESNES.

CYCLING NOTES.

The latest recruit to cycling in Germany is no less a person than Prince Hohenlohe, the Imperial Chancellor. In spite of the fact that His Highness is in his seventy-ninth year he has mastered the difficulties of "wheeling," and goes for a ride daily in the shady avenues of the Garden of the Radziwill Palais in the Wilhelmstrasse.—Boersen Courier.

NEW CYCLING RECORD.

FIRST WHEELMAN.—Swifte made a new record to-day.

SECOND WHEELMAN.—Yes. What was it?

FIRST WHEELMAN.—He ran over six old ladies in two miles.—*Answers.*

"Say, Uncle Bob, what's a pedestrian?"

"A pedestrian, my boy, is a man who cannot afford to buy a bicycle."—*Cycling.*

PARIS, SUNDAY, DECEMBER 13, 1896.

which also works by back- is called the "Frein Le pignon frein automatique"... when the place was left suddenly semi-darkness, some of the spect... not take a very...

OPENING OF THE SALON DU CYCLE.

Magnificent Exhibition — The Palais de l'Industrie Crowded.

AMERICAN MACHINES PROMINENT.

No Startling Novelties in Construction, but Many Improvements in Detail.

SOME NOTEWORTHY BRAKES.

Automatic Arrangements Put Into Operation by Back - Pedalling Likely to Be Popular.

A MAMMOTH BICYCLE.

Good Show of Automobiles—All the Leading Manufacturers Well Represented.

CLEVER TRICK-RIDING.

The Cycle Exhibition of 1896, which was opened yesterday at the Palais de l'Industrie, is a marked success.

It was opened at two o'clock in the afternoon by the Minister of Commerce, M. Boucher, amid an immense crowd of spectators, and from that time on to the closing of the doors of the exhibition, moving about the vast building was difficult and uncomfortable.

It cannot be denied that everything was not completely ready and in order when the show was opened; but this was not a serious matter under all the circumstances of the case.

For instance, the statue in front of the principal entrance was not complete and the pedestal was enveloped in canvas throughout the afternoon.

Many of the curiously inclined, however, managed to obtain a view. It is a very cleverly executed piece of workmanship and bears the name of Antonin Carles at its base. The principal figure is that of a beautiful woman with flowing robes steadying a bicycle with her right hand. The statue, which is in plaster,

MAMMOTH CLEVELAND WHEEL.

A MAMMOTH MACHINE.

As you enter the building one of the first things that strikes you is the Brobdingnagian machine, and the American giant, Mr. Joe W. Grimes, who nods and smiles on the crowds as they pass.

Mr. C. Bertrand, of the Cleveland Company, is very proud of his show and certainly it is a feature of the exhibition. The wheel in question is, as near as possible, a complete model of the Cleveland bicycle. It is 5½ yards high, 8 yards

M. LÉON BOLLÉE.

long, weighs 200lb. The tubing is of wood, but the tires are the B. F. Goodrich make. The rims are remarkable, and have been only lately introduced into America. They are made by Kuntz, of Cleveland, and are of rock elm. At first sight one would suppose that the rims are of one piece of wood, but this is not the case, as they are composed of three layers glued together, and the great advantage is that the spokes do not come into contact with the air chamber. There is no doubt that these rims are of decided value in the way of strength and elasticity. The big wheel cost 3,000fr.

On the saddle of this machine is another bicycle, a Liliputian toy, which was made in Paris.

AUTOMOBILE SHOW.

By far the most striking part of this year's exhibition is the part taken by automobilism. The show is a very representative one, and recalls the Paris-Marseilles race, when an important step was taken by the Automobile Club in bringing prominently before the public the possibilities of the horseless carriage and its uses in the near future.

Among the automobiles on view, the Bollée machine was quite as much admired as any, and there is no doubt that there are decided advantages in favor of the invention. The machines were both two-seated and single-seated.

That M. Léon Bollée is a very clever man has been proved already by the HERALD. His "calculating machine" is a wonder and his automobile carriage or "voiturette" is considered by many expert judges to be "the best idea" in automobilism at the present day.

Be that as it may, for simplicity, speed and general all-round convenience the Bollée machine is a very excellent one. The representative of M. Bollée told me that at their Paris office, rue Halévy, they were doing a very good business, and though only recently introduced into France, several hundreds had been already sold.

Military experts have long agreed that the bicycle will play an important part in the next war. France is seriously consider-ing the matter

BOLLÉE AUTOMOBILE.

MACHINE DESCRIBED.

The "voiturette" is something between an automobile carriage and a moto-cycle. It has three wheels and is very little bigger than an ordinary tricycle, and yet has comfortable seats for two persons, who sit tandem. Its weight is in all 160kilos.

The framework of the "voiturette" is made of steel tubes. The wheels have pneumatic tires, the caoutchouc being about two centimètres thick, so as to preclude the likelihood of their being burst. The back wheel only is worked by the motor. The two others in front have the steering gear attached. This arrangement insures considerable stability for the machine in turning. Its stability is further insured by the fact that the centre of gravity is very low.

Between the two wheels in front is placed the first seat on which the passenger sits. The second, which is as comfortable as the first, is used by the person who manages the machine. At his right hand he has the steering lever, and at his left a lever fulfilling the triple functions of brake, gearing controller and speed regulator.

The mineral essence motor is of two-horse power and works without water and without electricity. It will take the machine along at the rate of from 20kil. to 25kil. an hour.

The "voiturette" is not so long as it seems to be; in fact, the distance from the front wheels to the back wheel is not greater than that between the two wheels of a bicycle.

Sport came up to the stage erected for bicycle performers ... It was perfectly correct. M. Maurice Germaux, one of the teachers at the Palais-Sport, was riding a showy-looking bicycle about the stage and giving a most satisfactory account of himself in the way of "trick riding." Some of the feats are already known to HERALD readers. The "plongeon" was given with great success. Riding with the feet over the handle bar instead of the hands; jumping over the guidon and leaping over the saddle from the side, all the weight being thrown on the handle bar; leaning clear back to a horizontal position, with feet under the handle bar, and the "jockey trick," or jerking the front wheel violently so as to bring the wheel clear of

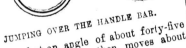

JUMPING OVER THE HANDLE BAR.

the ground at an angle of about forty-five degrees. The bicycle then moves about twelve or fifteen yards along the stage.

Maurice had another trick which is extremely clever and is for him quite new. He slips down to one side of the bicycle when it is in motion, and crawls under the bar connecting the wheels together, landing on his feet on the other side. He is as active as a cat and works with speed and precision. In a second he leaps on to the machine and pedals away with the hand. He has a number of other tricks which he performs with such rapidity that it is difficult to even follow him. Go and see "his attractions" and you will find it worth your while after four o'clock each afternoon.

TRICK RIDING.

ARMY CYCLISTS NOW A FACTOR.

Experiments Carried Out Under Captain Gerard Have Proved Their Superiority to Horsemen.

IN EVERY DIRECTION.

Can Be Used as Skirmishers and Also to Carry Machine Guns.

[From the *Daily Mail*.]

Military experts have long agreed that the bicycle will play an important part in the next war. France is seriously considering the matter, and if we can believe the information before us has already proved by severe tests that bicycle corps can be trained to very nearly take the place of cavalry.

Under the command of Captain Gerard, a young officer of the French army, a battalion of cyclist soldiers has been assiduously practising the feats which usually are performed by cavalry. In all cavalry schools the soldier is trained to cleave the Turk's head. Captain Gerard has been training his men to the performance of this feat with the bicycle instead of the horse.

It was found to be extremely difficult at first, and the slightest shift in the saddle caused a spill. But the men soon acquired great proficiency and demonstrated that the weight and impetus of the horse count as little and that the feat is accomplished by strength and dexterity alone.

CYCLE MAXIMS.

Rapid-firing machine guns are carried on several types of machines, including tandems, double tricycles and the regular bicycle. These guns are rigged in various ways in an effort to discover the best method for distributing their weight and that of the ammunition. On the regular safety the rapid-firing gun is fixed between the handles. It is an easy matter to perceive that a charge made by a couple of hundred men riding abreast and armed in this way would be more deadly than a charge of twice that number of cavalry.

The tricycle, or military duplex safety, as it is called, is thought of favorably, for the reason that the space between the two rear wheels is well adapted to the carrying of ammunition. The gun is rigged on a crossbar between two saddles, and is easily manipulated by one of the riders.

Another machine in use is a tandem fitted with two rapid-fire guns. The entire weight of the guns, ammunition and machine is less than 100lb. Of course, very fast time cannot be made, but two men can propel the cycle a greater distance and in much less time than would be the case with ordinary artillery.

The tandem skirmishers are specially formidable. They have a speed which no horse can attain. In times of danger the rider in front can bend low and work the pedals while his companion can fire over his shoulder.

It only remains to be added that tests are also being made with the motor-cycle, and that so far it has not proved itself so reliable as the machine propelled by foot power.

THE NEW YORK HERALD, PARIS, TUESDAY, JUNE 11, 1895.

PARIS TO BORDEAUX A

Over Thirty Starters Will Leave Versailles This Morning for th
President of the Republic Expected to be Present--New M
Petroleum and Steam Motors in Opp

And what is a horseless carriage ? one asks. Who is he who has dwelt in the capital f

"There is nothing new under the sun," said the ancients. "There is!" say we of modern date.

This morning, between nine and ten o'clock, about twenty-six horseless carriages —vehicles propelled by either petroleum or steam power, together with five or six petroleum bicycles, will leave the place de l'Etoile for the place des Armes at Versailles, the starting point for the great race to Bordeaux and back, of which so much has been talked of for many months past.

And what is a horseless carriage ? one asks. Who is he who has dwelt in the capital for a week at most who has not seen the electric tramway run from the Gare Saint-Lazare to Viccennes, and now and again a steam or petroleum vehicle dashing through the thoroughfares?

These, like the bicycle of old, are now stared at. So was the *diligence* in early days, and the George Stephenson railway engine caused no small amount of surprise. "The Rocket" and its successors "knocked out" the old road coach, and the horseless carriage and petroleum bicycle now bid fair to oust the present methods of locomotion.

Throughout the week there has been an exhibition of these "machines" at the Galerie Rapp in the Champ de Mars. They are certainly curious, and the scene is amusing, as each inventor claims that his system is the best. Each may be right, but from the experience that most of the members of the "fourth estate" have had, the only true and enjoyable state of "jumps" is on one of these machines, especially those moved by petroleum power.

These, by the way, are quicker than the "steam engines," but they are useless as far as draught is concerned. The parallel is easily drawn. Messrs. Peugeot Fils have the prettiest petroleum carriages at the exhibition—vis-à-vis, victoria and landaus, but Comte de Dion's "remorqueur" is serviceable, for it can take on any kind of carriage up to a family 'bus and then do twenty-five kilomètres per hour.

...feature
...ng chain, the
...mitting them
...eat length of
...red.
...ss and the
...ear and tear
...and requires

...ued Comte
... petroleum
...srs. Panhard
...Peugeot fils.
...er motors, a
...nt of which
...e first-named
...derfully well,
...the chain sys-
...them is the
...tors, which
...ndred revo-
...efore wear

...M. E. Roger's.
...nz petroleum
...om Germany.
...r bands play an

...our exhibits, a
...a brake. Both
...both the action
...eel blades bears
...back wheels.

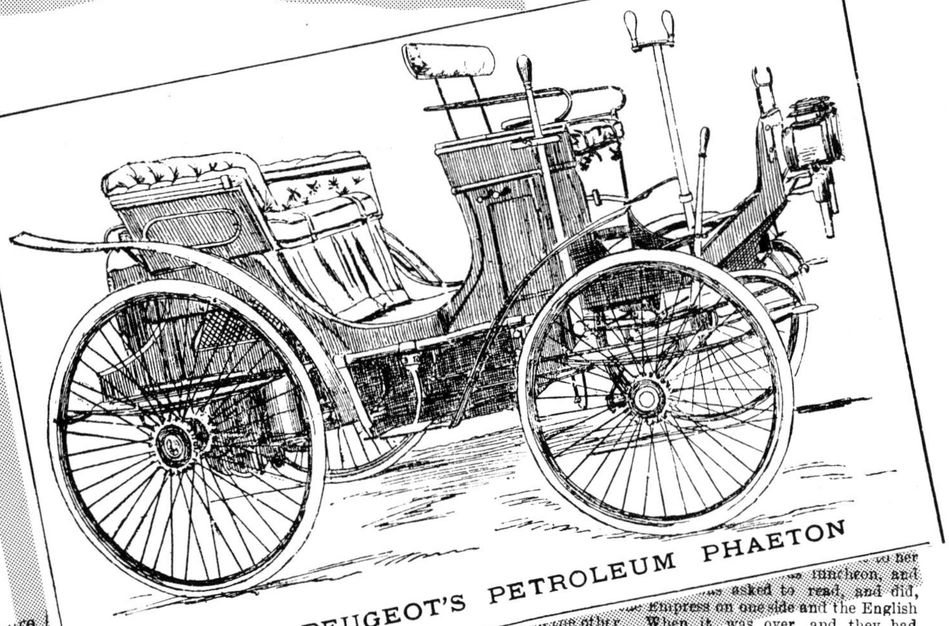

MESSRS. PEUGEOT'S PETROLEUM PHAETON

... vis-à-vis, | ... to her ... luncheon, and ... was asked to read, and did, ... the Empress on one side and the English ... the other. When it was over and they had gone up on deck, he asked the girl whether she thought the Empress liked it. "Well," answered she, "Her

MESSRS. PEUGEOT'S PETROLEUM VICTORIA.

victoria or phaeton. There are, however, many other comfortable vehicles, but as in mechanism so in outward appearance there is still lots of room left for improvement.

For the first time the petroleum bicyclette will take part in the race, and it goes

Majesty must have thought it a little unusual." "What do you mean?" "I mean that I don't think the Empress is in the habit of having her hand squeezed in public even by poets."

The poet afterwards made his humble apologies for his error, but the Empress only

'AGES.

D BACK.

Horseless Carriage Race--The
nods of Locomotion--
tion.

, carries its own coals
, and the heater is fed in exactly
the same way as a Choubersky."
"But," I asked, "taking all in all, is
petroleum preferable to steam?" Comte
de Dion was candid on the subject. Said
he: "Petroleum spirit is preferable for

snow. will do their best

This is the commencement of a
in road locomotion; one which will
cause a revolution, but which w
oust that noble animal, the horse.

RUN OVER BY A TRAIN.

A man named Poiat, a signalman in t
vice of the Vincennes Railway Compan

M. E. ROGER'S PETROLEUM "VIS-A-VIS."

MESSRS. DE DION AND BOUTON'S REMORQUEUR.

WALKING WILL SOON BE A LOST ART.

Automobiles and Bicycles Threaten to Supersede the Horse Altogether.

ANOTHER STREET PERIL.

Paris Police So Far Powerless to Prevent Furious Driving by Chauffeurs and Chauffeuses.

Not to be a "chauffeur" nowadays is be nobody. 'Chauffeur" is Parisian for automobilist. Put into English you would get "stoker," and it would be about as pretty.

It is astonishing how automobilism has spread within two years. It is now "chic" to pass an examination as your own "chauffeur." It is not as difficult as the Board of Trade examination, but it is the latest fad. Those who are newly converted say it is not a fad at all. On the contrary, they claim automobiles will drive carriages off the streets just as the locomotive has done with the mailcoach.

... welcome.

Automobiles are everywhere, e
...ge, for there is one in the

"I never see any one driving horses nowadays without thinking of Louis XIV.," said the other day one of the prettiest and wittiest women in Paris society.

It has not quite come to that yet, but the fashion is growing. Automobiles are as plentiful to-day as bicycles were a few years ago. It looks quite possible that they will really drive carriages off the road. That they may chase foot passengers out of the streets is also probable.

Their speed is the most terrible thing about them. They career along the crowded streets at a rate that would lead to the arrest at once of anyone driving a trap or a carriage. Timid walkers dread crossing the street as they do the plague. I saw an old lady the other day trying to get across the Champs-Elysées. Just as she made up her mind to attempt it an automobile whizzed by. The poor dame gave a little shriek and made a frantic break for cover. Evidently she only felt safe when she had got into a shop near by —where she may be yet if one is to judge from the look of relief on her face as she got there.

Many complaints been made with but little effect. M. Hugues Le Roux, the well-known writer, even sent a letter to the Prefect of Police a few days ago. He said his life, and those of his wife and children, had been so often imperilled by automobiles that he now promenaded the streets of Paris with a revolver in his pocket.

"The next 'chauffeur,'" he said, "who refuses to stop after nearly running over me will get shot."

He meant the warning seriously. The only thing apparently left for the automobilist to do is to go slowly or else run over M. Le Roux altogether if he doesn't want to be drilled by a bullet.

The police are handicapped when trying to stop a fast automobile. They cannot jump at the reins as they would at those of a runaway horse. They might just as well try to stop a railway engine. Accidents have been numerous. Indeed, if we are to listen to Alfred Capus, the "Figaro's" witty writer, the automobilist goes out in search of victims just as sportsmen go looking for game.

In fact, walking will soon be a lost art, for those who don't bicycle will surely automobile. Let us hope they will do it slowly.

SPORTING GOSSIP

PROMINENT "CHAUFFEURS" AND TYPES OF A

'TOMOBILES.

PARIS—AMSTERDAM—PARIS.

Thirty Automobiles, Composing the Tourist Section in the Great Race, Leave Villiers—Incidents at the Start—Complete List of the Competitors.

RACING DIVISION TO BE SENT ON THEIR JOURNEY TO-MORROW MORNING.

The great automobile race from Paris to Amsterdam and back has commenced. Yesterday the tourist division, consisting of thirty "chauffeurs"—there being but three absentees from the entry list—was sent on its journey.

It was a glorious morning, and the little village at La Fourche-de-Champigny, a quiet spot about twenty minutes' walk from lively Joinville-le-Pont, one of the Parisians' favorite Sunday resorts, was early astir, and from six o'clock the villagers commenced to assemble around the principal café, which was the rendezvous for those intending to participate in the race. Not, however, until nearly an hour later did the first of the competitors arrive, this being M. Ricard (124) on his two-place Peugeot. Others came in quick succession—vehicles of all kinds and shapes, with a good percentage of motocycles. The work of the Customs officers then commenced, a lead seal being attached to each machine, these assuring a free entry into France on the return journey across the Belgian frontier.

At half-past eight all were ready to proceed to La Fourchette at Bry, 2 kilomètres further on, where it was proposed to give the start. Here, at the wayside wineshop, the first control had been fixed, and mine host had made extensive preparations for breakfasts and luncheons. His disappointment was therefore great when, at the last moment, it was decided to change the starting-point to Villiers, another 3 kilomètres ahead, the reason for this being that this last-named place is situated in the Seine-et-Oise county, and that drivers, being outside the jurisdiction of the Seine departmental authorities—who have limited the speed of automobiles to 12 kilomètres in a town and 20 kilomètres in the open country—could "go as they pleased."

AT THE STARTING POINT.

On, then, we dashed through the narrow country road, with waving cornfields on each side, to Villiers, where the pace had to be slackened, as the high street was being repaired. Lucky that the race had not commenced! The scene here was amusing, for no sooner had the first "auto" made its appearance than the whole town turned out "en masse." One good woman, in her anxiety to see all, had donned her boy's soldier "kepi" by mistake, while he, with a broad grin on his face, held her straw hat behind him, and it was not until some passing cyclists chaffed her that she was aware of her mistake. It was an eventful day in Villiers.

Soon, however, the order to stop was given, and on a nice level piece of road about 18ft. wide, we all drew up. It took M. Herard and Comte de Lavalette but little time to get the starters one behind the other, 101 to 133 (109, 117 and 123 being absent) in line.

A slight incident occurred, M. Riguelle (107), on his De Dion motocycle was found to be missing. He had, it appears, taken "French leave," and without waiting to be timed, had proceeded. A consultation was held, and it was decided to inflict a twenty minutes' penalty.

At half-past nine exactly the first carriage, a six-place Panhard and Levassor, belonging to M. Pierron, was despatched, and from half minute to half minute the others were sent on their way. This was the moment for the kodak fiends, and the turn-outs and rig-outs, when reproduced, will cause many a round of laughter. The carriages were stripped of all unnecessary paraphernalia, the luggage consisting as a rule of hand bag and spare pneumatic tires; tins of naphtha served as footstools, and the occupants, dust and waterproof be-clad, look like grim executioners, with their peaked caps and large blue spectacles—a necessary precaution, by the way, as the clouds of dust the vehicles threw up behind them when they commenced racing were blinding.

As each "motor" moved off there was a cry of "bon voyage," and a waving of hands and hats, the Baronne Van Zuylen (133), driving her Panhard with M. Joseph Journu at her side, receiving hearty cheers. Dressed in a "hussard" blue jacket, dark gray skirt, and the conventional "chauffeur's" cap, this intrepid automobiliste looked charming. It was only two minutes before her turn to go came that she donned [illegible]ectacles, and then one knew that [illegible] despite the fact

seemed to be anyth
appeared to cover t
It was curious to
of the competitors
state that they cou
chines going, while
and Baronne Van Z
Dietrich and A. c
watch in one hand
The first stage
through Coulomm
Reims. The road
cellent, large notic
spot where a mist
made. To-day's
Château d'Ardenne
mètres.
The following is
starters:—

No.	Maker.	Horse Power
CLASS A (FIRST S		
104	Mors	5
105	Decauville	2½
106	Panhard	4
115	Dietrich	6
120	Panhard	6
124	Peugeot	6
126	Hurtu	4
128	Delahaye	6
133	Panhard	6
CLASS A (SECOND S		
103	Panhard	6
108	Soc. Franco-Belge	6
114	Dietrich	9
116	Dietrich	6
119	Damiler	8
121	Mors	6
125	Panhard	6
129	Delahaye	6
CLASS A (THIRD S		
101	Panhard	12
118	A. Bollée	9
130	Delahaye	8
131	Delahaye	8
132	Delahaye	8
CLASS B, TRIOYCLE		
107	De Dion	1¾
110	De Dion	1¾
111	Marot	1¾
112	Créanche	1¾
113	Créanche	1¾
122	Berthaume	1¾
CLASS B (		
102	Bollée	3
127	Bollée	3

The "Figaro" t
the result of the f
128, M. Delahaye,
2; No. 113, M. De
Pierron, 4, with th
So far, no serious
To-morrow the "
in number, follow.
La Fourche-de-Ch
the start from Vill
The Paris-Amste
is a decided success
By the way, th
run several brak
from 4 place de l'C
Champigny. Start
per place. Membe
ter their names as

CHARRON WINS THE AUTOMOBILE RACE.

Starting First from Villiers-sur-Marne He Makes the Fastest Time to Amsterdam and Back.

BOLLÉE "BATEAU" BEATEN.

Owing to Prefectorial Restrictions the Contest Ends at Montgeron Instead of Versailles.

The great automobile race from Paris to Amsterdam and back is over, and M. Charron, ex-cycling champion of France and now at the head of one of th

AUTOMOBILE CABS FOR PARIS.

Experiments Being Made by the Compagnie Générale des Voitures with Two Vehicles.

IN FIVE OR SIX MONTHS.

If the Cabs Meet with Public Approval the Scheme Will Be Largely Developed.

The problem of introducing electric cabs for the benefit of the public is now being solved by the Compagnie Générale des Voitures in Paris.

From time to time one sees a cab be-

THE NEW YORK HERALD.

FOUR YEARS OF PROGRE

A Triumph for French Brain and French Han
Material Represented in the Show, and
Square mètres of Ground not Half
Space--Every Constructor in

The opening of the International Automobile Exposition of 1899, under the auspices of the Automobile Club de France, marks the progress of the modern means of locomotion which is astonishing and grand.

The children of "The Coming Race," portrayed by Bulwer-Lytton, are the children of the dawn of the twentieth century—and the automobiles are their servants.

THE NEW YORK [H]E[RA]LD, PARIS, SUNDAY. APRIL 7, 1901.—WITH SUPPLEMENT.

THE REWARD OF PATIENCE.

"What are they waiting for?"
"Why! The great Automobile Parade

And what they saw.-

:. Denniston M. Bell's Enthusiasm Caused His Arrest in Newport.

3Y COMMERCIAL CABLE TO THE HERALD.]

R. I., Wednesday.—The sen- ... Mr. Den-

of tulle.

Miss Morgan has received a great number of superb wedding presents. From her father came a tiara and collar of diamonds of beautiful design, also a brooch or corsage ornament of pear-shaped diamonds set in a trefoil design. Mr. Morgan has also given his daughter ... amount of bonds and a country ... River.—Daily Tele-

How the President of the Republic Enjoyed His Run at the Exhibition at Vincennes.

M. JEANTAUD'S IMPRESSIONS.

Question of "Doping" Horses to Be Investigated at a Meeting in London

SEARCHING FOR THE TRUTH.

Owners, Trainers, Jockeys and Veterinary Surgeons to Discuss the Important Topic.

S, FRIDAY, JUNE 16, 1899.—EIGHT PAGES.

S IN HORSELESS CARRIAGES.

5

ork--Five Million Francs' Worth of Machinery and r Hundred Firms Exhibit--Thirty Thousand ge Enough to Meet all Applications for ance Working at Automobilism.

...ection with the meeting of ...rainers, jockeys, and veterinary ... which is to be held in the St. ...Hall, Piccadilly, on Monday after... ...t, says the "Daily Telegraph," ... John Atkinson, F.R.C.V.S., of ...e, who is organizing the move... ...aid the main object of the gather... ...to discuss the important question ... "doping" of racehorses. ... of the aims of the society was to ...in, as far as was possible, the exact ... respecting this system of "doping," ... was practised extensively in America ...nd, on a smaller scale, in this country. The expression "doping," was a pure Americanism, which found its equivalents here in the words "tampering with," or "faking."

Personally, he did not believe there was so much "doping" as was supposed in this country. As the result of two prolonged visits to the United States he acquired considerable experience of the American methods of horse training. "Doping" meant the administration to a horse of certain medical preparations with the object of either stimulating or retarding the animal's progress in a race.

With the Hypodermic Syringe.

One of the most objectionable forms of "doping," in his opinion, consisted in the use of a hypodermic syringe just before the race, by which means strychnine, nux vomica, phosphorus and other diffusable stimulants were injected. These were given with the specific object of increasing the animal's speed. On the other hand, if it was desired that the horse should not run in its true form, opiates of various kinds were administered.

At the forthcoming meeting he proposed to exhibit and explain an American appliance for the "doping" of horses, of which, so far as he was aware, but little was known in this country. This was an electric belt, with battery attached, which the jockey wore round his waist when riding in a race, the connections extending down the inside of both legs, and terminating in the boots at a point adjacent to the stirrups. The battery had only at the selected moment—usually a critical period in the race—to be turned on, and the jockey's heels pressed against the horse's sides, and the animal, nerved with the sudden galvanic shock, would gather fresh energy, and dash forward to the winning-post.

Undoubtedly these contrivances gave a jockey an enormous advantage over those rivals who did not have recourse to them, and who relied only on the whip. It should be borne in mind that the belt he had described was responsible for many a serious accident on racecourses in the United States. He had it on the authority of some of the most eminent veterinary surgeons in America that these belts were in extensive use there, and he had also heard it stated in authoritative quarters at home ... the appliance in question had on more ... occasion found its way to an Eng... That, however, was only ... hearsay evidence, for ... that, so far, no re... ...int had

...cause he ...

EW BELGIAN LEGATION OPEN.

...mtesse de Lichtervelde, Wife of Minister at Washington, Gives a Reception to Prince Henry de Croy.

BY COMMERCIAL CABLE TO THE HERALD.]

WASHINGTON, Wednesday.—Prince ...enry de Croy was the guest of honor a reception given here last night by ...mtesse de Lichtervelde, wife of the Bel...n Minister. The new Belgian Lega...n, 1,109 Sixteenth street, was thrown ...en for the first time for the social ...ent.

MISS MARY DALY ENGAGED.

...ughter of the Late Marcus Daly to Marry Mr. James W. Gerald, of New York.

BY COMMERCIAL CABLE TO THE HERALD.]

NEW YORK, Wednesday.—Announce...nt is made of the engagement of Miss ...ry Daly, daughter of the late million...e, Marcus Daly, to Mr. James W. ...rald, of the firm of Bowers and Sands, ...wyers.

WEDDINGS IN AMERICA.

:. Amos R. Pinchot Marries Miss Gertrude Minturn at St. George's Church, New York.

NEW YORK, Wednesday.—The wedding Miss Gertrude Minturn and Mr. Amos Pinchot was celebrated to-day at St. ...orge's Church. The ceremony was fol...wed by a large reception at the home the bride's mother, Mrs. Robert B. ...inturn, in Gramercy Park.

Miss Minturn, whose sister married the ...on. Alan Johnstone, British Chargé Affaires at Darmstadt, was given away ... her brother. Her only bridesmaid ...as her sister Mildred.

Mr. Pinchot's best man was his brother, ...r. Gifford Pinchot. Among the ushers the bride's brother, Mr. Hugh ... Mr. Henry Lane Eno, ...

Captain Cobie...

...man Have a Dispute w... with the Hounds.

An unfortunate incident, says the "Figaro," occurred yesterday at Fontainebleau, where MM. Pierre and Paul Lebaudy's hounds met. A dispute arose between the brother-in-law of one of the Masters and Captain Cobientz, whereupon the MM. Lebaudy stopped proceedings and sent the pack home.

INTERNATIONAL FOOTBALL.

A football match, under Rugby Union rules, will be played between the Racing Club de France and the Catford Bridge

...President's Civil Cabinet, occupied ... back seat.

"The President was delighted with the drive," said M. Jeantaud, in telling the story of the event. "We went about three kilomètres round the Daumesnil Lake in three minutes or so. There was quite an impromptu procession, for a couple of score of automobiles were following us.

"At first the speed was eighteen kilomètres an hour. I wanted to increase it a little, but M. Loubet exclaimed: 'Oh no, I beg you. I have a horror of speed.'

"But, monsieur le Président," replied

M. Millerand. M. Combarieu. M. Loubet. M. Jeantaud.

PRESIDENT LOUBET ENJOYING A RIDE IN AN AUTOMOBILE.

[By courtesy of the "Matin."]

Football Club, on Sunday afternoon, at the Vélodrome du Parc des Princes. The Racing Club team, which has not yet been defeated this year, includes eight internationals.

AUTOMOBILE CLUB DINNER.

[BY THE HERALD'S SPECIAL WIRE.]

LONDON, Thursday.—The annual dinner of the Automobile Club was held last evening at Whitehall Rooms, Mr. Roger ... W... ...hairman of the...

M. Jeantaud, "it is indispensable that you should know that we can go faster," and as he spoke he shifted the machinery to the second, then the third, and almost immediately to the fourth degree of speed. The pace went from 18 to 24 and then to 30 kilomètres, and then M. Loubet said: "Now, I really have the sensation of speed. It is delightful."

M. Jeantaud does not think ... the President is likely to ...

"I...

AUTOMOBILES. AUTOMOBILES.

Magnificent Manifestation of the Automobile and Cycle Industries Begins To-day in the Grand Palais by Old and New Firms.

Striking Exhibits of Germany, England, Belgium, Italy, Switzerland and America Found Side by Side With Those of France.

To-day the Automobile Salon opens—the Salon of 1904—that magnificent manifestation which brings together right in the heart of Paris the most perfect productions of the automobile and cycle industries.

France is the only country which at present is able to offer to the world the spectacle of an industry "de luxe" so flourishing, and of such a large number of manufacturers struggling unceasingly for the perfectionment of swift road transports. As in past years, the firms of Panhard et Levassor, Mors, Renault, Léon Bollée, Hotchkiss, Clément, Darracq, Richard-Brasier, Rochet-Schneider, etc., will be seen more flourishing than ever, and displaying vehicles more powerful, more robust, lighter and more simple. By the side of these are the new constructors, who enter upon their ... with the experience ...

BENZ AUTOMOBILES OF MANNHEIM.

... great merit. ... Switzerland have, in the Fiat, the Martini and the Dufaux, some productions of high value.

England and Belgium exhibit automobiles much more satisfactory than formerly, and which seem to be less copies executed without thought than they once were.

America finally, despite the distance, has managed to exhibit some of its machines which cannot yet be said to enter into competition with those of European manufacture, since they are not made for the same roads. But all the same the special manner in which they are constructed points to the fact that they will compete to some extent with automobiles made "wholesale" and "bon marché."

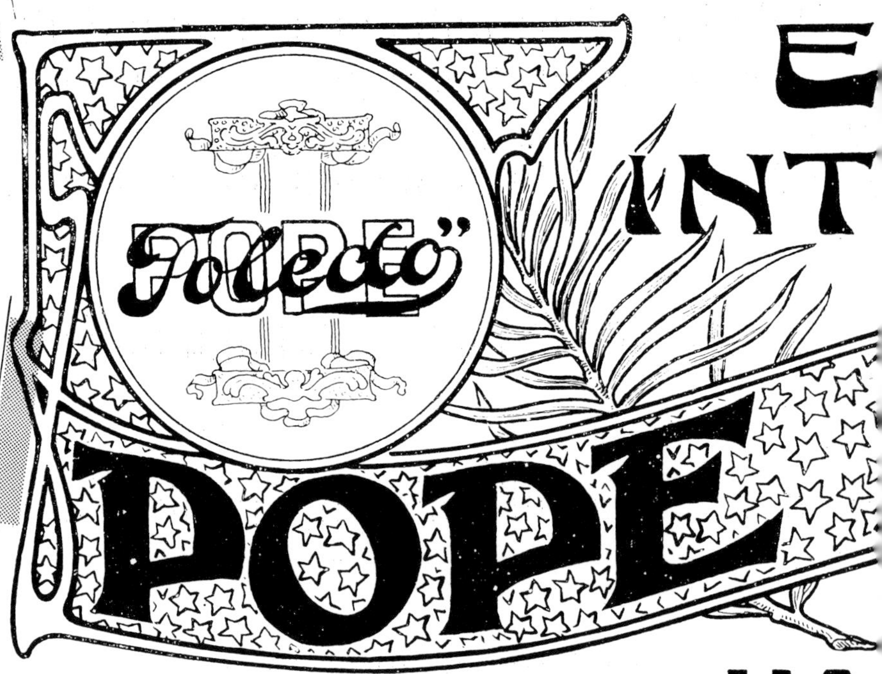

E

INT

HA

THE REPRESENTA

Highest Efficiency,

Comfort,

TWO

SALON D'AUT

INSPECTION INVITED.

POPE-TOLEDO GASOLINE.

Pope Automo

the GRAND

Loui

H.

AUTOMOBILES. | AUTOMOBILES. | AUTOMOBILES. | AUTOMOBILES.

POPE MFG. Co
TFORD, Conn. U.S.A.

IVE HIGH GRADE CARS OF AMERICA.

erfection of Details, Speed, Elegance;

Durability, Silent Running.

LARGE STANDS AT THE

MOBILES, GRAND PALAIS.

Demonstration Cars at the Service of Interested Parties.

Were Awarded IZE at the St. position.

Pope-Toledo 24 H.-P. STOCK CAR. Competing with 60 and 90 h.-p., Finished Third in the Vanderbilt Cup Races.

EUROPEAN REPRESENTATIVE:

NELSON, 24 Rue Cauchy, Paris.

TELEPHONE, 716.32

POPE-WAVERLEY ELECTRIC.

IN THE PADDOCK AT DEAUVILLE.

presented by all the well-known Parisian *étoiles*. In fact, a glance round the groups and over the tribunes justified the remark made by a friend: "One would think oneself at Longchamp, if this were not much prettier. Even Rochefort's white tuft and cynical smile are not lacking."

There was nothing else going on in the twin cities this afternoon, and the sun seemed to have only just risen when the streets were invaded with the cries of newsboys hurrying about with sporting papers.

There were six events on the card, and though the Grand Prix overshadowed all in the eyes of racing men, a vast amount of interest was to be found in the whole list. The meeting opened with the Prix de Fervacques, six starters facing the flag. Nemesis made a good showing, followed by Roncevaux. It was Confetti that eventually secured the lead, and in a fine spurt passed the post a head in front of Nemesis, with Roncevaux third, a length behind M. Devanlay's mare.

M. Holtzer's Iéna took off the Prix du Conseil Général, for two-year-olds, winning by three lengths. Four lengths separated ... second, from Gajeure, third.

... interesting race was seen for the ...ados, which fell to M. Edmond ...who led from start ...

SOCIETY AT TROUVILLE.

Princesse de Sagan's Dinner and Reception the "Clou" of the Season.

[SPECIAL DESPATCH TO THE HERALD.]

DEAUVILLE, August 16.—The dinner and reception given by the Princesse de Sagan last evening should form the *clou* of the season. It was given at the Hotel des Roches Noires, the salons being prettily decorated with flowers and plants. Indeed, it was a *fête des fleurs* for the ladies. All wore hats that were a mass of flowers, and as but a small number were invited to the reception after the dinner, an air of cosiness was felt that was infinitely pleasant.

Among the princess's guests were:—The Duc and Duchesse de Luynes, the Duc and Duchesse de Noailles, the Duc and Duchesse de Brissac, the Comtesse de Montgomery, Baron and Baronne Alphonse de Roth... Comte and Comtesse Murat, ...tesse de Chevigné, M. M...

TROTTING AT BADEN.

Eddie Hayes Wins the Matadoren Rennen in Splendid Style.

[SPECIAL DESPATCH TO THE HERALD.]

BADEN-BEI-WIEN, August 16.—At today s races the Matadoren Rennen, of 6,000 kronen, over 2,600 mètres, formed the great attraction. All the horses started scratch with the exception of the winner of the championship which had a penalty of 25 mètres. As Maggie Sherman, on account of the heavy rain and the consequent heavy track, remained in the stable, only seven starters came out, and cf these Valley Girl only ran in order to qualify.

When the flag fell Eddie Hayes took the lead and though hardly pressed first by Honeywood and then by Mi·s Bowerman, won after a splendid finish, beating the latter mare by a short head. The time was 3min. 56 1-10sec. Romola was a good third, beating Bellwether by a neck. The latter, in his turn, was separated by the same distance from Mattie H. Honeyw... ...hind. The ...

Department of the Marne in 1891, on th... occasion of the Vitry review; the large... demonstration which had been held sin... 1870.

M. Rambaud also spoke on the work ... M. Carnot as Chief of the State. His Pr...sidency, he declared, was truly the nation... defence against Cæsarism and again... anarchy.

A LABORATORY LAMP.

An Invention Likely to Assist Photographers in Getting More Sensitive Plates.

At MM. Gaumont & Co.'s, 57 rue Sain... Roch, I saw the other day in the photo...graphy department, a new laboratory lam... of a most ingenious character, recently in...vented by M. Carl de Mazibourg, a... amateur. I think this invention likely ... interest readers of the HERALD.

Hitherto all the lamps in use have bee... made either of tinned plate or iron, sub...stances not very well adapted to a perfe... adjustment. For example, most of suc... lamps allow white rays of light to escap... ...less to be detected by th... ... the work

DIAMOND JUBILEE WINS THE DERBY FOR THE PRINCE.

For the Second Time in Four Years His Royal Highness Captures the Blue Ribbon of the English Turf in Record Time.

A SCENE OF TREMENDOUS ENTHUSIASM.

[BY THE HERALD'S SPECIAL WIRE.]

LONDON, Thursday.—The Derby has been run and the Prince of Wales, for the second time in four years, has had the great satisfaction of owning the winner. It was a splendid race, and Diamond Jubilee, admirably handled by little Jones, scored by half a length, in 2min. 42sec., which equals the record time made by Persimmon in 1896.

The Duke of Portland's Simon Dale was second, and Mr. J. R. Keene's Disguise II., which carried the confidence of nearly every American present, was third, a length away.

To say that the cheering was deafening as the Royal colors shot past the post only faintly describes the enthusiasm displayed. A terrible roar of "The Prince wins" went up as soon as Jones took the lead on Diamond Jubilee, coming into the straight, and it continued like a roar of thunder right away down the course.

Pandemonium Breaks Loose.

Immediately No. 1 was hoisted, pandemonium broke out, and everyone on the stands and course seemed to go mad with joy. Hats and umbrellas were thrown into the air as if caused by a sudden explosion, and the cheering was prolonged for quite ten minutes after the winner had weighed in.

A somewhat gloomy morning in London did not prevent a large number of people traveling down by road.

The Downs were well covered with people, but it was not a record Derby so far as the attendance was concerned.

The Royal party included the Prince and Princess of Wales, the Duke of York, the Duke of Cambridge, Prince Christian and Princess Victoria and Princess Victoria of Wales.

In the Club Stand.

In the club stand were the Duke Duchess of Devonshire, Prince and cess Duleep Singh, the Marquis of mondeley, Earl Cadogan, Earl of Carn: the Earl and Countess of Coventry, Durham, Earl and Countess of Lord Falmouth, Lord Chelsea, Pri tykoff, Lord Harewood, Lord Lu Charles Montagu, Lord Farqu Ebury, Lord Russell of Killowen, niskillen, Earl of Ellesmere, Lo Beresford, Lord Marcus Ber Berkeley Paget, Sir E. Vir Maple, Mr. L. de Rot James I Geor

and Bona Rosa, 100 to 6 Simon Dale, 25 to 1 Sailor Lad, 33 to 1 Governor II., 40 to 1 Democrat, 50 to 1 Most Excellent, 66 to 1 First Principal and Sidus, 100 to 1 Frontignan, and 200

Places: 6 to 4 on Diamo guise II

Chev Forfars cellent, mond J tignan mile, L the ber front; Diamo Forfa ter o front tance separ fourt set u 1896.

EP Paws dor, 10lb.,

JU Doris 11lb. ran.

C Tal Duc 8st.

F gin. 9st. ran.

E Gig 8st. 3.

PRINCE OF WALES DELIGHTED.

Even More Pleased with Diamond Jubilee's Victory than that of Persimmon's.

[BY THE HERALD'S SPECIAL WIRE.]

LONDON, Thursday.—I think it may be safely put that yesterday's Derby was one of the most interesting on record: firstly there was the fact that for months past the favorites had alternated, one being first and the other second, and vice versâ. Mr. Dewar had been confident and was confident yesterday when I saw him, and when he told me his trainer was going to sleep in the stable with Forfarshire just for safety's sake.

The Prince of Wales had tipped all his friends to back Diamond Jubilee. He had backed the horse himself, and it is freely told about that he netted £60,000. Mr. J. R. Keene was just as sure as the owners of the two favorites that his horse, Disguise II., could win. Lord Rosebery thought he had a good chance with Sailor Lad, and Charlie Wood put most of his pals on to it as a good thing. A surprise was predicted to be brought off by Bona Rosa, and there were wild predictions about the French horse, Governor II.

The Prince of Wales behaved in a sportsmanlike way. Everyone knows that Diamond Jubilee is a bad tempered horse or at all events reputed to be so. Epsom is the noisiest and most provoking course for a nervous horse known. It might have been arranged that Diamond Jubilee should go directly to the post and avoid the paddock parade and the subsequent gallop up the course in front of the noisy crowd, but the Prince insisted that his horse should go through the entire mill from "A to Z," and so the horse did.

The expression of joy on the Prince's face as he led his horse in was remarked by all, much greater than that on the occasion of the Persimmon win.

The Prince of Wales gave a dinner party to the members of the Jockey Club last evening.

THE NEW LINER DEUTSCHLAND.

The Hamburg-American Line beg to announce that their magnificent new twin-screw express steamsh Commander Al at th

TF schland. unched anuary, w York from ne 13. n size. t, and ered tonquadruple velop 35,000 fully expected to speed of twenty-three efforts have been spared in the building to ma

RACING NEWS

SANDOWN PARK GRAND PRIZE.

Easy Victory of Mr. A. M. Kirker's Killyleagh Over Bird on the Wing and Cestus.

PIGEONS AT MONTE CARLO.

The Hon. P. Thellusson Defeats Messrs. Blake and Moncorgé in the Prix de l'Hôtel de Paris.

[BY THE HERALD'S SPECIAL WIRE.]

LONDON, Sunday.—The Sandown Park meeting was brought to a conclusion yesterday in very mild weather.

A feature of the afternoon, which proved a big attraction and helped to make the attendance one of the best on record for a National Hunt meeting, was the advertised sale of Manifesto, the favorite for the Grand National. Mr. Dyas's desire to sell his horse, however, was never taken altogether seriously, and when he learnt he would have to pay 2½ per cent. commission to the auctioneer on whatever reserve he placed upon the horse he naturally did not send him into the ring, Velox, Delvin, and Gentle Ida, belonging to the same gentleman, being also withdrawn. Just before the Sandown Grand Prize, however, Manifesto was sold to Mr. C. Grenfell, the owner of Father O'Flynn, acting on behalf of Mr. Bulteel, for 4,000 guineas, and he did not take part in the big race. Up Guards was also sold during the afternoon to Mr. C. Park, the price being 2,500 guineas.

Fossicker was always a hot favorite for the Grand Prize. He ran well till a quarter of a mile from home, when he was done with, and Killyleagh, who was beaten at both Dunstall Park and Birmingham, won in the commonest of canters. Results:—

SANDOWN GRAND PRIZE, a Handicap Hurdle Race of 500 sovs. Distance about two miles.

Mr. A. M. Kirker's Killyleagh (11st) Mr. Cullen 1
Major Edwards's Bird on the Wing (11st 1lb) Nolan 2
Mr. E. J. Percy's Cestus (11st 11lb) Mr. G. S. Davies 3

Also ran: Fossicker, Regret, Lahore, Bonnie Dundee, Cornbury, Glenbower, Priestsholme and Up Guards.

Betting: 5 to 2 Fossicker, 4 to 1 Regret, 6 to 1 Up Guards and Bird on the Wing, 10 to 1 Bonnie Dundee and Killyleagh, 100 to 8 Cestus, Priestholme and Glenbower, 100 to 6 Lahore and 20 to 1 Cornbury.

The Race.—Up Guards and Fossicker made joint running until two hurdles from home, where Killyleagh drew to the front, and drawing away with a clear lead after negotiating the last jump won by six lengths. Two lengths between second and third. Regret was fourth and Lahore last. Time 4min. 5sec. Winner is trained in Ireland.

MINOR EVENTS.

SELLING HURDLE RACE, two miles.—Mr. Agar's Chillingworth (8 to 1), Mr. H. Woodland, 1; Royal Charter II. (7 to 1), 2; Dabchick (11 to 2), 3. Won by three-quarters of a length. Ten ran.

FEBRUARY FOUR-YEAR-OLD STEEPLECHASE, two miles.—Mr. Dennehy's Windfall (5 to 1), Dowling, 1; Terpsichore II (9 to 2), 2; Daring Thief (7 to 1), 3. Won by three lengths. Twelve ran.

SELLING STEEPLECHASE, two miles.—Mr.

C.U.B.C., complai and B. H. Howell to row in the Uni that Mr. Howell, Boat Club, had us members of his co C.U.B.C.

Mr. R. B. Et confirmation of account of a con Mr. Howell who, substituting Mr. Dudley Ward as p

Mr. Howell repl influenced anybo Cambridge and Mr ment as to his pos

Mr. Lehmann e of the C.U.B.C. differences and Messrs. Bell and I position and ro eventually the m any definite se arranged.

CRICKET

Crushing Defea Eleven by D

[BY THE HER

LONDON, Sunda Sydney dated Frid mission, states t between Mr. Stodd sentative eleven of exciting finish w visitors' batting astounding manne runs were added t these Hayward ma

NEW S

1st innings.
Donnan, c Board b W wright.
Iredale, c Stoddart b B
Noble, c McLaren b ward
Mackenzie, c Haywar Hearne
Gregory, c and b Mason
Trumper, b Mason
Pye, not out
Kelly, b Stoddart
Newell, c Hirst b Stodd
McKibbin, c Druce b Br
Howell, b Mason
Extras
Total

MR. STO

1st innings.
J. R. Mason, b Noble
Wainwright, c Ho b Noble
K. S. Ranjitsinhji, Gregory b Noble
Hirst, c Newell b Noble
Hayward, c Howell b No
N. G. Druce, c Noble Trumper
Stoddart, c Iredale McKibbin
Briggs, c McKenzie McKibbin
A. C. McLaren, b Noble
Board, c McKenzie b Kibbin
Hearne, not out
Extras
Total

FOOTBALL

Results of Ye Matches Ur and R

[BY THE HERA

LONDON, Sunday final scores in the p contested yesterday

ENGLISH ASSOCIA —Newton Heath 0, Burslem Port Vale

YACHT RACING AT MARSEILLES.

The Mistral Abates and with a Steady Breeze Some Fair Contests Are Witnessed.

CHALLENGE CUP WINNERS.

The Gloria and Heartsease Both Successful—Results of the Minor Events.

MARSEILLES, Thursday.—The racing today was for the various challenge cups presented by the Marseilles Yacht Club and therefore the most important of the regatta.

As a strong mistral has been blowing for the last three days there was little hope of the fixture being kept, and it was an agreeable surprise to find the morning break clear and fine with a fairly steady nor'-wester blowing.

As there was but one competitor for the "Twenty Cup," a special rule applied to the race, namely, that the larger rating yacht must accomplish the course in less time than that taken by the first boat in the next class (counting time allowance). The results wer[e as] follows :—

Yachts from 1[...] cup, value 1,500fr. [...] 10 5 a.m.
Gloria (20), [...]

As the Gl[oria ...] this race an[...] against the [...] permitted [...]

Yachts [...] value 1,0[...]
Hearts[ease ...]
Semou[...]
Bonit[...]

The [...] pulled [...] the t[...] the r[...] spit[e ...] the [...] Th[...] pe[...] ta[...] a [...]

OPENING OF ROYAL HENLEY.

Favored by Fine Weather the Well-known Course Presents a Brilliant Scene.

ON HOUSEBOATS AND LAWNS.

First Heats in the Diamond Sculls, Grand Challenge Plate, and Other Events.

[BY THE HERALD'S SPECIAL WIRE.]

LONDON, Wednesday.—Henley, almost since its inception in 1839, has held and holds an unequalled position in the racing world. It is to aquatics what Ascot is to racing, the Royal reunion. In all other sports the less important fixtures lead up to gala days, but Henley, with one exception, has always inaugurated the regatta season.

Each Henley Regatta scene is practically a replica of its predecessor. This year, however, owing to the stringent regulations of the Thames Conservancy, houseboats are not nearly so numerous as in previous years, while the array of small boats is to all appearances below the average. Still, the river yesterday presented as gay and animated a scene as ever. Nowadays fashion tends to land stations. Thus innumerable club lawns extend almost from the winning post to Temple I[sland] ... these are tenanted wi[th] ... semblages, so ... nation ...

EXCITI[NG ...] AT [...]

[CON...]

boulevard d[...] hundred p[...] business [...] Dreyfus e[...] bas les j[...] charged [...] from th[...] lynched [...] fired an[...] of the [...]

A cro[wd ...] on the [...] window[...] heim. [...] on the [...] police [...] could b[...]

The [...] incident[...] and Picq[uart ...] were lea[...] themselv[es ...]

"You [...] Picquart. [...]

"You [...] "that I ho[...]

"I count[...] quart. "B[...] until after t[...]

"As you [...] And the t[...]

PARI[S ...]

Interview[s ...] Henri [...]

The p[...]

I noticed a beautiful dress in white slin with yellow guipure framing dallions in taffetas, on which were inted Pompadour bouquets. The cein re was made of an "enroulement" in ld, on which were also painted similar uquets. The sleeves and the empiècement were in lace. This dress was accompanied by a Louis XVI. hat in black e, with choux in sky-blue and pink lvet.

GOSSIP FROM TROUVILLE.

urire in Good Form—Record Night at the Cercle Trouvillais.

[SPECIAL TO THE HERALD.]

TROUVILLE, Friday.—The polo gymana will take place next Monday, also e pony races.

There are five gymkhana events and ree pony races, two on the flat and one steeplechase.

I saw Sénateur, the English horse enred for the Grand Prix de Deauville, is afternoon at exercise. He bolted and l to commence with, but then went a eady gallop of a mile and a half. Foure is going great guns and is considered most a certainty, as he likes the course.

Last night, or rather this morning, was record, so far as the Cercle Trouvillais concerned. The baccarat party broke at 11.15 this morning, when the heavyed punters, backers and croupiers, chanurs and commissaires du jeu walked disally out, with heavy eyes and weary nbs. This is a true holiday at the seade.

The Marquis de Massa's play next Mony is not the "revue" of last winter. It is new one, bringing in all the actualities Deauville.

A glove fight has been arranged to take lace on Sunday evening at the Théâtre unicipal between Tom Cooper and Tom arker.

PIGEON SHOOTING.

. Gayant Wins the Prix de la Societe des Casinos de Trouville.

[SPECIAL TO THE HERALD.]

TROUVILLE, Friday.—There was tendance to-day to shoot e la Société des Casi e competito

The Rainbow, 11h. 40min. 24sec.
The Mineola, 11h. 40min. 28sec.
The Yankee, 11h. 42min. 37sec.
The Virginia, 11h. 43min.

The course was a triangular one of fifteen miles to each leg, sailed twice over. Just before reaching the first mark the wind fell light, and canted to the eastward. The yachts rounded the mark as follows:—

The Rainbow, 12h. 2min.
The Mineola, 12h. 3min. 10sec.
The Yankee, 12h. 4min. 50sec.
The Virginia, 12h. 5min. 15sec.

To the next mark it was windward work. In the beat to the second mark the Yankee passed both the Rainbow and the Mineola, being well handled by Mr. Duryea, and on the run home she led the fleet by two and a half minutes.

The Rainbow was best handled in the second round, and cut down the lead of the Yankee, which, however, won by 52sec. The Virginia was 8min. behind the Rainbow. The result leaves the Yankee and Mineola a tie in the series.

ROYAL VICTORIA YACHT CLUB.

The Closing Day of the Regatta Favored by Splendid Weather.

[BY THE HERALD'S SPECIAL WIRE.]

LONDON, Saturday.—The Royal Victoria Yacht Club had grand weather, says the "Daily Mail" for the closing day of the regatta. There was a nice breeze at the start, but about noon the wind, which was from the north-west, dropped altogether, and the distances of all the races were reduced in consequence.

The first race sailed was for a challenge cup presented by the Earl of Desart, with £50 in money added. There were only two starters, famous cutters, Mr. Cook's the Senga and Mr. Burton's the Penitent, and the distance sailed was reduced from forty-eight to twenty-four miles. The Senga reached first the rounding mark nearly 3min. ahead of the Penitent, but lost her position in the beat to westward, and the Penitent won by nearly 3min.

The next race was for a cup given by the Vice-Commodore, but as Mr. Mellor's the Nan the only yacht entered she sai half the cup's value. The ich was the chief race of r a cup given by Mr.

NEWPORT.

Sensation Caused by Mrs. O. H. P. Belmont's Warrant for Mr. Ogden Mills.

TALK OF NEWPORT SOCIETY.

Mr. Lloyd Phoenix in the Intrepid Rescues a Schooner in Distress.

[BY COMMERCIAL CABLE TO THE HERALD.]

NEW YORK, Friday.—Mrs. O. H. P. Belmont's action in taking out a warrant for young Mr. Odgen Mills was the talk of Newport yesterday.

The New York "World's" correspondent sends the following despatch: "Although it had been reported on what was supposed to be reliable authority, that Mrs. Belmont had left for Saratoga, she put in her appearance at the Casino this morning, and gave a luncheon in the grill-room. The guests were Mrs. Stuyvesant Fish, Mrs. Hermann Oe Mr. and Mrs. George B. de For J. Cutting and Mrs. Herma house.

"Mrs. Belmont is the talk of folk to-day, and her action in re the trouble between her son, Mr. Vanderbilt, and Mr. Ogden Mills, bringing out some severe crit Sympathy is largely with Mrs. Mills

Newport's Peace Disturbed.

The NEW YORK HERALD despatch the same subject says: "What a life has Newport had, calm and peaceful the summer. There have been smoulde ing volcanoes, but no eruptions up to th present. Now everyone stands aghast What next? is the anxious query at the Casino. Everyone was wondering what would be the outcome of this latest social tornado."

"It was generally suggested that old scores were involved, and that warrants for the arrest were not slung about without grievous and heartgrinding provocation. Each side, of course, has its followers. Both women have been charmingly prominent in the gay world. Each is resolute and stiff as steel, and so the merry war is on once more.

"It was too funny to hear society's comments as people gathered together for the tennis matches at the Casino. "They say he's actually in jail," whispered one woman, referring to young Mr. Mills, "and his mother has taken him down some chicken sandwiches and pâté."

"Just then a policeman happened to his appearance in the Casino dozen men took cover and as many fringe th

"Th said one 'The mo

out for each other, the whole social structure falls to pieces, and it is "sauve qui peut."

The report of the illness of Mr. Harry Payne Whitney at Tucson, Arizona, cabled yesterday, was incorrect.

Rescue by the Intrepid.

Mr. Lloyd Phœnix had a party out on the Intrepid yesterday afternoon, when a small sloop was noticed near the breakers with a signal of distress flying. The Intrepid lost no time in passing her a line and towing her into Newport Harbor. But for the Intrepid's aid, the sloop, with her crew of three men, would probably have been lost.

The engagement is announced of Miss Carol Dubois, daughter of Dr. Frank L. Dubois, U.S.N., to Mr. Frank Clark Crosby, son of Pay Director Crosby, U.S.N.

TENNIS AT NEWPORT.

English Players Compete in the Great Tournament on the Grounds.

NEW YORK, Friday.—Glorious weather was enjoyed for the third day of the tennis tournament. The Englishmen, Messrs. Gore and Black, met this morning, the former winning three str ets. Mr. Black played as if s a foregone concl to-mor row o is extch for

FOOTBALL IN ENGLAND.

Results of Yesterday's Principal Matches Under Association and Rugby Rules.

[BY THE HERALD'S SPECIAL WIRE.]

LONDON, Sunday.—The following are the final scores in the principal football matches contested yesterday:—

ENGLISH ASSOCIATION CUP (second round)—Newton Heath 0, Liverpool 0; Burnley 3, Burslem Port Vale 0; Stoke 0, Everton 0; Derby County 1, Wolverhampton Wanderers 0; Southampton 1, Newcastle United 0; Bolton Wanderers 1, Manchester City 0; West Bromwich Albion 1, Sheffield Wednesday 0; Notts Forest 4, Gainsborough Trinity 0.

OTHER MATCHES.—Cambridge University 2, Old Carthusians 1; Sunderland 4, Aston Villa 1; Bristol City 2, Notts County 2; Wallsall 2, Darwen 1; Leicester Fosse 3, Lincoln City 1; Bury 1, Preston North End 0; Small Heath 4, Luton 2.

UNDER RUGBY RULES.

The principal Rugby matches resulted as follows:—

RUGBY UNION.—Blackheath 8 points, Cambridge University 3; London Scottish 11, R mond 0.

NORTHERN UNION.—Fleetwood 8 po Barton 0; Leeds 0, Bramley 0; Rochdale H 12, Morecambe 3; Ulverston 3, Birke Wanderers 0; Oldham 11, St Helens 0; Hudders ford 8, Manningham 2; Hull 8, Hunslet 20, Ho Wakefield 7, Halifax 5; Walkden 0, Lan Altrincham 6, Millom 0; Salford 6, Broughton Rangers 2.

FOOTBALL IN FRANC

Several interesting football mat Association rules, will be played a this afternoon.

In the HERALD'S Cup (ch competition, the Standard A. the United Sports Club or ground at Sèvres at 2.30 p.m same hour the kick-off will Vampires' ground at Vincen between the Paris Star and de France.

For the Lucenski Cup the Standard A.C. will the United Sports Club on ground at Billancourt and the Racing Club Levallois.

SAVOY HOT

The additional buil d considerably incre They c

4

LAWN TENNIS BY IMPERIAL PLAYERS.

H I H the Grand Duke Michael and H's Sister in the Homburg Tournament.

SOME FINE GAMES WERE SEEN

Among the Spectators was H.R.H. the Prince of Wales.

[FROM OUR SPECIAL CORRESPONDENT.]

HOMBURG, August 29.—Yesterday was an Imperial, Royal day in the lawn tennis tournament, not only as regards the weather, but a Grand Duke and Grand Duchess of Russia played and the Prince of Wales looked on.

In the gen'lemen's singles for the Challenge Cup, City of Homburg, it came in the fourth round to a warm fight between Count Voss-Schoenau and R. F. Doherty, with the latter as victor. Goodbody and Turner must settle it as to who will contest Doherty's grand prize.

doubles it will be de and Good-

fifteen Thomps There were n ne and in ybarita had to allow the Ho bine's allance being Cutting, the half distance. was selec the Sybarita was *débutante* thers, and saving on his vi ok the cup. The with her prize, and the New Yo The other cup represent port Knight's family. names w looked i

RING.

A Ger known jewel- a judge o ition at 21 his opinio the history season he open every Forbes, o gate (the Duk, of) ships. garian sta didn't I

WHER remem- opose?

" Hot many di man, as morning, " On t ness for ing like h " Why " Bec —Wash

H

PIGEON SHOOTING.

The Hon. P. Thellusson Defeats Messrs. Blake and Moncorgé at Monte Carlo.

[SPECIAL TO THE HERALD.]

MONTE CARLO, Saturday.—To-day was a bye-day, and we shot for a prize offered by the Hotel de Paris, consisting of a case of old brandy, added to a sweepstakes of 50fr. each.

The birds again were very good until the finish, when the betting was all in favor of the gun. The Hon. P. Thellusson was the only one to kill his twelve birds and consequently became the fond possessor of twelve bottles of *fine champagne* (1818), and also of the 1,055fr. Messrs. Blake and orgé took the second and third prizes, 700fr. and 500fr. respec- then contested, k place.

THE NEW YORK HERALD.

COMPLETE NUMBER 12 PAGES. EUROPEAN EDITION—PARIS. SATURDAY, APRIL 16, 1904. COMPLETE NUMBER 12 PAGES.

6
The Arts

THE HERALD'S ARCHIVES provide a useful insight into the turbulent world of the Impressionists. In April 1897, for example, the paper reported "A Battle Royal among Painters." Henri Rochefort, an art critic who was covering the Salon for the *Herald*, explained that two schools were in conflict – the official school of Gérôme and the Académie genre painters, and "an invasion by a species of art" (meaning Monet and others) "which is regarded as an extravagance by members of the Institute who protested furiously in an open letter to the Ministry of Arts. It is beyond doubt," Rochefort went on, "that we are passing a period when painting needs a renewal of some kind. However, it must be acknowledged that Delacroix, Rousseau, Corot and pupils were much greater artists than today's innovators."

But things changed fast and so did the *Herald*. Its later critic, Pierre Veber, was far more perceptive. As early as 1901, he wrote: "For a young collector, the school of 1830 is closed. A Corot, Delacroix or Millet, Rousseau or Daubigny would require millions, but with 200,000 francs, he [the collector] could buy a fine collection of Impressionists. Now is the time," he concluded. "In 20 years, those works will be as scarce as the works of 1830 are now."

Stories about Monet, Cézanne and Pissarro abound, as well as interviews with Helleu and Boldini whose languid paintings of Belle Epoque women helped to give the period its peculiar charm. The *Herald* carried a remarkable interview with Claude Monet, on the day he first exhibited his waterlilies ("Nympheas"). A modest, three-paragraph story, it appeared on page three, on November 22, 1900. Headlined "Claude Monet's Works – 25 of the Artist's Most Recent Creations in the Durand-Ruel Gallery," it read: "The works in the collection have been painted within the last ten years. But the series produced in 1899 and 1900 are the most interesting, especially that part which the artist has designated 'Bassin aux Nympheas.' They are about a dozen in number and consist of studies of a corner of his garden at Giverny, under the most varied aspects, chiefly on misty or sunny mornings.

"They are exquisite revelations of his comprehension of true light, of which he has made so careful a study. True, the pretty 'coin de nature' which he has represented in these works, catching the fugitive light of the sun playing amid the verdure, is extremely simple.

"As he explained to me," the critic added, "it is of his creation as it was planted by his own hands, some years ago. It is a charming bit of decorative landscape and will become famous, thanks to his magic brush."

Pissarro was also interviewed at the Durand-Ruel Gallery, earlier in the same year. He was exhibiting about fifty landscapes painted in and around Paris and Rouen. "I met the artist at the gallery," the critic reported, "and he expressed his regret that he did not become a citizen of the United States by the once-hoped-for annexation of the Island of Saint Thomas where he was born." (It was not annexed until 1917.)

"To my question: 'Which of his works in the gallery he preferred?' he told me that in his opinion, an artist could not like his own works until he saw them again after having lost sight of them for several years. 'I can have no preference for any of my pictures,' he said, 'for I am never completely satisfied with any of them.'"

The *Herald* critic found in all these pictures "an increasing charm and so clear a vision of nature and so much sincerity in the art that Mr. Pissarro's exhibition is well worth a visit from all who really care for art."

Famous artists were not immune to petty troubles and internal cabals. In 1896, Auguste Rodin was hard at work on a statue which, he said, "in one year will be the finest monument to Balzac." Instead, it became the center of a heated polemic. On May 17, 1898, "at a déjeuner given yesterday by M. Auguste Pellerin at Neuilly, Rodin sold that well-known collector his statue of Balzac for 20,000 francs to be erected on the lawns of Mr. Pellerin's property." A month later, the *Herald* announced that the statue had not been sold after all, but "It will be remembered that after the Société des Gens de Lettres had condemned Mr. Rodin's statue of Balzac, a subscription was opened for the purpose of purchasing it and erecting it on some public site in Paris. M. Rodin, however, has decided to keep it in his studio until the Salon is over and justice is done." The last of this story appeared on November 8, 1898, when the *Herald* announced that a new statue of Balzac, by Falguière this time, was now ready. "The famous author is represented in his long dressing gown, sitting on a bench. The sculptor, who is a great admirer of Mr. Rodin, has made no changes in the head but has slightly raised it and the monument will be both lifelike and pleasing."

Another artist having problems was Gustav Klimt, whose painting *Philosophy*, intended for the University of Vienna, was sent to be shown at the Paris Exhibition in April 1900. The painting had been presented to a few friends of Klimt, all professors at the University, who pronounced it beautiful. Yet they later refused to accept it. According to the *Herald* of April 19, 1900, with "bitter feelings," Klimt wrote a letter saying: "It is possible that I shall make some slight changes in this picture on its return from the Paris Exposition. But never will I make a stroke with my brush against my artistic convictions." The painter Karl Moll commented: "Think of the struggles of Ibsen and Wagner. Klimt is the first man in the Secession. After him is a large vacant space and then come the others." The celebrated Viennese architect Otto Wagner was quoted as saying: "This picture now hangs in the Grand Palais in Paris. To the true artist and art lover, it will be a monument showing in indelible letters the high place on which Austrian art stands in 1900."

Interviews with prominent art dealers gave a good idea of the art market and of the increasing success of the Impressionists. Durand-Ruel was a staunch and enlightened supporter of the Impressionists from the start. Asked on April 24, 1896, "Whose works are most in demand today?" he answered: "Puvis de Chavannes, but he is not a great producer." (In Puvis de Chavannes's obituary on October 25, 1898, the *Herald* quoted the painter's last wishes: "I desire that my funeral shall be very simple. Not a word must be pronounced over my tomb.")

Durand-Ruel stated that "Degas, Monet, Renoir always command a market. Among those who are gone, Manet, who, like Whistler, was refused at the salon of 1863, is readily bought." This opinion was later confirmed by another dealer, Bernheim Jeune, who said on February 12, 1901: "Impressionist work is booming. Here in Paris, the last 15 sales have consisted almost entirely of works of the School of 1870 – Degas, Manet, Sisley, Monet, Pissarro, Renoir, Cézanne, Jongkind, Daumier and Boudin. Indeed, one good work by any of them, which not long ago were vague numbers in a catalog, is an event. Germany, even America, have taken up the movement. The blind, or those who refuse to see and maintain that outside of the School of 1830, there is nothing, are no longer dangerous."

A less adventurous dealer, M. Sedelmeyer, who said he had given up dealing with modern art, told the *Herald* in 1896: "English masters are in demand and Dutch masters of the 17th century. America is ready, and the supply does not equal the demand. Museums are springing up everywhere to say nothing of private collections. People are beginning to understand. Americans also have the courage of their opinions and do not haggle over prices.

"A few years ago," he said, "the demand was all for the Barbizon school and Americans have secured the finest examples. Due to M. Henry G. Marquand, whose donations to the Metropolitan made his name famous, I was persuaded to send some old masters to America. I chose about 50 pictures, took them over and did not sell one. That was back in 1886. Now they would sell like hotcakes. Americans come all the time asking: 'Do you have a Rembrandt?' Nearly 30 Rembrandts have gone to America in the last four years. Buyers are beginning to see that modern painters' prices are too high."

Sedelmeyer, whose favorite painter was Rembrandt, reported that he was preparing a huge exhibition of 500 Rembrandt works for the autumn of 1897, of which one quarter were "inédits."

Mr. Tripp, of Messrs. Tripp and Arnold, who only dealt with paintings of the Barbizon School, did not believe in the Impressionists at all. "The Impressionists! Ah yes, it dispenses with the trouble of drawing. We don't have anything to do with it."

In spite of this point of view, one of the great events of the art world in 1901, the sale of the Feydeau collection, revealed that Impressionist pictures stood higher than ever in public favor. A great art connoisseur, Georges Feydeau found more pleasure in purchasing new pictures than in keeping them. The world-known playwright, author of *La Dame de Chez Maxim's* and other classical Belle Epoque farces, was selling about 100 paintings, including Corot's 'La Tour,' Sisley's 'Le Pont de Moret' – "a chef d'oeuvre," the *Herald* noted – Monet's 'View of Etretat,' plus a number of Pissarros, Courbets, Daumiers, Renoirs, Cézannes and particularly Boudin, "Feydeau being one of those who best know this painter."

The sale of this first-class collection surpassed all expectations. Its "clou," Sisley's 'Pont de Moret,' made 28,000 francs – or 8,000 more than the experts predicted. Monet did very well too, with 11,000 francs for a hoar frost effect but Renoir's 'Après le Bain' fetched only 1,275 francs. In short, the collection, which had cost Feydeau 380,000 francs, brought 513,000 francs.

An interesting comparison of values can be gleaned from another *Herald* story about the conventional and now forgotten painter, Henri Gervex, who worked four years on an immense painting of the coronation of the Tsar, which was valued around 1900 at 1,000,000 francs.

Much of the buying was from America, a great magnet with its new millionaires looking for respectability – as well as good investments – through art. A minor artist who visited there in March 1898 remarked: "Nothing seems capable of arresting the tide of migration to the United States that affects Parisian artists. Neither the threat of war nor custom house difficulties. At any rate, within the past 12 months, such eminent portraitists as Chartran, Madrazo and Boldini have in turn forsaken their Parisian studios." The writer, Carolus Duran, was taking no pictures with him. "Why should I? Americans know my work well enough. One of my latest portraits was, you probably remember, that of Miss Consuelo Vanderbilt, the present Duchess of Marlborough."

On January 18, 1903, Paul Helleu also visited the United States, where he was commissioned by a publisher named Russell to create an album representing twenty of the most famous beauties in New York. Helleu, who said that this commission was showered upon him literally from the skies, also thanked the *Herald* for their help in many interviews. "At the Waldorf where I am staying," he said, "the waiter, when I left the room, eagerly showed me numbers of the *Herald* containing reproductions of my work, which is so superior to those in other papers."

Among the portraits he did were those of the actress Ethel Barrymore, a Miss Warren and a Mrs. Edmund Junones. Helleu's opinion of American women? "Most exquisite, elegant and magnificently dressed. I might sum up my opinion in a sort of equation: one pretty Frenchwoman plus the chic of an Englishwoman equals one American woman."

In October 1904, at the Salon d'Automne, Pierre Veber hailed "the fabulous Fauves and Cézanne, Renoir, Lautrec, Bonnard, Vuillard, Puvis de Chavannes, Matisse, Odilon, Redon, Valtat." His lead read: "October 15, 1904 is a noteworthy date in the history of modern painting. The Indépendants took the Grand Palais by storm. Let us not complain. We shall never see its equal."

Veber's judgment was defective when it came to Cézanne, the "Pope of the Indépendants," of whom he said: "He has invented a new still life . . . and some varnished apples in badly balanced fruit dishes. The initiated," he mistakenly concluded, "will prefer the painter's portraits of himself." In fact, it was Cézanne's apples which later commanded some of the biggest prices ever paid.

On October 17, 1905, the *Herald* ran a supplement on the exceptional Salon d'Automne, which included Renoir, Cézanne, Guillaumin, Redon, Bonnard, Ingres, Manet, Vuillard and Villon. On May 11, 1906, "The Ultra-Impressionists are Getting Top Prices" at another memorable sale at Paris's auction house, the Hôtel Drouot. However, according to the *Herald*, Manet's watercolor of his celebrated "Le Déjeuner sur l'Herbe" failed to meet the 4,000-franc opening bid and was knocked down at 3,000 francs.

The Stage: Sarah Bernhardt

Imperious, irresistible Sarah Bernhardt – who was the equivalent of today's superstars – dominated the stage during the Belle Epoque. Seemingly inexhaustible reports of her activities ranged from the announcement in 1895 that she would write her memoirs "with a blue pencil but not until she retires from the stage," to her adventures in 1900 during a provincial tour. Traveling in a special carriage with members of her company and her favorite dog, she was asked by the ticket collector to put her dog into the pet carriage. When she refused, she was served with a summons and was very annoyed that the facts were getting into the papers.

At home she had fourteen dogs and four cats, and although she left most of her menagerie behind when she traveled, she kept getting into trouble. In 1901, she had to change plans in San Francisco when her dog was barred from the Palace Hotel. Once in New Orleans "Vexed Mme Bernhardt" wanted the music stopped right away because she had been given a suite near the dining room where an orchestra was playing. She also demanded that the occupant of the adjoining suite be moved out and her dogs moved in. When the manager refused, she sent him a note saying she was no longer on speaking terms with him.

Scandal exploded again in 1905 when eggs ("the decayed variety") were thrown at Sarah in Quebec, where she had given an interview uncomplimentary to the Canadians. Five days later, however, the *Herald* reported a triumphal entry in New York as she arrived at the Majestic Hotel. She had not been in New York for four years. Brass bands played the *Marseillaise* as she drove to the hotel, passersby applauded and she received an ovation from 1,000 people in the hotel's rotunda. That evening, when she opened in *La Sorcière*, the theater was sold out and critics lauded the "same old music of voice, the indescribable charm of her presence, her grace of pose." Since she did not like her dressing room at the theater, paperhangers were immediately summoned and the room was papered in a delicate rose color.

Earlier that year, she executed another prima donna coup on her arrival in New York by ship, when she fainted on the pier while impatiently waiting for her jewels to be examined. She had arrived on the SS *Touraine* which docked at 4.00 p.m. Her request for permission to go ashore before the customs check was denied and examination of her jewels began. So she fainted, was revived and was driven at once to the railroad station where a special train left for Chicago at 5.30.

When she was not keeping special trains waiting, the explosive Sarah was ordering a new locomotive – and getting it. In 1906, the headline "Interrupted in her Bath" informed the *Herald*'s readers that Sarah was in her bath as the train crossed Kentucky, when she was thrown out by a sudden jerking of the carriage. Physically unhurt, but much excited, she dressed very quickly and left the train, demanding a fresh engine. One was soon procured and the great actress resumed her journey.

From time to time, the *Herald* gave vivid accounts of Sarah's personal surroundings. In 1902, the paper's reporter described her large salon on Boulevard Pereire, "beautifully lighted from above and filled with charming works of art. Above the carved wood mantelpiece is Clairin's large portrait of her in white, lounging on a divan with a superb greyhound at her feet. Here too is another portrait by Walter Spindler, representing her in profile as a Muse and in a third, by Chartran, she appears as Gismonda.

"Beneath the feet are velvety carpets mingled with bearskins. A large divan, placed in one corner, indicates a favorite place judging from the heap of cushions bearing the impression of a body.

"One glass contains a quantity of jewels which have doubtless been worn in the principal parts played by the great actress. There are diamonds, pearls and turquoises, also waistbands and tiaras – and a pretty bibelot representing the gold masks of 'Tragedy' and 'Comedy' finely chased and fixed on laurel wreaths in emeralds. An enameled scroll, entwined among the leaves, bears the inscription: 'A Sarah Bernhardt, ses Admirateurs. 9 Decembre 1896.'"

While the reporter was admiring these treasures, Sarah entered "with a friendly greeting and a smile. She looks more radiant than ever; she is somewhat more slender than she was and there are some silver threads among the golden hair." She was wearing a charming ermine costume, a long jacket with a waistband of embroideries and a long stole bordered with ermine. The sleeves were finished off with lace frills.

Leaning against the mantelpiece and basking in the warmth of a bright fire, Sarah asked the reporter to be seated. "What do I think of the fashions?" she said. "Not very much. I live so completely beyond their tyranny that I never trouble myself about them. As regards others, I think the present fashion has made great progress in the direction of independence. When one thinks that in the days of Louis XV and XVI, a woman was only in the fashion when her nose was the right shape, one can realize what great progress has been made towards independence. . .

"Fashion ought to be personal," she added with good common sense, "and a woman's dress should be designed to set off any special charm that she may possess or to conceal some defect without any preoccupation as to what other women do. As for myself, I like beautiful materials and graceful folds. I like my dresses plain and straight in their lines, leaving the body free movement; and I like them long and wrapping."

Her activities when on tour in the United States were of great interest to the *Herald* and its readers. In 1901, they were told that she had been guest of honor at a tea at the French Embassy in Washington, in the music room hung with Gobelins tapestries. In 1905, she protested to the French Ambassador about "the action of a theatrical syndicate in closing the theaters of Texas." This resulted in a diplomatic correspondence between the French and American governments, with Sarah "smarting under the incident." As a result, she played Camille in Dallas under a huge tent that accommodated 42,000 people, and she received volleys of applause. Dallas was *en fête*. Excursion trains brought her fans from distant points. The people and press of the country were so interested that the French Postal Telegraph Co. equipped a station in the tent annex for reporters.

Sarah inaugurated the telegraph line herself with a telegram to her son Maurice. "I cable from this magnificent tent in which I play tonight. It is amusing and a fairyland. Adoration. Mother B.'" The *Herald* called it "the most extraordinary incident in Mme. Bernhardt's public career and in America's dramatic annals." In 1905, her career was at an all-time peak and her manager, William Connor, announced plans for a Sarah Bernhardt Theater in New York to be erected on the $1,000,000 site of the Audubon Hotel.

She was also a shrewd businesswoman who knew how to cash in on these highly profitable American tours (whose gross receipts in 1896 were, according to the *Herald*, up to the $1,000,000 mark). She also knew the value of publicity and every time she left for the United States, the Boulevard Pereire would be thronged with streams of friends coming to say goodbye.

She traveled in style, as indicated by an interview with Coquelin, an actor who crossed the Atlantic with her in 1900. "I called on Sarah. She is all right. A little apartment which is comparatively comfortable has been fitted for her. She has a cabinet de toilette, bedroom, dining room and a little drawing room. I asked her if she would like to take a walk on deck. 'Thanks, no!' she said. She doesn't like the sea, except from ashore. Sarah is never sea-sick but she will not leave her little domain where she has plenty of air and flowers. I passed an hour chatting with her. It was oh! so highly amusing for she has the gift, as only her friends know, of seeing and representing with irresistible humor the caricatured aspect of men and things."

Onstage, she was ever "The Divine Sarah." In 1898, she appeared in the memorable Paris premiere of Gabriele D'Annunzio's *La Ville Morte*. The theater was crowded with literary and artistic celebrities. During the evening, Bernhardt received a telegram from D'Annunzio's mistress, Eleonora Duse, in Rome. "I am delighted to hear of your triumph and, as an Italian, I am deeply grateful to you." Sarah declared herself "deeply touched by her delicate attention." When she played Edmond Rostand's *L'Aiglon* in New York, in 1900, she received an enthusiastic reception as public and critics agreed that the play was written for her.

Despite her theatrical success, Sarah was steadfastly refused the Legion of Honor. The *Herald* reported in 1906 that "The Council of the Legion of Honor considered her nomination for the second time and persisted in its refusal."

Authors

The *Herald* always showed an interest in culture and regularly published interviews with famous writers. One of the most significant, which ran in September 1895, was conducted in Russia by a Miss Isabel F. Hapgood, who had received an invitation from Leo Tolstoy. Hapgood started by asking the cab driver who drove her to the writer's home if he knew Tolstoy. His answer: "Everybody knows him. He is the first gentleman in the Empire." The driver had read every one of the count's books he could lay hands on, and from them he learned to love the world better and be a more honest man.

Hapgood described Tolstoy's study as very plain, lined with bookcases. The hall upstairs had polished floors, a set of very simple wicker furniture and portraits of ancestors, some of whom figured in *War and Peace*. "Cheap as the furniture is," she added, "he grumbled at it when he purchased it and still calls it 'sinful luxury.'" She also noted a piano, on which he sometimes played, and a large table, at every point emphasizing the simple character of it all in order to rectify what she called "an injustice," for the house had been described as a castle luxuriously furnished.

Tolstoy had been mowing and appeared at dinner in a grayish blouse and trousers and a soft white linen cap. He looked weatherbeaten. "His broad shoulders," Hapgood wrote, "seemed to preserve in their enhanced stoop a memory of recent toil."

He was described as a devoted father and husband who had lived for years in the country alone, fully determined never to marry. When he did, he made a "righteous choice. His wife is a heroine half his age. He brought her to this tiny wing and there she lived for 17 years." Hapgood noted the horrible loneliness of it, especially in winter, with not a neighbor for miles.

"Sophia Tolstoy was truly a heroine," Hapgood said, and it was to her self-denial and courage that the world owed *War and Peace* and *Anna Karenina*.

Another fascinating interview was with Anatole France, found among his books in the Villa Said, off the Avenue du Bois de Boulogne – a house full of bronzes, statuettes, pictures, china and rare editions. France's studio was a long lofty room lit by a diamond-paned window. Part of it was taken by a huge stone mantelpiece. The walls were hidden by books. His writing table close to the window was also thickly strewn with books. Stairs were improvised bookshelves, there were books on a window ledge, books burdened a cabinet inlaid with mother-of-pearl, littered the floor in piles, in heaps and mounds. Hapgood concluded: "All around is an orgy of books."

France was sitting in a capacious easy chair looking like a middle-aged Faust, in a thick gray dressing robe with tasseled cord and red silk skullcap perched on the back of his closely cropped head and smoking the caporal cigarettes of the Régie.

What was he like? "Full of indulgent wisdom and above vulgar prejudice."

Mark Twain was also interviewed on June 13, 1897, in London where he was then living.

His opening lines were grim: "Of course I'm dying," he said. "We're all dying." Nevertheless, he looked in good health and his snowy white hair was "as bushy as ever." Convinced that the writer was disturbed by worries, the reporter noted the hopeless resignation in his bearing, which contrasted with his once easy-going carefreeness. Twain did everything to reassure her. "I am as well as ever," he said. "You must not attach too much importance to Mrs. Clemens' remark that I was not in a condition to receive visitors. I was simply in bed, that's all. Now women think if a man does not get up before twelve o'clock he is not in good health – and I never get up before twelve." Since the death of his daughter a few months ago, Mark Twain had been trying to hide his grief and he had also suffered great losses when the Webster publishing firm engulfed his whole fortune. But he said: "Poverty is relative. I have been in poverty so often that it does not worry me."

Clemens also gave his secret for venting ill feelings. "I used to have a 'Rage' letterbox," he said, "and when I got into a temper about something, I'd sit down and write a letter, pouring out all my thoughts and all the bitterness, anger, contempt, indignation and invective in my heart. And when I had cleaned my heart, I put the letter in the box and Mrs Clemens would see to it that it did not go."

Rudyard Kipling was interviewed on January 20, 1901, at his home in Rottingdean, described as a picturesque village, less commonplace than an ordinary English village and as picturesque as Brittany. He did not look over thirty. His eyes especially, behind immovable spectacles, fixed the attention. Seated at his desk, his elbow resting on sheets of paper blackened with manuscript, he moved his shapely hands and his thick and hairy wrists and at times threw himself back in his chair with a frank, schoolboy laugh.

The conversation opened on the subject of India, a country which Kipling regarded with extreme tenderness. He knew Northern India best, loved the Russians "because they are so Oriental" and was a great admirer of Tolstoy. He did not like Wagner or Bach, liked Gounod but detested Beethoven, while his admiration of Offenbach verged on adoration. He also admired Rabelais, Maupassant and disapproved of D'Annunzio's "erotic fiction."

"It must be my Oriental leanings," he said, "but I do not like a woman outside of her house."

On December 1, 1900, the death of Oscar Wilde, "the once famous apostle of aesthetic art and literature," was reported: "yesterday, at 2:30 in a small hotel on the rue des Beaux Arts."

Wilde's superb arrogance had emerged in a *Herald* story on January 19, 1895. Under the headline "Oscar Wilde on Himself," he was quoted as saying: "Every play of Shakespeare is dominated by Shakespeare. Ibsen and Dumas dominate their works. My works are dominated by myself." Asked, "Do you think critics will understand your new play 'An Ideal Husband?' – 'I hope not,' replied Mr. Wilde. 'It is exquisitely trivial, a delicate bubble of fancy.'" Of his hero, he said: "I placed him in the highest rank of life merely because that is the side of social life with which I am best acquainted."

THE DIFFERENT ATTEMPTS AT RESTORATION

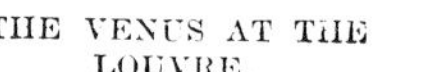

THE VENUS AT THE LOUVRE.

VENUS AND MARS.

VENUS WITH A MIRROR.

VENUS WITH WREATHS.

VENUS LEANING ON HER ELBOW.

VENUS WITH A DO

VENUS DE MILO HELD AN APPLE.

A Vivid Light Newly Thrown Upon the Much Disputed Mystery of This Lovely Creation.

WAS WHOLE WHEN FOUND.

[From the NEW YORK HERALD.]

There has always been considerable controversy over the actual original condition of that world-famed statue in the Louvre, the Venus de Milo. Who was its author? At what period was it conceived? And what was the position of those missing arms? M. Marcelles, in 1854, remarked: "It will not be very long before there is no one living who will be capable of lifting the mist of mystery which enshrouds the origin of the Venus de Milo."

In this statement he was mistaken. The very seemingly impenetrable mystery which enshrouded this goddess but whetted the impatience of the archæologists to unravel it. In 1874, just twenty years after M. Marcelles had spoken these words, a manuscript report was discovered by M. Jean Aicard, over the signature of one Dumont d'Urville, written at Milo April 16, 1820.

D'Urville claimed to have been one of the first to see the treasure. He was at that time only an ensign on board La Chevrette, a French naval vessel. In this report, addressed to his commandant, he relates the details of the discovery, which, according to him, was made at the end of the month of March, and he adds:—

"She (the statue) represents a nude woman; her left hand is uplifted and holds an apple; the right hand grasps a mantle, which is draped in graceful folds around the hips and falls to the feet, but unfortunately both the arms have been mutilated and are actually detached from the body."

Several foot notes by Lieutenant Matterer, another officer of the Chevrette, were added to this manuscript.

"When M. d'Urville and myself," he writes, "first saw the statue, the left arm was still attached to the body. The right was broken off at the wrist, but the left was still almost perfect. The hand was uplifted and held an apple. If M. d'Urville called this antique statue Venus Victrix it was because she was holding the apple in her left hand. Had both arms been broken, I do not think this idea would have occurred to him."

According to M. Matterer, Dumont d'Urville has misrepresented the truth a little in his official report. One naturally asks what could have been his object? This object was explained later in a memoir written by M. Matterer, in 1858, sixteen years after the death of his illustrious friend. Dumont d'Urville had been obliged to make an official statement which could be used as a safeguard against certain possibilities.

As every one knows, the Milo statue was purchased by M. de Marcelles for the Marquis de Rivière, then French Ambassador at Constantinople, and was shipped on board the gunboat Estafette. This acquisition and embarkation met with many more difficulties than were given out to the public at that time. For instance, there was considerable haggling over the price with the peasant whose spade had discovered the treasure, a very warm dispute with an Armenian priest and much red tape with the Pinnates of the island.

The truth, learned later by an admission made by M. Brest, Vice-Consul of France at Milo, and by the revelations of M. Matterer still later, was that fearing to lose the precious treasure on account of all the obstacles placed in their way the officers of the Estafette decided—encouraged, perhaps, by M. de Marcelles—to carry the statue away by force.

"Then ensued a regular battle," relates M. de Brest, "between the Grecian and Turkish sailors and the Frenchmen, and it was in this hand-to-hand struggle that the statue was mutilated."

At that time diplomatic incidents were not so easily managed as at the present day. The most important thing was to keep this squabble secret, not only to save the sailors from blame, who had only sinned in their [...]ess of zeal, but also to save M. de Mar[...] accusation of vandalism. It [...] the Venus of

"She was in a condition of good preservation. In one of her hands she held an apple, a fact which led him to suppose that she was the goddess of the island—as the word 'melos' in Greek signifies apple—but she could just as easily have been taken for a Venus. She is of marvellous beauty, the draperies being specially admirable."

The author of these lines, a nephew of the admiral of the same name, was himself a brilliant naval officer. A graduate of the Naval School and then of Angoulême, he gained great honors for his bravery at Navarino and Salamine. After the revolution of 1830 he sent in his resignation from active service.

IMPORTANT POINTS SETTLED.

His testimony in the question of the Venus de Milo is absolutely disinterested. He never for a moment thought of attaching any importance to his rôle in the affair. He simply wrote these daily notes for his own pleasure and perhaps because it was his duty to correct his daily observations, and they are simply what he heard and what he saw on the subject.

M. de Trogoff's story, which is absolutely trustworthy, settles and fixes two points in this historical controversy—first, that it was in March, 1820, from the 4th to the 11th, and not on April 8, as has been generally believed, that the statue was found; second, that both arms were intact and the Venus held an apple in one of her hands.

It is very improbable, however, that the archæologists will confess themselves vanquished. For nearly twenty years they have been promulgating systems without giving a thought to the witnesses who might overthrow them.

The different attempts made towards the restoration of this Venus de Milo offer some very amusing incidents. Fortunately, from the very beginning there was so much disagreement among the archæologists that Louis XVIII., finding himself in an embarrassing position when the Marquis de Rivière brought the marble to Paris, ordered the statue to be sent to the Louvre for public exhibition as it was found.

Being deterred by the Royal decision from trifling with the original marble, the archæologists called for competitive designs, showing how Venus probably looked before her mutilation, and this was followed by a

F THE VENUS DE MILO

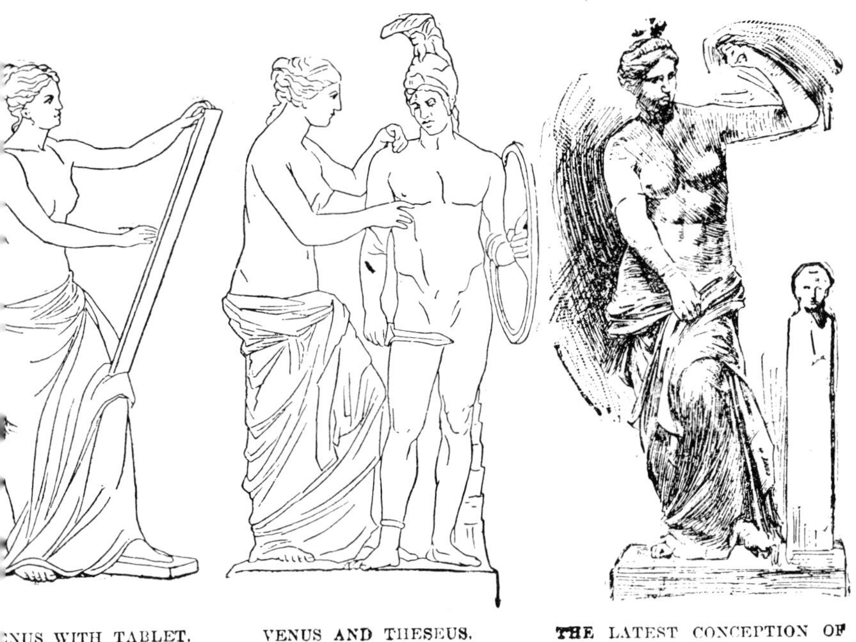

ENUS WITH TABLET. VENUS AND THESEUS. THE LATEST CONCEPTION OF THE STATUE.

e shield on
ne holds a
n inscrip-
y of the
Magazine,
y carefully,
of Victory,
scription on
r, gives us a
urel in each
ptor exhibited
toilet.
gler, Venus is
hand holding
eems to look
the subject,
e is a repro-
f Alexander,
n the time of
d the original
s welcoming into
ounder of Athens,
is sculptured out
has drawn forth
olomon that it is

ANCIENT STATUE OF GERMANICUS.

Archæologists Will Be Interested in a Discovery Recently Made in Asia Minor.

ONLY ONE KNOWN TO EXIST.

A discovery of great interest has been made recently at Cilicia in Asia Minor.

A number of portions of a bronze statue were found and these fragments are in the opinion of specialists on the subject parts of a statue of Germanicus, the Roman general.

This is the only known statue that was ever made of Germanicus, though many medallions have perpetuated his energetic features. The head of the statue is so well preserved that by a process of restoration performed by experts in this matter it has

FRAGMENT OF A STATUE OF GERMANICUS.

been made to reassume its former natural aspect, as will be seen by the accompanying picture.

These bronzes have great artistic and archæological value, for discoveries of this kind are getting very rare now.

Germanicus lived in the time of Jesus Christ, an interesting epoch, to say the least, and the conservators of the Louvre and several members of the Instit...
as MM. Hé...

WHAT

Maragliano'
Italia

CONTRADI

The serum t
of tuberculosis w
cussion at the me
recently held at
serum in particula
tapis. M. de Ren
excellent effect wi
the symptom feve
attributes this act
antitoxic substances
substances which ap
antidotes for the tub

M. Naseimbesse
a physician of Mila
cases of pulmonary t
eight were much b
treated with injecti
serum ; he even claim
plete recovery, and on
of failure.

M. Giura,
who practises in Rome,
that he had treated
gliano's method, one o
covered, while the other
improved.

Best of all,
however, was the paper re
in which he described h
rience for the benefit of h
became tubercular, and
the medications usually e
monary tuberculosis. In
he began the serum treatme
short time the fever, whi
been wasting his strength, l
of flesh stopped, and he beg
weight again, while the spe
completely disappeared from
he now considers himse
cured.

It is easy to understand
that in presence of such re
the physicians present at the
felt authorized in congratulatin
on the progress made in the
ment as recommended by Mara
fortunately, the successful case
to this method are still conf
country of the Genoese profe
even at the Rome meeting co
arose as to the effect of the s
attributing to it the power of lo
temperature in tuberculosis, othe
of the feverish reaction followin
jections. Maragliano himself ac
the injections do not always lower
perature and that it is not yet p
form a definite opinion as to the
of the improvement effected by th
tions of antitubercular serum.

As regards the cases
of improvement reported, the usua
tion arises as to the proportion due
better conditions of hygiene and al
tion under which the patients were
while being treated with the
Although in Italy the antitubercular
appears at present to work wond...
countries this...

n of
by
y the
lated
low a
and
f the
cked
e of
body
and
eight
dis-
tebral
tions.
ected,
hump
neck ;
dorsal
How-
p the
this
ained
s can
eased
itive
called
o first

COLOR PHOTOGRAPHS.

Mr. Frederick Ives has given a description of his method of photography in natural colors and exhibited a number of photographs so taken, at the Fine Art Society's Gallery. His system is an application of the principle that all the colors in nature are equivalent to mixtures of three colors of the spectrum itself. Three photographs are made of the object to be reproduced, each being taken by the joint action in due proportion of the respective fundamental color and all other hues into which it must enter in the reproduction. By means of a specially-constructed camera the necessary three negative images are taken at one exposure on one plate, and the contact positive from this negative is cut into three portions and mounted on a cardboard frame, which is dropped into the "kromskop," as the optical instrument is termed by which the three images are blended together. In this the red image is so placed that it is seen by reflection from the first surface of a transparent mirror of cyan-blue glass. The blue image is in like manner viewed through this glass by reflection from the first surface of a transparent mirror of yellow glass, while the green image is viewed directly through the cyan-blue and yellow transparent mirrors, both of which transmit the green light. Thus the three images appear as one to the eye and reproduce the object in its natural colors.—*Times.*

...ithout doubt the work of Cephisodate and ...arque, two sons of Praxiteles.
... Tarral, an Englishman living in Paris,
...I. Goeler von Ravensburg have ac-
...M. Dumont d'Urville's description of
...ss when first found at Milo, and
...een so completely corroborated
...idshipman's log book. The
... proposed by Mr. Tarral,
...e reproduce, is the
...the models so far
... nearer the trut...

THE SALON DES CHAMPS-ÉLYSÉES.

M. Henri Rochefort Writes of the Exhibition of the Société des Artistes Français Which Opens To-day.

IN THE PALAIS DE L'INDUSTRIE.

Severe Criticism of the Two Compositions which Have Been Most Talked About Previous to Their Exhibition.

M. TATTEGRAIN'S "SAUVETAGE EN PLEINE MER."

This and M. Louvet's "Ballade" the Most "Suggestive" Canvases in This Year's Salon.

M. BENJAMIN CONSTANT'S MASTERPIECE.

It seems to me a matter for deep regret that artists do not finish their pictures at least a year before exhibiting them. They would thus give their works time to dry, and enable time to impress upon them the effects which determine and consecrate the quality of a painting.

As it is they are nearly always at work on their exhibits up to the moment when the porters put in an appearance to carry them off on their *crochets*. Sometimes one even sees laggards giving the final touches to their canvases even in the dust of the varnishing, so-called because not a single picture is ever varnished.

The sinking in of the paint produced by the exposure of colors still damp thus gives the Salon which has just opened a grayish uniform veil, through which there is, at first, some difficulty in discerning the school, the style or the originality.

This is the first impression one receives in passing for the first time through the galleries of the exhibition in the Champs-Elysées. Little by little the fog disperses. Nevertheless it is some little time before the works which cover the walls appear to one what they really are.

Although there is no "Salon d'Honneur" in the Champs-Elysées Salon, and alth- the numbers attached to the fort- it imply neither superiori-

mental disorder. Titania is not the only one to allow herself to be captivated by the charms of a Bottom. Ask any mother who has daughters to marry. She will tell you that this kind of madness is true wisdom.

Room No. 1 shows us, besides, some women sewing the sails of a ship in blinding sunshine. This important picture, by a Spanish artist, M. Sorolla, is perhaps more crude than agreeable. But it is none the less the work of a powerful and sincere artist.

M. Surand also exhibits a poet dreaming, in a gray key—a work of much distinction. The women who appear to him in his dreams indicate an artist sure of his handling and of his modelling.

In this gallery, too, the public will crowd around a work which, from an architectural point of view, will dominate over all the rest: one of the three or four inaugurations of the Alexander III. bridge which were inevitable. This one is by M. Pierre Vauthier, who has treated it in a free manner and a bright note. It recalls to mind the splendid sunshine in which the day was bathed, and everything breathes the good humor and joy which m-

and ceiling, are reflected rays in the enormous bo- be more refreshing to t-

It is hard to pass thr- out stopping before leuse," by M. Eugène canvas of large size, purely impressionist not in the water look as if th- by a shower of confetti. boating on the Lake will my readers, pro- whether, even in the ever wore so strange

RO-

Although relative scarcely be able to will crowd in front tage en Plein Mer been inspired to t the sentiment of t- remember his pictu- "Useless Mouths Dr- City," who were wri- hunger. The scene His "Sauvetage" t- ing. The seamen, overturned boat, oth- ing wreckage on a feels to be of unfat- impression of ang- in vain is the work sionist painters. L- masted saving ship a which it has establis- a hand, a poor, cold and seen emerging from th- engulfed the rest of the appeal is frightful. that all the struggles of to the sea in ships and against the most impla- are concentrated on th-

M. Groiller has "pu- leine" that one wou- graphed from Henner's. not painted one, would have discovered the con- shadow, modelled that fi- those arms? It is pro- absolutely certain—that he given such an exact imit- *tiche* becomes a simple cop-

"La Première Commun- who is not the only one to with white—for there are bitions almost as many " "inquisitions"—inspire- sentiment than that of rash parents expose th- hands they place lig- of dresses and veil- the least breath of

ROOM 2.

The first thing that struck me in Room 2 was a group of kittens playing on the grass, exhibited by M. Thurner. Their velvet paws and pink coral noses, amid acanthus and borage leaves, are delightfully rendered, which is the more notable as nothing is so hard to transfer to canvas as the supple movements of a kitten.

Not far from this picture is the "Petite Gardeuse de Vaches," by M. Souza Pinto. The girl dreams while the cattle are grazing. She has nothing about her of Millet's peasants, but neither does she recall to mind those of Boucher. She seems as though she has sat to one of the early Italian painters, Giovanni Bellini or Beltraffio. But she is none the less charming, whatever school she may belong to, for in æsthetic and *genre* art there are only two classes of painters: those who have talent and those who have none.

In this room we find "Le puits algérien," at which Mr. Washington represents a body of Algerian cavalry. The figures are brilliant in color and are dazzling in the brilliant sunshine. One sees at a glance that the artist knows Algeria down to the very stones in the road. Courbet's *mot*, addressed to Fromentin, the Eastern painter: "You paint the Bedouins of the desert and you live in the place Pigalle," cannot be repeated in his case.

"L'Atelier," wherein M. Rosier shows a sculptor hard at work upon a "Milo of Crotona"—the model for which poses with conscientious energy—will attract attention on account of its exceptional suppleness.

M. Weingartner, whose name is unknown to me and who I fancy exhibits for the first time in the Champs-Elysées, sends a skilful picture of a cock-fight. We know, from the example set by M. Gérôme, that a début with a trifle of this kind may lead to anything. M. Weingartner has begun like the Member of the Institute. I will confine myself to wishing that he may not arrive at the same end.

There is the inevitable scene from the Inquisition, this time by M. Franz Schmid. Scenes from the Inquisition nearly always constitute the groundwork of a French exhibition. In M. Schmid's picture the victim has not yet undergone the torture of the red-hot iron, but she has just removed her last garment and the inquisitors seem to have devoted themselves less to their interrogation than to contemplation. Unfortunately the quality of the painting does not make up for the commonplace character of the subject.

-uch -tract -der- this time by M. Franz Schm- Scenes from the Inquisition nearly always constitute the groundwork of a French exhibition. In M. Schmid's picture the victi- twe- perl-

FIN DE SIÈCLE FRENCH ARTISTS.

Exhibition of Eccentric Pictures of All Kinds in the Durand-Ruel Gallery.

AN AMUSING SPECTACLE.

Globulists, Symphonists, Impressionists and Various Other "ists" to be Seen in Perfection.

It is not easy to classify in any known group of artists the painters who opened an exhibition of their works yesterday in the Durand-Ruel Gallery, 16 rue Laffitte.

They might be classed as independents, globulists, symphonists, impressionists, or any other "ists," or even "fumistes" if the known names of some of them did not preclude the idea. However that may be, those who prefer an amusing spectacle to an exhibition of pure art may spend a pleasant and exhilarating half hour in the gallery.

One cannot help laughing at M. Pierre Bonnard's "Enfants au Jardin," which look like embryos preserved in spirits; or the reminiscences of Italian pre-Raphaelites of which M. Maurice Denis' "Annonciation" is a caricature; or the wooden horses by M. Rippl Ronai, which look as though daubed over with soot; or the portraits and landscapes by MM. Petitjean Signac and Van Rysselberghe, wherein exaggeration is carried to the extreme of dotting the canvas all over with spots of the most improbable colors, producing the effect of a mosaic of Mid-Lent confetti.

M. Antoine de La Rochefoucauld has arrived at another result in his two religious subjects. The figures look like those of pre-Raphaelite artists copied by a Chinese.

Close by are the decorative panels of M. Sernsier, wherein the red-legged Breton women grouped around a fountain look more as though woven in colored wools than painted.

There is a view of a square, in summer, by Mr. André, the figures of which look as though worked with a tapestry needle. M. Odillon Redon's pastels, the prevailing colors in which are violet blues and yellow ochre, look as though they were produced by chance crushing of the colored chalk on the canvas. M. Louis Valtat's five exhibits are so daubed that it is impossible to make out what they represent.

Apart from a few studies by Ibels, and some drawings by Hermann Paul, and a few landscapes by M. Roussel Masure, which are not beyond comprehension, one wonders, after seeing the exhibition, whether it is not a wager, or a challenge to good taste and common-sense.

The other exhibitors are MM. Ranson, K. X. Roussel, Vuillard, Augrand, H. E. Cross, M. Luce, Daniel Monfreid, d'Espagnat, Emile Bernard, C. Fliger, A. M. Charpentier, Lacombe and Minne.

A CORRECTION.

To the Editor of the Herald:—

Here in Constantinople we were from time to time highly amused by the ingenious misstatements published in your columns as emanating from your local correspondent, but the ignorance of this individual has been eclipsed by the marvelous account of the London Drawing Room

ART EXHIBITION OPEN IN CAIRO.

English and American Painters Take a Prominent Place at the Cercle Artistique.

MAJOR MARCHAND'S PORTRAIT.

Some Pictures too Green, Some too Blue, Some too Yellow and a Few Badly Framed.

Cairo.—The exhibition of paintings and aquarelles at the Cercle Artistique continues to be the rendezvous of the Cairo fashionable world. Nobody should attempt a serious critique on an exhibition who has not made a study of art himself, and I am only going to tell you briefly what I saw and how I liked it, without any reference to art and technique strictly and purely considered. Of course, there is always that desire, that sometimes finds expression in manœuvring and influence brought to bear in any exhibition, to get one's pictures well hung. It must be admitted in this one that some of our best artists have come off rather badly, as referred to in my last letter. The general effect of the collection is pleasing, with a harmony of color pervading the whole, and in point of merit it is considerably above the exhibitions of previous years.

Two immense palettes, surmounted by banners, on the outer doorposts, call the attention of those driving along that the exhibition is there, while the internal decorations in the way of Oriental hangings, though few and simple, give an aspect of comfort to the suite of rooms in which the exhibition is held. The Rallis, the Bacons, the Easts, the Philippoteauxs, the Talbot Kellys are among those that are most admired. In the same category are two very good aquarelles by J. G. Rogers, "Sur le Nil" and "Le Cimetière Girget." Mr. Bacon's most important work, the "Secret of the Sphinx," is full of softness of color and delicateness of touch, and the Arab woman kneeling at sunrise before the spring which fills almost the entire background, symbolizes in an impressive manner Allah and eternity.

Mr. W. Brown's little picture, the "Mosquée à Boulac," is very pleasing, but hung a trifle too high.

"COQUELICOTS EN EVIDENCE."

Mr. Ralli's work is almost beyond praise. Mr. Ralli is very fond of red coquelicots; he has them on his "Médée" as she looks from a mellow background thoughtfully out of the frame; he has them on the head of his "Peplum" woman, a figure full of grace and beauty, standing on the steps of a Roman peristyle; he has them in a vase of his "Image Miraculeuse," and as the headdress on the "Marchande de Fleurs." I tried covering them with the hand and found it detracted from the beauty of the pictures. In his fine picture of the Jews weeping at the wall of the temple in Jerusalem, the grouping and coloring are exquisite.

Mr. E. Demirgian's "Café Arabe" carries out excellently the perspective of those vaulted cafés, with long archways ending on a street beyond. His "Rue à Boulac" is another portrayal of Oriental life. I stopped for a moment to look at Mr. N. Forcella's "Lecture du Coran" and his "Marchand de Cuivres," and passed on to Mr. Philippoteaux's "Sur la Digue de Ghizeh," representing a girl riding on a mospheres. His "Mer à Biarritz" takes us to the green seas.

Mr. Ogilvie's "Le Désert" is a fine large painting. The idea of solitude is faithfully expressed by two Arabs, the one on a camel, the other walking beside him, and away off across the eternal sands the setting sun.

Mr. Varley's "Rue de la Citadelle" is a very attractive painting. Mr. Talbot Kelly has several pictures of the highest artistic order. Mr. A. L. Rawlinson's "Lux in Tenebris" is an upright sepia in the Raphael angel style and attracts considerable attention.

Mr. H. Simpson's pictures are sketchy and artistic, and Mr. G. Munier has an aquarelle altogether remarkable as to execution, perspective and color, but rather architectural.

CARICATURES BY A PRINCE.

The Prince Mohamed Ali has three excellent pen-and-ink caricatures. The Cannes Golf Club ought to have his "Golfer's Delight," which represents a golfer leaning on his clubs with a caddy who smokes his pipe for him and a parrot to swear for him. Mr. E. Vernier's collection of bas-reliefs, bronze medallions, gold enamels, gold bracelet—representing "The Arts," and "The Three Ages of Life" (book cover) occupy the most prominent place in the room and are worthy of it. Commandant Marchand's portrait, standing, is very much "à la militaire," with an expression as if he was looking down the line; the likeness is striking. Near by is Mr. E. Bordes' fine portrait of M. de Cogordan, sitting, his quite thoughtful face true to the life.

Mrs. Rees' "Hamida" is an excellent piece of work, and merits a second visit. Mrs. Longworth has two "Nature Morte." Then there are good specimens of the works of Mme. L. Dubrucq, Mlle. Andlau, Mme. H. Parker, Mlle. Caprera, Mme. Waterford, Mme. Zoucas, Mlle. C. L. Sheppard, Mlle. Rawlinson and Mlle. Wilkinson. The Rossis, the Lyndons, the Royles and Mr. Tyndal's "Une Rue," deserve a more extended mention than space will permit me to give. Other exhibitors are: Messrs. Rossetti, Holst, Haddad, E. Schiffi, Dalbono, Brugo, Müsser, West, Schaüffel, Casse, R. Cavi, F. Ferraresi, etc. There are some "aquarelles" in the Salon des Amateurs showing decided talent. Among them are Mlle. Warnock's "Village à l'Abassieh" and Miss Campbell's "Tombeaux des Mameluks." Mlle. Becker has "dix aquarelles." Mlle. Castel has a lovely screen in the Watteau style.

In general the exhibition is a very good one; some of the pictures are too yellow, some too green, some too blue and a few badly framed or hung to disadvantage; but the work is superior to anything we have had here in previous years, and a credit to everybody concerned.

CONSTANTINOPLE NOTES.

Constantin[...] Monday.—The small steam yacht [...]nstructed at [...] Imperial d[...] Sultan to [...] has sailed [...] charge of [...] passed out o[...] day evening, [...] off Coom-Capo[...] morning. Orig[...] gunboat for r[...] commodation is [...] rich in decor[...] throughout by [...] cludes all app[...] waters of the [...] it is impossible [...] Boyana passage [...] ence some diff[...] quarters for his [...] granted for her [...] Cattaro Inlets, [...] hands.

The German [...] Loreley is abo[...] cruise of a few [...] the Mediterra[...] next for Salon[...] there will run[...]

set in Dresden ch[...] box, which have b[...] O'Hagan for the mi[...]

The men's handic[...] entries, among the[...] Count Voss, Mr. [...] Water, from Cann[...] M. Lamperti and M[...] Bordighera; Mr. M[...] tall, of St. Raphael[...] Monte Carlo. M[...] players are also en[...] two old members, M[...] and Mr. Gurney Sm[...] from London to rea[...]

MEN'S [...]

In the men's dou[...] and Count Voss pl[...] strongest pair ent[...] hind them come th[...] Ernest Renshaw an[...] pair to beat. Other[...] free and Morrison, F[...] hold the Swiss doubl[...] maire and Wills and [...]

For Mrs. O'Hagan's [...] of mixed doubles have[...] ladies have signed for [...] —in fact, a busy and [...] promised on the courts [...]

The grounds are in [...] the club committee are [...] of green canvas back of t[...] the light, especially in th[...] grounds are open to the [...] tournament on payment [...]

SERIOUS THEFT A[...] THE J[...]

Till Broken Open an[...] Thousand Fra[...] Off.

A few days ago the d[...] the Jockey Club was br[...] of 9,000fr. was carried [...] the theft was given to [...] Commissary, who open[...] the affair.

The "Temps" states th[...] ers at the club, while sw[...] yesterday morning disc[...] a corner, a sealed roll of [...] ed it up and carried it to [...] took it to the police stati[...] in his presence and was [...] nine bank notes of 1,00[...]

The manager of the [...] formed a suspicion as [...] the discovery of some [...] of paper confirmed. [...] ly been thrown duri[...] the corner where [...] having thus en[...] the inquiry [...] arrest [...]

M. RODIN'S BALZAC.

Purchased by M. Auguste Pellerin for Twenty Thousand Francs.

The "Figaro" states that at a déjeuner which was given yesterday by M. Auguste Pellerin, at Neuilly, M. Rodin sold that well known collector his statue of Balzac for 20,000fr. In accordance with agreement, the statue will be erected on one of the lawns of M. Pellerin's property at Neuilly. Should the committee which has just been formed collect sufficient money for the purchase of the statue it will be transferred to it by the present owner. The Paris municipality has not succeeded in purchasing M. Rodin's "Le Baiser." This group was commissioned by the State in 1889.

AT THE GALERIE PETIT

Twenty-seven Oil Paintings by the Late Alfred Sisley Now on View.

GIFTS FROM FRENCH ARTISTS.

Among the twenty-seven oil-paintings about to be sold in consequence of the recent death of Alfred Sisley, which I saw yesterday in the Georges Petit Gallery, rue de Sèze, where they will be on view again to-day, I noticed some very interesting works.

Without indulging in the blind admiration which so many amateurs lavish on all the productions of certain artists, one must admit the real talent of Sisley, at the same time discriminating between his productions.

The best of his pictures on view yesterday, or at any rate those which will please his admirers most, though they may not reach the highest prices at the sale, are the following

No. 11, an ancient church lighted up by the sun, very warm and glowing; No. 12, "Les Bords du Loing," with the river full of transparency; No. 2, "Le Pont de Moret," with remarkably pellucid water; and No. 3, "Un Coup de Soleil," an evening effect on the road to Grez, most glowing with color.

At one end of the gallery is the picture intended for the Luxembourg Gallery. It represents a canal bordered with trees, which runs away in the background till lost in the distance. The keynote of the picture is a tender pink.

There are also numerous views of the old church at Moret, painted at different times of day, and landscapes and views near Cardiff and in the neighborhood of Moret, which give a faint idea of what the artist could do, as his best works are naturally not there.

I do not admire the six pastels in the gallery any more than I do the pastels in general by this artist. Among the fifty pictures, more or less, sent by various artists to be sold for the benefit of their late colleague's family, I especially admired "La Balayeuse," by Renoir, a small figure extremely delicate in handling, wherein the subdued tone of pink is remarkably effective.

No. 38, "L'Aube," a female figure, by Albert Besnard, is a remarkable study in white.

No. 64, "Jugement de Paris," is a fine drawing in green crayon, by Menard.

No. 77, "Lavoir à Issoudun," by Thaulow, gives a great impression of truth and of limpidity in the water.

No. 68, "Tuileries on a Winter Afternoon," is by Pissaro.

No. 55 is a pretty pastel drawing, full of light, by Walter Gay. It represents a little girl in pink, in a luxurious drawing room.

No. 69, "Balayeur," by Raffaelli, is not a success; the figure looks wooden.

As to No. 39, given by Claude Monet, a Norwegian village snowed up, I confess I fail to see its beauties, if it has any. It is hard, badly conceived, and incomprehensible. A study of a landscape, by Brangwyn, is interesting.

Besides the above there is a landscape by Cazin, a pastel, "La Toilette," by Degas; a drawing in sanguine by Helleu, and "Les Meules de Blé," a pastel by Lhermitte.

The pictures will be sold to-morrow by MM. Chevallier and Petit.

AT THE HOTEL DROUOT.

Impressionist Pictures by Well-known Artists Sell for Very High Prices.

There will be no exhibition to-day at the Hotel des Ventes, rue Drouot.

The sale of modern pictures by MM. Chevallier and Bernheim jeune, in Room 11, yesterday, brought in a total of 35,988fr., of which the following prices were the best:—

No. 1, "L'Amour Maternal," by Carrière, 2,300fr.; No. 2, "La Dame à l'Eventail," by Cassat, 1,900fr.; "La Cour de Ferme," by Cezanne, 1,550fr.; No. 4, "Une Rue d'Alger," by Dagnan-Bouveret, 810fr.; No. 5, "Le Bain," by Daumier, 3,500fr.; No. 6, "Five o'Clock," by Maurice Denis, 720fr.; Nos. 7 and 8, two pastels by Fauché, 33fr.; No. 10, "Bords de la Seine" (moonlight effect), by Guillaux, 300fr.; No. 11, "Figure of a Woman," by Toulouse Lautrec, 1,400fr.; No. 12, "Falaise de Varengeville," by Claude Monet, 3,460fr.; No. 13, portrait by Berthe Morizot, 4,000fr.; No. 14, "Vue de Pontoise," by Pissaro, 4,050fr.; No. 15, "La Route," by Pissaro, 3,050fr.; No. 16, "Jeune Fille Lisant," by Renoir, 4,950fr.; No. 17, "Le Loing à Moret," by Sisley, 2,995fr.; No. 18, "La Voie Ferrée," pastel by Sisley, 1,000fr.

None of the pictures in the sale were of a quality to justify the high prices obtained.

In a sale of pictures in Room 1, conducted by MM. Chevallier and Féral, the modern pictures disposed of, which were not impressionist, went much lower. It is true they were mostly very commonplace. No. 17, a "Jeune Musicienne," by Corot, sold for 1,600fr.; No. 18, "Peasant Girl and Cow," 290fr.; No. 25, "Horses," by Alfred de Dreux, 500fr.; No. 75, "Le Repasseur," by Ribot, 1,000fr.; No. 84, "Dog and Fowl," by Troyon, 1,550fr.; Nos. 85 and 86, landscapes, by Troyon, 210fr. and 620fr., and No. 99, "Spanish Scene," by Worms, 700fr.

M. LOUBET AT THE SALONS.

The President of the Republic visited the Salons yesterday afternoon and formally opened them. He was escorted through them, says the "Temps," by the presidents of the respective societies, who introduced to him the artists whose works had specially attracted his attention.

DEATH OF A CENTENARIAN.

The "Temps" hears from Camon that Mme. veuve Brigitte Lefebvre, who reached her 104th year on April 4 last, died on Friday. She was born at Camon on the 14th Germinal of the Year III. Up to the very last her mind and faculties were unimpaired.

CHÉR

Few Bu
bi

DOG S

The week
Chéri's, rue d
day, Wednesd
been the occa
hunters.

Among those
MM. Lemonnie
tavice, Baron de
Le Mire, Major
seur, de Jacquel
MM. Chabert, Er
lerand, Chenu, C
miche, Arnold, M
Ameline, Guénaud,
comte Arthur de C
du Nord, Baron de C
MM. H. Hawes, Ern
Kahn, J. Lieux, Wi
Mayer, Rondet, Mori

The pair 30 and 31,
marked yesterday as
matched, were sold
2,000fr.

Officier (16), whic
lent points, was b
1,900fr.

M. Perdry paid
bay mare.

The following a
sale:—

2. Bay mare, 3 yrs.,
4. Bay mare, 7 yrs., 1m
6. Jack, dark bay, 10
gnet ....
7. Jupiter, chestnut geldi
Dr. Pornequet ....
8. Toby, bay gelding, 8 yrs.
10. Tarbi, gray pony, 7 yrs
Worms ....

MYSTERY OF A DESERTED HOUSE.

Small Hotel in the Rue Monsigny Which Contains Many Works by Great Masters.

AN ART COLLECTOR'S COOK.

She Came Into the Property But Ignored the Value of Its Contents.

A curious story of long-hidden art treasures was made public yesterday in connection with a deserted house within hail of the grand boulevards.

Facing the Théatre des Bouffes-Parisiens, at No. 7 in the quiet little rue Monsigny, stands the house in question. For ten years past its shutters have been up, and people had almost forgotten at one time it was inhabited by a M. Chocquet, a chief of Department at the Ministry of the Interior.

Curiosity was awakened among the neighbors some two months ago when M. Péchard, police commissary for the quarter, came to seal the doors. It then began to be rumored that the house concealed great treasures. M. Chocquet, who died twenty years ago, was a well known art-collector. He had amassed, says the "Temps," a great quantity of valuable "bric-à-brac," porcelains and paintings, among the latter being canvases by Eugène Delacroix, Manet, Tassaert, Ingrès, Claude Monet, Sisley, Pissaro, Cezanne and other masters.

M. Chocquet had married his cook and made her his universal legatee. The widow being quite ignorant of the value of her possessions, forsook the little hotel in the rue Monsigny and took up her abode at Yvetot.

She died intestate some two months ago, and the "juge de paix" of Yvetot proceeded to administer the estate. By his orders the house in the rue Monsigny was sealed.

Then began a hunt for the heirs. Half a dozen have been traced, nephews and great-nephews of the deceased, all in very modest circumstances. One is a porter at the Paris Halles, another a dock-laborer at Havre. There is also a nursemaid and a dealer in insecticide powders.

LEAGUE BASEBALL GAMES.

The following table gives the standing of the League baseball clubs in the United States at the close of play on June 1:—

Club.	W.	L.	P.C.	Club.	W.	L	P.C.

SHIPPING NEWS.

TAVERNIER PICTURE SALE.

Record Price of Forty-three Thousand Francs Made for a Masterpiece by Sisley.

BOOM IN IMPRESSIONISM.

Works by Claud Monet, Daumier, Degas, Jongkind and Lepine Go Off Well.

The sale of modern pictures consisting of the collection of M. Adolphe Tavernier, which took place in the Petit Gallery yesterday, was conducted by Me. Chevallier, the auctioneer who presides at most of the great art sales. It was a great success, as the results far surpassed the estimates of the experts, MM. Georges Petit and Bernheim Jeune. There was a great gathering of collectors, artists, amateurs and dealers, and the total product of the 155 specimens was 422,627fr.

The success of the sale may be judged from the subjoined list of prices:—

The most important work in the sale was No. 68, "L'Inondation," a masterpiece by the great impressionist artist Sisley, for which the experts asked 25,000fr. Not only did it reach this price, but the biddings ran up within measurable distance of twice as much, when the hammer fell to a bid of 43,000 fr. from Comte de Camondo, amid general applause. This picture, as stated in the HERALD, yesterday, was sold by the artist off the easel for 40fr., and about ten years later fetched 87fr. at an auction at Bordeaux. It should be noted that works by Claude Monet, the leader of the living impressionist artists, also sold very well. The leading prices were as follows:—

The other canvases by the same master realized prices which have fixed his position in the world of art. It will be seen from the following list that "Sisleys" are moving steadily upwards: No. 69, "Une Rue à Ville d'Avray," 6,600fr. (M. Lazare Weiler); No. 70, "Maison sur les Bords du Loing," 6,000fr.; No. 71, "La Première Neige à Veneux-Nadon," 5,100fr. (M. Mancini). This work was bought by M. Durand Ruel at the Vever sale, three years ago for 1,150fr.

No. 72, "Les chalands berrichons, sur le canal du Loing," 5,150fr. This picture realized 4,600fr. at the Sisley sale last year. No. 73, "Meule de paille en octobre," 7,100fr.; No. 74, "Une Rue à Sèvres," 7,600fr.; No. 76, "La Route de Versailles," 8,050fr.

No. 62, "La Vigilance," by Puvis de Chavannes," made 10,700fr.

Works by Claude Monet: No. 55, "La Falaise à Pourville," 7,500fr.: No. 56, "L'Eglise de Vernon," 9,500fr. (brought 7,000fr. at the Desfossés sale); No. 57, "Vue de Hollande," 8,300fr.; No. 58, "Vue de Sainte-Adresse," 8,800fr.

Pictures by Renoir sold as follows: No. 64, "La Place Clichy," 6,000fr.; No. 65, "Allant au Conservatoire," 1,730fr., and No. 66, "La Jeune Fille au Cygne," 3,200fr. "Le Faucheur," by Corot, made only 6,100fr.

Works by Fantin Latour went as follows: No. 18, "La Toilette," 13,000fr. (M. Charles Ferry); No. 19, "Ariane Abandonnée," 5,300fr. (M. Lindet); No. "Un Déjeuner," 90fr. By Vuillard: No. 105, "La Tasse de Thé," 1,100fr.

PASTELS AND WATER-COLORS.

The pastels and watercolors reached relatively as high prices as the paintings. The works of Daumier and Degas appeared to be the most in request.

Works by Degas: No. 114, "La Sortie du Bain," 6,800fr.; No. 115, "Ballabile," 7,800fr.; No. 116, "Les Pointes," 11,600 fr.; No. 117, "Le Ballet," 14,100fr. (M. Durand Ruel); No. 118, "Arlequin et Colombine," 6,900fr.; No. 119, "La Coiffure au Bain," 3,050fr.

Watercolors by Daumier: No. 107, "Avant l'Audience," 4,100fr.; No. 108, "La Chanson à Boire," 10,700fr.; No. 109, "Les Confrères," 3,250fr.; No. 110, "Une Histoire Plaisante," 460fr.; No. 111, "La Plaidoirie," 3,300fr.; No. 112, "Un Dernier Mot," 390fr., and No. 113, "Portrait de Carrier-Belleuse," 160fr.

By Bonvin: No. 106, "La Religieuse," 230fr.

By Delacroix: No. 120, "Royal Tiger," 1,000fr.

By Forain: "Souvenir du Bal," 520fr.; No. 122, "Dans les Coulisses," 500fr.; No. 123, "Au Foyer de la Danse," 450fr.; No. 124, "Aux Folies-Bergère," 480fr.; No. 125, "Le Favori," 885fr.; No. 126, "A la Terrasse du Café," 290fr.

By Helleu: "Le Repos," 455fr.; No. 128, "Page d'Enfants," 500fr.

By Jongkind: No. 129, "Le Faubourg, Havre," 550fr.; No. 130, "Rotterdam," 1,680fr.; No. 131, "Dutch Windmill," 555fr.; No. 132, "Moonlight on a Canal," 760fr.; No. 133, "La Grande Ferme, Honfleur," 425fr.; No. 134, "Le Vieux Bassin, Bruxelles," 1,000fr.; No. 135, "Le Bassin, Honfleur," 930fr.; No. 136, "Saint-Parize le Châtel," 410fr.; No. 137, "Canal Scene," 380fr.; No. 138, "Chemin Devant la Ferme," 850fr.; No. 139, "The Rhône at Lyons," 400fr.; No. 140, "Tour Goguin, Nevers," 560fr.; No. 141, "Trees on Bank of Canal," 2,009fr.; No. 142, "Old Houses at Morlaix," 480fr.; No. 143, "The Scheldt at Antwerp," 390fr.; No. 144, "The Drac at Grenoble," 445fr.; No. 145, "Rue St. Genest, at Nevers," 1,950fr.

By Henri Monnier: No. 146, "Une Assemblée," 270fr.; No. 147, "Les Diseurs de Riens," 500fr.

By Berthe Morizot: No. 148, "Young Girl Seated," 300fr.

By Raffaelli: No. 149, "Le Bon Compagnon," 310fr. By Renoir: No. 150, "La Petite Liseuse," 1,990fr. By Saint-Marcel: No. 151, "Lion Couché," 52fr.; No. 152, "Panthère aux aguets," 30fr.; No. 153, "Lion Dormant," 45fr., and No. 154, "Tigre couché," 500fr.

AT THE HOTEL DROUOT.

In Room 6 at the Hotel des Ventes, rue Drouot, there will be an exhibition of works of art, furniture, and tapestry from the Stolypine collection.

In Room 7 there will be on view a collection of watercolors and drawings by Reps.

In Room 10 there will be a sale of fine jewels, and in the Petit Gallery, rue de Sèze, the private view of the collection of M. Auguste Rousseau, composed of small landscapes by masters of the French school of 1830.

"SAPHO" BLOCKS BROADWAY.

Advance Sale of Seats at Wallack's Theatre Amounted to $60,000.

NEW YORK, Tuesday.—When the police stopped the performances of "Sapho," Broadway, the thoroughfare on which Wallack's Theatre is situated, was blocked with people, the advance sale of seats having amounted to $60,000.

To-night Miss Nethersole puts on the "Second Mrs. Tanqueray."—Daily Telegraph.

THEATRICAL NOTES.

FA
F

Items of
ing P
"H

NEW KN

The Duke o
Horse,

[BY TH
LONDON,
Telegraph" p
of fashionable
Her Majest
ment of the
Knight of t
late Duke
who is in h
the Horse
torian Ord
Lord Eg
pointed Lo
Chester, i
Westminst
The Du
and suite
morning, a
one of Lord
has been p
the complet
residence o
in the day
the second L
Lord-Lieuten
The membe
1765-85 dined
Hotel Metropo
morate the bat
Admiral Henry
guest of the ev
Sir Joseph Phil
laid for fifty.

FROM THIS

To-day's "Daily
lowing:—
Lady White,
the defender o
Windsor Castle
ceived by the
with the Impe
India. Lady S
Stewart, was
honor.
Lord and La
Tring Park.
Mrs. Harry
daughter by he
the Drawing Ro
Sir Kenneth a
who have been
of the winter i
Queen Anne's
Lady de B
mouth, as the
journey to t
intended to
cent attack
Winifred,
is now at he
will probably
her adventur
perienced tra
peditions to re
ied even by a m
to go to South A
Isaac Gordon,
England, died in

ROSA BONHEUR STUDIO SALE.

Proceeds of the First Day Amount to More Than Half a Million Francs.

OXEN MOST IN DEMAND.

Stags Also Fetch Very High Prices—Felidae Come Next, While Horses Are a Drug.

The crowd which thronged the Petit Gallery yesterday, when the sale of paintings and studies by Rosa Bonheur began, was of quite a special character, the room being filled with foreigners of all nationalities. Naturally, the Paris picture dealers were present in force, and the numbers put up were rapidly carried off, the total proceeds of the day being 565,000fr.

The sale began at two o'clock, and it was a quarter past six o'clock when the last lot, No. 29, a figure of a lion, was knocked down to M. Bernheim, amid general satisfaction to see so long a sitting brought to an end.

The highest price of the day was that made by No. 198, a team of Nivernais oxen. This picture was keenly disputed by MM. Schaus, Georges Lebreton and Bourgeois, of Cologne. The latter eventually secured the picture for 33,600fr. The highest price paid for a stag was 21,300fr., paid by M. Knoedler for No. 320, "Cerf écoutant passer le Vent."

No. 200, "Oxen in a Meadow," fetched 17,500fr., and a forest scene, No. 323, went to M. Montagnac for 20,200fr.

No. 201, a fine picture of a Scotch ox, made 10,800fr. No. 1, a lion lying down, for which M. Petit, the expert in charge, asked 20,000fr., was bought by M. Tedesco for 15,400fr., and No. 24, a figure of a panther lying down, brought 11,500fr. The best prices were made for oxen; then came the stags, and after them the wild beasts.

The horses were not so much in demand. The highest price for a single specimen was 8,200fr., a white horse in a meadow, No. 80, "Horses in a Meadow," the principal subject of which is a fine white animal, in bright sunlight, was bought cheap by M. Lebreton for 4,700fr.

The best prices for dogs were: No. 445, a portrait of a black dog, 3,600fr.; No. 446, another portrait, "Ravajo," 7,500fr., and No. 750, "Matamore and Flambart," 7,200fr.

No. 470, a flock of sheep in a field, found a buyer at 5,500fr., and No. 471, a group of black sheep, went for 4,000fr.

The sheep and goats were less apppreciated. No. 585, a painting of moufflons, only fetched 2,950fr., and No. 586, "L'Hôte de la Montagne," 2,600fr.; No. 608, "Battage du Blé," a study six mètres long, which is only suitable for a museum, was bought by M. Georges Petit for 10,000fr.

The best of the three studies made for the "Horse Fair," No. 617, was bought by M. Bourgeois for 13,000fr.; No. 615 fetched 6,800fr. and No. 616 made 9,300fr.

No. 736, "Le Printemps au Bois," in spite of its remarkable qualities, fell to M. Hochon for 1,150fr. Had there been any sort of an animal in it, it would have fetched ten times as much.

The foxes did not take; the best price, 1,154fr. was paid for No. 438. The wild boars went rather better, No. 417, a study of these animals in a forest, making

of art tha
the divor
French sc
wife. The
In Roon
tion of wa
by Allong
ture, pict
rooms.

RA

Good Fi
Yest

Thursday
Friday ...

Althoug
ening yes
lombes th
for gentle
M. Stern
and by M
Fontarce
Hermine
as there w
second, a
away.
Nab' h
could not
at a dist
the Duc d
Railleu
lombes co
winning
Trencsi
final hur
on in a
got him
The D
eral Pea
colors fo
next We
J. Cla
the Gran
be on R
There
day, but
large; a
ners.

COLON

PRIX DE S
mètres
M. I. Wyso
M. H. de
M. Ch. Lié
Also ran
Won by
and third.
Betting:
10 to 1 Fu
Paris-Mut
places, 13fr
8fr. 50c.; p
PRIX JEA
Gentlem
and thr
M. P. Aum
M. P. Teiss
Vicomte de
Also ran
75½k., Gab
ly, 77k.,
67½k., Cob
Won by
Winner tra
Betting:
Ecole, 8 to
Whig, 14 t
Beryl, Mer
Paris-Mu
places, 19f
Winner, 27
PRIX D'AC
four an
M. H. de
M. I. Wyso
M. Ch. Lié
Also ran
46½k.
Won by
third. Wi
Betting:
d'Eau, 9 to
viette.
Paris-Mu
places, 21fr
50c.; place
PRIX JUM
ers, H
mètres
Comte G. d

the eminent novel-
rated his literary
an important work
(The Cruel), the
appear in the Jan-
Russkaya Mysl."
g, Chamberlain and
l nobility, has left
F. A. Meyendorff,
al of Nobility for
G. Doukmasoff,
Corps, have ar-
sti.
e an editorial
honor of its
journals re-
he "Russkaya
aie," "Pravo,"
rier," "Sever-
k." Prince V.
the "Severny
uch-applauded
ded with song
Imes. Bolska,
Z. N. Mour-

AND.

hat Indif-
Owing

WIRE.]

g those who
rday for the
s the "Daily
Mrs. and Miss
rafford, Major
Beresford, Mr.
ell, Mr. Muntz,
Mr. Harry Bent-

st drawn, and a
but lost, after
d forwards be-
l Wood. Swin-
n blank, but
anford Hall
g run by
however,
e thick
nade the

has been
ph," by
ss. Dur-
H. Heath,
vel, near
of

CLAUDE MONET'S WORKS.

Twenty-five of the Artist's Most Recent Creations in the Durand-Ruel Gallery.

M. Durand Ruel has just organized in his galleries, rue Laffitte, an exhibition of the latest works of Claude Monet, which will be on view until December 15.

All the works in the collection have been painted within the last ten years, but the series produced in 1899 and 1900 are the most interesting, especially that part which the artist has designated "Bassin aux Nymphéas." These are about a dozen in number, and consist of studies of a corner of his garden at Giverny, under the most varied aspects, chiefly on misty or sunny mornings. They are exquisite revelations of his comprehension of true light, of which he has made so careful a study.

True, the pretty "coin de nature" which he has represented in these works, catching the fugitive light of the sun playing amid the verdure, is extremely simple. As he explained to me, it is of his creation, as it was planted by his own hands some years ago. It is a charming bit of decorative landscape, and will become famous, thanks to his magic brush.

Imagine a quiet pond, crossed by a rustic bridge, in the midst of a vast thicket, crowded, like Zola's "Jardin du Paradou," with masses of verdure and unkempt trees, with their long and thick foliage drooping over the transparent water, the surface of which is covered with iris, nympheas, and water-lilies. In this corner of a garden he has succeeded in committing to canvas the lights, in their most fugitive aspect, in one and all of the pictures: they are, in fact, so many repetitions of the same subject, with impressions of something widely differing. Each of the twelve canvases represents the same subject, executed by the same hand, but every one of them is absolutely unlike the rest.

Selections from these works have already been made by MM. de Camondo, Georges Petit, de Montaignac, and Georges Kohn.

There are also in M. Monet's collection landscapes representing scenes in Norway, Dieppe, and Giverny, but all of them pale before these studies of the "Mare des Nymphéas."

BAR A...

part which the artist has designated "Bassin aux Nymphéas." These are about a dozen in number, and consist of studies of a corner of his garden at Giverny, under the most varied aspects, chiefly on misty or sunny mornings. They are exquisite revelations of his comprehension

nts, has not since
"General Zabotkin"
scended in charge of
anko, accompanied by
soff. Leaving the gas-
, it sailed away in a
ection. At 10.8 a.m.
rd the sound of waves
they were all the time
They concluded that
loga, and calculated it
e to four hours more to
te shore.
was sent up to a height
s, the temperature being
At 3.23 p.m. a landing
the district of Olonetsk,
St. Petersburg. The aero-
get back till three days
s the third time a military
rossed the lake.

UNTS AT ODDS.

Suit Brought by Count P. ...tieff Against Count V. S. Tyszkiewicz.

(From the "Kievskoe Slovo.")

...eresting case will be tried in a ... before the tribunal at Lipowiec. ... S. Tyszkiewicz is accused by ... N. Ignatieff of fouling the water ... allowing refuse from the ... to float into

PICTURE SALE.

Modern Paintings by French and Dutch Masters Disposed of at Very Moderate Prices.

PRINTS TO BE ON VIEW TO-DAY.

Exhibition of the Most Recent Works of Claude Monet in the Durand-Ruel Gallery.

In Room 7 at the Hotel Drouot yesterday, Me. Guillet, assisted by Me. Belval as expert, disposed of the thirty-nine paintings in the collection of M. Maillet. It is probable that in some cases the reserve prices were not reached, which would not be surprising at a moment when pictures, if not by great masters, or by fashionable painters, are hard to dispose of. In any case, the following were the prices realized yesterday: No. 1, "L'Enlèvement," by Bensa, 430fr.; No. 2, "Interior of an Ox Stall," by Brascassat, 630fr.; No. 3, "Marine Painting," by ...0fr.; No. 4, "An Interior," ...r 370fr.; No.

EXHIBITION OF PICTURES.

Works by Mlle Louise Abbema and M. René Foy in the Georges Petit Gallery.

VINCENT VAN GOGH'S PICTURES.

Show of the Societe Nouvelle de Peintres et Sculpteurs in the Rue de Seze.

An interesting exhibition of seventy-five pictures, studies and watercolors, by Mlle. Louise Abbema, who is a past-mistress in the art of painting flowers, has just been opened in the Petit Gallery.

All the gamut of the most varied species of flora has been exhausted to enable the artist to display her marvellous talent. Among the numerous compositions also exhibited by her I must mention some decorative designs for "salles de fête," and a sketch of a "Gismonda" for the crush-room of the Théâtre Sarah Bernhardt. These are interesting artistic efforts for a woman. This exhibition, which will remain open till the end of the month, is well worth a visit.

Artistic Jewels.

The same may be said of the collection of artistic jewels by M. René Foy, which are exhibited in the same gallery. This artist, whose work has been frequently mentioned in the HERALD, shows a fan, the leaves of which are covered with an allegorical composition by Mlle. Abbema, "La Naissance de la Perle." Each stick is a figurine of a woman, whose only adornment is a girdle of precious stones of different colors. The ends are decorated with mistletoe carved in ivory.

I should also mention a lorgnette handle, representing a girl enrolled in goat's beard; a silver waistband plate, with a head of a woman marvellously carved in ivory, and several pendants in exquisite taste, among them one decorated with designs inspired by pinks and set off with rose diamonds.

"Societe Nouvelle" Exhibition.

I was only able yesterday to visit the exhibition of the Société Nouvelle de Peintres et Sculpteurs in the rue de Seze. If I speak of it at this late period, it is because I was greatly interested in some of the works, which will be on view until the 29th inst. M. René Prinet exhibits, among other things, three pictures which I consider remarkably fine. They are admirably drawn, especially the one entitled "Convalescence." They are at the same time vigorous, and yet quiet and severe in tone, especially a figure of a woman on a sofa beside the fire.

M. Gaston La Touche exhibits six most pleasing canvases. "L'Après-Midi," a composition singular, and extremely original, and "Le Dernier Chapître," a picture with two half-length figures, are marvellously lighted up by rays coming through a curtain. A small canvas, "Le Bal," wherein the artist has succeeded in catching the movement and whirl of a ballroom in the midst of blazing warm light, is in every way remarkable.

The above, with the figure pictures by M. Aman Jean, and the small interiors by Mr. Walter Gay, who particularly excels in this style, are the best things in the

...tached. ...y to Get ...d by an ...d by the ...g in the ...eregrine ...is; "Bol- ...S. Cou- ..." by J. ... Land- ..." by T.

...Dignity ...ne very ...engrav- ...another, ...as "The ...t, of which ..., and "The

...signed by ...sting to ...lt in such ...good, to

...n Land- ...d which ...est, that ...ed by T. ...great at-

...of the ...nter and ... Random ...airy Maid ...ll; "The ...er; "The ...1; "The ...ood Dog ...sing the

...Georges Griveau, Henri Duhem, André Dauchez, Charles Cottet, and Albert Baertsvel.

Ultra-Impressionism.

The small congregation of ultra-impressionists are in a state of great delight over the works of the late Vincent van Gogh, in the Bernheim Jeune exhibition, rue Laffitte. In spite of my sincere admiration for some of the painters of the young school, in spite of the place occupied by the works of some of the great impressionist landscape painters, in spite of my eclectic taste in matters of art, my delight in the exhibition of Van Gogh's works resolves itself into mild hilarity.

Portraits painted in globules, which look as if made with multi-colored wafers; sunflowers on a blue ground as a floral decoration; landscapes in which the palette knife has traced deep furrows in monochrome paste—these are the features over which very serious amateurs and erudite critics run wild. I am neither one nor the other; I can only laugh.

As to the artist, I gather from the correspondence introduced into the preface of the catalogue, that he was "intoxicated with colors." That is no doubt why he could not see straight. To delight in colors and to empty bladders of ultramarine, chrome or vermilion, on a malachite table does not suffice to render a man a painter.

I cannot seriously discuss any of the pictures that I saw, but I advise all those who like facetious things and caricatures to go to the Bernheim Jeune Gallery, rue Laffite. They will not regret their visit.

An exhibition of the works of Trouillebert, recently deceased, will open to-day in the Galerie des Artistes Modernes, rue Caumartin.

JURY ... THE SALON

Tyers had ...

BOSTON ... Liverpool. NEW Y... from Live... from Sout... QUEEN... New York... pool. KINSAL... York, for New York. DOVER, ... from Brem... HURST... land, from ... CHERBO... for New Yo...

W...

Mar. 22 ...
Mar. 23 ...
Mar. 23 ...
Mar. 25 ...

TRA...

TO LONDON ...

MAIL. 1st & 2nd cl... Via Calais. *9.30a.m.

4.55p.m.

Via Calais. 9.00a.m.

*4.45p.m.

NOTE.—Th... dence with t... 9 a.m. and 9... from Charin... The 9.30 a... toria, Cann... Paris and ... Charing C... Victoria ...

Claude Monet's Works.

First of all I will mention Claude Monet, five of whose works figure in the catalogue, two of them in the first rank. No. 14, "Le Bassin d'Argenteuil," is an exquisite landscape, exquisitely delicate and full of luminous qualities. It measures 86cm. across by 60cm. high.

No. 17, "Vue de Sardaam," by the same artist, is considered the gem of the sale. It is one of those views in Holland in which a canal is depicted, bordered with windmills and red-roofed houses, beneath a blue sky flecked with white clouds, reflected in its calm waters. The coloring is warm and golden, and time has given it an admirable patina. In spite of its great qualities I prefer the first-named picture to it. M. Strauss, the great picture collector, who bought Sisley's "Pont de Moret," at the Feydeau sale, admired it greatly yesterday, and will certainly not fail to watch over its destiny at the sale.

Daubigny, the famous landscape painter, who greatly admired Claude Monet, ... introduced him to M. Durand... thirty years ago, bought ... him, and had it in his ... At the sale in 1878 ... considered worthy o... bigny's works, and i... a second sale of the ... Daubigny's studio. ... was the buyer. He ... do not expect it will ... to-morrow.

I do not care much f... de la Creuse," nor for ... du Havre," but I great... "Le Pont d'Argenteui... trifle sad-looking, for i... twilight, the reflections ... transparent, and the pic... teresting.

Monet, who has succeeded in seizing and fixing effects of light, which had up to his time been regarded as beyond the reach of the artist's brush, revealed a new method of impression, and, as M. Thiébaud Sisson so justly says, has widened the limits of art.

Jongkind figures in the catalogue, but only with a small canvas of no ... portance. No. 8, a D... light, which ...

...transparent, and the picture is most in- teresting.

Monet, who has succeeded in seizing and fixing effects of light, which had up to his time been regarded as beyond the reach of the artist's brush, revealed a new method of impression, and, as M. Thiébaud Sisson so justly says, has widened the limits of art.

Jongkind figures in the catalogue, but

SALES AT THE HOTEL DROUOT.

Important Impressionist Pictures by Monet, Sisley and Pissarro to Be Disposed Of To-morrow.

BEAUFRERE EFFECTS ON VIEW.

Many Drawings and Small Artistic Curios to Be Seen in Rooms 10 and 11 This Afternoon.

The collection of pictures formed by M. X——, which were on view privately yesterday, will be open to the public this afternoon in Room 6 at the Hotel Drouot. There are only thirty-eight works, but they indicate that the collector had a pronounced taste for the impressionist school, or, as M. Bernheim, the young expert in charge of the sale, well characterizes it, the school of 1870.

The names of Sisley, Claude Monet and Pissarro, in fact, occupy the chief place in the catalogue, and beneath them Guillaumin, Lebourg, Cottet, Gauguin and Vogler.

As is always the case on such occasions, there was a good deal of discussion yesterday on the merits of the collection as a whole, or of one or another isolated work. It would be out of place to sum up the various opinions that I heard, some based on personal interests, others on a manner of appreciation, due either to a too-advanced or too-incomplete education in art. I shall give my own opinion, which is extremely favorable to some of which will not fail to be made on it as a whole.

Last year saw also the discovery in the Wallace collection of a masterpiece of a much greater standard of merit, Titian's "Perseus and Andromeda," that is now re-installed in its rightful position of honor by Mr. Claude Phillips, to whom is due

-garding affairs in

urned from the is-
did not consider
convention in re-
dment as final.
Cubans will finally

nt has received a
y against the en-
necessary quaran-
ssels clearing from

OGRESSING ANAL TREATY.

sions on Alaskan
nge for Abro-
nt Treaty.

y.—The HERALD's
ent telegraphs that
r. Hay have so far
gotiations for the
ave agreed upon a
a tentative draft
submission to the
Kinley departs on
reported that the
roposes to accept
kan frontier in re-
the abrogation of
aty.—Globe.

T TO ERICAN MEAT.

ion the Foreign
Boycotting of
Products.

—Mr. Hay has in-
investigate and re-
nected with the al-
at Britain not to
at for the British

at the prohibition
ent applies to re-
The United States
est, but it is like-
deem it expedient
on the subject to
ffice.—Daily Tele-

MON LEADER.

y.—The death, at
George Q. Cannon,
n. leader, is an-
was for nearly
wer in the Mormon
City, and during
ted Utah in the
Jnited States Con-

ARD'S RETURN.

nited States Paris
are to be removed
and will be located
ue Decamps. The
-General, Mr. B.
t arrived in Paris,
rom the accident
oyage from Paris to
the direction of the
ission.

V DISCOVERED.

VANISHING PAINTINGS.

Masterpiece by Titian Stowed Away in a Bathroom for Over Twenty-Five Years.

LORD CREWE'S CUT PORTRAITS.

Story of a Madonna Cut in Two and the Halves Divided Between Two Claimants.

[BY THE HERALD'S SPECIAL WIRE.]

LONDON, Sunday.— The recovery of the famous missing Gainsborough has awakened an almost universal interest in the now celebrated Wynn-Ellis picture. The beautiful duchess seemed to be painted in Gainsborough's most popular and sought-for manner, and, indeed, remains to-day the most Gainsboroughesque Gainsborough of any of his works.

The picture is so well known that to merely mention the title recalls the charming lady. Three-quarter length she is shown, facing the left, her arms demurely folded, catching up the loose pannier of her skirt, with the characteristic soft muslin fichu folded around her shoulders, and at her breast a single rose, lightly attached. Her hair, "semi-poudré," falls in ringlets over her shoulders, and the large Nell Gwynne-like hat, placed askew upon her head, without coquettishness, adds a dignity of feeling that is equally maintained throughout the figure. At the Wynn-Ellis sale at Christie's, in 1876, the picture realized ten thousand one hundred guineas, the then record price for a picture at a public auction. It will not be the least surprising to hear that a lapse of twenty-five years has more than doubled its value.

Sir Walter Armstrong, in his erudite folio book "The Life of Gainsborough," says that "doubts have been cast with some degree of probability on the authenticity of this too famous portrait," but it will be interesting to carefully follow the varying criticisms that will be showered upon this portrait picture by present day judges, when they have had the promised opportunity of a careful inspection at Messrs. Agnew's always interesting galleries.

Other Missing Masterpieces.

Last year saw also the discovery in the Wallace collection of a masterpiece of a much greater standard of merit, Titian's "Perseus and Andromeda," that is now re-installed in its rightful position of honor by Mr. Claude Phillips, to whom is due the credit of finding this famous treasure. When the Wallace collection at Hertford House was in course of arrangement the picture was found in a bathroom, behind a wardrobe, where it had rested for more than a quarter of a century. It now takes its place on one of the best "hangs" in the large gallery at Hertford House. In Mr. Phillips' account of this picture, which appeared in the "Nineteenth Century," he shows it to have been painted for that great patron of arts, Philip II. of Spain.

In the past other great pictures have disappeared mysteriously. The Countess of Derby, by Sir Joshua Reynolds, vanished shortly after it was painted, never to appear again. It was believed by many to have been destroyed at the instigation of the earl, on account of a serious quarrel he had with the portrayed countess.

In Lord Crewe's gallery is a mutilated picture of a past son and daughter of the house; at least, the son no longer exists on the canvas, having been cut out, it is said, in spite, on account of a family quarrel. A century after, the head of the boy, who is fancifully portrayed as a cupid, turned up in the market, and was identified as the original head cut from the canvas. Naturally, it was eagerly sought for, and purchased by Lord Crewe, but has never been replaced in the group, as the picture had already been skilfully repaired.

A Raphael Cut in Two.

In the famous Bridgwater House Galleries, Lord Ellesmere possesses a Madonna by Raphael, on panel, that owing to a past family dispute as to its ownership was cut in two down the centre of the face, and the claims of the contending parties satisfied by each taking half. After many years the respective owners of the halves came to an agreement and the two parts were re-united. The picture now appears as a perfect whole, so skilfully has the damage been rectified, but in certain lights the join down the centre of the face is clearly visible.

So much for the past; as for the future we may hear some day of a Georgione, vaguely described by a painted inscription on the frame as "belonging to the school of Titian," that has for half a century adorned one of the lesser sitting-rooms at Buckingham Palace.

DECORATIVE ART AT SALON D'AUTOMNE

Not a Very Strong Showing This Year, but Hopes for Future Exhibitions.

THE NOCTURNAL "VERNISSAGE."

A Novelty Likely to Attract the Thousands to the Petit Palais This Evening.

A nocturnal "vernissage" is a novelty even for Paris, so it will not be surprising if the number of those who accept the gracious invitation of the committee of the Salon d'Automne to be present at the opening of their exhibition in the Petit Palais to-night is legion. After all, one does not go to a "vernissage" to see the pictures. And persons may certainly be seen to advantage by electric light. The idea of the nocturnal "vernissage" should therefore prove contagious and permanent.

A marquee constructed of heavy mahogany timbers supporting a handsome transparency has just been erected at the corner of the Petit Palais, near the Champs-Elysées. It is there to indicate the entrance to this third Salon, which, beginning with this evening, becomes a part of the artistic life of Paris.

It is only a beginner as yet, a "young Salon," to which the city has amiably lent the basement of one of its palaces—the Petit—of which the charming writer on art topics, M. Henri Lapauze, has lately been made the curator.

An Adjuvant.

Just opposite its elder brethren—the Spring Salons—this one is announced as opening wide its portals to decorative art which should serve as adjuvant to the other, to the great art, and mingle with it. Alas! it must take a humbler place. The catalogue gives but forty numbers in this section as against 905 reserved to the others.

Let us hope that the showing will be larger next year, above all as regards furniture, which to me seems very poorly represented. What there is, is exhibited in the remotest extremity of the basement, almost underground, but still very well lighted by daylight or, better yet, by the thousands of electric lights that drive all gloom away.

In these galleries are many pictures and bits of sculpture of which it is not my business here to speak, many potted plants and draperies and also the conventional decoration of handsome Oriental carpets, which, at the time of my visit, were being artistically arranged by M. Dalsème. But how hard it was to discover the forty numbers devoted to decorative art! Most of the show cases were empty, and will be up to the moment of the opening, which as usually happens at all exhibitions.

However, I did notice several plaster casts by M. Ernest Carrière—albatrosses, penguins and other sea-birds strangely interpreted; some artistic bindings by M. Kieffer; artistic potteries by Mr. William Lee and gray and blue ceramics by M. André Mithey.

Bats and Grasshoppers.

There was also the mounting for an alms-box designed with bats and an umbrella-handle of grasshopper form by M. Eguer, and small enamelled plates with a double circlet of gem-mounted silver, by M. A. Jacquin.

A burnished metal pot in the form of a gourd by M. Camille Lefèvre struck me as very artistic. He exhibits also a very spiritual bust of Mme. Willette.

Further on I saw some gold and silver jewels by M. Vigan, a decorative panel in cloth mosaic by M. Belville, art windows by M. Labouret and a statuette in bronze by M. Blairsy.

Apropos of the small sculptured pieces, I should mention the charming terra-cotta bust of a woman entitled "Rieuse," by M. Vasselot, and of a colored plaster head, possessing great character, by M. Fix Mosseau, as well as M. Navellier's little bronzes.

That was all that I could discover yesterday. To-day, perhaps, more things will be visible. M. Jansen, the carpet dealer and decorator, organized the decoration that will be admired here this evening.

IN IMPORTS VER CIGARETTES.

for "Fragrant Weed" ctured in America Has lined Considerably.

UDGET WAS PRESENTED

lieved in Some Quarters to e to Resentment Against the Trust.

Friday.—Not only have im- merican-made cigarettes fallen in London since Mr. Austen in submitted his first budget

...ere so... the tobacco war thing to do with the former ...s, and possibly the present ...igher price has curtailed the ...mewhat, but I believe that Bri- ...ition to the American Trust is ...he bottom of the reduced sale. Virginia tobacco is used ex- in England for cigarettes, and ...ill be continued. But small ...anufacturers are making their ...ds, and are not as keen for articles as formerly."

...ity.

Salmon and Gluckstein main- ...retail shops in the city under ...e, though their business is now of the Imperial Tobacco Com- ...ich attends to the British dis- of the Consolidated Tobacco ...s brands. Naturally the officials ...m were reluctant to speak for ...n on the subject, and referred ...e head offices for information. ...in charge of several of the above ...he Strand and Cheapside, how- ...e freely. They told of the fall- sales in American cigarettes, ...entally paid their respects to ...management, which they said ...as liberal to branch-shop mana- ...ere the men in control under ...rder of things. They knew no- ...ever of the effects of the new

A Gainsborough Which Was Disposed of for £12,705

LONDON, Wednesday.—By the courtesy of Messrs. Agnew, the HERALD is enabled to present the reproduction of the Gainsborough portrait, which achieved the record figure of £12,705 at the sale of the late Duke of Cambridge's pictures at Christie's on Saturday last.

This Gainsborough portrait represents Maria Walpole, Countess Waldegrave, Duchess of Gloucester, in gold-tinted dress with pearl ornaments, leaning her head upon her left arm, which rests upon a pedestal, her hair done high and powdered, size 35¼in. by 27¼in.

Although Messrs. Obach and Co., the vendors of Whistler's peacock room, refuse to divulge the name of the American collector to whom they have sold this masterpiece of decorative art, I hear from another source that the mysterious purchaser is Mr. Charles L. Freer, of Detroit, who already owns the finest collection of paintings by the American master.

On the other hand, I am able to contradict the rumor that the Gainsborough portrait acquired by Messrs. Agnew has been or is about to be sold for America. Whatever the eventual fate of the picture may be, at present such a rumor is premature.

MARIA WALPOLE, Duchess of Gloucester, by Gainsborough

WHISTLER'S PEACOCK ROOM.

OBJETS D'ART FOR SALE IN LONDON.

Grand Collection of Antiquities on View at the Waring Galleries.

WELL SELECTED FURNITURE.

From Henri II. to the Present Day—Almost Every English Style Splendidly Represented.

LONDON, Thursday.—At Messrs. Waring's antique galleries a sale is taking place this week of a grand collection of antique furniture, tapestry and objects d'art. From the Henri II. period to the beginning of the nineteenth century almost every style and country is splendidly represented in the furniture section, and the pictures include a fine Bellini from Mr. G. Donaldson's collection, a Jan Steen, and an early Italian view of Verona, with a cavalcade in the foreground.

From Mr. Donaldson's collection again is a magnificent upright cabinet, the inner lining of which is decorated with small paintings by Rubens, representing the "Judgment of Paris," the "Finding of Moses," and other subjects.

There is also a complete Queen Anne room, in pine, which has recently been taken down from an old manor house at Enfield; an exceptionally perfect and interesting example of the period, probably from the designs of James Paine, about 1740. A sixteenth century carved oak Italian confessional-box, by Prucellini, is equally remarkable for the beauty of its carved decoration, as for the inappropriateness of its motifs and cupids and amatory trophies.

Fine Chimneypiece.

Nothing could be finer in its way than an imposing chimneypiece, 12ft. wide, of the sixteenth century. The frieze is carved in high relief, with four figures representing the quarters of the globe, and the middle panel with the shield of the arms of the Collingwood family. Two large carved panels represent Abraham's Sacrifice and Salome receiving the head of the Baptist. The chimneypiece stood formerly in the Turk's Head Inn at Newcastle-on-Tyne, the residence of the Collingwood family

Early French furniture is represented by a boldly carved François Ier cabinet, with heads in high relief; a mantelpiece of the same period, and a splendid Henri II. credence. Among numerous genuine pieces of the Louis XV. and Louis XVI. period I noticed a remarkably faithful copy of the famous Louis XV. commode, formerly in the Hamilton Palace collection, and one of a Louis XV. commode by Riesener.

The English decorative furniture section is naturally the most complete. Sheraton, Chippendale, Hepplewhite and Adam can be studied in many characteristic examples, while there is no lack of Charles II., James II., Queen Anne and William and Mary specimens.

Most of the walls are hung with rare pieces of French and Flemish tapestry, and on sideboards, cabinets and show-cases can be found good specimens of old English china, pewter and French

MME. ... A...

Murder... Th...

ABODE...

Attempt... Res...

ST. P... St. Pete... little wh... throw o... most fas... wife of ... murdered... manserva... smashed ... What ... all St. P... up its m... scandal ... happily, ... murderer... gated by ... of the h... in the cr... The HERALD ... Catharin... by her ... ties of je... her apar... The cr... malevole... sons ver... people b... have bee...

Lived i...

Mme. ... parative ... of her d... and Bar... person o... an enor... twenty-e... one man... lived at ... in a sma... from the... trance. ... seldom a... The r... art and ... opened, ... and a b... given, a... Mme. S... relations... casions ... The de... time in ... wealth, ... gnoir, w... enormou... gnon st... very late... ures the... She p... Antoinet... ordinary... self each... with he... At the... Mme. S... sent fro...

everywhere.
eab'e com-
presentative
veled in the
nd without
ost identical
s the result

s most im-

y yet that
pay in view
opening of
new lines,
The chief
cited similar

ance in the
ing on the
York and
ondon, with
Singapore.
ge of quick,
ion between
of the same
nd for its
f delay is a
ling Japan,
nen proudly
the canal
and I have
emark that
e she would
were it in

e main part
time is at
story, but in
shall deter-
s bordering
eady for the
canal, the
Argue as
ays and the
dering the
g the very
st have the
ilt the Fa-
and able to
At present
ed to the
is strong in
the hands
use the boy

ost reaches
great en-
pushed on
d fifty mil-
noted, is no
rican trade,
will follow
onstruction,
tige and in
from the
trade of
ned nearly
00,000 com-
eeing other
were, from

be a score
s, climate,
But where
day if she
que in her
nent in the
m, national
re? Great
ependency,
nd France a
y had not
nations are
e creation,
y succumb

ght quote
in rebuttal
onents, but
n is above
nal issue—
the honors
tions, one

"LA DAME AUX CAMÉLIAS."

Mme. Sarah Bernhardt Opens Her Winter Season at the Renaissance.

STILL PLEASES THE PUBLIC.

Costumes of the 1840 Period Used Both for the Ladies and the Men.

After a long absence from the stage in Paris, Mme. Sarah Bernhardt opened at the Renaissance last night with a revival of "La Dame aux Camélias."

Except to say that the ever-popular work of the younger Dumas, with all the romantic incidents associated with it, still has its old charm for the public, and that Mme. Bernhardt acts the part of Marguerite with her usual power of passion, no comment would be required to place on record the revival of such a well-known play. But on this occasion Mme. Bernhardt has ventured an innovation.

Up to the present it has been usual to play the piece in the costumes of the day. The idea has been that, the interest of the drama lying wholly in its emotional character, the costumes were a matter of no importance. Mme. Bernhardt has however, used dresses such as were worn in 1840, at which date the events which form the subject of the play actually occurred. For, as is well known, in "La Dame aux Camélias," Dumas put into dramatic form certain incidents in his own life.

A good deal of curiosity was aroused by the announcement of this innovation, especially in regard to the costumes of the men, for ladies fashions have these latter years to a large extent resembled those of the 1840 period.

M. Henri Fouquier, in the *Figaro* this morning, says, at the conclusion of his notice: "To give you my impression frankly, the 1840 costumes did not seem to me to look very well for the men, but they were completely forgotten in the poignant emotion of the last acts."

M. Fouquier considers the 1840 style notably unsuitable for M. Guitry, who takes the part of Armand Duval; as for the rest, they looked neither better nor worse than usual.

Just at first one felt a little surprised at seeing the men wearing long-pleated frock coats with waists to them, trousers wide at the top and narrow at the bottom and hats with broad curled-up brims. The *coiffure à rouleau* also looked a little strange. But the impression soon passed off, and in addition to the sentimental enthrallment of the drama one had an interesting picture of the dress and manners of people who lived sixty years ago.

The opening of the Renaissance's winter season has been a distinctly successful one.

THEATRICAL NOTES.

The Comédie-Française will be closed on Tuesday night, the night before the gala performance there, to allow of the decorating of the auditorium.—*Journal des Débats.*

"Hamlet" will be given at the Opéra on Saturday night, on the occasion of the first

POWER

[CO

who soug
the numbe
The ships
come so m
escape the n
the much-c
nesday last
which gave
"Levanter."
wind began
clouds a h
from the r
bills aroun
mist and t

A four
Grozyast
the shore
rowed a
going fo
steam la
manage
great di
way ag
water.
The
the I
French
Italian
and t
there
In fac
comin
the s
A.
have
Govern
a telegr
but teleg
written in
men the w
CON
We have
gratulate Sir
acquired K.
tioned the
Alfred, wor
leagues and
A consul's
place like t
developed,
clever enou
and with
and the C
vice not c
Governor.
served and t
heartily pleas
A good r
turned up-
and are o
estimate th
probably a
burnt. In
doubt as t
described
tians. N
number
have ye
peasants
peasant
imagina
any oliv
ficant in
villages
destroyed
Efforts
Turkish
their h
not wi
sent to
may ob
be give
my hou
that the
it seems
his reaso

GLORIFYING THE DRAMA'S STAR.

Mme. Sarah Bernhardt Fêted by the Notabilities of French Literature, Art and Society.

POETS SING HER PRAISES.

Congratulatory Telegrams Received from Sir Henry Irving and Others.

The imposing fête held yesterday in honor of Mme. Sarah Bernhardt could not have been more successful than it was.

The proceedings began with a banquet at one o'clock in the Salle du Zodiaque of the Grand Hotel. They were continued in the afternoon at the Renaissance Theatre, when the celebrated actress appeared in "Phèdre" and "Rome Vaincue," and where French poets recited sonnets in her honor.

Shortly after the assembling of the guests and subscribers at the Grand Hotel Mme. Bernhardt arrived, leaning upon the arm of M. Victorien Sardou. Then followed MM. François Coppée, Ludovic Halévy, Jules Lemaître, Henry Bauër and several other friends.

Above the central part of the *table d'honneur*, says the *Temps*, was a large canopy made of green velvet and an Aubusson tapestry, the design upon which represented Time. At this table were seated: On the right of Mme. Sarah Bernhardt, M. Victorien Sardou; on her left, M. Henry Bauër; then on each side of the actress, Mme. de Najac, Mme. Maurice Bernhardt, MM. Ludovic Halévy, François Coppée, Catulle Mendès, Henri de Bornier, Jules Lemaître, Coquelin, André Theuriet, de Rodays, Périvier, Edouard Colonne, Pierné, Clairin, Maurice Bernhardt, Armand Silvestre, Charpentier, Haraucourt, Robert de Montesquiou, Jean Lorrain, Lavedan and Rostand.

At the ten tables, which filled the room, were more than six hundred covers. To give the names of those present, including all the literary, artistic and dramatic personages of Paris, would be to give a *liste de première.*

At dessert, M. Sardou rose and improvised the following toast:—

"Gentlemen, I leave to the poets the honor of praising better than I could do the incomparable *tragedienne*, the artiste without rival whom we glory in to-day. A true creator of the rôles she interprets, a queen of the dramatic art, she is applauded as such all the world over.

"It is not given to all those who have applauded and admired her to have known her intimately, and after having applauded the *tragédienne* to have appreciated the kindliness, the generosity of soul, the exquisite goodness of the woman. I have been able to enjoy this inappreciable happiness, and that is why I raise my glass to the health of that one, who is not only the great, but also the good Sarah!"

This toast was received with three rounds of applause. Mme. Bernhardt then rose and said these words: "A vous tous qui êtes ici, d'un cœur ému et reconnaissant, je dis merci, merci merci."

Again there was applause and the whole of those present rose to their feet, cheering Mme. Bernhardt, who warmly shook M. Sardou by the hand.

de Blowitz, Colonel and moin, Lavoignat, Clunet, Georg Meyer, Georges Boyer, Rochard, Mariani, Comtesse de and Mlle. Vervoort, Mmes. Maur Mora, Claire Lemaître, Louise Bi Magnier, Lina Munte, Angèle, I vivier, Blanche Thyl, Lender, Blan Angèle Moreau, Gilberte, MM. Ed taille, Mézières, Poincaré, Victor Dr. Péan, Edmond Lepelletier, G F. de Curel, Paul Meurice, I Brieux, Pierre Decourcelle, de La Motte, Michel Heine, L nesse, Henri Letellier, Fenoux T Mmes. Héglon, Paul Saunière, Céline mont, Marthe Brandès, Marguerite Marni, Félicia Mallet, "Gyp," Sév Jeanne Granier, Rostand, Amel, Saylor vigne, Darlaud, Segond-Weber, Abb Sorel, Lucy Gérard, Sisos, Darmières, lix, Yves Rolland, Lola and Peppa Inverni MM. Le Bargy, Feydeau, Henry Lee, Mai roy, Georges Docquois, Auguste Germa Guiches, Croze, Paul Grosian, Nadar, Noble Dujardin, Guitry, Jules Roques, Fasquell Eugène Tardieu, Depas, Bérard, Crozie Dr. Apostoli, Dubufe, Paul Tissier, Baduel Maurice Barrès, Jules Renard, Léon and Lucien Daudet, Borda, Angelo, Talasso, Charles Akar, Jean Stevens, Juven, Chancel, Dr. Louis Jullien, Clerget, Strong, Douglas, Ajalbert, Alex. Bisson, Debruyère, Stephan Lafarge, Edouard Noël, Paul Gavaud, Pierre de Cottens.

The *salle* was tastefully decorated with plants and flowers. The distribution of the *livre d'or* containing the sonnets of MM. Catulle Mendès, André Theuriet, François Coppée, Edmond Haraucourt and Edmond Rostand, was made in the *foyer*. These were recited after the act of "Rome Vaincue" and a short interval. The curtain was drawn up and Mme. Sarah Bernhardt was seen seated on a "stalle," decorated with flowers, having on her left the company of the Renaissance theatre, and on her right the poets, who one by one came forward and recited their poems. In addition to those already mentioned M. Morand read a sonnet by M. José-Maria de Heredia, whose name did not appear on the programme.

Before the conclusion of the performance M. Tixier, president of the committee of the Association des Etudiants, presented to Mme. Bernhardt an immense wreath of flowers bearing an inscription "From the Jeunesse des Ecoles."

A large number of congratulatory telegrams, says the *Figaro*, arrived yesterday. One of these was from Sir Henry Irving, as follows: "Your brother and sister artistes of the Lyceum Theatre send their love and salutations. Your chosen art and all other arts render homage to you, and we, your comrades in another country where your genius is held in such high esteem, are happy to add our tribute to the great honor which you merit." Other telegrams were received from Mme. Emma Calvé, who is at present in New York; Mme. Réjane, M. Gabriel d'Annunzio, Mr. Wilson Barrett, of the Lyric Theatre; Mr. Bronson Howard, President of the American Dramatic Club of New York; the Russian students in St. Petersburg, the artistes of the St. James's Theatre, London; Mme. Melba and others.

THEATRICAL NOTES.

MM. Martial Teneo and Alexandre Trebitsch's recently finished play has been named "L'Ornière."—*Gaulois.*

A special matinée performance will be given at half-past two o'clock to-day at the Folies-Bergère. Little Tich will make an appearance.

Mlle. Karina, of the Ambassadeurs and Scala music-halls, has left Paris for New

MME. SARAH BERNHARDT.

... Française ... and in verse which ... produced on December 21 at the performance given on the occasion of the anniversary of the birth of Racine.—*Temps.*

The *Temps* reports a serious accident which happened on Monday evening at the Théâtre du Mans. A pistol fired by M. Delaunay, who was taking the rôle of Desotteux in "Hoche," burst and so seriously injured his left hand that it is feared the member will have to be amputated.

ON THE LONDON STAGE.

Miss Ellen Terry's health still leaves much to be desired. She has had to undergo several slight operations recently, whilst appearing in "Cymbeline."—*Daily Mail.*

Mr. S. Creagh Henry is reported to be getting ahead with his version of "The Sorrows of Satan," which, under the title of "The Prince of Darkness," is to be produced at the Theatre Royal, Plymouth, next week. There is some talk of this version coming to London by-and-by.—*Daily Mail.*

I hear glowing accounts of the preparations for "The Pilgrim's Progress" at the Olympic Theatre. No expense is to be spared in the production. The story is to be brought thoroughly up to date and made in keeping with the festive season of Christmas. Gounod's "Ave Maria" and other examples of modern music have been added.—*Daily Mail.*

"The Woman's World," by Mr. J. P. Hurst, was produced at the Court Theatre on Tuesday afternoon. It satirizes the "New Woman"—as did Molière and Shakespeare! Study of the London papers has not disclosed whether the production was a success or a failure. The *Standard* says: "Mr. J. P. Hurst has met with some success as a playwright, but it is to be feared that the sum of his good fortune will not be increased by his comedy."

M. Loub... subject.
The r... no modif... ing newsp... will remai... cognito, is...
The fol... auguratio... published...
The cer... the Pont... Exhibitio... necessita... a large n... other ha... impossible... whatever... ladies.
At the s... be used b... part of t... enclosure... Cours-la-R... which is r... and the me... only two k... stand and...
Cards ... enclosure... in whose... must be... invitatio... doors.
Membe... on the pr...
The *T*... of Com... of the in... used by ... dent of t... *procès ver*... first stone...
The Sta... plied an... character... an idea of... taken fro... magnifice... Tsar as a...

MADAME BERNHARDT TRIUMPHS.

Her Production of M. Rostand's "L'Aiglon" an Event in Stage History.

IMMENSE ALL-ROUND SUCCESS.

Madame Bernhardt as the Aiglon and Guitry as Flambard Share the Honors.

ADMIRABLE INTERPRETATION.

Drama Superbly Placed on the Stage, and Historical Scenery Perfectly Reproduced in All Details.

THEATRE SARAH-BERNHARDT. — "L'Aiglon," a drama in verse in six acts, by M. Edmond Rostand.

The production of the much-talked-of drama "L'Aiglon" (Young Eagle), by M. Rostand, written expressly for Mme. Sarah Bernhardt, with the part of the Duc de Reichstadt especially intended to be filled by her, will mark a date in the history of the Paris stage. So says M. Henry Fouquier, of the "Figaro," who asserts

M. EDMOND ROSTAND.
(The successful author.)

that beside being a magnificent success for the theatre, the poet and his interpreter, it is an evolution—even more than was "Cyrano de Bergerac"—of historic drama.

The "Aiglon," it is unnecessary to say, is the son of Napoleon I. and the Empress Maria Louisa. In the first act he appears at the Court of Austria under the charge of Prince Metternich, to whose care he has been confided by the allied Powers of Europe.

Around the young man is a group of Bonapartist conspirators, who fondly ... to see him on the throne ... father was ...

MME. SARAH BERNHARDT
(As the Aiglon.)

... the assemblage ... the "Figaro" cite ... Mme. ... Casimir-Perier, M. ... Leygues, M. and Mm... Pierre Baudin, M. and Mme. Louis Ba... thou, M. and Mme. Lépine, MM. Vic... torien Sardou, Ludovic Halévy, Paul Her... vieu, Albert Vandal, Henri Houssaye, An... atole France, Jules Lemaitre, Marquis de Castellane, MM. Vlasto, L. Bourgeois, Baronne Salomon de Gursbourg, M. and Mme. Gandrey, M. and Mme. Strauss, M. and Mme. Albert Cahen, Comte Robert de Montesquiou, Comte and Comtesse d'Haussonville, M. and Mme. Maurice Bernard, M. and Mme. G. de Caillavet, Baron Legoux, M. Louis Varney, M. Ph. Crozier, Charles Ephrussi, Baron Edouard de Rothschild, M. and Mme. Fasquelle, M. Paul Ollendorff, M. and Mme. Pierre Decourcelle, Mme. Brugère, M. Paul David, M. and Mme. Fère, M. Jacques Liouville, M. René Waldeck-Rousseau, Comtesse de Loynes, M. Quentin-Bauchart, General Zurlinden, M. Coquelin, M. Coquelin cadet, M. and Mme. Worms, M. and Mme. Febvre, M. Ganderax, etc. In the stage box were: Comtesse Greffulhe, the Duc and Duchesse de Rohan, Prince and Princesse Murat.

THEATRICAL NOTES.

"Véronique" will be revived at the Bouffes this evening.—Figaro.

"La Duchesse de Berry," a five-act drama, by M. Arthur Bernède, will be produced at the Ambigu this evening.—Figaro.

M. Hardy Thé will sing and M. Lazarus Levy will play at the matinée musicale of Mr. Sebastian B. Schlesinger and Baronne de Reibnitz on Saturday next.

"Le Bijou Perdu" was given at the Lyrique-Renaissance last night instead of "Martin et Martine," in consequence of the indisposition of M. Dantu.—Figaro.

Herr Reichmann, the well-known German singer, who is to appear at the Colonne Concert on Sunday, has arrived in Paris and is stopping at the Hotel Saint-Pétersbourg.

MM. Camille Chévillard, Maurice Hayot and Joseph Salmon, assisted by MM. Firmin Touche and Bailly, will give a concert of chamber music at 9 p.m. on Tuesday next, at the Salle Pleyel.

Mrs. Welman's second Kipling concert in aid of the Permanent Homes for Disabled Soldiers at Bisley (patroness, H.R.H. Princess Christian), will take place in the Salle des Agriculteurs on Thursday evening, April 5.

M. Alfred Bruneau, in to-day's "Figaro," says of M. Massenet's oratorio, given last night at the church of Saint-Eustache: "Conceived for performance in a vast nave, the work affects a violently decorative character, uniting the austerities of the classical fugue with the luxury of modern methods. I need scarcely say that had the performance not been in a church it would have been ... plauded."

... t... d... at... dr... con... its ... brill... that ... More... Lilies... the f...
The ... and un... devolv... State f... handso... beautif... Duchess... the princ... by the sp... diamonds...
Lady E... her sister... her marria... soft pearl ... Viscounte... white point... was of pink... monds and c... loop, one be... of white orch...
Mrs. Willia... white satin dre... XV. bows, with... with white silk...
Miss Maude ... was of white C... white Scotch ros... bodice draped ... of chiffon, and ... with a cluster of ... train was prettily ...
Lady Tracy, ... Tracy, was attired ... velvet bodice, cleve... velvet, with rare o... qué.
Mrs. Walpole Gre... ivory satin embroid... diamonds and per... Her bolero was of ... broidered like the sat... periwinkle chiffon.
A graceful-looking ... Lady Emily Hart-Dyk... her youngest daughter... China crape, with a s... incrusted with designs o... spangled with steel... with na...

MR. CONRIED WILL RIVAL BAYREUTH.

The "Parsifal" Production Will Equal Anything Given at the Shrine of Wagnerism.

NOT AFRAID OF FRAU WAGNER.

She is Not in a Position to Interfere With the Production of the Opera.

NEW YORK, Thursday. — "Parsifal" will be presented at the Metropolitan Opera House in Christmas week, if Mr. Heinrich Conried's plans are carried out. Sitting in Mr. Grau's old chair yesterday, Mr. Conried talked interestingly of his aims, and said:

"I shall give an opera presentation equal in beauty and completeness to any ever given in Bayreuth. Herr Burgstaller will sing the title-rôle, and Herr van Romy will be Ahfortas. I think that Fräulein Ternina will be Kundry, although I have not engaged her. Herr Blass will be Gurnemanz. The rest of the cast will be of the first rank. Herr Burgstaller was afraid at first to sign a contract to sing Parsifal here. He was afraid of Frau Wagner.

"Dr. Hertz, who went on the same steamer to Europe, has cabled that Herr Burgstaller signed on the way over."

Mr. Conried added that he bought his score of "Parsifal" in London eight years ago. The sale was absolutely without restrictions. He was positive of his rights in the matter and of Frau Wagner's inability to interfere with the production.

Mr. Conried said, regarding salaries: "M. Jean de Reszke wants $4,000 a performance for twenty performances, and, in addition, a contract for his brother Edouard for sixty performances at $700 each. I have offered Jean $2,500 per performance and have told Edouard I shall not want him if Jean does not come."

He said he would have Mme. Calvé and Mme. Melba if they would not ask for the gross receipts. He sails for Europe on Tuesday to engage additional artists.—Daily Telegraph.

MRS. LANGTRY'S RETURN.

She Says She Never Made So Much Money in America As This Time.

NEW YORK, Thursday.—Among the passengers yesterday on the Philadelphia for Southampton was Mrs. Lily Langtry. She said she expected to return to New York next winter, and added: "I have never before made so much money in America as I did this season, and now I am going home to rest a while and enjoy myself. I have two new plays for next season, but Mr. Frohman asked me not to tell what they are.

"When I get home I am going to place a large bit of my earnings on my horses, particularly on Smilax, the unbeaten three-year-old, whom I am backing to win the Coronation Plate at Epsom."—Daily Telegraph.

Mme. Calvé Narrowly Escapes Death by Poison.

Just before the curtain rose on the "Damnation de Faust," at the Théâtre Sarah-Bernhardt yesterday evening, the manager appeared on the stage and announced that Mme. Calvé was unable to appear. The celebrated singer, he stated, had by accident taken an overdose of aconite and was in a serious condition.

The "Matin" this morning gives the following details of the accident. Mme. Calvé, being somewhat hoarse yesterday afternoon, took a dose of tincture of aconite. She, however, took an excessive quantity, and about four o'clock felt seriously indisposed. Two hours later her state inspired the gravest anxiety. The persons of her entourage thought that her death was imminent.

Happily, medical aid proved efficacious, and, thanks to energetic treatment, by yesterday evening the great singer was out of danger. Mme. Calvé has intimated to M. Gunsbourg that she hopes to resume her rôle on Saturday evening.

DEADLY RIOTING

Two H…
as …

ALSO …

Sy…

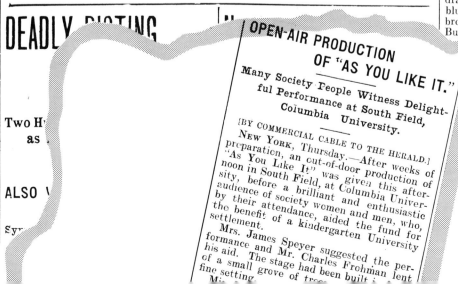

OPEN-AIR PRODUCTION OF "AS YOU LIKE IT."

Many Society People Witness Delightful Performance at South Field, Columbia University.

[BY COMMERCIAL CABLE TO THE HERALD.]

NEW YORK, Thursday.—After weeks of preparation, an out-of-door production of "As You Like It" was given this afternoon in South Field, at Columbia University, before a brilliant and enthusiastic audience of society women and men, who, by their attendance, aided the fund for the benefit of a kindergarten University settlement.

Mrs. James Speyer suggested the performance and Mr. Charles Frohman lent his aid. The stage had been built … of a small grove of tre… fine setting…

CHINESE S… AT M…

Sailor Novelist … Exotic Enter… Roche…

TO MEET "C…

Annamite Schoo… Ou-Tse-Tsien, …lestial" Be…

Pierre Loti gave … Rochefort on Tues… a red-letter day in … taining. A corresp… gives a graphic des…

The invitation … ous request that … before ten o'cloc… Imperial Majest… press of China … the homage of t… once the wome…

In the "Rapl… red velvet, Mm… sumptuous Chin… and orange, emb… ceived the guests … nieces, also in Ch… was invisible. … quette required … attendance on t…

Amid all the … forms of admi… peculiarly cha… the scene. At … had arrived, and … announced that … to appear had so…

Mme. Loti le… room in which th… before the gaze … women. Halbe… Middle Ages m… staircase leading…

A Japanese Pri…

The guests ass… room. A stroke … nerves, and a he… mous gold drag… garment over his … coming of a Japane…

Slowly she made … human flower, w… draped in a lon… blue relieved … broidered … Buddh…

CHINA
OS RAPIDLY

e Reported Along
ailway and Also
foo.

ORS SUCCUMB.

Virulent Type
municated by
Contact.

HE HERALD.)
ERALD BUREAU,
QUARTER, PEKING.
. — Dr. Hsu, a
ad at Harbin; Dr.
man, is dead at
nese doctor has died
ach case the plague
contact.
a Chinese graduate
is in charge at Fu-
s to the HERALD's
ll are agreed that
e worst known in
infection is taken
e virulence of the
as it passes from
is never safe."
y anxious inquiries
United States and
D. Owens, U.S.N.,
Legation Quarter
equests the HERALD
riences at Harbin,
ere show that for-
oper sanitary sur-
le danger from the
nent, is verified in
t the Russian Lega-
neral Horvat, pre-
e Eastern Railway.

ors.

n Harbin General
the deaths from
ans are confined to
ical attendants who
ntact with infected
wer-class people liv-
ese.
reports that there
Fuchiatien yester-
orvat says that at
rate is fully 200.
ports a rapid spread
the railway in all
in, despite the stop-
ing third and fourth

recrudescence of the
Ashiho shows 100
Kwanchengtse the
tically every town
us of 150 miles from
nd most of them are
medical aid. The
s are panicky and

ces the inception of
nters bringing Tar-
iberia. The disease
anchuli in October.
e city at Harbin in
nand for the skins
n Europe and Ame-

"Der Rosenkavalier," Strauss' Latest Opera, Given at Court Theatre, Dresden

COUNT FRITZ VON SEEBACH.

HERR RICHARD STRAUSS.

THE ROYAL OPERA HOUSE, DRESDEN.

Brilliant Production Shows the Great Composer in New Light as a Humorist.

(SPECIAL TO THE HERALD.)

DRESDEN, Thursday. — Amid brilliant surroundings, Richard Strauss' latest opera, "Der Rosenkavalier," was produced for the first time on the stage at the Dresden Court Theatre to-night.

This work has been a subject of discussion in the columns of the newspapers for some months past, several incidents arising out of the arrangements for its production having already been made public. Thus, for instance, Strauss handed over the opera to Count Seebach, the intendant-general, and Herr Foller, the manager of the Court Theatre, without having then given it a definite title, and he bound them to maintain secrecy regarding the nature of his work. Shortly afterwards there appeared in the press an announcement to the effect that the opera was called "Baron Ochs," after the principal personage. Strauss on seeing this promptly gave his work the name of "Der Rosenkavalier."

As interest in the forthcoming production increased Strauss later on declared that he would not allow his opera to be performed unless Count Seebach also bound himself to produce at least four times a year all the other Strauss operas, particularly "Salome" and "Elektra." Other theatres which had arranged to produce the new opera, among them the New York Opera House, had to accept the same conditions.

To-day's performance, however, was proof that "Der Rosenkavalier" did not require any advance advertising. It was effective from its own force and showed Strauss in a new light—namely, as a brilliant humorist.

The libretto of "Der Rosenkavalier" of a notorious dive. Baron Ochs is unmasked and seeks to hide his shame in flight. However unsympathetic the rôle of Baron Ochs may be from a moral point of view, Strauss has devoted much care to the part as regards the music. Baron Ochs is the musical centre of the opera. He sings a song full of life and fire when he approaches Sophie, and again when he drinks with Faninal. The orchestra mocks at the baron when he is caught in the tavern and scoffs at him as he runs away disgraced. Under the influence of the jubilant music of the orchestra, Sophie becomes engaged to Octavian.

Octavian also has charming musical themes, particularly when he sings with the princess in Act I. and in his duet with Sophie.

In the art of delineating character in music, Strauss, in "Der Rosenkavalier," has been even more original than before. He always knew how to express all kinds of events in music, but this time he expresses things which it would seem almost impossible to represent, such, for instance, as the asthma of a notary and the cackling of a tenor who has lost his voice. But these are amusing musical incidents which must not be allowed to divert attention from the magnificent music of the orchestra conducted by Herr Sucher.

Gaiety Combined With Art.

Strauss' music in "Der Rosenkavalier" marks the carrying out of a hitherto unfulfilled public desire that opera music should be gay as well as artistic. Herr Strauss is reported to have said: "You want dance music? Well, I will give it you; but I shall not give you merely trivial rythm. When I see fit I shall break off in the middle of a waltz and give what is required by the general tone and spirit of the scene."

Fräulein Margarete Siems excelled all the singers of the evening, giving a most noble performance. The part of Octavian also requires a skilful actress as well as a singer, and it was splendidly act ended with a great outburst of applause.

After the second act Herr Strauss remarked to friends: "It is wonderful how Herr Schuch (the orchestra conductor) has discarded the usual heavy opera style and has found soundly adequate expression in conducting musical comedy, for that is what I wish 'Der Rosenkavalier' to be regarded as."

The opera contains thirty rôles, chief among which are the princess (soprano), Baron Ochs (bass), Octavian (mezzo soprano) and Faninal (high baritone).

Count Seebach, the intendant-general, has spared no pains and no expense to obtain the most beautiful and appropriate scenery, and experienced intendants-general who were present, such as Count Hulsen (Berlin), Herr von Putliz (Stuttgart), Herr Mutzenbecher (Wiesbaden) and Herr von Seidel (Munich), described the staging as marvellous.

The opera already has been accepted by twenty theatres.

Distinguished Audience Present.

(SPECIAL TO THE HERALD.)

DRESDEN, Thursday.—A large and distinguished audience was present at the performance of Strauss' "Der Rosenkavalier" at the Court Theatre to-night.

Among those present were Princess Johann Georg of Saxony, Prince and Princess Fürstenberg, Prince and Princess Alexander of Thurn and Taxis and Princess Maximilian of Thurn and Taxis, Sir Edgar and Lady Speyer, Prince and Princess Karl Lichnovsky, Mr. and Mrs. Coats, of London; M. André Messager, director of the Paris Opera; M. Gabriel Astruc, Herr Humperdinck, Signor Sonzogno, Princesse de Polignac, Count Frankenberg, Count Béthusy-Huc, Herr Bütler, Herr Köttig. Herr von Metzsch, General von Klemperer, Baroness Kaskel, Countess Vitzthum, Countess Schönburg-Glauchau, Signor Mingardi, of Milan; Herr von Mendelssohn, the directors and orchestra conductors of the leading German and Austrian theatres; the American Consul in Dresden and

RECIPROCI
EXCEED

Sweeping Reduction
ment Betwee
United

PRESIDENT UP

New England Leg
Free Fish and
Undecided

(BY COMMERCIAL CA
WASHINGTON, Th
scope than the mos
tions is the recipro
da made public t
taneously in the tw
Taft has sent a
strongly recommen
the United States c
He says: "No y
the benefit to the
freer commercial i
not in violation of
ciple because protec
a tariff between s
whose conditions ar
Speaking of the
ing on the free lis
this may not at on
food it will preven
tions and postpone
ther increase in th
ing into the cost c
dent says he feels
terprets the wish o
and earnestly hope
will be promptly en
Mr. Taft and th
have boldly throw
battle to the stan
hand and the free
the agricultural Sta
the free list go g
cluding wheat, fish
products, fruits, ve
try, cattle and all o
ton, seed oil and ro
nada, and tin plate
the United States.

To Make Print Pa

Print paper is ma
of all restrictions b
inces on the expor
Canada and the Ur
tually reduced the
meats, fresh and c
vegetables, flour a
foodstuffs, and re
vided on automobil
watches, plate glas
printing ink. Cana
cents a ton, and t
duces iron ore to 10
The United Stat
free articles valu
$39,811,000 and t
articles worth $7,5
poses to make free
at $21,968,000 and
articles worth $25,8
assurance that it w
of $1.50 a ton on
ing in Canadian w
The liveliest inte
Congress regarding

"MARK TWAIN."

"MARK TWAIN" INTERVIEWED IN LONDON.

A "Herald" Correspondent Has a Talk with the Veteran Humorist.

NOW LIVING IN CHELSEA.

Working Hard on "The Surviving Innocent Abroad," Not Dying in Poverty.

HIS LOAD OF DIFFICULTIES.

Philosophy Regarding the Coincidence of Impulse and Opportunity —French Law Criticized.

SOME MORE GOOD STORIES.

[FROM OUR SPECIAL CORRESPONDENT.]

LONDON, June 10.—"Of course I'm dying." "Mark Twain" smiled grimly. "We're all dying. But I don't know that I am doing it any faster than anybody else. As for dying in poverty: I'd just as soon die in poverty in London as anywhere. It would be a little more difficult, that's all; because I have got quite a number of friends here, any one of whom, I believe, would be good for a month's provisions, and that would drag out the agony a fairly long time."

I could not help thinking there was something forced in the careless tone. Was it possible the reverses of fortune of the author of so many works bubbling over with wit and humor, and philosophy and high spirits, were as serious as has been recently stated?

It is true Mr. Clemens has denied the report first published, namely, that he was dying in a state of extreme poverty. And certainly he looked in fairly good health when I saw him a couple of days ago in his house at Chelsea. And yet there was a difference in his physiognomy: it was more lined and much thinner than when I saw him last. His hair, as bushy as ever, is now almost snowy white. And there was a species of hopeless resignation in his bearing, in painful contrast to his one-time easy-going carelessness. And in spite of his disclaimer, in spite of his assertion that he was perfectly well, I felt convinced that if his physical health were of the best, he was, nevertheless, so disturbed by mental worries that the report of his failing condition was practically well founded.

"No, I assure you," he added, "I am as well as ever I was. You see you must not attach too much importance to Mrs. Clemens's remark that I was not in a condition to receive visitors. That simply meant I was in bed! Now most women think if a man does not get up before twelve o'clock there must be something wrong with him, and as I never do get up before twelve o'clock my wife thinks I am not in good health.

"As a matter of fact, when you were announced I wanted to have you shown up to my room. But Mrs. Clemens heard me, and as you can never persuade a tidy woman to show a stranger into an untidy bedroom, that idea did not work.

"I said to her: 'Let him come to my room. Send up some cigars with him; I am comfortable enough.'

"'Yes,' she said, 'but what about him?'

"'Oh,' I said, 'if you want him to be as comfortable as I am, let him have a bed made up in the other corner of the room.' . . . That did not work either. So I thought the best thing to do was to get up and come and see you."

"What are you working upon just now?"

"On my journey round the world. Everybody has done his little circumnavigation act, and I thought it was about time I did mine. So I have been getting it ready for the press since I have been here, and before, for the matter of that. The book is just my impressions of the world at large. I go into no details. I never do. Details are not my strong point, unless I choose for my own pleasure to go into them seriously. Besides, I am under no contract to supply details to the reader. All that I undertake to do is to interest him. If I instruct him that is his 'fat.' He is that much ahead. . . .

"I had thought of calling it *Another Innocent Abroad*, but following advice, as the lawyers say, I have decided to call it *The Surviving Innocent Abroad*.

"Now Mrs. Clemens said: 'But that is not true. You know there's so-and-so in Cleveland, and this, that and the other in Philadelphia!'

"But I said to her, 'I'll fix that.' So I am going to put a little explanatory note to that title, pointing out that although there are still in existence some eight or ten of the pilgrims who went on the 'Quaker City' expedition some twenty-eight years ago, I am the only surviving one who has remained innocent. In fact that title *The Innocents Abroad* was only strictly applicable to two of the pilgrims even at the time it was written, and the other is dead."

"When do you expect the 'Survivor' to appear?"

"Oh, about Christmas," said Mark. "Christmas is a good time to bring out a book. Everybody is thinking about Christmas presents, and the pious are hoping Divine providence may send an answer to prayer, giving them some clue as to what to give. And a book, if it comes just at the right time, is about as good a thing as one could desire. It must come just at the right time though. In other words, the opportunity to secure a present must happen just at the moment the impulse to give one is felt.

"It is a strange thing," he went on, musingly, "how much more charity there would be in this world if the opportunity only coincided with the impulse. The trouble is that too much time often intervenes. I was making a maxim the other day about this very matter. And I said: 'If you want to be economical in your charity count twenty before you give anything. You will generally save 50 per cent. in this way. If you will count forty you will save 75 per cent. and if you count a hundred you will not give anything at all—a distinct saving of 100 per cent.!' . . .

"The basis of French legal procedure is humor, and, like the best humor, it is made up of tragedy. What, for instance, can be more ludicrous from the point of view of justice, and more tragic from the point of view of humanity, than the examination of a prisoner. Think of it! A man is accused of a crime and his judge appears to bend all his energies, not upon discovering the truth, but upon proving him guilty. He usurps in a certain way the functions of the Almighty. In fact, if all those tricks to entrap a man into convicting himself were adopted at the last judgment, even reverence would not prevent you saying that it was a low-down trick on the part of the great Judge. . . . It appears to me all right that a lawyer should be paid to prosecute and should do his duty loyally to convict you if you are guilty. It is equally right that a lawyer should be paid to defend you. But that a judge should interfere, and in fact should do anything except take into consideration the evidence and weigh the probabilities in obscure points, is monstrous.

"I once thought of writing about French law, for it is a most engrossing subject. I many a time ask myself what was the good of tearing down the Bastille if the machinery it contained were saved? They simply took the abuses somewhere else and destroyed a piece of valuable property—which was a foolish waste both of time and material! The system of punishment, too, seems to me utterly wrong. I am not speaking about the case of the Anarchists in Spain, which as far as one can judge, seems to have been an abominable affair. But imagine the sentence passed on the man Acciarito, who attempted to stab the King of Italy. Think of it! Seven years' complete, absolute, solitary confinement! Why no crime a man can do merits such a punishment! I often think there is a great void which requires filling in the education of our judges. If a man came to me and wanted to paint my picture, a man of whom I had heard nothing before, and he told me: 'I studied drawing under so-and-so, and anatomy under this celebrated artist, and coloring under that great man,' I should say: 'Yes, that's all right. You have learnt the details of your art, but did you ever paint a picture?'"

studying medicine. H
Adams, the ringleader
bears the same nam
was educated in Sy
complete history of hi
including a descriptio
of the people from
Island in 1856, whic
published in London

GENERA

Accordin
terday to t
Minister o
who is at
his journe
He will o
will visit
to Antan
of the N

Mail
morning
Ibis RU

"And if he said 'No,' I should say: 'Well, you are not an artist until you have done so.' Similarly we make a lawyer study Blackstone, and Statute law, and Common law; and we try him before a jury and see what his skill as an orator is. But we never ask him the crucial question: 'Have you ever committed a crime? Have you ever undergone a term of imprisonment?'

"Because until that has been done a man is not fit to sit in judgment upon his fellow creatures.

"It is such a little thing that stands between all of us and crime at one time or another of our lives. As I said about charity, if the impulse to kill and the opportunity to kill came always at the same instant how many of us would escape hanging?

"We have all of us, at one time or another, felt like killing something, and we have all of us, at one time or another, had the opportunity to kill something, but—luckily for us—the impulse and the opportunity did not coincide. If a man is rich and he wants to kill something, he can take his gun and go out and shoot. He lets off steam in that way, and the sore place gives over hurting. I used to have a 'Rage' letter box, and when I got into a temper about something, if any one had done something to me that annoyed me or put me out, I would sit down and write a letter to him, and I would pour out all my thoughts and all the bitterness and anger and contempt and indignation and invective in my heart. And when I had cleaned myself out thoroughly I would put that letter in the box—And Mrs. Clemens would see that it did not go. She used to say when she saw me sitting down:—

"'What are you going to do?'

"'I am going to answer this letter,' I would say.

"'But you know you won't send it.'

"'I know that; but, by George, I'm going to write it!'"

And Mark Twain laughed as though he enjoyed the matter very much, adding: "I'm sorry many a time those letters were not kept, because when a man is in a thorough-going temper he now and again finds things to say that are worth preserving."

THE "BRISTO…
UNIT…

SIGNOR GABRIELE D'ANNUNZIO.

D'ANNUNZIO AT HIS SEASIDE HOME.

A "Herald" Correspondent Visits the Italian Novelist at Francavilla-al-Mare.

HIS THEORY OF LIFE.

Preaches a Renaissance of the Antique Adoration of Beauty and Worship of Art.

Francavilla-al-mare: such a big name, such a tiny place. Nine hours or so by train from Rome; nine hours that is, in the time-table. . . . Oh, those Italian time-tables! . . . The route lies through the very heart of the Abruzzi mountains, through scenery as wild as it is sad, immortalized in color by Michetti, in poetry by Byron, in music by Berlioz. Life seems narrowed there, where the horizon is so wide . . . landscape is enshroud…

Now and again a sun-kissed woman looks listlessly out upon the train moving past, or bare-legged children stare fearfully at the few passengers. To right, to left, the white-tipped mountains: above, the livid winter sky. At Pescara another train is taken when, at last it arrives. . . . Now along the Adriatic southward in the company of English people bound for Brindisi and the East. Then appears a hamlet, a mere group of cottages perched aloft on the hill. This is Francavilla and here lives Gabriele D'Annunzio.

An odd, inaccessible place for a novelist to live, and particularly, for a novelist who paints society. But then, few men have been so sated with the social life of big cities, have sounded its profoundest depths so thoroughly, have gone through its entire gamut so completely, as has the young Italian writer D'Annunzio. Besides, the *mal du pays* may have drawn him home. That low red villa we passed before arriving at Pescara, the Villa del Fuoco, was where his childhood was passed. Ortona, down yonder to the south, saw some of the scenes of his turbulent youth, told in *Trionfo della Morte* (the *Triumph of Death*). And that dilapidated convent, the Convento di Santa Maria Maggiore, you see up on the slope in its grove of orange trees, was where most of his novels and almost all his poems have been written.

"I live here because the ambient beauty makes me quiver with ecstasy," he said speaking of his retreat. And the murmur… the Adriatic accompanied his words… gentle lullaby. "It is quiet, it … away, that no one can disturb m… none of the distractions of… make artistic work impossi… novelist ought to know th…

Gabriele d'A…
There was th…
the station w…
arrived one e…
standing on t…
"Signor D…
At the name…
they whisper…
reverence fo…
gered in this…
not give an o…
sous and he…
again the so…
Guides m…
"the poet.'…
"*Ecco!*" on…
fore one of t…
enough in It…
equally both…
though this…
Francavilla!…
within reach…
in at the ver…
"He is in…
guides. "Loo…
I could see t…
mysterious aw…
whispers, and…
door she put h…
silence before…
the poet-nov…
heavily tap…
Delilah" c…
window…
every…

…asked. …*poeta!*" …the ancient …or, still lin…ld. Did I …couple of … "Behold … …d me to …ly, then …e stood be…s, common …to shut out …g curiosity, …feared at … was almost

number of the … *Grazia* and *L*… spoken of, the… months, April … *Fuoco*, and th… *Vita* are to fo…

One stan… fecundity. A… of phrasal gra… tion of the sub… an unflagging… zio himself … create anew… his successive… creations, have… broken virgin s… are suffused, wi… fact of living, a… glad flame into t… pessimism clos… literature. Be… century "Roma… *Innocente* and … nunzio seems to … rapture, though m… a pæan of happine… of sadness is the s… the series has gro… his theory, if you… He regards be… part of life: … though some fac… ness…

"Did not the splendor of this idea blaze forth in the art of antique Greece and in that of our Renaissance? Art must represent in living forms the ideal of life, must glorify, above all things, the beauty and power of dominant humanity. The New Renaissance, then, ought to commence with the re-establishment of the cult of Man. And the new artist, like the old, will share with science the faculty of creating, will continue the work of nature in its highest manifestation and noblest form by holding up to man an Ideal. Guided by the ancient spirit the artist to-day must join art and life indissolubly, discovering truth, creating beauty and distributing joy. . . ."

Taine asked what manner of man was he who wrote the manuscripts of old. Similarly one asks: Whence comes this reincarnation of the *quattrocentist* spirit in the nineteenth…

"… kn… los… we … me … cau… bro… wo… mu… an… for… str… tha… the… the… ag… of … its … tim… ext… str… an… Bo… of … per… of … the…
"… po… an… nu… we… wh… Ita… *int*… vic…

w… lo… sc… by… is … by… w… of… is … B… su… to… B… vi… as… th… li… in… g… p…

MR. KIPLING INTERVIEWED.

Sketch of the Famous Author from th Pen of an Eminent French Littérateur.

ACTION HIS CARDINAL VIRTUE.

His Views on Music, Art, Literature and Fiction; His Sympathy and Liking for France.

A correspondent of the "Temps," whose identity is veiled by the initials "R. d'H.," recently interviewed Mr. Rudyard Kipling at his home, at Rottingdean, which is described as "a picturesque village, less commonplace than the ordinary English village, and as picturesque as Brittany." The correspondent finds the famous author extended on a sofa; but he springs up, and with a hearty welcome calls for "tea, tea!"

Here is the correspondent's description of the poet of "Tommy Atkins":—

"He (Kipling) does not look over thirty. Nicholson's engraving makes him look too old. His frank, open expression is only to be found in the portrait of him by the Hon. John Collier. The eyes especially fix the attention, behind the immovable spectacles; full of light, sympathy and gaiety, keen to take in every form of life. His chestnut hair is cut short across the forehead. His thick-set body is singularly agile: there is nothing of the "wooden" movements of ordinary Englishmen about him.

"Seated at his desk, his elbows resting on sheets of paper blackened with manuscript, he moves his shapely hands and his thick and hairy wrists, and at times throws himself back in his chair with a frank, schoolboy laugh. This man, loaded with honor and glory, in whom, for the first time, the obscure self-consciousness of an entire race manifests itself, is the quintessence of simplicity."

Oriental Proclivities.

The conversation opens with India, a country which Mr. Kipling regards with extreme tenderness. He speaks Hindustani with perfection, which serves as a passport among the 270 idioms that exist between the Himalayas and Cape Comorin. But he knows Northern India best, and smiles when he is told that he has been accused in Southern Presidencies of Northern prejudices. He loves the Russians because they are so Oriental, and is a great admirer of Tolstoy.

Mr. Rudyard Kipling talks on all sorts of subjects. His musical taste is characteristic. He does not like Wagner, nor does he like Bach much. He likes Gounod, but detests Beethoven, while his admiration of Offenbach is akin to adoration. In regard to art, he asks: "After all, what is the use of it?" He frankly avows his taste for qualities of action. He is no idealist, and the cardinal virtue with him, as with his race, is energy.

Questioned respecting French prose writers, he names as his favorite authors Rabelais and Maupassant, though he confesses to a strong liking for Edmond About. A mention of D'Annunzio elicits from him a strong protest against erotic fiction.

"It must be my Oriental leanings," he says, "but I do not like woman outside of her house. She is charming in life, but she has been somewhat misused in literature. There are so many other subjects" (for fiction).

Sympathy with France.

Mr. Kipling expressed great sympathy with France. It is quite a mistake to depict him as fierce and provocatory. He said, quite sincerely, though with a touch of Irish humor, that it would grieve him to see war break out between his country and that of the best story-tellers in the world. He waxed enthusiastic over the pleasures of life on the hospitable soil of France, and said that his father had just spent a fortnight among the fishermen on the coast of Normandy. In reply to a remark that the excessive charms of France engendered in her sons a spirit of prodigality, want of energy, and vain indifference, he cried: "Yes! they are too well off. They should be kept out of Paris for a century. You would see how they would develop!"

In accompanying his visitors to the station, Mr. Kipling assured him, laughingly, that Rottingdean was one of the points of disembarkation for the French squadron which was to attack England. Adding: "I don't believe in invasion. Is there really any chance of war?"

The "Temps" correspondent adds that Mr. Kipling's visit to the Cape is not due to political motives, but is on account of the salubrious climate and agreeable temperature.

MASK FO... SES."

Protectio...
mobi...

One ... ventio... which ... tria.

As ... above ... mobil ... made ...

an or ... thus ... can ... ing ... the ...

I... we ... m... the ... fair sex to ... future.

SI...

Little I... goin' to be...

Accepte... the day y... in long en...

Little B... all her e... Tit-Bits.

M. FEBVRE'S SURVEY OF AMERICA'S STAGE.

The Vice-Doyen of the Comédie Française Praises Little and Condemns Much.

SCENERY AN OBJECT OF CARE.

Mr. Puff Speaking of "Trilby" as Ridiculous as Telephones in "Madame Sans-Gène."

[From the New York Herald.]

I easily remember the period—now long distant—when an individual who had been, so it was said, as far as Constantinople, was regarded with a sentiment of curiosity, mingled with respect, whenever he showed himself in a drawing-room.

How the times have changed! That traveler who seemed to "hold the record" for long distances then would find himself to-day the object of the most complete indifference. Distance no longer exists. The first comer may purchase his ticket for Jerusalem, there and back, Bethlehem—with ten minutes' stop for refreshment at the buffet!

One of my friends who was traveling in the Holy Land told me that he once interrogated the landlord of a hotel as to how he could best pass his evening.

The worthy Boniface replied:—

"As yet we have not got a Casino, but you might go and smoke your cigar on the Mount of Olives!"

The lovers of color, the fervent admirers ...que, had better make haste. ...d variety in cos... dis... ...gs, ...ms, ...elty ... have ...ating ... that, ... of its ... which ... when ...ng some ... to one's ...lly sur... the time ... on board ...appy ones ...o the gene... ...e ingenuity ...d assiduous ...ainments!

*

...w York.

...ct a complete ... the great city. ...d be more than ... outrecuidance." ...pressed to me in ... to give with the ...ion of the theatri...rious city, which ...uch hospitality to those amo... ...des who have had the happiness of being heard here and of being applauded.

Chance conducted me to Daly's Theatre upon my first evening, where I saw "The Orient Express," an English adaptation of

M. FRÉDÉRIC FEBVRE.

see an author su... classic—suffer f... adaptation?

Why not resp... and the style of ...

To hear Mr. ... Rehearsed" sp... dainty little mat... opinion, as thoug... in "Madame Sa... phone at the Pal...

My second e... Metropolitan, as ... "Manon" give... troupe.

SARDOU AS...

Then I saw "... Broadway Theat...

This time I h... a sufficiently fai... popular play, one... step by step, a... expressions a lit... in the mouth o... Augustus Pitou ... he had been able... proverb: "Trad...

Miss Kathryn... Sans-Gêne, is a... She has, above ... grace.

I will not pay ... ment of institu... her and Mlle. F... line by Ponsard ...

One insults those...

Besides, why ... sons? Why n... the good qualit... sesses?

Mr. Augustus ... Napoleon. He ... and the build of ...

To attack this ... redoubtable task... being ridiculed w... Mr. Cook has do... to compose the ... great authority. ... the part, which ... object of very c... study upon th... actor.

Scenery, furn... all at this theatr... reproductions ... Paris.

But for a Fr... thing it is to he... I am aware that... useful to him la... Sir Hudson Low... Helena. But do... dear readers, tha... into the future? ...

Being anxious ... city, I went t... which is being ... Palmer's Theatr...

The *mise-en*... arranged. You... regulated here ... Hazard—that g...

I shall not pay... probabilities of ... childish points ... who are living ... cognising each c... shoulders in clos... been concerned ... by their eccentr... in even the mos... have passed ove... the drama, yet—... two alone has a... mained exactly ... recognition take...

One might pl... of him who esca...

"My dear f...

SOME IMPORTANT TENDENCIES.

Finally, after a conscientious examination of the New York theatres, I was struck, I was even grieved, by the amount of imagination, of ingenuity, dispensed every evening without serious profit for dramatic art.

This whimsical caprice, a little gross at times, is, it must be admitted, but the small change of wit, and decorum runs a great risk of disappearing in its midst.

Such unfortunate tendencies corrupt both the taste of the spectator and of the actor at one and the same time; for that they provoke a laugh is not sufficient excuse for certain follies of the pen or the interpretation.

It is for the real lovers of the theatre, for the gourmet, that the actor ought to play, disdainful of applause given by the masses whose taste is far from being of an irreproachable purity.

To believe that it is necessary to shout very loudly in the drama, or that it is not sufficient to adopt a natural, truthful tone in the comedy, ought to be the belief alone of very mediocre actors, who thus retain in the minds of the public gross and culpable errors.

After having visited most of the principal theatres, and after having heard the best comedians of the city, it appears to me that in the opinion of all real lovers of dramatic art—and every one knows to what point the American loves this art—the establishment of a national conservatory of declamation—drama and comedy—must be a most imperious necessity.

There is no art without its grammar. One does not catch the comedian's art as one does a cold! It ought to be the result of a vocation and not the mere choice of a profession.

The young people who attack with such temerity a career which is so difficult and so interesting in this sense, that the last word in it is never spoken, make me think of those so-called musicians who play upon the piano waltzes and polkas without ever having practised an elementary scale.

The school would bring in its train style, that masterly quality which characterises the great artist.

How can one interpret Shakespeare, Goethe, Schiller, Corneille, Racine, without any preliminary notions of prosody and punctuation?

No matter what language one speaks when one interprets an author, the simple art of pronouncing the words distinctly and correctly demands a patient, laborious and indispensable study.

For there is no necessity to bring to life again the remark of a celebrated critic:—

"In England," he said, "there are for the comedian as many different ways of speaking English as there are English comedians to speak it."

A national school of declamation is the only way of realising this dream, "the unity of the language."

IMPORTANCE OF PANTOMIME.

Several months ago, before my departure for America, I formed part of a commission charged with the duty of revising the statutes of the Conservatoire de Déclamation at Paris, and I proposed to my honorable colleagues the formation of a chair of pantomime. Understand me well—not a school of deportment, which the greater part of the time results only in affectation and mannerism! No, I mean a school of pantomime; that is to say, instruction in gesture, much more correctly, into the thought of the author, realising, as much as it is possible to do, the ideal that has been preconceived by the spectator.

Almost all the great actors have been finished masters in this art of pantomime. Garrick, Kean, Kemble, in England; Frederick Lemaitre, in France, are so many examples to prove what I advance.

Fleury, in his memoirs, wrote that an actor ought to be brought up in the lap of a duchess. For my part I should have asked for nothing better.

When Mr. Henry Irving allows the arms with which he is about to take his life to be torn from his hands, in "Olivia," there takes place a little bit of silent acting that proves conclusively what force, what authority, what power, for the public, can lie in an action, mute, it is true, but of an undeniable intensity, by the mere force of facial expression.

At this moment there are no words which could be so eloquent as the pantomime that takes place between the gentle vicar and his too culpable daughter.

I know that there have been in New York attempts at instruction, but private attempts, apart from governmental aid—that is to say, attempts that had to submit to any fluctuations of events, and to all the caprices of the Maecenas.

And, in taking my leave, bearing away with me many pleasant souvenirs of the courteous reception I found here, if I might be permitted to express a last wish it would be that some one might invent a means of locomotion that would permit one to come quickly—very quickly—to New York, and, crowning point of progress, a means of departing but slowly—very slowly.

Amen! FRÉDÉRIC FEBVRE.

TUESDAY, MAY 14. 1895.

"TANNHAEUSER" AT THE PARIS OPÉRA.

A French Audience Makes Amends for 1861—Enthusiastically Applauded.

M. VAN DYCK'S TRIUMPH.

His Superb Rendering of the Title Rôle—The First Dramatic Tenor of the Day.

The Parisian public did its best yesterday to make the artistic world forget the evening of March 13, 1861, when, for reasons which had nothing whatever to do with either art or music, it hissed the work of Richard Wagner. The evening was a triumphal one and worthy of the music which was listened to. It would be useless to deny that the audience at the Opéra, accustomed as it is to hear music which is easily understood, found the second act rather long, but this impression could be remedied without difficulty by making the cuts which were made at the Vienna Opera House. In any case the sublime beauties of the third act were acclaimed as they deserved, and there is every reason to believe that "Tannhaeuser," after having gone triumphantly round the world, will end by obtaining rights of citizenship in the répertoire of the Opéra of Paris.

Act I. Scene I. The Venusberg. Abandoning the poetic contests, the knight Tannhaeuser has gone to the Venusberg, whence travelers hear love songs proceeding and see strange lights shining by night. Venus has yielded herself to him, but a day comes when Tannhaeuser wishes to see the light again. The goddess lavishes her caresses on him in vain; he invokes the Blessed Virgin and the Venusberg disappears.

Near the Wartburg. Tannhaeuser ... ds himself again near the ...

THE MUSIC.

The music of "Tannhaeuser" is known to everyone. The first scene contains all that Wagner added in 1861 to his work, which dates from 1842. It is in Wagner's second style, energetic, violent, impetuous, but sublime. The second act contains the shepherd's song, which was not very well sung, and the septette of the friends who have recovered Tannhaeuser, which is one of the finest pieces of part music in existence. In the second act there is the march, which did not produce as much effect yesterday as at the concerts, and the powerfully sonorous finale. In the third act all is beautiful without exception: the prayer of Elizabeth, the song to the Star, the sublime recital of Tannhaeuser as a pilgrim and the end of the work, unfortunately curtailed at the Opéra.

THE INTERPRETATION.

First of all must be mentioned M. Van Dyck, who sang the rôle yesterday for the first time, but who sang it as it can never be sung by another. M. Van Dyck is simply the first dramatic tenor of our time. He transported the audience of the Opéra yesterday. He found poses more beautiful than the greatest sculptor could find. He gave everyone the very impression of the mystic life and it is impossible to form an idea of what this admirable artist was. After him the greatest success was for M. Renaud, who has a superb voice and sang very well—though a little too much in the Italian style—the pretty melodies of the rôle of Wolfram von Eschenbach.

Unfortunately the female rôles are less well filled, and in spite of the applause of an audience which is always grateful to artists for past impressions, it must be confessed that Mme. Caron has no longer her beautiful voice of the days of old, though she still retains her art and her charm. As for Mlle. Bréval, frankly she is not good. She has failed to understand the part of Venus, and it is a pity for the young actress.

The evening was a triumphant one for the work of Wagner. All the actors were recalled after each act, but the recalls of M. Van Dyck assumed the proportions of veritable and well-deserved ovations.

The audience was a brilliant one. Among those present were the Comte and Comtesse de Castellane, Mme. Jules Porgès, Mme. Maurice Ephrussi, the Comtesse Greffulhe, Comtesse Greden, the Comte de Montesquiou, the Prince de Sagan, Comte de Valon, Comtesse Hallez-Claparède, M. and Mme. J. Ricard, M. Hennessy, M. and Mme. Zola, M. Brunetière, the Comte de Gontaut, the Comte de Niermont, M. Lefèvre, M. Elias, M. and Mme. Poidatz, M. and Mme. Edgar Stern, M. Lamoureux, ... M. Edouard Dujardin ... Dr. and ...

RACES.

... ner Run ... A

... RPRISES.

... Won by ... by the ... sy.

... ENT.] ... rnational ... n tons ... nt club, ... ght four ... Vednesday, ... Taormina, ... e and the

... he Taormina ... ed by the ... lvadore and ... ed in the ... at 3h. ... Salvadore ... Taormina

... e north-east ... The prizes ... of a total ... prize 2,500

... DY. ... for yachts ... ten knots, ... ok place

... everyone, ... emselves ... y, Count ... off first ... Icipici, ... way.

INCOME TAX ... LIKEL ...

Justice Jackson Sa... with the Others ... the La...

DEATH OF PROFES...

Temperature in ... Falls Rapidly an... Kills the Grape ...

[BY COMMERCIAL CABLE TO TH...

NEW YORK, May 13.—The ... a vote was taken on ... Supreme Court ... Jack...

M. PAUL BOURGET.

PAUL BOURGET ON COSMOPOLITANISM.

He Forecasts to a "Herald" Correspondent the Literature of the Future.

"What of cosmopolitanism in literature?"

"By cosmopolitanism I mean that the time of local literature has completely passed. It is impossible to ignore the influence of different peoples upon one another nowadays. And I believe we are advancing toward a world, as distinguished from a national, literature. I may even say it already exists with the characteristic varieties proper to each division. The influence of authors of different countries upon each other is prominent in all. It would be difficult to summarize the proofs of this in a few words, but look at the facility with which the works of German, French, Russian and Norwegian writers have penetrated Italy and have been assimilated by Italian writers. Then see how Italian, Norwegian, Russian and German writers have become popular here, in France. When I was in America I remember to have heard lectures on Ibsen and Zola, to have read articles about Tolstoy, D'Annunzio, myself. And all is due to the cosmopolitanization of literature.

"The only country I find somewhat outside this movement is England. I am astounded to see how the great English writers such as George Eliot, Robert Louis Stevenson, Thackeray or George Meredith are but slightly appreciated by my countrymen. But the insularity of England is slowly disappearing and I believe we are drawing near to a cosmopolitan literature in the best sense of the word."

"Do you think the movement a good one?"

"Oh, that question is very difficult to answer. It is manifest that true literary work to-day is beginning to lose a certain savor, and, above all, that the world is losing its picturesque characteristics. But it seems to me that a great literary cosmopolitanism will result in laying bare depths of the soul that have not yet been sounded or explored. And in any case, now, when nations are multiplying engines of war, is not the moment to regret that there exists a means of drawing the peoples closer together. To those who dream of the United States of Europe, while longing for the United States of the World, anything that can help races to a better understanding one of the other, is a boon to humanity.

"And this is the mission of Literature!"

APRIL 11, 1897.-

ANATOLE FRANCE AMONG HIS BOOKS.

Interviewed by a "Herald" Correspondent in His Book-Lined Study.

THE WORK OF HIS LIFE.

His History of Jeanne d'Arc—How He Works Out an Idea Into a Story.

"That," said M. France, speaking of the sheet of manuscript I was looking at, "is a page of my *Jeanne d'Arc*. For thirty years I have been working on a history of the Maid of Orleans. It is a subject full of charm to me. And the research among archives, documents and particularly ecclesiastical reports, has taken a great deal of time. I want the book to be as complete as possible. I don't mean by 'complete' that I want to make it a mass of evidence quoted from official records. When you read the history of any one, I think you ought to feel at the end that you know the person spoken of, that you realize not so much what he did, as why he did it; that you appreciate the motives that led to the events described.

"This is what I have been [illegible] to find

When the novelist sits down to write, the story is thus complete, and his work is simply a matter of style. "Easy writing," said Sheridan, "is devilish hard reading." The wonderful limpidity of M. France's style is not got easily. The phrases are polished and changed and corrected time and again, until they are crystallized in the form that satisfies his fastidiousness. He showed me a page of manuscript, a small sheet of coarse paper covered with a network of corrections, the lines of the text all sloping up to the right in a curiously aggressive way. There was an air of philosophic combativeness about the very handwriting

M. ANATOLE FRANCE.

PIERRE LOTI AND HIS BASQUE FRIEND.

A "Herald" Correspondent Interviews the Sailor-Academician at Hendaye.

ON THE SPANISH FRONTIER.

How He Got Material for "Ramuntcho"—The Naval Officer and Novelist at Home.

It had begun to look as though I should never find Pierre Loti! He was as elusive as the charm his own books exhale. . . . In Paris every one said: "What, Loti? Oh, he is always in Rochefort—Rochefort-sur-mer, you know! . . . He lives there." Eight or nine hours later I was in Rochefort, only to be told: "M. Loti? Oh, he is always in Hendaye, down on the Spanish frontier, below Biarritz! . . . He is stationed there in command of the Javelot!" . . . Another seven hours' journey by railway. Somewhere between eleven o'clock and midnight the train stopped at Hendaye. Only a very few passengers descended. Most ... in the om-nibus running fr... village. And at... reached, for, in r... you know whe... just now?" tl... *Monsieur!* W... omnibus with...

Again he l... traveled toge... dined in th... tables; in... mounted th... ing across... and we ha... laughed w...

M. Loti'... the Bidas... creep up... crowns, s... From th... the appr... river an... Pyrene... castle... ornate... bearin... turies... noon... sugg... ness... tha... loo... an... Sp... u...

s... j...

frontier. ... anything you like ... band, but a scruple of cons... prevents them smuggling anything back...

he, himself, accomplishes rather than with what his contemporaries create.

"My interest in the movement of current literature is bounded by my personal preferences," he said. "I have so little time for reading and certain phases of modern thought alone occupy my attention. I receive no journals; indeed, often for weeks together I never even see one. Thus I know next to nothing of what is going on, and as for the literary world I am so far from it and have so little time at my disposal that even if the inclination were there I could not keep in touch with it.

"Of course I have my favorites among modern writers. I like, for example, the literature of the Rosnys, for they are marvellous when they take the trouble to write, that is, I mean, when they are occupied with serious work, and not with a couple of columns for the first page of a journal. I must admit, though, that I cannot understand how two writers can possibly work in collaboration. I should find it totally impossible. I must write as I feel inclined, when the mood is on me, quite independent of the tendencies of another mind. It is true," he added, with his faint smile, "my books are accused of having neither head nor tail, and it may possibly come from my refractoriness to extrinsic mental influences in writing them! . . .

"Then, again, it seems to me that collaborators in literary work must take a method almost totally opposed to the one I have followed. Most of my works have been drawn from my journal, one I have kept regularly since I was fourteen. Take my first book, for example. A friend, looking over some passages in my diary one day, insisted that I ought to extract a connected narrative from its pages. I did so and published *Aziyade*. Then *Madame* ... simply consists of pages from ... touched with only ... My

M. PIERRE LOTI.

M. MARCEL PRÉVOST.

MARCEL PRÉVOST ON MODERN LITERATURE.

He Explains His Intellectual Attitude to a Correspondent of the "Herald."

WHAT READERS WANT NOW.

"Nowadays," He Says, "We Exact More than Mere Amusement from Fiction."

One day Marcel Prévost looked over the field of contemporary French literature. This was something like nine or ten years ago, it may be even more. The young French writer was already practised, his pen was already sure. In him fecund imagination was allied with powers of subtle analysis and ready expression; a broad education had polished a naturally graceful style and a touch of irony in his way of regarding things gave raciness to his utterance; he had ideas, perspicacity and a rare knowledge of men, or, rather let us say, women . . . a knowledge part experience, part intuition.

So he looked over the field of contemporary French literature, seeking some unworked corner for himself.

At first he saw none—saw nothing but swarming activity all around him. Every "school" had its army of defenders: the naturalistic, the idealistic, the symbolical; the realistic, the psychological, even the *rosse* . . . And the world seemed weary of them all, of the grossness of one and the vagueness of the other; of the mysticism of this and the diffuseness of that.

But M. Prévost had his own theory ripening. Romanticism, he may have mused, is as dead as Charlemagne and no one is any the worse. . . . Yet it had charm; it might still flourish in a regenerated form if vigorous sap were only infused into it. Now

the story, by the char... laying bare of psychol... for all," and in Prévos... surprised to note what... motives and passions a... has left with you, ho... learned of the storms t...

It was essentially a w... I found M. Prévost. T... his *appartement* in the... long bookcase, with no... space in it, lined the bot... and a big table covere... and books occupied th... the works were in fore... being the prevailing on...

"I am very agreea... England," said M. Pré... recent visit paid to t... Ireland. "I think th... the curious discipline w... late matters of every... delightful thing. It se... sort of business exac... social life, for examp... English customs must... have been brought in... and particularly by the... something entirely exc... which they have littl... frankly, I can conceiv... hideous than an Anglici... England, in itself, is on... tive places to visit."

M. Prévost's travel... interfere with his work... long list of books he ha... few years. Without co... of journalistic work t... the care he devotes to... work, M. Prévost is one... writers of the day. Th... had hardly appeared... *Lettres* were published,... the *Demi-Vierges* is st... the literary world when... issued. And he is at... novel to be issued sho... that will soon be seen... vard theatres.

Referring to what... New Latin Renaissance,...

"It is true there h... manifested recently to... there has been an... to resuscitate literary... excellent in the... them into being. Bu... one as rather like th...

SUNDAY, MAY 2, 1897.

have
Sté-
rwise
they
nsuls
sured
taken
urunu
afety
d of

bom-
reeks
d not
tan—
l the
thout
ladies
d get
here.
ment
grow
town
c are

ow in
reeks,
peror
f the
er of
were
up to
oever
The
eyes
thus

f by
some
rman
sent
vene.
st of

the
ry to
now
man-
of all
vords
rkish
to
was
d:—
will
He
food.
fast,
order
e we
olute
vhat-
o the

oured
indi-
ldier

M. BRUNETIÈRE SCORES M. ZOLA.

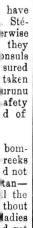

The Academician Says the Novelist Has Degraded France and Dishonored Literature.

GERMAN-AMERICAN CITIZENS

Great Earthquake in the Leeward Islands, Causing Much Damage at Montserrat.

[SPECIAL DESPATCH TO THE HERALD.]

(By Commercial Cable.)

NEW YORK, May 1.—In his farewell lecture here last night M. Brunetière scarified M. Zola, saying that he had simply degraded France and dishonored literature.

M. Zola, he said, had betrayed art and

M. BRUNETIÈRE.

knew nothing of French history, French society or French morality.

He declared that M. Zola's *bourgeois*, his workman, his peasant and—adding with the vehemence of outraged patriotism—his soldier, were no Frenchmen.

THE "FIGARO'S" COMMENTS.

The *Figaro* this morning says :—

"Le NEW YORK HERALD a reçu de New York une dépêche sur la conf... faite ...

reached the ...
telegraph fro...
It is stated ...
has made no ...
condition o...
looked for b...

Spain'...
[SPECIAL ...

WASHING...
introduced ...
officers of ...
are here on ...
The State ...
of the releas...
authorities i...

CHINES...

Though on ...

VANCOUVE...
dinary affair...
arrival of the ...
from Shangh...
on board, and ...
regulations th...
to undergo fu...
Among thos...
Chinese Ambas...
the Emperor of ...
London and ...
Chang distinctly ...
gation and has ...
and Lord Salisb...
obnoxious perf...
On the other ...
clare that unl...
lation he wi...
Chang has ...
would be pr...
he will lose ...
disobeying ...
He declar...
upon him ...
Britain. At p...
ship, and the ...
Ottawa for in...

WEST IN...

All the Buildi...
and Antigua ...
[SPECIAL DE...
(By C...
KINGSTON, JA...
ing are all the po...
to the earthqual...
A slight sho...
This was fol...
by others, ea...
violent.
Last ...

M. ZOLA.

WEDNESDAY, JANUARY 19, 1898.

COMPLAINT AGAINST M. EMILE ZOLA.

Minister of War Places the Matter in the Hands of the Minister of Justice.

TIVOLI-VAUXHALL MEETING.

Exciting Scenes in the Main Thoroughfares of Paris—Disturbances in the Departments.

The attention of the meeting of the Cabinet Council which was held yesterday morning at the Elysée under the presidency of M. Félix Faure, was exclusively devoted to the subject of the Dreyfus case. The Minister of War placed in the hands of his colleague the Minister of Justice a complaint against the *gérant* of the *Aurore* and against M. Emile Zola. This complaint will be handed on to the Procurator-General.

We have reason to believe says the *Temps*, that proceedings will be taken for defamation before the Seine Assizes. The case cannot be heard before the first fortnight in February.

The *Liberté* states that M. Zola will be defended by Me. Fernand Labori, who acted for Mme. Alfred Dreyfus in connection with the Esterhazy court-martial.

AT THE TIVOLI-VAUXHALL.

Anarchists and Antisemites Come ... Blows—Police Charge Studen... in the Fog.

M. ZOLA STIRS UP THE DREYFUS CASE.

The Famous Novelist's Letter to the President of the Republic Discussed in the Chamber.

PROSECUTION ANNOUNCED

Lieut.-Colonel Picquart Arrested and Imprisoned—Major Esterhazy Asks to Be Retired.

M. Emile Zola's letter to the President of the Republic, which was published in the *Aurore* yesterday morning, accusing General Billot, the Minister of War, with having in his possession the proofs of Dreyfus' innocence, created a great sensation in Paris. The matter came before the Chamber of Deputies at a quarter past five o'clock yesterday afternoon, and the Government announced that proceedings were going to be taken to put a stop to the campaign which was being waged against the army.

It was the Comte de Mun, the well-known Catholic Deputy, who brought the question before the Chamber by interpellating the Minister of War.

M. Méline, President of the Council, stated in reply that M. Zola's article would be reported to the judicial authorities, though he did not disguise the fact that these proceedings were sought for and that they were destined to prolong the deplorable state of agitation of the country.

The Comte de Mun replied that these words facilitated his task, but it was necessary that the Minister of War should also reply from the tribune to the abominable accusations which had been brought against the army.

General Billot then spoke.

"It is the fourth time during the past year," he said, "that I have defended the *chose jugée* from the tribune."

M. Chauvin : "*A huis-clos!*" (Disturbance.)

General Billot : "The army is above all attacks. Its honor is like the sun—what matter a few spots! It did not the less shine with incomparable brilliancy. But is it not a lamentable spectacle to see this honor the object of such audacious accusations before Europe which is watching us?. . . Can we compromise the National Defence for which we have sacrificed everything? Do we wish this country, every citizen of which is a soldier, no longer to follow its leaders in the time of danger? The Government is ready, it is determined to put an end to such a situation, and to defend the honor of the army, the respect of the decisions of the court-martial and the interests of the country."

This declaration was received with loud applause.

M. JAURES NOT SATISFIED.

But M. Jaurès was not satisfied. He asked in the name of the Socialists why the court-martial had held its sittings with closed doors; why did they not wish the country to judge of events? Storms of applause came from the Socialist benches when the speaker declared that :—

"If it is true that, in the case in question, irregularities in procedure have been committed, it is necessary that these revolutionary acts accomplished for the country should be openly admitted by the responsible authority. But no! they ask for mystery and secrecy. The military authorities hear all cases of treason with closed doors. But at the same time they daily beg at the doors of the newspapers that they should invoke the interests of the National Defence in its favor."

"J'ACCUSE! . . ."

M. Alphonse Humbert: "It is false. I deny it."

M. Jaurès: "What, then, was the step taken by the orderly officer of the chief of the general staff in regard to the manager of a newspaper?"

The speaker refused to sanction such abuses, one of the great principles of the Republic being the subordination of the military to the civil authority. Let them beware! They were about to hand over the Republic to the generals!

IT WAS SUPPORTING ZOLA.

Such a declaration as this was, in the opinion of General Billot, renewing and at the same time aggravating the attacks of M. Zola. He asked the Chamber to allow the army to devote itself silently to its sacred mission, the defence of the country.

M. Cavaignac also protested against M. Jaurès' words, but he nevertheless wanted to know whether the Government had done everything which it ought. He pointed out that the Minister of War might have stopped the campaign by a single word. In the *dossier* was a document which might be made known without compromising the interests of the National Defence; there existed written testimony, contemporary with the Dreyfus case and from which it resulted, that the sentenced man confessed to having handed over unimportant documents to a foreign Power so as to obtain more important ones in return. That was not all. There had been seized by an officer of the staff documents appearing to incriminate Major Esterhazy. After an inquiry the Minister had placed them aside; why had he not done so at once when the newspapers got hold of them?

The President of the Council stated that had the Government done as M. Cavaignac wished, the Dreyfus case would have had to be reopened, which was just what M. Scheurer-Kestner wanted.

Several orders of the day were proposed. MM. Rouanet, Jaurès and Gérault-Richard asked the Government to return to the Republican tradition; MM. Marty and Lieut.-Colonel Guérin approved of the Government's declarations; Comte de Mun proposed that "The Chamber, relying upon the Government to take the necessary measures to put a stop to the campaign against the honor of the army, passes to the order of the day," and M. Cavaignac proposed a vote mildly censuring the Government.

The Chamber finally adopted by 312 votes to 122 the following order of the day, made up of the propositions put forward by Comte de Mun and MM. Marty and Guérin:—

"The Chamber, approving of the declarations of the Government, and relying upon it to take the necessary measures to put a stop to the campaign against the honor of the army, passes to the order of the day."

"J'ACCUSE! . . ."

M. Emile Zola's Letter to the President of the Republic.

The letter which M. Emile Zola publishes in the *Aurore* under the title of "J'accuse. . ." is addressed to the President of the Republic. He appeals to M. Félix Faure to intervene in favor of what he declares to be truth and justice.

M. Zola's contention is that the *deus ex machina* of the Dreyfus case is Colonel du Paty de Clam. This officer, he states, delights in romantic intrigues, anonymous letters, mysterious women who at night carry about with them crushing proofs. He it was who thought of dictating the *bordereau* to Dreyfus; who dreamed of studying him in a room, the walls, ceiling and floor of which were covered with mirrors; who wished to enter Captain Dreyfus' cell and cast upon the face of the sleeping man a flood of light from a dark lantern with the object of surprising his crime in the emotion of his sudden awakening. It was Colonel du Paty de Clam who arrested Dreyfus and placed him in secret, and who then went to the house of Mme. Dreyfus to tell her that if she spoke a word her husband was lost!

After laying particular emphasis on the worthlessness of the indictment, the writer comes to the Esterhazy case and says that the only honest man in the whole affair is Lieut.-Colonel Picquart, who is charged with having forged the card-telegram, which put the Ministry of War into a state of consternation, because the officials saw that there was a danger of the Dreyfus case being reopened.

M. Zola further contends that they could not hope that the second court-martial would undo the work of the first.

The writer then brings a series of charges against Colonel du Paty de Clam, General Mercier, General Billot, General de Boisdeffre, and General Gonze, General de Pellieux and Major Ravary; the three experts, Belhomme, Varinard and Couard; against the officials of the Ministry of War for having carried on an "abominable" press campaign, and against the first court-martial for having convicted a man on secret evidence.

M. Emile Zola concludes as follows:—

"By bringing these charges I am not ignorant that I bring myself under Articles 30 and 31 of the Press Law of July 29, 1881, which punishes for defamation. I am voluntarily running the risk.

"As to the men I accuse, I do not know them, I have never seen them, I have against them neither rancor nor hatred. To me they are only beings, spirits of social wrong-doing. And the act which I accomplish here is only a revolutionary means of hastening the outburst of truth and justice.

"I have only one passion, that for light, in the name of humanity which has suffered so much and which has a right to happiness. My passionate protest is but the cry of my soul. Let them dare then to bring me before the Assizes and hold the inquiry in the light of day!

"I wait."

JURISDICTION IN THE ZOLA CASE.

The *Figaro* states that it is possible for the Zola case to come before the Assizes in the second fortnight in January. There can be no question of arrest.

It is not certain that the case will be judged in public. The law, in fact, authorizes the *huis-clos* when the Court considers that publicity is dangerous to good morals and also to public order.

LIEUT.-COLONEL PICQUART.

Arrested Yesterday Morning and Taken to Mont-Valérien.

Lieut.-Colonel Picquart has been arrested. Such was the news which the Ministry of War announced yesterday afternoon in a note communicated to the news agencies. The note was as follows:—

"In consequence of facts brought to light by the inquiry and the proceedings of the Esterhazy case, Lieut.-Colonel Picquart ... fortress under arrest ...

THE SEINE ASSIZES.

...xplain the interest ... Clam's evidence ... Picquart was ... and Mlle. ... Com- being signed ... Lieut.- this ... over ... had ... he ...

necessary to justice. General Mercier, according to M. Zola, had communicated to the court-martial ...

2ND EDITION.

LORD QUEENSBERRY IN THE DOCK.

Mr. Oscar Wilde's Action for Criminal Libel Begun at the Old Bailey.

A "CAUSE CÉLÈBRE."

The Court Crowded in Every Part by Barristers, Solicitors and Public.

SOME REMARKABLE LETTERS.

Counsel Reads the Prosecutor's Correspondence with Lord Alfred Douglas.

SEVERE CROSS-EXAMINATION.

[BY THE HERALD'S SPECIAL WIRE.]

LONDON, April 4.—For the first time in the history of the Old Bailey the dock of that Court was yesterday occupied by a peer of the realm. This was John Sholto Douglas, Marquis of Queensberry, who stood there to answer a charge of criminal libel against Mr. Oscar Wilde, yet though it was the marquis who was technically in the dock it was quite evident that before the day's

THE MARQUIS OF QUEENSBERRY.

proceedings finished it was his accuser, the heavily jowled, broad-shouldered person lounging ungracefully over the front of the witness-box, who really stood on his defence before the world. The case was interesting throughout. The trial, as the day waned and the centre of gravity, as it were, shifted from the defendant to the prosecutor, became absolutely dramatic, and I have never seen so crowded a court preserve such

Mr. Wilde the original, he gave another half sovereign. This letter, according to his counsel, Mr. Wilde regarded as a prose sonnet, and, indeed, since then, in May, 1893, it had appeared in sonnet form in the *Spirit Lamp*, an æsthetic magazine edited by Lord A. Douglas. The letter was as follows, written from Torquay:—

My own dear boy—

Your sonnet is quite lovely and it is a marvel that those red roseleaf lips of yours should be made no less for the music of song than for the madness of kissing. Your slim gilt soul walks between passion and poetry. I know that Hyacinthus, whom Apollo loved so madly, was you in Greek days. Why are you alone in London and when do you go to Salisbury? Do go there and cool your hands in the gray twilight of Gothic things and come here whenever you like. It is a lovely place; it only lacks you, but go to Salisbury first. Always with undying love, yours. OSCAR.

THE MARQUIS AT THE ST. JAMES'S.

In mentioning later on the fact that the Marquis went to the St. James's Theatre on the first night of "The Importance of Being Earnest," carrying a bouquet of vegetables he was refused admittance, Sir E. Clarke suggested that there was a doubt as to whether the Marquis was always responsible for his actions. He then took up the last two statements added to the plea of justification, which were to the effect that Mr. Wilde in July, 1890, wrote and published a certain immoral and obscene work in the form of a narrative entitled *The Picture of Dorian Grey*, and that in December, 1894, was published a certain other immoral and obscene work in the form of a magazine, entitled *The Chameleon*, which contained divers obscene matters, and that he contributed thereto certain immoral maxims as the introduction to the same under the title of "Phrases and Philosophies for the Use of the Young."

The gist of this last accusation, as Sir Edward pointed out, was that one contribution to the magazine in question was entitled "The Priest and the Acolyte," which was of such a nature that even Mr. Wilde's counsel characterized it as a disgrace to literature, expressing his amazement that anyone should write it, and his still greater amazement that any decent publishers should publish it. Sir Edward wound up his address by giving with effective skill, which did not, however (as he was careful later on to make clear) quite satisfy Mr. Wilde's artistic judgment, a synopsis of the plot of *Dorian Grey*, which he said was the story of a young man of good birth, great wealth and much personal beauty.

Certainly, the vices in which this youth eventually indulges were hinted at, said Sir Edward, but he should be surprised if his learned friend could point to any passage which did more than describe, as novelists and dramatists must, passions and vices of life which they might desire to reproduce in a work of art.

EVIDENCE OF THE LIBEL.

This ended Sir Edward's address, and after calling the porter of the Albemarle Club to give formal evidence as to the publication of the libel, Mr. O. Wilde was asked to step into the witness box. He strode deliberately thereinto and occupied a few seconds after he was sworn in arranging, in convenient proximity to his elbow, a glass of water. He then lounged over the rail of the stand, as I have already said, in a clumsy posture, clasping his hands nervously in front of him over a pair of dogskin gloves he held, and occasionally wiping his forehead with his hand or with his handkerchief.

He was asked to take a seat but preferred the ungraceful posture which I have described. Close behind him sat the fragile-looking Lord A. Douglas and the sturdier and more manly looking Lord Douglas of Hawick. With an occasional suggestion of flippancy he bore out the opening statement

extraordinary was called forth by the reading of a letter from him to Lord Alfred, which began—

Savoy Hotel.

Dearest of all boys,

Your letter was delightful red and yellow wine to me, for I am sad and out of sorts.

And ended—

My bill here is £49 for a week, but why are you not here, my dear own boy? Fear I must leave. No money, no credit, and a heart of lead.

From your own OSCAR.

In regard to one of the alleged blackmailers, named Wood, Mr. Wilde admitted he had met him at the Café Royal, and on the first night he saw him he took him to supper in a private room at the Hotel Florence, in Rupert-street, and gave him £2, though he was neither an artist nor a literary man, nor a man of his own social position. He also admitted that afterwards he gave Wood £2, with which to go to America. He also gave him a farewell luncheon. He called Wood Alfred and Wood called him Oscar, as did also the other alleged blackmailer Taylor. He also admitted that none of his many letters to Lord Alfred save the one which was discovered had been subsequently turned into sonnets or characterised by him as prose poems. All the letters, however, were beautiful.

FURTHER CROSS-EXAMINATION.

Leaving discussion of Mr. Wilde's literature aside for the moment Mr. Carson proceeded to question him as to his intimacy with a young man in the employment of Messrs. Elkin Matthews and John Lane, publishers of *The Yellow Book*. Mr. Wilde objected to the youth being termed an office boy, but admitted he was very fond of him and had taken him to the theatre, to the Lyric Club, to the Café Royal and to a private room at Kettmans' and also the Albemarle Hotel, and had on various occasions given him money.

He also admitted he knew a lad at Worthing, named Alfonso Conway, who, according to Mr. Carson, sold newspapers at that place and "enjoyed himself in being idle." He was a lad of no literary ambition and of but little education. He had given him a suit of clothes, a walking-stick, which was produced in court, a straw hat, which was likewise on exhibit, and a cigarette case and a photograph of himself, not to make him look like his equal, "for he could never look like that, but because he was a pleasant nice creature."

THE CASE ADJOURNED.

At this point the case was adjourned, the defendant, somewhat significantly, being allowed to depart on his own recognisances in the sum of £500, a reduction ... he former bail of £2,000.

The eno...

MR. OSCAR WILDE.

THREE MERCHANTS REPORTED DROW...

Rumored Fatal Ending to ... in Biscayne ... Florida.

MRS. PARAN S...

Mr. Nat Herres... ing, and the ... Progres...

[BY COMMERCIAL ...

NEW YORK, Ap... current here to-... Ziegler, the multim... Mr. John H. Flagl... merchant; and Mr. ... minent merchant, have ... cruising in the Biscayne ...

MAYOR STRONG...

The "Herald" Approve... Changes in the Poli...

[BY COMMERCIAL CABLE T...

NEW YORK, April 3.—T... leading editorial this m... Mayor Strong in his ... against "bossism," a... intended removal of M...

The HERALD also poi... of care being exercise... cessors to the Police Co...

The Mayor, by the ... Edward Mitchell to acc... but an answer has not ...

The names of Mr. F... Theodore Roosevelt ar... the vacancies.

The Mayor's message ... many's juggling with ... city finances has cause...

The tone of the edit... that the city has be... moment too soon fro... ring.

Sickness Foils Mr...

[BY COMMERCIAL CAB...

NEW YORK, April ... scheme to force the ... Bi-partisan Police B... failed, owing to th... Senators, without cou... barely the requisite sev...

The bill has been s... The leading Republicans ... issued an address beggin... of the State to influence ... o aid Platt's schemes.

Republican Gains in S...

...BY COMMERCIAL CABLE...

NEW YORK, April 3.—... ...tions have resulted ... ...lican sweeps except ... and Wisconsin. ...can Mayor of Chic... ...lity and St. Louis ... ...y routed.

...tmaster-General V...

...OMMERCIAL CABLE...

NEW YORK, April 3.—West Virginia, was sworn

SUNDAY, APRIL 7, 1895. TEN PAGES.

OSCAR WILDE AND HIS COMPANION.

Appear Before the Magistrate at Bow Street—Remanded Till Thursday.

PRISONERS REFUSED BAIL.

Congratulations Showering upon Lord Queensberry—Rumors of Another Arrest.

[BY THE HERALD'S SPECIAL WIRE.]

LONDON, April 7.—Yesterday London spent another day of ferment in connection with the sickening case of Oscar Wilde. Never has a matter of this nature—and it is perhaps as well that it should have been so—taken so complete a hold upon the public mind and especially upon the mind of that portion of the public which occupies a higher social position.

The reason for this is not to be found alone in the personality of the accused, though, of course, the familiarity of his name and the popularity of his dramatic works have increased the sensation of shuddering disgust which has been universally felt. As I hinted yesterday, the real reason is ethical rather than personal. It is felt that a cankering sore has for long been eating into the body of London society, and that it is just as well that for a brief period it should have been exposed in all its horrors to the public gaze, thus a service to morality has been rendered by the painful trial which was on Friday concluded so shamefully at the Old Bailey.

It is now, however, the general feeling—so far as I have been able to fathom it in conversation with people of varying importance—that the proceedings taken by the country against this wretched man, who now lies in a prison cell, should be conducted with as little publicity as possible.

OSCAR WILDE AT BOW STREET.

It is universally hoped, indeed, that when the prisoner is committed for trial ... Old Bailey, as he ...

Little College street formerly occupied by Taylor, spoke of the number of young men who frequented the house and of their character. She also described the way in which the rooms were furnished and lighted.

Alfred Wood, a fair young man dressed in black, who described himself as a clerk, also testified after the same fashion, and also told how he received a sum of £20 from Wilde to purchase his passage to America after he had given him back the incriminating letters. The last witness was Sidney Arthur Mavor, who seemed to be of a different social position to the other youths, but whose evidence was similar in character.

Mr. Humphrey, on Mr. Wilde's behalf, reserved his right to cross examine all or any of the witnesses.

Finally the case was adjourned until next Thursday, and though bail was applied for on behalf of Wilde, it was, of course, refused, and he and Taylor were led away in custody.

I may add that there is a well-defined rumor in circulation to the effect that a warrant has been issued for the arrest of another prominent figure in the case, but up to a late hour last night no action had been taken in the matter.

A RECTIFICATION.

The Marquis of Queensberry asked me yesterday to mention particularly that in his message to Oscar Wilde, to which he referred in the interview which appeared in yesterday's HERALD, he did not threaten actually to shoot Wilde, but merely said he would be justified in so doing if he cared to take the trouble. Lord Queensberry further told me that letters and telegrams of congratulation continued to pour in upon him, and he referred with evident pleasure to two telegrams reading: "Well done, old chap," and signed by two of his old shipmates who are now post-captains in the Royal Navy.

He expressed himself as having a sort of pity for the probable fate of his late prosecutor. As to what this fate will be, should he be found guilty, I understand that the particular section of the Criminal Law Amendment Act under which he is charged allows of so short a term of imprisonment as two years. This is interesting in view of the general impression that prevails among the public that ten years' penal servitude is the least punishment that can be awarded.

I hear, by the way, that Sir Edward Clarke has offered to defend Wilde without a fee.

PHILOSOPHIC MORAL OF THE CASE.

The *Figaro* this morning points a philosophic moral to the story of Oscar Wilde. Referring to his case our contemporary says:—

"It is the natural and regular physiological result of a literary and æsthetic effort and from that point of view it demands the reflections of all thinkers. It demonstrates the influence which the deviation of certain literary faculties in the direction of a refined sensualism can exercise over the intelligence and over the morals of men undoubtedly gifted. . . . Fatal degeneracy will ensue when intellectual effort is made the result and not the principle of sensations. . . . We must beg our æsthetes to be moderate."

UMB... P...SONERS.

Li...

SATURDAY, APRIL 27, 1895.

...'s article ...ion of the ...vy, but en... he delay in

...E NAVY. ...es the slowness ...es navy. In

... dwelling for a United States and continuity ...ays been found on them and ...ig. But it is the State than ...ard advance- among the the different ...*ates of youth* ...*t of the sea.*"

...MENT.

...lde Rather

...HE HERALD.]

... Platt is deter... s Senators, Mr. Mr. Robertson. ... organ, to day bribery in con... of the bill to ...s. ...e, which was ...he facts, sum... ...o testify. He ... To-day the ...he was sum... killed himself stand. ...g other wit... ...e memories ...was a corrup... ...lbany.

...ent.

...HE HERALD.]

...essrs. Edward ...ash settlement ...f their liabilities,

...K FIRM

...me E. S Jaffray & Robert Jaffray as ...which he and his ...ontrolled. In 1833 the son of John R ...ry, being at that It was his energy ...eatest success and S. Jaffray & Co., or partner.

...ENDER.

...lates to be Used

OSCAR WILDE'S TRIAL BEGINS.

The Whilom Æsthete Appears at the Bar of the Old Bailey.

ON ARMENIAN ATROCITIES.

Mr. Gladstone Says the Sultan Is Indelibly Disgraced—Naval Fund Meeting.

[BY THE HERALD'S SPECIAL WIRE.]

LONDON, April 27.—It might almost have been assumed that by this time people were tired of fighting to get a glimpse of Oscar Wilde's face; but I found the crowd almost as large as ever at the Old Bailey yesterday when the whilom æsthete, in company with the very unæsthetic Taylor, appeared before Mr. Justice Charles for trial. The Court was filled with a struggling crowd the moment the doors opened.

Wilde looked much thinner than when he was at Bow Street and his hair was shorter. Sir Edward Clarke interposed at an early stage with the objection that the accused could not be called upon at the same time to plead to an indictment which contained charges under the Criminal Law Amendment Act and also the charges of conspiracy first named. The judge, however, overruled the objection and both prisoners at once pleaded not guilty.

Mr. C. F. Gill then opened the case in a speech which simply went over the ground now quite familiar to the public and Charles Parker was called as the first witness. Some doubt had been expressed as to whether the witnesses against Wilde would stand to the statements they had already made, but Parker soon dismissed all apprehension on this score. He was quite firm on all points already brought out and besides made new admissions tending to increase the gravity of the charges.

His evidence, however, was of a character similar to that elicited at Bow Street. His brother followed him into the box and other evidence not of great importance having been taken the case was adjourned for the day.

THE ... DISGRACED.

MA...

Chine... Pr...

TO ...

Cha... V...

[...

PEK... at pre... has b... and its... The... war a... Hung... the ra... that so... Japan far too... The... promin... dispos... ratifica... Sho... predict... affecti... to ano... Li-H... events. be mad... and to the Pe... that th... should Chow a...

FRA...

Russia... Me...

[SPE...

St P... in St. ... that Ja... Thes... torious gorical least ...

... suppressed at the stern instance of the judge. According to the prosecutor the interview ended by Lord Queensberry threatening to thrash him if he caught him at any public restaurant with his son, and Mr. Wilde replied: "I don't know what the Queensberry rules are, but the Wilde rules are to shoot at sight."

ANNOUNCEMENTS.

HORSELESS CARRIAGES.

All persons interested in, or desirous of becoming acquainted with, the working of "Horseless Carriages," which have such a promising future, can gain all information by writing to the AGENCE PARISIENNE (Office Générale), PALAIS DE LA BOURSE DU COMMERCE, PARIS.